# MANAGED FUTURES FOR INSTITUTIONAL INVESTORS

Since 1996, Bloomberg Press has published books for financial professionals on investing, economics, and policy affecting investors. Titles are written by leading practitioners and authorities, and have been translated into more than 20 languages.

The Bloomberg Financial Series provides both core reference knowledge and actionable information for financial professionals. The books are written by experts familiar with the work flows, challenges, and demands of investment professionals who trade the markets, manage money, and analyze investments in their capacity of growing and protecting wealth, hedging risk, and generating revenue.

For a list of available titles, visit our Web site at www.wiley.com/go/bloombergpress.

# MANAGED FUTURES FOR INSTITUTIONAL INVESTORS

*Analysis and Portfolio Construction*

**Galen Burghardt**
**Brian Walls**

BLOOMBERG PRESS
An Imprint of
WILEY

Published by John Wiley & Sons, Inc., Hoboken, New Jersey.
Published simultaneously in Canada.

For general information on our other products and services or for technical support, please contact our
Customer Care Department within the United States at (800) 762-2974, outside the United States at
(317) 572-3993 or fax (317) 572-4002.

AlternativeEdge is a registered trademark of Newedge Group.

Wiley also publishes its books in a variety of electronic formats. Some content that appears in print may
not be available in electronic books. For more information about Wiley products, visit our web site at
http://www.wiley.com.

*Library of Congress Cataloging-in-Publication Data:*

Burghardt, Galen.
   Managed futures for institutional investors : analysis and portfolio construction /
Galen Burghardt, Brian Walls.
      p. cm. – (Bloomberg financial series)
   Includes bibliographical references and indexes.
      ISBN 978-1-57660-374-1 (cloth); ISBN 978-0-47087-922-1 (ebk); ISBN 978-1-11810-315-9 (ebk);
ISBN 978-1-11810-312-8 (ebk)
   1. Futures.   2. Portfolio management.   3. Institutional investors.   I. Walls, Brian.   II. Title.
   HG6024.A3B88 2011
   332.64'52–dc22

                                                                           2010048911

Printed in the United States of America.

10   9   8   7   6   5   4   3   2   1

*We dedicate this book to our mothers, Joyce Burghardt and Helen Walls, who are responsible for every good thing we have ever done.*

# Contents

## PART II: BUILDING BLOCKS

## CHAPTER 4
### How Trend Following Works                                      **75**

## CHAPTER 5
### Two Benchmarks for Momentum Trading                           **99**

## CHAPTER 6
### The Value of Daily Return Data                                **129**

## PART III: PORTFOLIO CONSTRUCTION

## CHAPTER 12
### Superstars versus Teamwork                                   **253**

## CHAPTER 13
### A New Look at Constructing Teamwork Portfolios               **279**

## CHAPTER 14
### Correlations and Holding Periods: The Research Basis for the *Newedge AlternativeEdge Short-Term Traders Index*                                                **297**

# Acknowledgments

We want to take this opportunity to thank those who have helped us bring this book to fruition and to extend an open invitation to its readers to approach us any time with the kinds of questions we wrestle with in this book. The young people who work behind the counter at our local Potbelly's wear t-shirts that say, "Get in here before we both starve." We feel the same about questions and animated conversations. Without them, we would starve.

First, we want to thank our colleague, Leslie Richman. Leslie co-founded our manager research forums, the first of which was held in 2002 and which have been the equivalent of a research nebula. Launching these forums required a tremendous commitment from all involved because the rules were so completely at odds with the usual kind of cap intro events to which managers and investors typically would be invited. The presenting managers were not allowed to talk about their firms, their trading programs, or their track records. Instead, their marching orders were to talk about some interesting piece of research that would help everyone think more fruitfully about trading and investing.

Second, we want to acknowledge all of the managers and investors who have participated in these research forums over the past eight years. It was from these forums that we were able to glean and distill the kinds of questions that weighted most heavily on managers' and investors' minds. These forums also have given us a place to try out our work with highly motivated listeners and to learn from their comments and criticisms. We have borrowed shamelessly from their insights.

One example is the work that appears in the chapter on drawdowns. The inspiration for that research was a rough survey we took at one of our earliest conferences. We had asked everyone what they thought the most useful measure of risk was, and a very large majority replied "drawdown." This outcome produced a firestorm of protest from those managers who had been around for a long time and from those whose targeted return volatilities were relatively high. The conversations that took place around the breakfast and dinner tables the next day provided some of the key insights that shaped our work.

Another example that we love is in Chapter 13, where you will find a scatter plot that shows past and future average pairwise correlations for groups of 10 managers. When we first displayed that scatter plot at one of the May conferences, Rishi Narang (author of *Inside the Black Box*, Wiley, 2009) wanted to know why it looked like a football. The answer to his question proved to be a huge improvement in the way we thought about past and future correlations and why one could have confidence in averages of low pairwise correlations even though one could not have much confidence in low values of any one pairwise correlation estimate.

There are many more examples, but what we want to convey here is our gratitude for the kind of open and critical minds that people have brought to our conferences and the kinds of conversations they have produced. We cannot thank these managers and investors enough for allowing us to do much of our learning in public and to benefit from any mistakes we have made. We certainly cannot thank them all by name, but they know who they are and will recognize the influence they have had on our work.

We want to thank our colleagues in research at Newedge, especially Lianyan Liu and Ryan Duncan, both of whom appear as co-authors on many of the research notes you will find listed in the bibliography. Both of them have been rock-solid and have, over the years, propelled us forward in our understanding of thorny statistical and portfolio construction problems. Their theoretical acumen combined with their capacity for dealing with huge quantities of detail and data have been a godsend for us. We also would like to thank Lauren Lei, whose work on market liquidity and transactions costs has been integral to those parts of our work dealing with costs of trading and active portfolio management.

We want to thank everyone who helped pull this volume together. Molly Dziedzic, in particular, was tireless and unfailingly good humored throughout the entire process, especially when crunch times loomed. Hal Wadsworth has been our go-to guy for publishing for years and did not let us down here. Our editors at Wiley worked wonders, too, for which we are extremely grateful.

And finally, we must say just how thankful we are to have been able to work in a corporate culture that values the pursuit of knowledge, both here at Newedge and earlier at Calyon Financial. The pressures in this world to make more money faster are extreme. So it is all the more to our colleagues' credit that they have supported us so completely and enthusiastically while we were pursuing insights into the questions addressed in this book.

# Introduction: Why Invest in CTAs?

This book is intended to be an introduction to the world of Commodity Trading Advisors (CTAs) for savvy high-net-worth and institutional investors who are looking for an edge and who are willing to invest the time and attention required to take full advantage of what CTAs have to offer.

For the most part, the book is written for those who are persuaded that investing in CTAs promises to improve the performance of their portfolios. Before we get to the main body of the text, however, we want to make the best case we can for why you should invest. In doing so, we address these questions:

- What kind of hedge fund is a CTA?
- Do CTAs make money?
- How are CTAs' returns correlated with those on conventional assets?
- Why do CTAs make money?
- How much should you invest?
- What about the risks?
- Why are futures a good fit for pension funds and other institutional investors?

## What Kind of Hedge Fund Is a CTA?

Managed futures denotes the sector of the investment industry in which professional money managers actively manage client assets using global futures and other derivative securities as the investment instruments. Managed futures managers are also known as Commodity Trading Advisors (CTAs),

1

and The National Futures Association (NFA) is their self-regulatory organization. The first managed futures fund started in 1948; however, managed
futures did not take off as an industry until the 1980s.*

Like most hedge funds, CTAs deal with institutional and high-net-worth
individual investors who are financially sophisticated, who have specific investment requirements, and who need asset diversification. At the same time,
CTAs' returns exhibit much lower correlations with those on conventional
assets and so afford much better diversification than do private equity, venture capital, or conventional hedge funds. Further, CTAs provide far more
liquidity.
Investors who want to invest in alternatives need to understand CTAs.

## Why Do CTAs Make Money?

If CTAs did not hold out the promise of positive expected excess returns—that
is, returns in excess of what could be earned by low-risk or no-risk money
market investments—there would be no point in considering them as an
investment outlet. In fact, the evidence on this point is fairly compelling, at
least for the subset of CTAs whose returns are reflected in the Barclay Hedge
and Newedge CTA indexes.
Consider the evidence provided in Exhibit I.1, which shows three net
asset value series—one for the S&P 500, one for Barclay Hedge Capital
U.S. Aggregate Bond Index, and one for CTAs. The CTA series has been
constructed by concatenating the Barclay CTA Index from 1990 through
1999 and the Newedge CTA Index from 2000 through 2009. All three series
start and end in roughly the same places, delivering average returns of around
7 percent for bonds and CTAs and 8 percent for the S&P 500. Over this
period, the dollar performance of global stocks underperformed the other
four investment classes by a substantial amount. The paths they followed are
obviously quite different, and it will be no surprise that when we consider
what the optimal portfolio weights would have been for stocks, bonds, and

*Peng Chen, et al., "Managed Futures and Asset Allocation," February 2005 working paper
from IbbotsonAssociates. The authors also provide in a footnote: From a legal standpoint, CTAs
must register with the Commodity Futures Trading Commission (CFTC) in according with
the U.S. Commodity Exchange Act (Title 7, Chapter 1, Section 6n). Similar obligations exist
for firms located outside of the United States (e.g., the Commodity Investment Regulations
in Japan). CTAs are typically organized as Limited Partnerships and have offshore structures
reminiscent of those created for hedge funds.

**EXHIBIT I.1** Net Asset Values for Stocks, Bonds, and CTAs

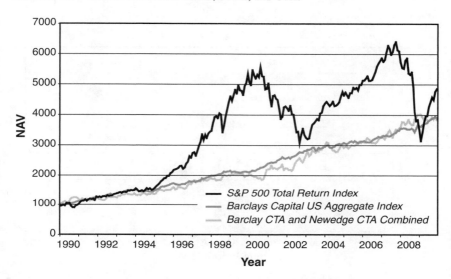

*Source:* Barclay Hedge, Bloomberg, Newedge Prime Brokerage Research.

CTAs over the past 20 years, we will find that equities merited a fairly low weight, while CTAs would have been accorded a fairly high weight.

The important thing to note about this CTA series is that it represents the results of a very real CTA investment portfolio. The index, at least since 2000, has comprised CTAs who are large, open to investment, and willing to provide daily return data to Barclay Hedge, which is the index calculation agent. The index is reconstructed once a year for each calendar year. There is no backfill in these results, and no optimization. As such, there is no so-called "selection bias." And there is survivor bias only in the sense that by focusing on the largest CTAs, the index follows the fortunes of those CTAs who have been successful enough over time to persuade many investors to invest substantial amounts of money.

Of course not all CTAs will make money. There are no barriers to entry, except for the regulatory requirements that govern the industry. Anyone with an idea about how to trade can become a CTA, and we know for a fact that many spend a little time in the financial sun, and then disappear from sight.

As a rule, though, if the broad index of CTA performance has done well, one finds CTAs tend to do well. The upper panel of Exhibit I.2 shows the distribution returns for 410 CTAs who reported monthly returns in 2003, which was a good year for the index. Most of this distribution lies to the

**EXHIBIT I.2**  Distributions of CTA Returns (2003 and 2009)

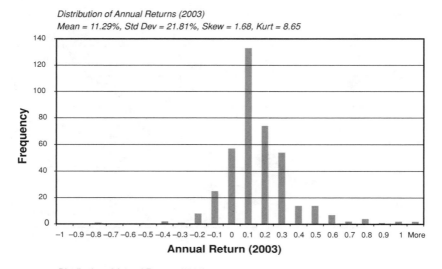

*Distribution of Annual Returns (2003)*
*Mean = 11.29%, Std Dev = 21.81%, Skew = 1.68, Kurt = 8.65*

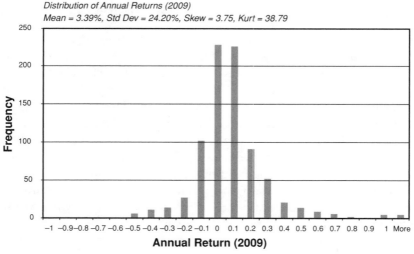

*Distribution of Annual Returns (2009)*
*Mean = 3.39%, Std Dev = 24.20%, Skew = 3.75, Kurt = 38.79*

*Source:* Barclay Hedge.

right of zero. The average of these returns was 11.29 percent. And of the 410 CTAs, 307 reported positive returns. The lower panel, however, shows a return distribution for the 821 CTAs who reported monthly returns for 2009, which was a decent year for the CTAs in the index. The average of these returns was positive at 3.39 percent, but of the 821 total, 432 reported losses.

Being large is no sure thing, either. Bernie Madoff convinced a lot of people to invest a lot of money in his operation, and it turned out to be a sham. But then his operation was hardly transparent.

Perhaps the toughest question we face is from investors who are new to the CTA or managed futures space and ask, rightly, why CTAs should make money. After all, investments in most hedge funds in general and CTAs in particular are not investments in conventional assets such as stocks, bonds, and real estate. Stocks, bonds and real estate represent ownership claims on real assets that generate real yields or income.

Before tackling the question, though, we would like to push back a little and point out that anyone who asks this question about CTAs or other hedge funds really has to ask the same question about any kind of portfolio manager who does not hold the world's assets in exactly the same proportions as they exist in the world. A dollar-based investor who holds only U.S.-based assets, for example, is overweighting the United States and underweighting the rest of the world. Or an active portfolio manager who varies the mix of stocks, bonds, and real estate to adapt to what he or she sees are changing economic conditions is overweighting some assets and underweighting others. In either case, the manager's contribution is a function entirely of bets made on prices—that some asset prices will rise more than others.

When viewed this way, the difference between a hedge fund and someone we would describe as a conventional, active portfolio manager is only one of degree, not of kind. The business of deconstructing assets and recombining the parts is now old hat. Salomon Brothers pioneered the practice of stripping the coupons from Treasury bonds to create customized bond portfolios. Hedge funds, which focus on strategies like long/short equity, convertible arb, and credit spreads have simply taken this idea to its logical conclusion.

So if we are going to ask why CTAs make money, we really have to ask why anyone who deviates from the world portfolio—including conventional, active portfolio managers—makes money. In fact, the literature on this question is not especially encouraging. It is not at all obvious that portfolio managers beat standard asset indexes with any regularity, or by amounts that are statistically significant.

In the case of CTAs, we have yet to hear a completely satisfactory response, but several plausible reasons merit your consideration.

For one thing, we know that asset and currency prices go through long stretches of what economists would consider mispricings. Purchasing power parity, for example, does a terrible job of explaining why currency prices do what they do. Robert Shiller and others have argued that stock prices are far too volatile. Anti Illmanen, in a marvelous series that he wrote for Salomon

Brothers, argues that investors do not earn a premium for taking duration risk in bonds beyond two years. There is a subset of academics who pursue serious research in psychological finance, and they are taken seriously. And even the late Paul Samuelson found enough merit in the idea of market inefficiencies to invest both time and money in establishing a trading firm called Commodities Corporation. Commodities Corporation in turn became the cornerstone of Goldman Sachs Asset Management's hedge fund business.*

In such a world, CTAs bring an interesting set of tools to bear. For one thing, many CTAs are systematic trend followers. In a world in which prices trend, CTAs can make money. Our own work on simple trend following models bears this out. In Chapters 4 and 5, for example, we show that a broadly diversified, volatility-weighted portfolios of futures positions driven by very simple moving average crossover and breakout models tend to make money and tend to be robust. We don't know why, and of course results like this drive people from the University of Chicago crazy, but these models worked when we published our first note on this topic in 2005, and were still working when we revisited the topic in 2010.

Then there is the systematic part of what they do. Systematic, or quantitative, traders are often excoriated in the press for employing "black boxes." But the black boxes are nothing more than tools that enable traders to discipline themselves and to avoid the traps and pitfalls that so often accompany discretionary trading. Rishi Narang has written a very approachable description of this part of trading life called *Inside the Black Box* (Wiley, 2009).

The CTA space is one of the few in which traders are as likely to be short as long. Shorting is anathema for many investors and portfolio managers. Worse, the world's portfolios as an aggregate are stuck with the world's assets. Someone has to own all the stocks, bonds, and real estate. Even long/short equity hedge funds tend to be long stocks. As a result, CTAs can actually make money from price decreases that long-only investors must simply suffer through.

And then, too, successful CTAs are very effective at managing risk. You will see this in the way they combine markets or trading horizons to produce a volatility of returns that allows them to retain the confidence of their investors—that is, to control their losses and to avoid unusually large

---

*"[Samuelson] was always interested in markets, in money markets in particular. He knew Warren Buffett, was pals with John Bogle, and when in 1968 Stanley Marsh called him away from a game of tennis to pepper him with questions, the conversation led to the founding of Commodities Corp., an early and successful hedge fund (sold to Goldman Sachs in 1997)." See Paul Samuelson's Legacy, economicprincipals.com, December 20, 2009.

**EXHIBIT I.3**   Past and Future CTA Volatility

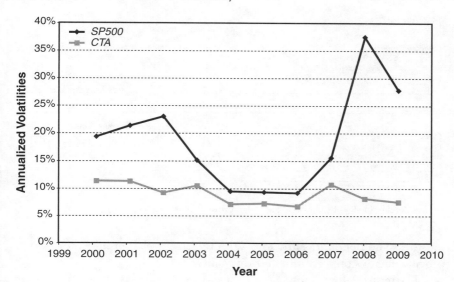

*Source:* Bloomberg, Newedge Prime Brokerage Research.

drawdowns. CTAs' control over return volatility is in sharp contrast to the world of conventional money managers who are more or less stuck with the volatilities that the market delivers. Exhibit I.3 compares the volatility of returns on the S&P 500 with the volatility of returns for the Newedge CTA Index for 2000 through 2009. During these years, while the stock market was going through extended periods of volatility, quiet, and crisis, CTA return volatilities chugged along steadily in a range around 10 percent.

None of these arguments are likely to satisfy the truly skeptical investor, and it is not our hope to do so. At the same time, we are confident that a CTA who turned in a performance similar to that of the S&P 500 would not keep his job or his investors for long. He might have been able to raise a lot of money in the 1990s, but his performance from 2000 through 2003 would have led to substantial redemptions. And even if he managed to raise money again, his losses in 2008 would almost certainly have led to further redemptions.

## How Much Should You Invest?

The answer is a surprisingly large number—or at least it can be. In the first place, as shown in Exhibit I.4, the correlations of CTA returns with those

**EXHIBIT I.4**   Return Correlations (1990–2009)

U.S. Assets and CTAs

| Category | Index | Annual Rate of Return (Arithmetic) | Annual Standard Deviation | Maximum Drawdown | Return / Risk | Optimal Weight* |
|---|---|---|---|---|---|---|
| Equity | S& P 500 Total Return Index | 9.43% | 14.96% | 50.95% | 0.63 | 5.61% |
| Bond | Barclays Capital U.S. Aggregate Bond Index | 6.96% | 3.85% | 5.15% | 1.81 | 82.57% |
| CTA | Barclay CTA and Newedge CTA Combined | 7.11% | 9.37% | 10.31% | 0.76 | 11.82% |
| Portfolio | | 7.12% | 3.71% | 4.53% | 1.92 | 100% |

*Global Assets and CTAs*

| Category | Index | Annual Rate of Return (Arithmetic) | Annual Standard Deviation | Maximum Drawdown | Return / Risk | Optimal Weight* |
|---|---|---|---|---|---|---|
| Equity | MSCI World Index | 6.07% | 15.36% | 53.58% | 0.40 | 5.60% |
| Bond | JP Morgan Global Aggregate Bond Index | 7.43% | 6.04% | 9.42% | 1.23 | 69.85% |
| CTA | Barclay CTA and Newedge CTA Combined | 7.11% | 9.37% | 10.31% | 0.76 | 24.55% |
| Portfolio | | 7.28% | 5.37% | 7.86% | 1.35 | 100% |

* *Weights chosen to maximize return/risk ratio.*

*Source:* Barclay Hedge, Bloomberg, Newedge Prime Brokerage Research.

on stocks and bonds are fairly low. With return correlations like these, CTAs provide obvious opportunities for diversification.

The return information provided in Exhibit I.5 sheds some useful light on the choices investors might face. During the two decades from 1990 through 2009, stocks delivered reasonably high returns for dollar-based investors, at least on average. The 1990s were an almost uninterrupted bull market, while the 2000s were more like a rollercoaster. By the time these two decades had drawn to a close, the S&P 500 had produced an average annual return of 9.43 percent, which was much higher than the average return on a diversified bond portfolio (6.96%) or on a portfolio of CTAs (7.11%).

But the risks in equity returns were off the charts. Annualized volatility was nearly 15 percent, and the maximum drawdown in equities was more than 50 percent. Bonds, in contrast, produced their returns with little or no volatility and a maximum drawdown of just over 5 percent. CTAs came in somewhere in the middle with returns more volatile than those on bonds but less volatile than those on stocks. Also, both bonds and CTAs delivered much smaller maximum drawdowns than those experienced by equity investors. In sharp contrast to the 50 percent drawdown in stocks, the worst drawdown for bonds was just over 5 percent, and for CTAs was just over 10 percent.

The combined effect of these returns, volatilities, and correlations is an optimal 20/20 hindsight portfolio that would have contained only slightly more than 5 percent stocks, nearly 12 percent CTAs, and 83 percent bonds. And, as shown in the lower panel of Exhibit I.5, a dollar-based investor with a globally diversified portfolio would have done best with a portfolio comprising almost 25 percent CTAs, 70 percent bonds, and 5 percent stocks.

**EXHIBIT I.5**  Return Histories (1990–2009, Dollars) with Optimal Weights

*1990 through 2009*

|  | S&P | MSCI W | U.S. Bonds | Glbl Bds | CTAs |
|---|---|---|---|---|---|
| S&P500 | 1.00 | 0.89 | 0.19 | 0.13 | −0.16 |
| MSCI World | 0.89 | 1.00 | 0.16 | 0.25 | −0.14 |
| Barclays U.S. Bond Index | 0.19 | 0.16 | 1.00 | 0.70 | 0.15 |
| JP Morgan Global Bond Index | 0.13 | 0.25 | 0.70 | 1.00 | 0.19 |
| CTAs | −0.16 | −0.14 | 0.15 | 0.19 | 1.00 |

*2000 through 2009*

|  | S&P | MSCI W | U.S. Bonds | Glbl Bds | CTAs |
|---|---|---|---|---|---|
| S&P500 | 1.00 | 0.97 | −0.01 | 0.10 | −0.22 |
| MSCI World | 0.97 | 1.00 | 0.03 | 0.20 | −0.15 |
| Barclays U.S. Bond Index | −0.01 | 0.03 | 1.00 | 0.77 | 0.18 |
| JP Morgan Global Bond Index | 0.10 | 0.20 | 0.77 | 1.00 | 0.28 |
| CTAs | −0.22 | −0.15 | 0.18 | 0.28 | 1.00 |

*Source:* Barclay Hedge, Bloomberg, Newedge Prime Brokerage Research.

Of course, the world cannot allocate this much of its global portfolio to CTAs. The total value of real money portfolios in the world is measured in the tens of trillions of dollars, while the total value of money managed by this subset of hedge funds is closer to $200 billion. Stephen Ross rightly characterized the entire hedge fund space, which might control $2 trillion or so, as a rounding error on the world's portfolio. As a result, the world is constrained to hold only a small fraction of its portfolio in this form.

Individual money managers, in contrast, are not constrained by the size of the CTA market. They may be constrained by investment covenants or deterred by skepticism, but in principle, even the largest of the world's pension funds would be able to assign much higher weights to CTAs than they do.

## What About the Risks?

Futures are often characterized as risky, mainly because they afford as much leverage as they do. But, as we show in Chapter 1, the risk in a portfolio based on futures is under the portfolio manager's complete control and depends entirely on how positions are combined with one another and how much cash is combined with the futures. In principle, futures, if combined with the right amount of cash, exhibit exactly the same risk as the underlying assets or commodities.

In practice, because of the transparency and liquidity that are the hallmarks of futures, CTAs represent the most liquid subset of the hedge fund space. In 2008, when investors needed cash from their investments, they learned that CTAs were by far the most reliable source of liquidity.

It is worth noting, too, that the clearing house system that allows the futures industry to settle up gains and losses every day in cash and to protect clients' cash or securities that they post to guarantee performance has proven itself to be very effective. Futures markets have handled enormous gains and losses during times of financial crisis without any stress on the system at all. And the futures market practice of segregating customers' funds has worked well, even though the level of protection varies with the regulatory environment.

Anyone who knows anything about over-the-counter markets and derivatives markets knows that futures markets are a model of risk management. With each passing year, risk management in the over-the-counter swaps market looks more and more like what futures have always done. More often than not, swaps require collateral, provisions for settling up gains and losses in cash, and netting. And in discussions of regulatory reform, one often hears the idea of a clearing house proposed as one solution to the problems that beset the over-the-counter derivatives market.

## They're a Good Fit for Institutional Investors

Actually, they're not a good fit for everyone. But for those investors who choose to invest, CTAs afford a number of advantages that flow through to the investor. These include:

Transparency: Futures prices are determined competitively, and futures positions are marked to market daily. The fact that futures prices tend to be determined in single price discovery markets in which everyone can see the limit order book and in which the settlement price is a real tradable price makes them more accurate and more reliable than prices determined in nearly any other market. The prices used to mark portfolios to market are not stale. There are no "dark pools" of liquidity like those one finds in equity markets. There are no massive interpolation schemes that one finds in most bond markets where only a handful of bonds actually trade on any given day. And there are no models needed to determine the value of structured securities. Futures prices are real, competitive prices.

As a result, the returns you see are real and have not been smoothed. One simply does not find any of the serial correlation in returns associated with the discretion other hedge funds have in when and how much to revalue a portfolio when market prices change.

**Liquidity:** We've already mentioned liquidity, but only in the context of liquidating positions and extracting cash. In fact, transactions costs in futures are lower than in their underlying cash markets. As a result, the benefits of the kind of active management and trading that CTAs do are available with much less drag from market impact than one would have to incur doing the same kinds of trading in underlying markets.

**No withholding taxes:** In a number of the world's stock and bond markets, foreign investors are taxed more heavily than domestic investors. With futures, all of the tax benefits that accrue to domestic investors can be passed through to those who use futures in the form of simple cash/futures arbitrage.

**Very low foreign exchange risk:** Futures on foreign assets or commodities come with built-in hedges against foreign exchange risk. A futures contract has no net liquidating value. As a result, being long European equity index futures has no exposure to the change in the price of the Euro, while an investment in European equities exposes the investor not only to changes in the price of European stocks, but to changes in the price of the Euro as well. In the case of futures, the investor's currency risk is limited to the comparatively small amounts of margin that must be posted at exchanges around the world and to any realized profit or loss that has not yet been converted back into the investor's home currency.

This is not a complete list of the benefits associated with using futures as part of any actively managed portfolio. But it should be apparent that any hedge fund or investor that does not use futures to implement their market views has a lot of explaining to do.

## How the Book Is Structured

In our role as brokers, we are privy to some pointed questions and intense conversations about the ways CTAs work—how they make their money, the environments in which they are more or less successful, the risks they face, and ways to improve your own returns on investments in CTAs. We also enjoy the luxury of objectivity, mainly because we do not have to defend a track record. The only real sense in which our research is self-serving is that we believe we will do better if everyone in the industry, both managers and investors, share a common understanding of the challenges they face and are free to make informed decisions.

The rest of the book is for those who want to explore the possibility of investing in CTAs and to know how to do it well if they do. To this end, we have organized the material into three broad sections: a practical guide to the industry, building blocks, and portfolio construction.

**Part 1: A Practical Guide to the Industry**
Chapter 1: Understanding Returns
Chapter 2: Where Are the Data?
Chapter 3: Structuring Your Investment: Frequently Asked Questions

This section is a nuts-and-bolts guide to how the industry works. In Chapter 1, for example, we explain the industry's cash management practices, single currency margining, and what it means to calculate a rate of return on something that has no net liquidating value. In Chapter 2, we show you where to find the data and how to wrestle with problems of self-reporting and survivorship bias. Chapter 3 walks you through the most common vehicles for investing in CTAs, including funds, platforms, and managed accounts.

**Part 2: Building Blocks**
Chapter 4: How Trend Following Works
Chapter 5: Two Benchmarks for Momentum Trading
Chapter 6: The Value of Daily Return Data
Chapter 7: Every Drought Ends in a Rainstorm: Mean Reversion, Momentum, or Serial Independence?
Chapter 8: Understanding Drawdowns
Chapter 9: How Stock Price Volatility Affects Returns
Chapter 10: The Costs of Active Management
Chapter 11: Measuring Market Impact and Liquidity

Each chapter in this section grew out of some fairly intensive research into each of these questions. Some clients, frustrated by CTAs' unwillingness to reveal much about the ways they actually trade, wanted to know how trend following works. The industry is migrating from monthly to daily data as a standard, which has its advantages and its challenges. Some investors truly believe that they can time their investments in CTAs (and we doubt it) by investing on drawdowns or selling on high-water marks. We show how to put CTAs' drawdown experience into perspective given the length of their track records and the volatilities of their returns. We take a close look at how the single most important source of volatility in world financial markets affects the relationship between stock returns and CTA returns. We put real numbers on what active management of CTA investments costs. And we report out on the work we have done on market impact in futures markets.

**Part 3: Portfolio Construction**
Chapter 12: Superstars versus Teamwork
Chapter 13: A New Look at Constructing Teamwork Portfolios
Chapter 14: Correlations and Holding Periods: The Research Basis for the *Newedge AlternativeEdge Short-Term Traders Index*
Chapter 15: "There Are Known Unknowns": The Drag of Imperfect Estimates

The only free lunch in portfolio management is diversification. Everything else comes at a high price. But knowing how to use basic portfolio construction tools to your advantage can pay great dividends.

One investor we know likes to say that the thing he understands most is transactions costs. Transactions costs are highly predictable and highly controllable. Next on his list is volatility and correlation. Volatility and correlation tend to be fairly predictable and fairly controllable. The last thing on his list, the thing he understands least, is returns. Past returns tell us almost nothing about future returns and can't be predicted or controlled at all.

Our own research bears this out, and to our advantage. Futures markets exist only because the costs of trading are lower than they are in their underlying markets. And, in the third section, we report on what we have learned about volatility and correlation and how their predictability can be used to build portfolios that perform really well.

What we contribute to this conversation, then, are insights into those things that you can use effectively to create well-diversified portfolios and those things that you cannot. We show how to identify low correlation reliably and where the past in fact does reveal something useful about the future. We also face up to the empirical hurdles that get in the way of knowing whether one is doing a good job. This problem is hardly unique to CTA investments, but the standards to which CTAs are held tend to be higher than those used to evaluate conventional real money managers, so it is good to know just what those standards imply.

Happy reading.

# PART I

# A Practical Guide to the Industry

# CHAPTER 1

# Understanding Returns

The purpose of this chapter is to bridge the gap between the world of conventional money management, where return has a natural and well-understood meaning, and the world of futures, where the idea of return by itself makes no sense. The disconnect between the two markets is simply this: Real assets tie up real cash. To buy a portfolio of real stocks, for example, one invests real cash. The stocks then spin off dividends, which constitute part of the return, and the prices of the stocks rise or fall, which constitutes the rest. The resulting gains or losses are converted into a return using a denominator equal to the value of the cash invested in the stocks.

Once you leave the world of fully invested, conventional assets, reckoning returns becomes more of a challenge. What, for example, is the return to a long/short strategy in which the market values of your positions are exactly offsetting? This is, in fact, the case with futures, which behave like fully leveraged or geared positions in the underlying commodity. Their purpose in applied finance is to capture changes in the price of the underlying, which allows them to be used equally well for both hedging and trading. The real usefulness of futures stems from the fact that they are almost always less expensive to trade than are their underlying commodities. And in the hands of CTAs, they are building blocks from which highly diversified portfolios of positions—both long and short—in the world's financial and commodities markets can be built.

To understand how a CTA works and how to interpret a CTA's returns, you need to know a few key things about how futures and the futures industry works. In the sections that follow, we cover most of what you will need to feel comfortable with the industry. The key points include:

- Risk and cash management in futures markets
- Trading levels, funding levels, and the idea of notional funding

17

- Stability of CTAs' return volatilities
- Basic futures mechanics (using S&P 500 futures as a worked example)
- Managing cash and collateral
- A typical trend-following CTA's portfolio of futures
- Converting profits and losses into returns and return volatilities
- Different share classes in CTA funds

## Risk and Cash Management

Although futures are like forwards in the sense that they both behave like fully leveraged positions in the underlying commodity, the futures industry has must stricter risk and cash management practices than the over-the-counter derivatives market. And the way the futures market approaches risk has important implications for the way CTAs do business and for the way you may choose to invest in this market.

As a stepping-off point, consider these three key points:

1. Futures markets require gains and losses to be settled in cash daily.
2. Futures contracts have no net liquidating value.
3. Futures markets require participants to post collateral to cover potential daily losses.

The first point has important consequences for the way you organize your investment in CTAs. The practice of settling up gains and losses every day in cash produces an ongoing stream of small transactions costs. Minimizing these costs is an important objective for CTAs and their investors. The cash that flows into or out of your account also affects your ultimate return. Cash that flows in can be invested, while the cash that flows out must be financed, either explicitly or out of pocket.

The second point actually follows from the first and is truly fundamental. Because all gains and losses are settled in cash daily, futures contracts never have any net liquidating value except for whatever they accumulate over the course of a single trading day. As a result, there is no natural denominator for reckoning the return on a futures position.

The importance of the third point also becomes apparent when you decide how to structure your investment in CTAs. In Chapter 3 we walk you through a decision process that allows you to compare an investment in CTAs' funds with an investment in managed accounts, or with a hybrid investment using a CTA investment platform. What you earn on any cash or collateral invested in a fund or posted as collateral in a managed account is part of your return. You also care about the security of your cash investment.

## Trading, Funding, and Notional Levels

To cope with these features of the futures market, the CTA industry has adopted three specialized terms that investors must know—trading level, funding level, and notional level.

The three terms can be defined as:

**Trading level:** Trading level is simply the choice of denominator. It is the dollar number that the CTA uses to translate futures profits and losses into returns. It is also the dollar number that the CTA uses to calculate ongoing management fees.

**Funding level:** Funding level is the total amount of cash or collateral that you post or invest. The rock-bottom minimum funding level for any futures position or portfolio is the total value of margin collateral required by the various futures exchanges.

**Notional level:** Exchange margins tend to be small relative to the face values or portfolio equivalent values of the contracts themselves. And in a diversified portfolio of futures contracts, the actual day-to-day risk in the portfolio can be smaller still. As a result, funding levels can be lower than trading levels. If they are, the difference between the trading and the funding levels is known as the *notional level* or as *notional funding*.

## The Stability of Return Volatilities

One of the important consequences of the way CTAs approach their choice of trading level is that they can control the volatility of their returns. For that matter, unlike real money managers, who must live with the return volatility they are given in their respective stock and bond markets, CTAs appear to actively manage the size and mix of their futures positions so that, given their choices of trading levels, their returns exhibit a high degree of predictability from year to year.

Exhibit 1.1 illustrates this point. For a collection of 54 CTAs (chosen because they all had $100 million or more under management and four years of reported returns), we have calculated the annualized volatilities of reported

**EXHIBIT 1.1**  Past and Future Return Volatility

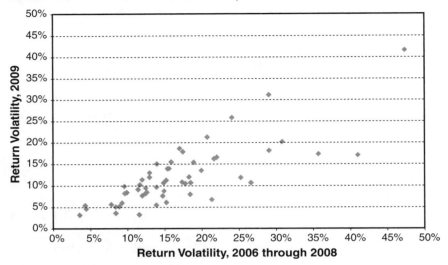

*Source:* Barclay Hedge.

returns for 2006 through 2008, which are measured on the horizontal axis, and for 2009, which are measured on the vertical axis. We say a lot more about this in Chapter 11, but for now it is enough to know that this kind of relationship is typical. You can choose nearly any look-back and look-forward periods you like, and you will find that a CTA whose returns are low this year (or for the past two or three years) will be likely to have low returns next year (or for the next two or three years).

This kind of predictable return volatility is extremely helpful when constructing portfolios of CTAs.

## Basic Futures Mechanics

Most of what you need to know about futures and futures markets can be illustrated using one of the industry's most actively traded contracts—the E-mini S&P 500 contract. It is especially helpful that the underlying is a widely recognized index of stock prices and that the futures contract, when combined with the appropriate amount of cash, can behave like a small diversified portfolio of stocks. In this section, we cover basic contract terms, the S&P 500 futures contract, cash/future price relationships, and combining futures with cash to create a synthetic stock portfolio.

## Contract Terms

Strictly speaking, futures are governed by exchange rule books, which lay out in considerable detail just how various members of the exchange are to deal with the exchange and, if they have any, with their non-member clients. Many of the rules are common to all of the futures traded on the exchange, but each futures contract requires a few key contract specifications that govern that particular contract. These basic terms include, at a minimum:

- A definition of the underlying commodity or index
- The dollar (or other currency) value of a 1-point change in the price of the commodity or of the value of the index
- The minimum change in the futures price
- The months in which the contract expires
- Last trading day
- Final settlement terms
- Ticker symbol(s)
- Limit price moves

The exchange, or its clearing house, also determines the amounts of margin collateral that must be maintained by the clearing broker to support any open futures positions.

## The S&P 500 Futures Contract

All of the important features of futures can be illustrated with the E-mini S&P 500 futures contract. The relevant contract terms, as they apply to users, are shown in Exhibit 1.2, which is a standard page available on Bloomberg. In this case, we are looking at the September 2009 contract. Its ticker symbol is ESU9, in which the *ES* stands for the E-mini S&P 500 contract, the *U* stands for September (don't ask), and the *9* stands for 2009. It is typical to use a 2-letter code for the market, a 1-letter code for the contract's expiration or delivery month, and a single numeral to describe the year.

The underlying is the SPX index, which is simply the S&P 500 stock price index. The contract size is said to be $50 times the value of the index, which means that each index point is worth $50. The tick size is the minimum price change allowed by the exchange and is set at 0.25 price points, which makes the value of a tick $12.50 [= $50 · 0.25]. The value of the contract's price at the time this snapshot was taken on June 25, 2009 was 915.50. When multiplied by $50, we find a contract value of $45,775 [= $50 · 915.50].

**EXHIBIT 1.2**    S&P 500 Contract Specifications

DES                                                                    Msg: ECO STATS

| 22) News |                                   Futures Contract Description

Notes
Description: E-mini S&P 500 Futures

Exchange ticker: ES

25) View All Notes

| Contract Specifications | | Trading Hours | | |
| Name S&P500 EMINI FUT Sep09 | | | Exchange | Local |
| 26) Ticker ESU9 Index | | | 15:30-15:15 | 16:30-16:15 |
| 27) Exchange CME-Chicago Mercantile Exchange | | | | |
| Underlying SPX Index | | | | |
| Contract Size 50 $ × index | | | | |
| Value of 1.0 pt $ 50 | | Related Dates | | |
| Tick Size 0.25 | | Cash Settled | | |
| Tick Value $ 12.5 | | First Trade Mon Jun 23, 2008 | | |
| 28) Price 915.50 index points | | Last Trade Fri Sep 18, 2009 | | |
| Contract Value $ 45,775 @ 13:41:19 | | Valuation Date Fri Sep 18, 2009 | | |

Margin Limits

|  | Speculator | Hedger | Price Range | |
| Initial | 5,625 | 4,500 | Up Limit 968.00 | Life High 1,339.50 |
| Secondary | 4,500 | 4,500 | Down Limit 828.00 | Life Low 662.00 |

Cycle    –    –    Mar    –    –    Jun    –    –    Sep    –    –    Dec
| 1) Future | 2) Option | 3) Spread | 4) Generic | 5) Monthly |

Australia 61 2 9777 8600    Brazil 5511 3048 4500    Europe 44 20 7330 7500    Germany 49 69 9204 1210    Hong Kong 852 2977 6000
Japan 81 3 3201 8900    Singapore 65 6212 1000    U.S. 1 212 318 2000    Copyright 2009 Bloomberg Finance L.P.
SN 223810 G566-163-1 25-Jun-2009 13:51:28

*Source:* Bloomberg Financial LP.

The exchange has set initial and secondary margin limits for speculators and hedgers. As a practical matter, once a position is open and maintained from day to day, the relevant number from the exchange's standpoint is $4,500.

Under related dates, you can see that the contract was first listed for trading on June 23, 2008. Its last trade date is Friday, September 18, 2009. The contract is said to be cash settled, which means that its final settlement price is set equal to the value of the S&P 500 at the time the contract expires. In this case, the final settlement value is set equal to the value of the index calculated using prices for all 500 stocks as established at the market open for each stock.

## Cash/Futures Price Relationships

The force that ties a futures price to the price of the underlying commodity or asset is *arbitrage*. If futures are rich relative to fair value, the arbitrageur can buy the underlying asset and sell the futures. Or if futures are cheap relative to fair value, the arbitrageur can sell the underlying asset and buy the futures. Just how effective these arbitrage forces are depends on the costs of buying and selling the underlying commodity, the costs of financing, availability of arbitrage capital, and so on.

Because of these arbitrage forces, the relationship between futures prices and spot prices can be thought of generally as:

Futures price = Spot price + Financing and other storage costs − Convenience yield

where spot price represents the price of the underlying asset of commodity.

For financial assets, financing is the main cost of holding or storing the asset. For physical assets, holding costs can include wastage, the costs of maintaining a ranch or drilling platform, and so on. Convenience yield depends on the asset or commodity. For equities, convenience yield would include dividends and, possibly, income from securities lending. For bonds, convenience yield would include accrued coupon income. For currencies, convenience yield would include interest on the foreign currency. For physical assets, convenience yields are small, although those who hold gold may enjoy some rental income.

The way this relationship works for the E-mini S&P 500 contract is illustrated in Exhibit 1.3, which is another standard Bloomberg page. This snapshot was taken on June 25, 2009. Under "Cash," you find that the value of the S&P 500 index is 918.87. From this, the reasoning is that one could buy a diversified portfolio of stocks using the S&P 500 index weights as a guide to how much of each of the 500 stocks one would hold. At $50 per index point, the total value of this diversified portfolio would be $45,943.50 [= $50 · 918.87].

The cost of financing this purchase is assumed to be the risk-free rate of 0.60 percent. The contract expires September 18, 2009, which is 85 days from June 25.

The convenience yield includes expected dividends, which are calculated in index points. Between June 25 and September 18, Bloomberg's *consensus* sources suggest that the holder of the portfolio can expect to receive dividends worth 5.16 index points.

Taken together, these pieces of information suggest that the fair value of the September 2009 futures contract is

$$Fair\ Futures = Spot\left(1 + Financing\ rate\frac{Days}{360}\right) - Dividends$$

**EXHIBIT 1.3**   S&P 500 Futures Fair Value

```
<HELP> for explanation.                                          Index FVD
ENTER ALL VALUES AND HIT <GO>
              EQUITY INDEX FAIR VALUE (DETAIL)
```

| S&P 500 INDEX | Cash | Future | Theo. Future | Fair Value | Spread (Basis) | Upper Bound | Lower Bound |
|---|---|---|---|---|---|---|---|
| 1) ESU9vsSPX | 918.87 | 915.00 | 915.02 | −3.85 | −3.87 | −2.69 | −5.01 |
| Risk Free: | .60% | Expire: | 9/18/09 | Dividend: | 5.16 | Dvd Yld: | 2.38% |
| Implied Rate: | .59% | Days: | 85 | Percent of Gross Dividend : | | | 100.0% |
| | | | | Enter 3<GO> for BDVD projections | | | |
| 2) ESZ9vsSPX | 918.87 | 911.25 | 913.14 | −5.73 | −7.62 | −4.57 | −6.90 |
| Risk Free: | 1.07% | Expire: | 12/18/09 | Dividend: | 10.55 | Dvd Yld: | 2.35% |
| Implied Rate: | .65% | Days: | 176 | Percent of Gross Dividend : | | | 100.0% |
| | | | | Enter 4<GO> for BDVD projections | | | |

```
      Note: use RDFL <go> for the risk free rate default.
■ Percent/Index Points            Transaction Costs
  Buy-Stocks Sell-Futures    (Upper Bound)      Sell-Stocks Buy-Futures    (Lower Bound)
  Stock Bid/Ask Spread       = ███              Stock Bid/Ask Spread       = ███
                                                Stock Borrowing Cost       = ███
  Stock Commission           = ███              Stock Commission           = ███
  Future Bid/Ask Spread      = ███              Future Bid/Ask Spread      = ███
  Commission Futures         = ███              Commission Futures         = ███
  Other (Stamp, Currcy..)    = ███              Other (Stamp, Currcy..)    = ███
  Total Transaction Cost     = 0.13%  1.16      Total Transaction Cost     = 0.13%  1.16
```

```
      Hit <#> Go to monitor the intra-day spread of cash & futures (Basis)
Australia 61 2 9777 8600  Brazil 5511 3048 4500  Europe 44 20 7330 7500  Germany 49 69 9204 1210  Hong Kong 852 2977 6000
Japan 81 3 3201 8900      Singapore 65 6212 1000    U.S. 1 212 318 2000          Copyright 2009 Bloomberg Finance L.P.
                                                        SN 223810 G566-163-1 25-Jun-2009 13:54:09
```

*Source:* Bloomberg Financial LP.

which, in this example, becomes

$$915.01 = 918.87 \left(1 + .006\frac{85}{360}\right) - 5.16$$

which is .01 less than Bloomberg's 915.02 because of a small amount of rounding. Notice that the market value of the futures price is shown as 915.00, which is less than its calculated fair value. This same relationship is also illustrated in Exhibit 1.4.

The futures price in this case is below the spot price because expected dividend income is greater than the cost of financing the position. The fair value of the "spread" or difference between the futures and spot prices is shown as −3.85 [= 915.02 − 918.87] while its market value of basis is shown as −3.87 [= 915.00 − 918.87].

With any three pieces of information, one can use the above expression to solve for the fourth. For example, using the cash and futures prices of 918.87

**EXHIBIT 1.4**   Fair Value of an S&P 500 Futures Contract

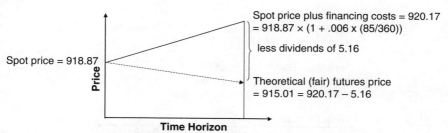

Bloomberg shows a fair futures price of 915.02, which reflects a rounding error somewhere.

and 915.00 and the expected dividend value of 5.16, one can solve for the financing rate that would cause the futures price to be "fair." This is shown as the implied rate of 0.59 percent.

## Creating a Synthetic Stock Portfolio

This cash/futures arithmetic can be used to combine cash and futures to create a synthetic alternative to an actual stock portfolio. Instead of buying stock, one could combine $45,943.50 invested in an 85-day term money market instrument with one long futures contract. The resulting combination would, to a very close approximation, exhibit the same gains and losses as those on a real stock portfolio. Moreover, the returns on the synthetic portfolio would be identical to those on the underlying stock. In other words, a futures position, when combined with the appropriate amount of cash, exhibits the same risk as the underlying asset.

To confirm that this is true, consider the possible outcomes shown in Exhibit 1.5, which shows the gains or losses on two portfolios—one a fully invested position of $45,943.50 in real stocks, the other a combination of futures and an amount of cash equal to the value of the real stock portfolio. Three outcomes are shown: stock prices (the index value) unchanged at 918.87, stock prices down 50 points to 868.87, and stock prices up 50 points to 968.87.

Consider the unchanged case first. The real stock portfolio produces dividend income of $258.00 [= 50 · $5.61] and no capital gain or loss for a total gain of $258.00. The synthetic stock portfolio produces interest income of $65.09 [= .006 · 85/360 · $45,943.50] and a gain on the futures contract of $193.00 [= $50 · (918.87 − 915.01)] because at expiration the futures price equals the value of the stock index. Notice that the gain on the futures contract makes up exactly for the difference in the dividend income on the

**EXHIBIT 1.5**    Returns on Real and Synthetic Stock Portfolios as Stock Prices Rise and Fall

**Portfolio 1 (Stock)**
Buy $45,943.50 of a diversified portfolio of stock at
an index value of 918.87

**Portfolio 2 (Synthetic stock)**
Buy 1 futures contract at 915.01
Invest $45,943.50 at 0.6% for 85 days

**Portfolio Gains and Losses**

|  | S&P500 at Futures Expiration | | |
|---|---|---|---|
|  | 868.87 | 918.87 | 968.87 |
| **Stock Portfolio** | | | |
| Stock | −2500.00 | 0.00 | 2500.00 |
| Dividends | 258.00 | 258.00 | 258.00 |
| *Total* | *−2242.00* | *258.00* | *2758.00* |
| **Synthetic Stock Portfolio (Futures Plus Cash)** | | | |
| Futures | −2307.00 | 193.00 | 2693.00 |
| Interest | 65.09 | 65.09 | 65.09 |
| *Total* | *−2241.91* | *258.09* | *2758.09* |

*Source:* Bloomberg, Newedge Prime Brokerage Research.

stock and the interest income on the cash. As a result, the two portfolios produce the same final gain, just in different combinations. (The extra $.09 on the synthetic futures portfolio is there because we assume we buy the futures at 915.01, which is ever so slightly lower than the contract's fair value of 915.0117.)

In the other two cases, the two portfolios produce the same loss or the same gain, in both cases because what you lose on the futures is less than what you lose on the stock, or what you make on the futures is more than what you make on the stock. In both cases, the differences are the difference between dividend income on the stocks and interest income on the cash.

In practice, on the days between contract expirations, the futures price may trade either higher or lower than fair value by amounts that are limited by the possibilities of cash/futures arbitrage. For the most part, these departures from fair value are small, and if we were to track the return volatility on the synthetic stock portfolio, it would look almost exactly like the return volatility on the real stock portfolio. One would hardly be able to slide a piece of paper between the two series.

However, the futures position could be made to appear a lot riskier by combining with futures only with enough cash to cover the exchange's required margin of $4,500 (the secondary or hedger margin shown in Exhibit 1.2).

Because this is roughly 10 percent of the portfolio equivalent value of the contract, the resulting return volatility would be roughly 10 times higher. With stock price volatility that varies between 10 and 20 percent, the leverage portfolio could be made to exhibit volatilities of 100 to 200 percent if desired.

In contrast, the riskiness of a futures position can be reduced to zero—or to that of a money market instrument, by combining the futures with an offsetting position in the underlying stock. That is, the same arithmetic can be used to create a synthetic term money market instrument. If one were to buy the stock outright and sell the futures, the resulting position would pay an 85-day term money market return of 0.59 percent, and it would exhibit the price risk of an 85-day term money market investment.

## A Typical Futures Portfolio

One way to make this more concrete is to consider a futures portfolio that would be typical, or at least representative, of the kind of portfolio one would find with a CTA described as a systematic trend follower. We track several generic trend-following models on a daily basis. The portfolio shown in Exhibit 1.6 shows the positions that a 20/140-day moving average crossover model might have held on March 9, 2010. We explain how such a model works and the reasoning behind the choices of numbers of contracts in Chapter 4.

The example is a good one because it shows how one can have exposure to a broad range of financial and commodities markets. In this case, the contract mix covers equities, interest rates, foreign exchange, and commodities. The mix of contracts within each sector has been chosen to give roughly equal volatility weighting to each contract. The sizes of the four sectors have been chosen in this example so that roughly 30 percent of the portfolio's return volatility comes from each of the three financial sectors and 10 percent of its volatility from commodities. The overall position sizes have been chosen to produce a return volatility of approximately 15 percent on a $2 billion portfolio, although the numbers of contracts in each market have been limited to no more than 1 percent of open interest and 5 percent of average daily volume in their respective markets.

This example is also good because it is both rich and realistic and allows us to illustrate a wide range of issues related to how cash is used in such a trading model. In the course of this discussion, we will touch on the following:

• Minimum (SPAN) margin requirements
• Multi- and single currency margining

**EXHIBIT 1.6** Sample Futures Portfolio for 20/140 Moving Average Model (March 9, 2010)

| Market and Contract | Position |
|---|---|
| **Equity** | |
| SPI 200 | −499 |
| CAC 40 | −731 |
| DAX | −214 |
| Euro S TOXX 50 | −969 |
| FTSE 100 | 499 |
| Hang Seng | −242 |
| IBEX 35 | −267 |
| KOSPI | 473 |
| MIB | −241 |
| NASDAQ 100 Mini | 1,271 |
| Nikkei 225 | 325 |
| S& P 500 E-mini | 744 |
| Swedish OMX | 3,110 |
| Russell 2000 Mini | 573 |
| **Interest Rates** | |
| Australian 10 Year | 1,566 |
| Australian 3 Month | 1,083 |
| Euro 3 Month Rate (Euribor) | 6,475 |
| German 5 Year (BOBL) | 2,197 |
| German 10 Year (BUND) | 1,412 |
| German Schatz | 5,206 |
| Japan 10 Year (JGB) | 261 |
| Japan 3 Month | 990 |
| UK 10 Year (Gilt) | −1,023 |
| UK Short Sterling | 3,435 |
| US 10 Year | 1,474 |
| US 2 Year | 2,853 |
| US 30 Year | −971 |
| US 3 Month Rate (Eurodollar) | 4,989 |
| US 5 Year | 2,265 |
| **Foreign Exchange** | |
| British Pound | −1,812 |
| Canadian Dollar | 1,899 |
| Euro | −1,114 |
| Japanese Yen | 1,466 |
| Mexican Peso | 4,223 |
| New Zealand Dollar | −1,935 |
| Swiss Franc | −1,570 |
| Australian Dollar | 1,499 |
| **Commodity** | |
| Cocoa | −358 |
| Coffee | −545 |
| Copper | 135 |
| Corn | −1,972 |
| Cotton #2 | 553 |
| Crude Oil | −461 |
| Gold | 760 |
| Heating Oil | −420 |
| Lean Hog | 654 |
| Live Cattle | −810 |
| Natural Gas | −527 |
| RBOB | 426 |
| Silver | −584 |
| Soybean Oil | −952 |
| Soybeans | −875 |
| Sugar # 11 | 2,688 |
| Wheat | −1,001 |

*Source:* Bloomberg, Newedge Prime Brokerage.

- Daily variation margin settlements
- Exposure to foreign currency risk
- Interest income and cash management costs
- Margin-to-equity ratios
- Trading and funding levels

## Minimum (SPAN) Margin Requirements

First, Exhibit 1.7 shows how much margin would have been required in various currencies for such a portfolio on March 9, 2010. The total dollar margin shown in the exhibit is $131,845,566.99. This is the minimum value of the collateral that the various exchanges would require the clearing broker to post to guarantee performance. The trader's clearing broker is free to require more.

The industry standard for determining minimum margin or collateral requirements is known as SPAN, which is derived loosely from Standard Portfolio Analysis of Risk. The system was designed originally by the Chicago Mercantile Exchange to integrate positions that included both futures and options on those futures by doing scenario or "what-if" analysis as a way of dealing with the nonlinear risks in options. It has since been expanded and extended to allow for the effects of diversification on risk in a futures portfolio.

The basic objective of SPAN margins is to make sure that on most days, the amount of margin on hand would be enough to cover the day's losses. As a rule of thumb, these minimum SPAN margins are considered adequate if they cover roughly 95 percent of all losses, which would correspond to a couple of standard deviations' worth of changes in the portfolio's value.

In fact, the minimum margin on a globally diversified portfolio would be more than enough to meet this objective because allowances for diversification

**EXHIBIT 1.7** Margin, Collateral, and Cash Summary for Sample Portfolio

| Market by Currency | Margin 3/9/10 | P/L | Margin | FX Rates ($/FX) | |
|---|---|---|---|---|---|
| | | 3/10/10 | | 3/9/10 | 3/10/10 |
| U.S. dollar | 83,229,369.00 | −6,166,097.69 | 83,229,369.00 | 1.00000 | 1.00000 |
| Australian dollar | 7,370,730.00 | −74,492.06 | 7,370,730.00 | 0.91345 | 0.91585 |
| Euro | 18,076,359.50 | −2,275,927.50 | 18,111,973.50 | 1.35945 | 1.36530 |
| Swedish kroner | 0.00 | 4,198,500.00 | 0.00 | 1.49870 | 1.49800 |
| British pound | 3,578,829.00 | 483,817.50 | 3,578,829.00 | 0.12885 | 0.12885 |
| Hong Kong dollar | 15,584,800.00 | 605,000.00 | 15,584,800.00 | 0.01112 | 0.01105 |
| Japanese yen | 281,580,000.00 | 17,672,500.00 | 281,580,000.00 | 0.14015 | 0.14045 |
| Korean won | 7,727,164,500.00 | 47,300,000.00 | 7,727,164,500.00 | 0.00088 | 0.00089 |
| Converted total | 131,845,566.99 | −7,739,778.80 | 132,028,927.42 | | |

*Source:* Bloomberg, Newedge Prime Brokerage Research.

are made only within a given clearing house. In this portfolio, several clearing houses are involved. Each clearing house assesses margins that cover the risks in the contracts that it clears without regard to positions held in other markets.

## Multi- and Single-Currency Margining

In practice, each clearing house requires that margins be posted in their local currency. In our example, the trader's clearing broker would have to have posted margin in seven different currencies—U.S. dollars, Australian dollars, euros, British pounds, Hong Kong dollars, Japanese yen, and Korean won—in the amounts shown in Exhibit 1.7.

One way for the trading client to handle this, of course, would be to maintain pools of appropriate collateral denominated in each of these currencies. The chief advantage of securing one's positions this way would be the elimination of transactions costs associated with daily conversions of one currency into another to keep all positions square. The chief disadvantage would be the exposure to changes in foreign currency prices associated with the cash positions one would have in each of these currencies.

The solution to *multi-currency margining* from the client's standpoint is known as *single-currency margining*. With this approach, as the name suggests, the trading client can post the full margin in the form of dollars (or euros, or any other currency shown in the exhibit). Under this arrangement, the clearing firm is responsible for converting the client's cash into collateral that is acceptable to the various exchanges around the world.

## Daily Variation Margin Settlements

Second, you can see that the passing of one day produced gains and losses in various currencies. It is standard practice in futures markets to settle all gains and losses in cash every day. These daily cash settlements of gains and losses are sometimes known as *variation margin*. In this example, the gains in Swedish kroner, British pounds, Hong Kong dollars, Japanese yen, and Korean won would represent inflows of cash in those currencies. The losses in U.S. and Australian dollars would represent cash outflows in those currencies. Part of the clearing broker's job is to handle these cash flows efficiently on a daily basis.

You can also see that the margin requirement to continue holding the position increased slightly as of the close of business on March 10. The positions haven't changed, but the margin required to hold European positions has increased slightly.

## Foreign Currency Exposure

One benefit of using futures to take market positions is that they come with a built-in currency hedge. This is because futures contracts have no net liquidating value. As a result, a position in Eurostoxx futures makes or loses money only when the index rises or falls. A change in the dollar price of the euro would by itself produce neither a gain nor a loss because you have no cash position in euros.

In contrast, the return to a fully funded, unhedged dollar investment in Eurostoxx would be, to a first approximation, the sum of the return on Eurostoxx as viewed by a euro-based investor and the dollar return on the euro. Conventional money managers are well aware of the problems raised by currency risk because currency risk is potentially very large. Exhibit 1.8, for example, plots monthly changes in the dollar price of the euro against monthly changes in the value of the Stoxx index. From this scatter, one can see that returns on the Stoxx index are somewhat more widely distributed than are dollar returns on the euro, but not by much. During most of the months for the past 20-plus years, currency risk could be counted on to be as important a source of risk to a dollar-based investor as was risk in the foreign asset.

**EXHIBIT 1.8** Sources of Risk in a Dollar-based Investment in European Stocks (Monthly Percent Changes in Stoxx and Dollar Price of the Euro, 1987–2010, correlation = –0.17)

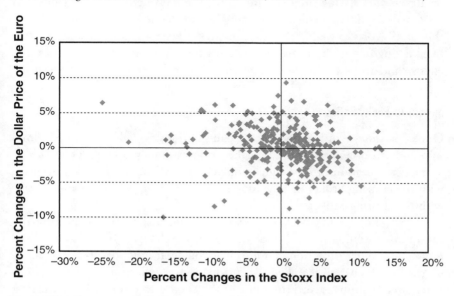

*Source:* Bloomberg, Newedge Prime Brokerage Research.

For CTAs, the only foreign currency risk associated with using futures to trade comes from the value of cash or collateral balances that are the result of posting margin collateral or that are the result of accumulating gains or losses in currencies in which the contracts are denominated. Because these balances tend to be small relative to the notional values of the positions taken, foreign currency risk is, for all practical purposes, decoupled from the risks associated with the underlying assets or commodities. This decoupling allows CTAs to take much more nuanced views on currency exposure than is possible for most conventional money managers, for whom hedging currency exposure can be costly.

### Interest Income and Cash Management Costs

The collateral posted by the trading client with the clearing broker remains the property of the trading client and is frequently segregated from the clearing broker's funds. In principle, then, the client stands to earn interest or dividends on whatever collateral he has posted. Just how much, though, is limited by the costs of managing cash and the kind of collateral that the various clearing houses require. Unless the trading client posts exactly the kind of collateral that each clearing house requires and in exactly the right amounts, the clearing broker will incur costs in converting whatever the client has deposited into whatever the clearing houses want. Also, the daily settlement of gains and losses will require that collateral be bought and sold in various currencies, and this entails costs as well. As a result, the trader faces a steady tension between maximizing income and minimizing costs that occupies a great deal of time, energy, and attention in managing a futures portfolio efficiently and well.

### Margin-to-Equity Ratios

One consequence of having to settle gains and losses daily is that cash flows into and out of an account as it makes or loses money overall. This leads to a practical question of how much collateral the client will be asked to leave with the clearing broker or how much collateral the client will want to leave with the clearing broker.

From the clearing broker's perspective, the task is one of posting the minimum amounts of margin at the various exchanges. If a client has lost money at any clearing house, additional collateral must be posted to make up the loss. However, if a client has made money, collateral may be freed up. If required margins exceed the value of the client's account with the clearing broker, the clearing broker is required to incur a capital charge. Therefore, it is in the clearing broker's interest to have a collateral cushion that allows losses to be covered in a timely way.

From the trading client's perspective, there is a clear advantage of maintaining control over collateral, but there is an ongoing cost to wiring money in and out of an account on a regular basis. Therefore, it is in the trading client's interest to maintain a cash buffer with the clearing broker that absorbs typical flows of cash into and out of the account on a daily basis.

Just how large the buffer should or must be is the result of the clearing broker and the trading client balancing risks and costs. Whatever the outcome, though, it is common for the trading client's equity (i.e., open trade equity) to exceed the margin required by the various clearing houses. This results in a margin-to-equity ratio, or margin/equity ratio, that is less than 1.0.

## Turning Profits and Losses into Rates of Return

To expand on this example, consider the daily gains and losses produced in 2009 by a 20/140 moving average crossover system with the kind of contract weights shown in Exhibit 1.6. Daily profits and losses are charted in Exhibit 1.9, and the distribution of these daily gains and losses is shown in

**EXHIBIT 1.9** Daily Gains and Losses for a 20/140 Moving Average Model (Dollars, 2009)

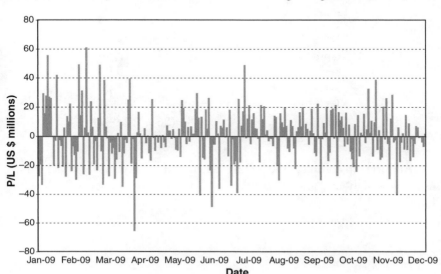

*Source:* Bloomberg, Newedge Prime Brokerage Research.

**EXHIBIT 1.10**  Distribution of Daily Gains and Losses for a 20/140 Moving Average
Model (Dollars, 2009)

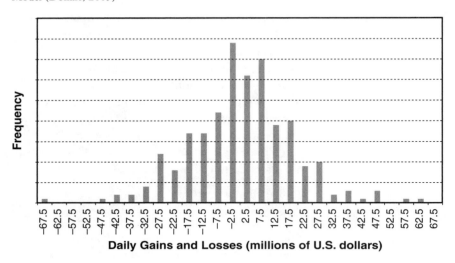

*Source:* Bloomberg, Newedge Prime Brokerage Research.

Exhibit 1.10. As it happened, the key summary statistics for this distribution
were:

| | |
|---|---:|
| Mean | $650.94 |
| Standard Deviation | $18,041,348 |
| Skew | 0.06 |
| Excess Kurtosis | 1.08 |
| Maximum | $60,712,266 |
| Minimum | ($65,217,082) |

And to help complete the picture, a net asset value analysis, which allows
us to track high- and low-water marks and drawdown experience, is shown in
Exhibit 1.11.

**EXHIBIT 1.11A** P/L Summary for Model MA20–140 in 2009 Inception Analysis (January 2, 2009–December 31, 2009), Distribution of Daily Returns

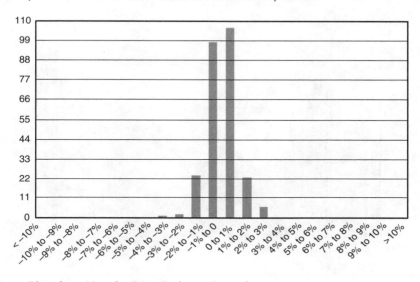

*Source:* Bloomberg, Newedge Prime Brokerage Research.

| | Summary Stats | |
|---|---|---|
| | **Arithmetic** | **Logarithmic** |
| **Rates of Return** | | |
| Daily | 0.04% | 0.03% |
| Annual | 8.83% | 7.87% |
| **Standard Deviations** | | |
| Daily | 0.87% | 0.87% |
| Annual | 13.89% | 13.88% |
| **Shape** | | |
| Skewness | 0.08 | 0.04 |
| Kurtosis (Excess) | 1.15 | 1.15 |
| **Risk/Return** | | |
| Sharpe Ratio | 0.62 | 0.56 |
| Return/Risk | 0.64 | 0.57 |
| Sortino Ratio (0%) | 0.94 | 0.83 |

**EXHIBIT 1.11B** P/L Summary for Model MA20–140 in 2009 Inception Analysis (January 2, 2009–December 31, 2009), NAV Analysis

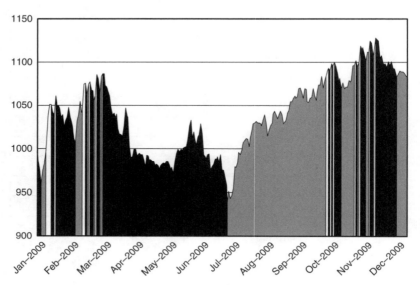

*Source:* Bloomberg, Newedge Prime Brokerage Research.

### Drawdown Stats

| Period | Drawdown |
|---|---|
| Mar. 6, 2009–Jul. 8, 2009 | −13.60% |
| Jan. 20, 2009–Feb. 9, 2009 | −5.08% |
| Dec. 1, 2009–Dec. 22, 2009 | −3.94% |
| Jan. 1, 2009–Jan. 6, 2009 | −3.94% |
| Oct. 21, 2009–Oct. 28, 2009 | −2.78% |
| Feb. 23, 2009–Feb. 26, 2009 | −2.06% |
| Mar. 2, 2009–Mar. 4, 2009 | −1.96% |
| Nov. 16, 2009–Nov. 20, 2009 | −1.52% |
| Nov. 25, 2009–Nov. 27, 2009 | −1.48% |
| Feb. 18, 2009–Feb. 19, 2009 | −1.21% |
| Jan. 15, 2009–Jan. 19, 2009 | −1.04% |

Assets under management: 0.0 Mil.

**EXHIBIT 1.11C** P/L Summary for Model MA20–140 in 2009 Inception Analysis (January 2, 2009–December 31, 2009), Drawdown Analysis

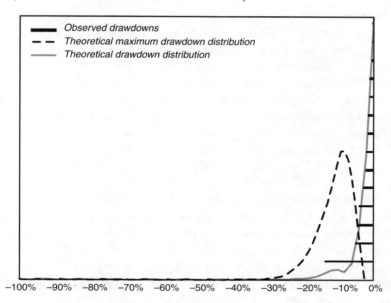

*Source:* Bloomberg, Newedge Prime Brokerage Research.

## Rates of Return

First consider the question of turning these profits and losses into rates of return. As we explain in some detail in Chapter 4, we chose this particular collection of futures to produce an expected volatility of returns of 15 percent on a $2 billion portfolio. As it turned out, if we had begun the year with $2 billion, the resulting year's arithmetic return was 8.83 percent with an annualized standard deviation of 13.89 percent, which was close to the 15 percent target.

The $2 billion as our choice of denominator is arbitrary, of course, and could as easily have been $1 billion or $4 billion, in which case the annualized return volatilities could have been almost 28 percent or just under 7 percent.

## Trading, Funding, and Notional Levels

In the terminology of managed futures, the $2 billion denominator, if that is what the CTA chooses, is known as the trading level. There remains, then, the question of actual funding level and its complement, the notional funding level.

In many CTAs' funds, you would be fully invested in cash so your funding level would equal your trading level. In fact, however, the trading program does not require this much cash. For example, in Exhibit 1.7, we see that the minimum exchange margin for a similar portfolio, although on a different day, was $131.8 million, which is far less than $2 billion. And in Exhibit 1.10, we see that the program's maximum drawdown during the year was 13.6 percent. Of course, the maximum drawdown could have been worse, but at 13.6 percent, one could have posted an additional $272 million [= 0.136 · $2 billion] and not have had a margin call at any time during the year.

In fact, one of the advantages of managed accounts and of CTA investment platforms, which we discuss at length in Chapter 3, is that they allow you to economize on the use of cash. In the fully invested program, you are counting on the CTA to invest the excess cash wisely and well. In a managed account, you invest the excess cash in whatever way suits you best. In a managed account, the funding level is negotiated, and the difference between the trading level and this mutually agreed-upon funding level is known as the *notional funding* level. The CTA does not actually have the cash, but the sum of the actual and notional funding levels produces the hypothetical trading level on which all return and fee calculations are based.

## Where Is the Cash and How Is it Managed?

Once you get to the point of investing in a CTA, you will find that the devil is in the details. It is one thing to talk about cash, collateral, and foreign exchange in the abstract. But the difference between a good CTA and an excellent CTA will come down to the way they handle the complexities of collateral, segregated funds (various forms and provisions), single-currency margining, and costs and noise in managing forex balances.

Exchanges have well-defined ideas about the kinds of collateral they accept, while many investors have strong ideas of their own about the kinds of collateral they want to hold. Segregation of funds is common in the futures industry, but the regulatory meaning of segregation can vary in hugely important ways across jurisdictions. Futures clearing firms can provide single-currency margining for their clients, but extract a fee for the service. CTAs can be highly attentive to their control of foreign currency exposure or they can be relaxed. All of these considerations can have important effects on your rates of return and on the safety of your cash and collateral investments.

How and where cash and collateral are managed and held are important considerations also in whether you are more comfortable with an investment in a CTA's fund or with a managed account. With a fund, your cash is controlled by the CTA. With a managed account, your cash is controlled by you. Each approach has its strengths and drawbacks, and examples like those provided in this chapter can be used as a foundation for evaluating the two approaches, which we address at some length in Chapter 3.

# CHAPTER 2

# Where Are the Data?

Investors in conventional assets—stocks, bonds, and asset-backed securities—are accustomed to dealing with challenges in their data sets. Equity prices can be stale. Most bond prices—especially corporate and municipal bonds prices—are the results of elaborate interpolation routines. Asset-backed securities are notoriously difficult to price. But at least the assets exist somewhere and have some kind of price history from the time they came into existence.

What is most challenging about the managed futures industry is that the data on CTAs and their returns pose significant challenges to proper use and interpretation—even though the underlying futures markets suffer from almost none of these problems. Most of these problems stem from the fact that CTA returns are self-reported. CTAs choose when to start reporting returns, and they have considerable control over when to stop reporting returns. Also, while reporting conventions are improving over time, they are not entirely uniform. You must keep in mind, too, that the returns you find in publicly available databases are not audited. For audited returns, you must turn to each CTA directly and ask for them.

With these challenges in mind, we review in this chapter the most widely used data sources—both for indexes and for the track records of individual CTAs. As we go, we try to keep in mind the fact that your objective is to use your time well and to interpret what you find correctly. To that end, we discuss:

- Sources of data on CTAs
- The CTA universe and your range of choices
- Measuring assets under management
- Flows into and out of databases
- Backfilled returns

- Trading programs and lengths of track records
- Returns net of fees and the use of share classes
- Sources of data for indexes of CTA performance

Although the subject of data has real potential for being dull, the consequences of knowing what goes into these sets are huge for potential investors.

## The CTA Universe and Your Range of Choices

The first step in your search is to get a sense of what the universe of CTAs looks like. How many are there? How much money do they manage? How long have they been around? How many CTAs do I have to investigate as part of my investment process?

For information about individual CTAs, you may turn to any of the databases listed in Exhibit 2.1. The oldest and most comprehensive of these data sets is the one provided by Barclay Hedge, which has been tracking individual CTAs since 1985. As of October 18, 2010, their database contained track records for 980 CTA programs reporting live returns and historical information about 2,313 so-called "dead" CTAs—those who once reported but no longer do.

In the interest of full disclosure, we should note that Barclay Hedge has had a longstanding business relationship with what is now Newedge. They published the index that was known as the Carr/Barclay Hedge CTA Index, which is now the Newedge CTA Index, and they are the index calculation agent for the AlternativeEdge Short-Term Traders Index. For these reasons, we work extensively with their data and are most comfortable describing the characteristics of their data sets.

**EXHIBIT 2.1**   Sources of Data on CTA Returns

| Databases | Number of Active CTAs |
|---|---|
| Barclay Hedge | 980 |
| CISDM (Global Trend) | 607 |
| CISDM (Global Non-Trend) | 288 |
| IASG | 524 |
| AutumnGold | 410 |

*Source:* Barclay Hedge, Morningstar Alternative Investment Center, IASG, AutumnGold (as of 10/18/2010).

**EXHIBIT 2.2**   CTAs and Assets Under Management

| Year | Total Active # of CTAs | Total Active Cumulative AUM ($bn) | AUM > $100M # of CTAs | AUM > $100M Cumulative AUM ($bn) | Track > 3 Years # of CTAs | Track > 3 Years Cumulative AUM ($bn) | AUM>$100M and Track > 3 Years # of C TAs | AUM>$100M and Track > 3 Years Cumulative AUM ($bn) |
|---|---|---|---|---|---|---|---|---|
| 2003 | 401 | 59.1 | 88 | 53.4 | 290 | 55.3 | 77 | 51.0 |
| 2004 | 531 | 98.2 | 111 | 90.7 | 335 | 91.1 | 92 | 85.7 |
| 2005 | 609 | 86.1 | 119 | 77.9 | 378 | 79.2 | 102 | 73.6 |
| 2006 | 663 | 129.1 | 135 | 119.5 | 396 | 115.3 | 114 | 109.5 |
| 2007 | 714 | 156.7 | 141 | 146.2 | 439 | 146.2 | 117 | 139.2 |
| 2008 | 780 | 171.7 | 162 | 161.1 | 489 | 161.5 | 139 | 154.6 |
| 2009 | 821 | 208.5 | 170 | 197.9 | 523 | 200.2 | 147 | 192.4 |

Data include lead funds only.
These numbers may change for the following reasons:
1. Manager was previously misclassified (addition/removal changes the CTA count).
2. Data usage was changed (manager previously marked private for some reason).

*Source:* Barclay Hedge (as of 10/18/2010).

Exhibit 2.2 provides an overview of the size of the industry, both in numbers and assets under management, and a brief history of how the size has changed over the past few years. At the end of 2009, there were 821 CTAs reporting program returns to Barclay Hedge. And, after correcting for double counting, we find that they represent assets under management of $208.5 billion. Over the six years from 2003 to 2009, the number of CTAs in the data set roughly doubled, and the amount of money they managed more than tripled.

The next three sets of columns in Exhibit 2.2 show what happens to the set of eligible CTAs as you narrow your search, either in terms of assets under management, length of track record, or both. The numbers we have chosen for this exercise are standard rules of thumb—assets under management of at least $100 million, a track record of at least three years, or both.

The $100 million minimum had the greatest effect on the number of CTAs from which you could choose. If you require your CTA to have at least $100 million under management, the number of programs available to you fell from 821 to 170 at the end of 2009. Because these were, however, the largest CTAs, the assets under their control fell only from $208.5 billion to $197.9 billion. So the cost of this rule is comparatively small.

Requiring a minimum track record of three years had a smaller effect on the number of eligible CTAs—from 821 to 523—and roughly the same effect on assets under management.

And then, requiring both $100 million and a three-year track record reduced the number of eligible CTAs to 147 managers, but left you with $192.4 billion under management. As a practical matter, these 147 CTAs would be the focus of most investors' attention and due diligence.

**A Cautionary Note about Reported Assets Under Management** ━━━━━━

One of the notes to Exhibit 2.2 indicates that the assets under management are for "lead funds only." The reason for this note is simply this: A CTA may offer identical programs—one onshore and one offshore, for example—and manage a combined value of $500 million in the two. When asked about assets under management, the CTA may well report $500 million for each of the two, identical programs. This way of reporting assets under management obviously can lead to an inflated idea of just how much money a CTA manages. If one were to take the $500 million reported for each program at face value, the result would seem to be $1 billion under management. At the same time, it has the virtue of informing potential investors about the true scale of a program. For example, the offshore program may control only $50 million, while the onshore program controls $450 million. As far as investors in either program are concerned, the underlying trading program has attracted $500 million.

To deal with the problem of double counting, Barclay Hedge began asking CTAs to designate one of these programs as the "lead program," and to tie all assets managed under this and its twins to this lead program.

## The Fluid Composition of a Database

One of the problems with self-reporting is that CTAs enter and leave the databases. The main reason for entering a database is clear enough. The CTA firm wants its performance to be a matter of record that is accessible to potential investors. The reasons for leaving a database, however, vary. Some leave because the CTA stops trading and liquidates the fund. Some leave because the CTA simply decides to stop reporting, even though the CTA still trades actively. You will find this happening chiefly when a CTA firm has reached what it considers its capacity and reasons that the costs of reporting no longer merit the trouble.

As shown in Exhibit 2.3, the number of CTAs actively reporting returns to Barclay Hedge grew from 609 at the end of 2005 to 821 at the end of 2009. But the overall increase of 212 was small when compared to the additions and deletions each year along the way. In all, from 2006 through 2009, 947 CTAs entered the database and 735 left.

Our interest in the fluidity of the database stems from our need to use historical track records to make decisions about investments and our need to evaluate our decisions. Any time spent analyzing a CTA who then stops reporting is time wasted, or at least time not well spent. And all the nagging questions about survivorship bias that go with the disappearance of CTAs

**EXHIBIT 2.3** Flows Into and Out of a Database

| Year | Active by Year End | Addition | Deletion | Liquidated | Delisted | Unknown |
|---|---|---|---|---|---|---|
| 2005 | 609 | 207 | 100 | | | |
| 2006 | 663 | 198 | 144 | 54 | 25 | 65 |
| 2007 | 714 | 221 | 170 | 75 | 57 | 38 |
| 2008 | 780 | 250 | 184 | 96 | 34 | 54 |
| 2009 | 821 | 278 | 237 | 108 | 71 | 58 |

*Source:* Barclay Hedge (as of 10/18/2010).

from the data sets cast doubt on any conclusions one might otherwise draw from one's research.

In 2006, Barclay Hedge added a feature to their data set that allows the user to drill down a little bit on why CTAs dropped out of the database. In particular, where possible, they make note of whether the departure was voluntary (i.e., delisted), involuntary (i.e., liquidated), or simply unknown. According to Barclay Hedge's language:

- *Liquidated:* Manager informed Barclay Hedge that the fund is no longer trading and therefore will not report performance.
- *Delisted:* Manager informed Barclay Hedge that the fund is still trading but will no longer report its performance (closed to new investments, no longer marketing, etc.).
- *Unknown:* Manager stopped reporting to Barclay Hedge and is not responsive to follow-up emails and phone calls (stale performance data).

Given the voluntary nature of CTA reporting, it seems that Barclay Hedge has been relatively successful in establishing why CTAs drop out. The first year, 45 percent of the deletions fell in the unknown category. The next two years, fewer than 30 percent were unknown.

As one might expect, there were noticeable differences between CTAs who were liquidated and those who were simply delisted. Exhibit 2.4, for example, shows that the probability of remaining in the data set (which we call "survival") increased with assets under management and tended to increase with length of track record. As a practical matter, this means that focusing on CTAs with more assets under management or longer track records will tend to provide longer returns histories to study.

As a working hypothesis, it is reasonable to suppose that CTAs who fall into the liquidated category were not doing as well as those who simply

**EXHIBIT 2.4**   Chances of Staying in a Database

| Probability of Survival by AUM (2009) | | | |
|---|---|---|---|
| | Start | End | % |
| < $ 100 M | 618 | 462 | 75% |
| $100 to $500 M | 112 | 99 | 88% |
| > $500 M | 50 | 45 | 90% |
| ALL | 780 | 606 | 78% |
| Probability of Survival by Length of Track Record (2009) | | | |
| | Started | Ended | % |
| < 3 years | 291 | 200 | 69% |
| 3 years to 5 years | 179 | 151 | 84% |
| > 5 years | 310 | 255 | 82% |
| ALL | 780 | 606 | 78% |

*Source:* Barclay Hedge (as of 10/18/2010).

delisted. The evidence in Exhibit 2.5, which covers CTAs who left the set in 2009, tends to bear this out. In the top panel, you find the distribution of returns for the 12 months just before delisting for each CTA. And, while there were some large gains and some large losses, the average for this set was 0.9 percent. In contrast, the average 12-month return for those who liquidated was −6.09 percent and was skewed quite a bit to the loss side of the distribution. Interestingly enough, the "unknowns" experienced an average gain of 3.56 percent, which leaves their reasons for leaving the database a mystery.

## How Backfilled Data Can Mislead

Another aspect of voluntarily reported track records is an understandable bias toward programs that have been successful. By the time a CTA chooses to expose a track record to public scrutiny, one can expect that the CTA has had a comparatively good run. The challenge for an investor, then, is to be able to distinguish between those parts of a CTA's track record that are backfilled and those parts that one would consider to be out of sample or "live."

The amount of backfill in track records can vary quite a lot. Exhibit 2.6 shows the distribution of backfilled months for managers who entered the data set in 2009. Of the total of 278 newly reporting CTAs, roughly half reported less than a year's worth of backfilled returns, and about two-thirds reported less than two years of backfill. However, there were a few who reported several years of backfilled returns, with one CTA reporting more than 15 years of past returns.

**EXHIBIT 2.5** CTAs' Returns During the Year before Dropping Out of a Database

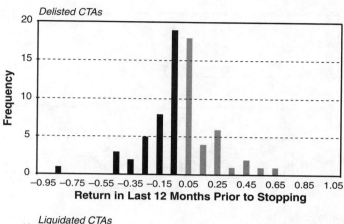

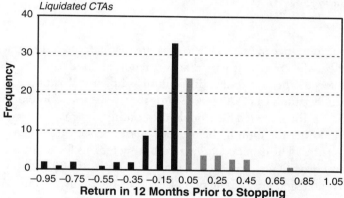

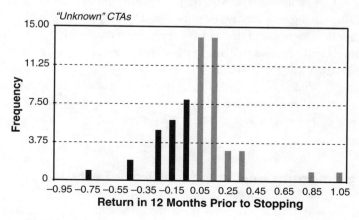

*Source:* Barclay Hedge.

**EXHIBIT 2.6**   Backfilled Months for Programs Added in 2009

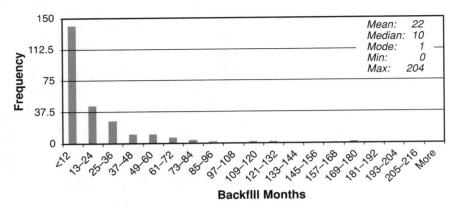

*Source:* Barclay Hedge (as of Oct. 18, 2010).

The importance of being able to separate that part of a CTA's track record that was backfill from that part that was reported "live" or "out of sample" is illustrated by the two return distributions shown in Exhibit 2.7. For this illustration, we took all CTA track records that were created in Barclay Hedge in 2009. We then created two pools of monthly returns. One contains all monthly returns for months before each series was created. These are the backfill returns. The other contains all monthly returns for months after each series was created. We then drew a random sample of 500 monthly returns from each pool and created the two histograms shown in Exhibit 2.7.

Your eye will confirm what you might already have expected—that back-filled returns are higher than live or out-of-sample returns. The higher return buckets contain more backfilled returns than live returns, while the reverse is true for lower and negative returns. In these two samples, the average monthly backfilled return was 1.42 percent, while the average monthly live return was 0.22 percent. When compounded to annualized returns, the differences are huge. The annualized backfilled return would have been 18.4 percent, while the annualized live return would be been 2.6 percent.

## Trading Programs and Lengths of Track Records

By itself, the length of a program's track record will not tell you everything you need to know about the CTA. Many CTAs run more than one program.

**EXHIBIT 2.7** The Difference between Backfilled and "Live" Returns

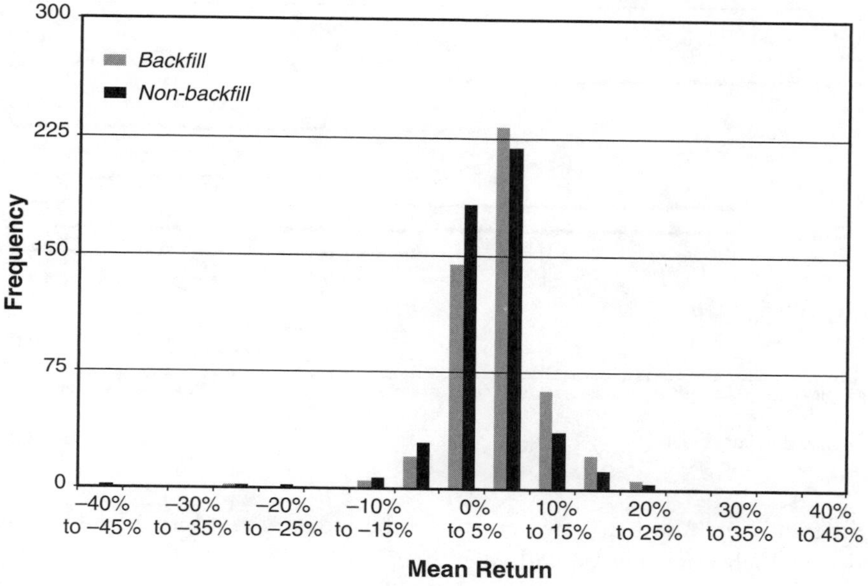

*Source:* Barclay Hedge (as of Oct. 27, 2010).

As an example, we have diagrammed the timelines of various programs run by Crabel, a short-term diversified CTA that has proven to be both successful and durable (Exhibit 2.8). In all, they have run 13 distinct programs, of which seven were still active as of the end of 2009.

The diagram makes it clear that any one program's length of track record does not reveal all you need to know about Crabel's performance. For example, none of the active programs stretch back to 1989. (In fact, Crabel first began trading as a CTA in 1989.) And the six discontinued programs provide great fodder for your due diligence. Why were they discontinued? Were they replaced with other configurations?

## Returns Net of Fees and Share Classes

It is the practice of the industry to report returns net of fees. The challenge for someone studying track records, however, is that not all investors pay the same fees. One reason, of course, is that different investors may negotiate

**EXHIBIT 2.8** Generations of Trading Programs at Crabel Capital Management, LLC

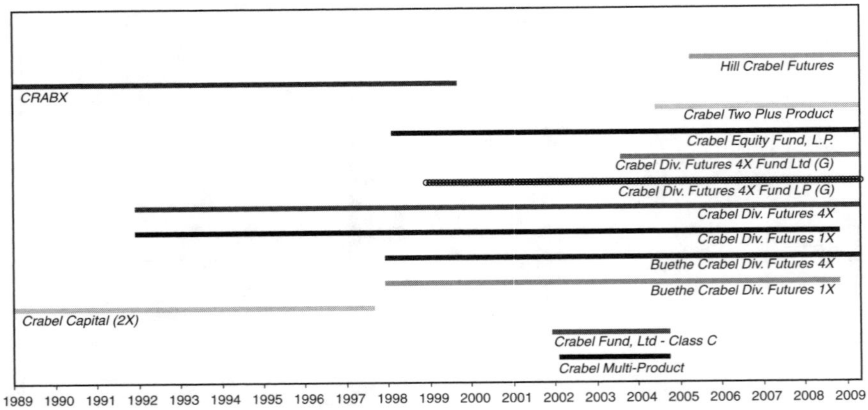

Hill Crabel Futures

CRABX

Crabel Two Plus Product

Crabel Equity Fund, L.P.

Crabel Div. Futures 4X Fund Ltd (G)

Crabel Div. Futures 4X Fund LP (G)

Crabel Div. Futures 4X

Crabel Div. Futures 1X

Buethe Crabel Div. Futures 4X

Buethe Crabel Div. Futures 1X

Crabel Capital (2X)

Crabel Fund, Ltd - Class C

Crabel Multi-Product

1989 1990 1991 1992 1993 1994 1995 1996 1997 1998 1999 2000 2001 2002 2003 2004 2005 2006 2007 2008 2009

*Source:* Barclay Hedge.

different fees. Another, however, is that the industry's performance fees are tied to high-water marks, and when you invest in a CTA's fund, the high-water mark used to calculate your fees will very likely be different from the high-water mark used to calculate the fees for those who invested earlier.

To deal with new investors in their funds, CTAs assign new share classes to new investors, and the high-water mark for a new share class typically is the net asset value of the fund at the time the new investment is made. Under this arrangement, because CTAs are under water most of the time, it is very possible for older share classes to be under water while newer share classes are above water.

What this means, of course, is that any kind of what-if analysis has to carry with it a cautionary note that your returns net of fees might not have been those reported by the CTA for existing investors. This difference, of course, would disappear once the CTA hits a new high-water mark for all investors. When this happens, all outstanding share classes are typically rolled into one that shares a common high-water mark.

## Sources of Data for Indexes of CTA Performance

Exhibit 2.9 provides a thumbnail listing of some of the more widely used indexes of CTA performance. They differ in many respects, including coverage, weighting, and frequency both of reporting and of reconstitution. They

**EXHIBIT 2.9** Sources of Data on CTA Return Indexes

| CTA Indices | Weighting Methodology | Data Frequency | Start Date |
|---|---|---|---|
| Newedge CTA Index | Equal weighted | Daily | 1/1/00 |
| Barclay CTA Index | Equal weighted | Monthly | 1/1/80 |
| CISDM CTA Index (asset weighted) | Asset weighted | Monthly | 1/1/80 |
| CISDM CTA Index (equal weighted) | Equal weighted | Monthly | 1/1/80 |
| Dow Jones/Credit Suisse Managed Futures Index | Asset weighted | Monthly | 1/1/94 |

*Source:* Newedge, Barclay Hedge, CASAM, Credit Suisse.

also differ in their usefulness as standards of performance. On this point, the *Newedge CTA Index* may be one of the best performance measures from the perspective of an institutional investor. To be included in this index, the CTA must be large, open to investment, and willing to report returns daily. This means that the index tracks the returns on a portfolio that is both plausible and practical and that does not suffer from selection bias—apart from the fact that the component CTAs have managed to attract substantial assets under management—or survivor bias.

# CHAPTER 3

# Structuring Your Investment

## Frequently Asked Questions

Once you decide to invest in managed futures, you must tackle the problem of just how to structure your investment. To do this, you embark on a decision process that proceeds roughly like this:

First, how many CTAs do you want in your portfolio? Many family offices, and even some larger institutional investors, will choose one. This choice has the virtue of simplicity and is possible to accomplish by choosing one of a handful of well-known CTA firms such as AHL, BlueCrest, Transtrend, or Winton, whose performance will correlate very highly with a benchmark like the *Newedge CTA Index*. If you go this route, then you will want to focus your attention on the differences between investing in a CTA's fund or in a managed account.

We think the single-CTA route is risky, though, chiefly because it is riskier than a diversified approach. Your objective may well be to improve the overall performance of your portfolio, and for this all you need is a positive expected return from the CTA and low correlation. What we find, though, is that the investment will almost certainly be evaluated on a standalone basis. And if it is, you will want something that has better risk-adjusted returns than a single CTA's returns can offer and that allows you to diversify away some of the business risk.

We discuss correlation and diversification in CTA portfolios at some length in Chapter 5, but for the purposes of jump-starting this discussion, we

53

think it is enough to say that you should shoot for at least five CTAs in your portfolio. If you follow the diversified approach, then the important questions hinge on how much you plan to invest. For purposes of your thinking at this point, we offer two rules of thumb. As with any rules of thumb, the truth is more complex, but we find these rules helpful.

*First rule of thumb:* If you plan to invest less than $250 million, then the most cost-efficient way to achieve diversification is through a multi-CTA fund. If you plan to invest more than $250 million, then you may want to use the fees you would pay the multi-CTA manager to create your own fund of funds.

*Second rule of thumb:* The next breakeven point is somewhere around $500 million. At this point, you will find that the scale of your investment warrants consideration of managed accounts. Managed accounts afford a number of very important advantages—transparency, security of collateral, ease of opening and closing positions—over investments in CTA funds. They also require you to have experienced people and reliable systems in place that are costly to run.

In the material that follows, we address what we have found to be the questions that investors ask most frequently. The list is by no means exhaustive, and at the end of this chapter we provide a brief list of things we have not covered because they are so far outside our range of experience and competence. But our years of experience working both with CTAs and their investors have prepared us to comment on the questions that follow:

- How many managers should you choose?
- What are CTA funds?
- What are multi-CTA funds?
- What are managed accounts?
- What are platforms?
- How do you compare and contrast these choices?

Other questions include:

- Who regulates CTAs?
- How are structured notes and total return swaps used by CTA investors?
- What are the account opening procedures?
- What is the minimum investment in a CTA?
- What does it mean when a manager is closed?
- What are the subscription procedures for a fund?

**EXHIBIT 3.1** Annual Returns for Randomly Formed CTA Portfolios

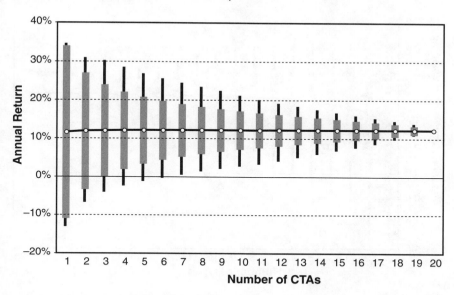

*Source:* Barclay Hedge, Newedge Prime Brokerage Research (2008).

## How Many Managers Should You Choose?

This question lends itself to an interesting analysis of what you are trying to accomplish. Consider, for example, that your objective is to do a tolerably good job of tracking the *Newedge CTA Index*. This is a plausible goal because the index is a widely used benchmark and the CTAs whose returns make up this index are among the largest in the business, are all open for business, and all provide daily returns. We use 2008 returns for this example, chiefly because the returns were positive, which allows us to examine risk-adjusted returns in a meaningful way.[*]

In Exhibit 3.1, we show the range of returns you would have realized on randomly formed and equally weighted portfolios that included anywhere from 1 to 20 of the 20 CTAs whose returns made up the index. The index return in 2008 was about 12 percent. From this exhibit, we learn that the main effect of increasing the number of CTAs in the portfolio is a decrease in the amount by which you might overperform or underperform the index. With a

---

[*]See Chapter 12 for a brief discussion of why negative Sharpe ratios cannot be used to rank outcomes.

**EXHIBIT 3.2**   Sharpe Ratios for Randomly Formed CTA Portfolios

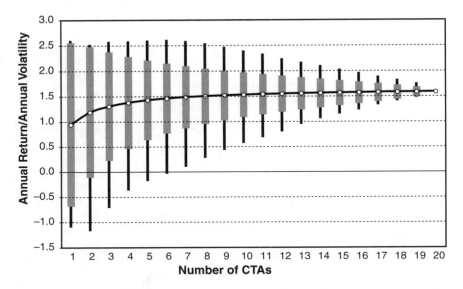

*Source:* Barclay Hedge, Newedge Prime Brokerage Research (2008).

single CTA portfolio, you might have outperformed the index by as much as 22 percent, but we could also have lost money on our own investment when the industry was, on average, making money. From there, the main question is how much tolerance you have for slippage. In this example, it would take 10 CTAs to bring the range of over- or underperformance down to 5 percent. And with five or six CTAs, you could have reduced nearly to zero the chance of losing money when the industry was making money.

Another consideration is risk-adjusted return. The effects of diversification will, as shown in Exhibit 3.2, tend to bring up the ratio of expected return to the volatility of returns. For the index, the ratio of return to standard deviation of returns was about 1.6. With a single advisor, your expected risk-adjusted return would have been less than 1.0. It is apparent from the curve that most of the expected gains from diversification are realized by the time your portfolio contains five or six CTAs. After this, diversification still helps, but less so.

Still another issue is the outright expected return, irrespective of risk. The reason for bringing this into the discussion is shown in Exhibit 3.3, which shows the returns for each of the 20 managers in the *Newedge CTA Index*. For the purposes of this exhibit, we have organized the trend-following CTAs

**EXHIBIT 3.3** Returns of the CTAs in the *Newedge CTA Index* (2008)

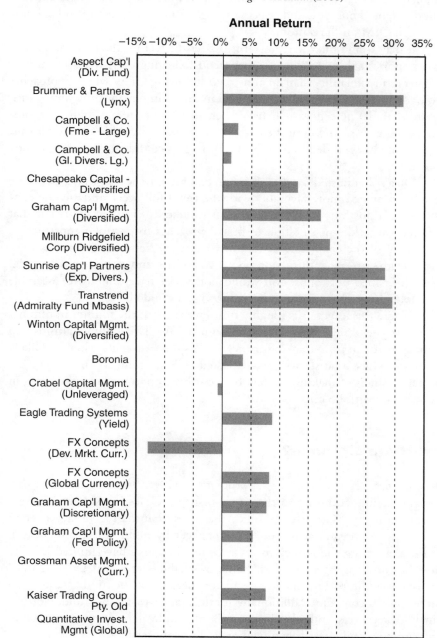

*Source:* Barclay Hedge, Newedge Prime Brokerage Research.

alphabetically on the left and the non-trend-following CTAs alphabetically on the right. Thus, you find Aspect through Winton on the top and Boronia through QIM on the bottom.

It may seem unfair to show returns after the fact for the two groups, but the important thing to know is that trend-following CTAs tend to target a higher return volatility than do non-trend-following CTAs, whose approaches to trading strive for more diversity. And in this example, the only way to earn more than 10 percent would have been to focus your portfolio on trend-following CTAs. And even then, given the variability of this group's returns, you would have needed four or five CTAs to gain confidence in the portfolio's outcome.

On a risk-adjusted basis, as shown in Exhibit 3.4, the non-trend-following group compared more favorably with the trend followers, and anyone constructing a portfolio of CTAs will want to take this into account. For that matter, we tackle the question of best approaches to portfolio construction in several of the chapters that follow. Chapters 12 and 13 tackle the question of how to use information about volatilities and correlations to build well-diversified portfolios. You would not, as we have done here, assemble portfolios at random. Instead, as we show, you can do better.

Where this leaves us is roughly this: Five is about the minimum number of CTAs you would want in a portfolio of CTAs. This number affords you some protection from tracking error, provides some diversification, and likely would produce a satisfactory risk-adjusted return. From five on up, you are in the business of making smaller, but possibly important, improvements in what your portfolio does for you.

## What Are CTA Funds?

A *CTA fund* is a separate legal corporation with a board of directors that assigns trading authority to the single-manager CTA's investment management company. With a CTA fund, the investor turns the money over to the company organized by the CTA manager by filling out a subscription form and wiring the money to the account. Investors have limited liability for the fund manager's actions. Some oversight is provided by such third parties as auditors, brokers, and regulators because of the fund's status as an independent company. Additionally, for the manager's flagship fund, industry analysts, reporters, and other investors in the fund will be paying attention to performance and effectively providing additional oversight.

**EXHIBIT 3.4** Sharpe Ratios of the CTAs in the *Newedge CTA Index* (2008)

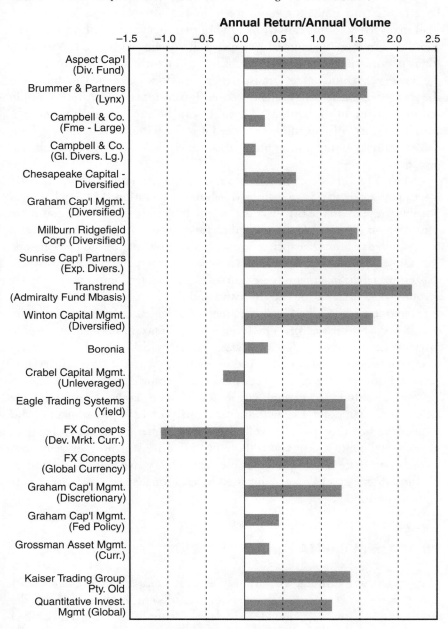

*Source:* Barclay Hedge, Newedge Prime Brokerage Research.

Fund investors have a broad choice of managers, because most managers have funds, and funds are more likely to accommodate smaller investors than managed accounts can. (A handful of managers will take only managed accounts, but those are unusual.) Managers like dealing with investors through funds because there are standard terms for risk, return, and liquidity.

However, a fund has less transparency than does a managed account, and the amount of transparency can be variable. It is customary to provide monthly returns and monthly liquidity. Liquidity can be just as variable, though, with managers offering different schedules for withdrawals ranging from daily to annual and requiring notice in advance of the scheduled withdrawal period.

Most CTA funds are managed through offshore accounts. A typical fund is set up as a Cayman Islands limited liability corporation (LLC), where it is possible to appeal to the British court system, but only after the local courts are consulted on disputes. The outside directors are chosen by the manager and have varying amounts of experience in corporate governance and investments.

These accounts generally have a *master–feeder* structure. Under a typical master–feeder arrangement, there are two funds that feed into a single master account. One feeder is for U.S. investors and the other for overseas investors. Their money is combined in the master fund, which opens the trading accounts at the brokerage firm. This setup is done for tax purposes; the non-U.S. investors do not have to deal with U.S. tax authorities, while U.S. investors receive the documentation they need to square up with the Internal Revenue Service. Both sets of investors receive the same performance.

Some funds are structured with different share classes. The classes may differ on fee structure and withdrawal rights. For example, someone who wants daily liquidity might be willing to pay a higher management fee than someone willing to accept annual liquidity. New investments may be held in a temporary share class until it has the same high-water mark as the rest of the fund. Some classes may be invested in additional assets that are not part of the main fund.

## What Are Multi-CTA Funds?

Multi-CTA funds are known variously as *CTA funds of funds* or *commodity pool operators (CPOs)*. From the investor's standpoint, both accomplish the same thing—that is, they provide a single vehicle for investing in a diversified portfolio of CTAs. The differences are chiefly regulatory and relate to the way the funds are structured and where they are offered. CPOs, for example, focus on vehicles that are distributed in the United States and are common investment vehicles for retail investors, high-net-worth individuals, and even some small institutions. Funds of funds, however, specialize in offshore funds and tend to focus on larger institutional investors. The expression "fund of funds" derives from a time when the primary investment vehicle at the individual CTA level was a fund. As the industry has evolved, multi-manager funds have migrated to the use of managed accounts.

The primary benefits of a multi-CTA fund structure are expertise in choosing the managers, structuring the portfolio, performing both investment and operational due diligence, performance reporting, risk monitoring, and accounting. In addition they perform less obvious tasks such as collecting data, meeting many managers, running background checks, analyzing performance and strategies (such as a continuity check, which means testing the stated strategy to see whether it, indeed, would generate the stated performance), negotiating contracts and fees, and then monitoring performance and rebalancing as necessary. The investment offering and services consolidate much of the work into choosing and reviewing a single organization.

Different multi-CTA funds have different investment objectives, so investors need to find a fund that is consistent with needs of their portfolios. They also need to find one that operates consistently with their organizational needs; different investors have different requirements for reporting and transparency.

With a multi-CTA fund, the manager assembles a portfolio of CTAs and then accepts investments in the entire portfolio. The multi-CTA manager charges a fee for the portfolio construction and oversight services, and of course each of the managers in the fund has its own fee. Investors have to negotiate contracts and fees with the multi-CTA manager, and although consolidated into a single organization, they still have due diligence and monitoring obligations.

The fees charged by multi-CTA managers raise two important questions about how you want to structure your investment. As we mentioned at the outset of this chapter, if you invest $250 million in CTAs, you may find that you could do much of what the multi-CTA manager does. At that level, the fee savings would be enough to hire the staff and consultants you would need to select CTAs, do the due diligence, construct the portfolios, and so on.

At this level, however, you likely would be investing in CTAs' funds rather than setting up managed accounts. Managed accounts, which are the vehicle of choice for most multi-CTA managers, are a much bigger undertaking. To warrant the work involved in setting up brokerage accounts, negotiating agreements, monitoring the accounts, reconciling trades, complying with anti-money laundering regulations, managing cash flows, and so forth, we think a reasonable breakeven point is an investment of around $500 million.

## What Are Managed Accounts?

*Managed accounts* are brokerage accounts held by a brokerage firm that is also registered as a futures commission merchant, where investment discretion has been assigned to the CTA manager. The investor is responsible for opening and maintaining the account; reconciling brokerage statements and maintaining cash controls; and negotiating contracts with managers, including investment management agreements and powers of attorney. The limited power of attorney gives the manager authority to trade on the investor's behalf, but the money has to remain in the investor's account. The investor controls the terms of the power of attorney, including the right to revoke trading privileges.

The key advantage to a managed account is complete control. By pulling trading privileges, the investor has the ability to manage the cash and liquidate the account at any time. In theory, this gives the investor better than daily liquidity, as the account can be liquidated whenever the market is open. That alone is enough that some investors demand managed accounts, especially investors that have in-house staff to handle the paperwork.

Managed accounts have other advantages. The money is in the investor's control at all times, not the fund manager's. The accounts offer complete transparency. The investor can see the positions, trades, and details at any time. The investor can choose the parameters for leverage based on the investor's targeted volatility of returns. The choice of leverage makes it easier for the investor to manage the underlying cash. In fact, this type of CTA account structure is often looked at as an overlay on the cash position in an investor's portfolio rather than as a separate asset class.

Of course these advantages come at a cost. The first is the reduced pool of managers to choose from. Many large managers do not accept managed accounts and those that do have some pretty hefty minimum account sizes and other administrative requirements. In addition, the previously mentioned complete transparency and control comes with the responsibility for establishing and maintaining brokerage accounts that require sophisticated understanding of all the legal, administrative, risk, and investment issues to meet your organization's investment standards. And, unless procured by the investor, there is no administrator or auditor.

Managed accounts can be set up several different ways to meet different portfolio policy requirements. Exhibit 3.5 shows some of the more common structures that we have seen in the market.

In many managed-account situations, the investor starts by setting up a *special-purpose vehicle (SPV)* or other holding entity to fence off any trading liabilities from the rest of the money that the investor controls. It is not a necessary step, however, as there are other ways to manage the potential liability. We're not offering legal advice, of course, just describing what we have seen our clients do. If a special-purpose vehicle is used, though, the account would look like the first three examples in Exhibit 3.5.

In Example 1, Allocation to a Single Manager, the investor uses the special-purpose vehicle to open an account at a brokerage firm where the CTA manager has trading authority. The investor gives the manager the authority to trade in the account.

In Example 2, Allocation to Multiple Managers, a single investment account is set up by the special-purpose vehicle at the futures brokerage firm. The account has subaccounts allocated to different trading managers with three different powers of attorney. There is just one legal entity. This is a simple way to set up several managed accounts; the paperwork and credit

**EXHIBIT 3.5A**  Managed Account Structures (*Example 1*)

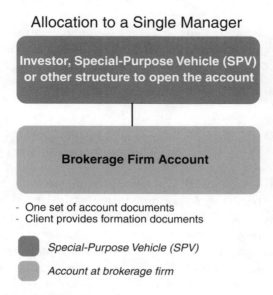

## Allocation to a Single Manager

Investor, Special-Purpose Vehicle (SPV) or other structure to open the account

Brokerage Firm Account

- One set of account documents
- Client provides formation documents

*Special-Purpose Vehicle (SPV)*

*Account at brokerage firm*

*Source:* Newedge Prime Brokerage Research.

**EXHIBIT 3.5B**   Managed Account Structures (*Example 2*)

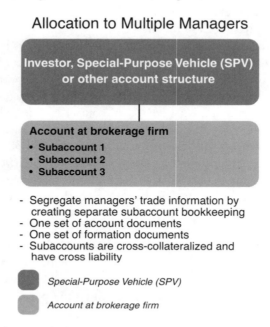

## Allocation to Multiple Managers

Investor, Special-Purpose Vehicle (SPV)
or other account structure

**Account at brokerage firm**
- Subaccount 1
- Subaccount 2
- Subaccount 3

- Segregate managers' trade information by
  creating separate subaccount bookkeeping
- One set of account documents
- One set of formation documents
- Subaccounts are cross-collateralized and
  have cross liability

*Special-Purpose Vehicle (SPV)*

*Account at brokerage firm*

*Source:* Newedge Prime Brokerage Research.

checks need to be done only once. Net margining across the accounts is allowed because one legal entity owns them all. As there is no firewall between the different accounts, the performance and value of the accounts is netted together.

Example 3 is an expansion of Example 1. It allows for allocation to multiple managers by setting up three different special-purpose vehicles; each SPV opens an account using a different CTA manager. Each account requires its own paperwork and credit check, but the performance of the managers is separated.

Example 4 is a Protected Cell Company, an account structure that is allowed in many regulatory jurisdictions including the United States. It allows for a simplified account setup and firewalls between the money managers trading for it. This is becoming the most common way to set up a multiple-manager CTA account, replacing Examples 1 and 2. A protected cell company structure combines the simplicity of opening one account with the ability to separate performance in order to better evaluate the effects of manager selection. It allows for greater customization of the CTA investment.

**EXHIBIT 3.5C** Managed Account Structures (*Example 3*)

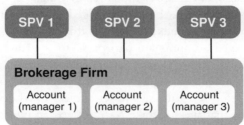

## Allocation to Multiple Managers

- Segregate investments by forming separate SPVs
- Each SPV opens an account
- Each SPV completes account documents
- Each SPV provides formation documents
- No cross liability between the accounts—no cross collateral

■ *Special-Purpose Vehicle (SPV)*

■ *Account at brokerage firm*

*Source:* Newedge Prime Brokerage Research.

**EXHIBIT 3.5D** Managed Account Structures (*Example 4*)

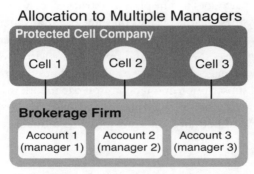

## Allocation to Multiple Managers

- Segregate managers by forming a protected cell company (PCC) with multiple cells
- The PCC completes one set of account documents and provides addendums for each cell
- The PCC provides one set of formation documents
- No cross-liability between subaccounts if the PCC and cells are formed correctly

■ *Special-Purpose Vehicle (SPV)*

■ *Account at brokerage firm*

*Source:* Newedge Prime Brokerage Research.

Which is best? As with so many matters involving CTA, it all depends on the needs of the investor. We find that clients make the decision based on their own organizational culture as much as anything.

The CTA managers who handle managed accounts may also manage CTA funds and other investment vehicles. If this is the case, investors should ask whether managed accounts are pari passu to the fund, or whether the investments will be different. If so, how will they differ?

Unfortunately, not all managers handle managed accounts, so an investor who insists on this option will have fewer choices in strategy and manager. The willingness of managers to take on managed accounts has varied over time.

## What Are Platforms?

The fourth way to structure a CTA investment is through a *platform*. This is a relatively new product offered by a handful of financial services firms and operates almost like a multi-CTA fund except that the investor can select the portfolio. A series of funds are offered through the platform, and investors can choose their own leverage and create their own portfolio from the mix.

Platforms argue that some of the advantages are objective, independent boards of directors and vendors. Instead of the manager choosing these parties, the platform company does it. The platform structure may also reduce custody concerns. Usually these platforms pass on some of the advantages of managed accounts such as transparency, liquidity, and customized leverage.

Investors can have a series of fund investments with the platform's participating money managers, receiving consolidated performance information and consolidated subscription and redemption paperwork from the platform. It is relatively easy to move money from one manager to another. Because of the transparency and liquidity, these are a hybrid of managed accounts and CTA funds.

## How Do You Compare and Contrast These Offerings?

Exhibit 3.6 consolidates many of the previous answers into a summary table. It provides answers to the primary questions for the four different categories of investment structures: CTA funds, multi-CTA funds, managed accounts, and platforms. While there definitely are exceptions to our answers in this table, it should serve as a good starting point when considering your investment structure.

**EXHIBIT 3.6** Managed Accounts versus Fund Investments

| | Liability | Liquidity | Funding & Leverage | Oversight & Control of Assets | Terms & Fees for Service Providers | Maintenance | Position & Trade Transparency | Availability | Due Diligence Burden |
|---|---|---|---|---|---|---|---|---|---|
| CTA's Funds | Limited | Monthly | Manager-Determined | Directors selected by manager | Directors selected by manager | Low | Usually not | Most managers offer flagship fund | Medium |
| Multi-CTA Fund | Limited | Weekly/Monthly | Manager-Determined | Directors selected by manager | Directors selected by manager | Low | Usually not | Most managers offer flagship fund | Low |
| Managed Accounts | Unlimited | Daily | Customer-Determined | Investor | Investor | High | Yes | Not all managers accept managed accounts | High |
| Platforms | Limited | Weekly/Monthly | Hybrid | Directors selected by platform | Directors selected by platform | Medium | Varies; manager determined | Not all managers have an established relationship with a platform | Low |

*Source:* Newedge Prime Brokerage Research.

Where possible we list some specific answers such as who appoints directors. And when it comes to the cost of resources or the difficulty of a function,
we have resorted to simple rankings of low, medium, and high. These rankings
are based on years of direct experience, but are just our general opinions.

It is useful to look at these answers together. Investors following the path
of managed accounts might not have considered the high cost of maintenance
or limited manager availability. They would be well served to have a more
thorough dialog with multi-CTA funds or platforms to see whether their
structuring needs can be accommodated. Having said that, if full control of
the assets and daily liquidity is a must, they just might have to accept the
costs.

## Who Regulates CTAs?

CTAs in the United States are regulated by the Commodity Futures Trading
Commission (CFTC), and CTA managers are registered with the National
Futures Association (NFA). In fact, you can look up the regulatory status of a
CTA firm or employee at the NFA's web site, www.nfa.futures.org/basicnet/,
an important first step in due diligence.

The terms *Commodity Trading Advisor* and *CTA* have precise definitions
under CFTC regulations, but they also have generic usage as money managers
who specialize in options and futures trading. Likewise, some funds prefer to
be known as hedge funds or systematic futures managers even though they are
registered with the CFTC as CTAs. Any advisor managing an account with
a total value of $2,000,000 or more that has 10 percent or more of its assets
allocated to commodity trading has to be registered as a CTA. But there are
smaller managers that trade in futures exclusively, and larger accounts that
are required to be registered but follow broader, macro-investment strategies
rather than concentrating on futures.

An account that handles more than just options and futures may also be
registered with the Securities and Exchange Commission, but it does not have
to be. Likewise, the personnel may have a dual registration with the Financial
Industry Regulatory Authority (FINRA); those licenses can be checked at
www.finra.org/Investors/ToolsCalculators/BrokerCheck/index.htm.

Accounts that are managed outside of the United States may be registered
with other national authorities or may not be registered at all. The registration
status should be asked about and checked during due diligence. In addition,
investors should find out what court system would oversee any complaints.

## How Are Structured Notes and Total Return Swaps Used by CTA Investors?

An alternative way to pick up CTA exposure is through structured principal-protected notes or total return swaps. Structured notes typically are designed to guarantee the return of principal upon maturity, with the coupon tied to the rate of return on a managed futures account. Similarly, total return swaps provide a return indexed to an account managed by the CTA and are usually structured through documentation of the International Swap Dealers Association (ISDA). Because CTA accounts are so heavily weighted with cash, these may be a good way to customize investments and improve return for a given level of risk. Either of these can limit the amount of drawdown, assuming that the issuing bank has enough credit to make good at maturity. Because these are sold and managed differently from traditional CTA accounts, we have not included them in the chart above.

## What Are the Account Opening Procedures for a Managed Account?

Opening a CTA account is similar to opening other types of institutional brokerage accounts, although there may be some aspects that are new to those who have never been involved with derivatives before. All it means is a little more disclosure and a few more forms, but it is helpful to know what to expect.

### The Information Request

The basic information request usually covers such things as certificate of incorporation, memorandum and articles of association, and register of directors. From these, the brokerage firm has the official legal names and regulatory structures needed to determine the appropriate documentation for the account. Then, the investor fills out other sets of forms related to its status and the type of account being opened. Some typical supplemental documents include agreements with the fund manager, a power of attorney to allow the manager to execute trades, and give-up agreements. A standard disclosure statement will have to be signed, depending on the products being traded, to ensure that the investor is informed of the risks involved. An ISDA (Institutional Standard Derivative Agreement) or an IFEMA (International Foreign

Exchange Master Agreement) may be needed for products that are not traded on exchanges, most usually foreign currency. A customer based outside of the United States will have to file a Form W-8 for the U.S. Internal Revenue Service.

## Providing Account Information

The investor will receive the relevant documents to sign along with a request for information needed for credit approval and to comply with anti-money laundering regulations (AMLs). The forms included in the packet will vary with the type of account being opened, but the minimum requirements will include information about how much money will be used to fund the new account and where it comes from, audited financial statements, and copies of the passports of the account-holders' directors. This helps the brokerage firm know that the investor is legitimate and set appropriate position levels.

Many CTA accounts are designed for accredited investors or qualified purchasers. The fund operator does not have to register under the Securities and Exchange Commission's Rule 501 as long as it deals only with investors who are perceived to be sophisticated enough to handle risk. These have strict legal definitions; an accredited investor is an individual or married couple with a net worth of at least $1 million or an annual income of $200,000 ($300,000 if married couple), while a qualified purchaser is an individual, business, or institution with a net worth of at least $5 million. The SEC has revised those levels over time. The most recent revision was in 1982, but it could change in the future. Not all CTAs will need proof that an investor meets these standards; some simply require a high enough minimum investment that the matter is irrelevant.

## Approvals

Once the documents are submitted, the brokerage firm will review the financial information and the anticipated level of trading activity to determine how much leverage is appropriate for the client. CTAs are inherently leveraged, but some use more margin as a percentage of assets under management than others do to execute their strategies. The firm's risk managers may need more information about the account characteristics or the officers and directors to ensure that all regulations are met and that the client isn't taking on unsuitable risk.

## What Is the Minimum Investment in a CTA?

Different managers have different requirements. The minimum amount for an investment is stated on subscription forms or in other offering documents. The manager will set a minimum based on the trading strategy and business issues. The manager will usually have a minimum portfolio size in order to trade the target strategy as many contracts have a minimum margin requirement. The business burden of setting up a customized managed account for an investor can vary widely on the organization and the trading strategy. Strategies that have very short holding periods and trade numerous exchanges usually require higher minimums. The manager might institute a minimum portfolio increment, which is another way of saying a large enough change to make a difference in the portfolio. For example, Japanese government bond (JGB) contracts require $100,000 in minimum margin to control $1 million in contracts, and that margin must be posted in $100,000 increments. If a manager is trading JGB futures, and they represent 5 percent of the margin requirements, an incremental $10,000 investment is of no use.

Some managers have a maximum investment, in order to keep any one client from becoming too great a part of the business.

## What Does It Mean When a Manager Is Closed?

A manager will sometimes close its fund or its managed account services to new investors. This means that it is not accepting more money. Some managers will close to all new investments, and some will close to only new investments; some will stay closed for a period of time and then reopen after existing investors redeem funds or when market conditions change. The more difficult status to describe is *soft closed*, what we often think of as "selectively open upon review." This means that the manager is publicly closed to new investments, but the manager will accept investments of a certain size or from certain types of investors.

## What Are the Subscription Procedures for a Fund?

One does not open an account with a fund; one *subscribes to it*. The subscription procedures for a fund are less burdensome than those for opening a managed account, but they are not trivial. Investors need to have proof of identity and suitability; funds will also want evidence that the money comes from legitimate sources.

## Conclusion

While we are confident that this chapter will go a long way toward helping you make good decisions, there is much we have not covered. Among other things, we have avoided any discussion of:

- Taxes and tax law
- Credit risk
- Tracking error
- Due diligence
- Negotiation of terms and documents
- Operational issues and the reconciliation of statements
- Legal structures

Then again, most of these issues are common to any investment that an institutional investor makes, and so we are just as confident that once you get this far, you will find the help you need among the resources you already have.

# PART II

# Building Blocks

# CHAPTER 4

# How Trend Following Works

Medium- to long-term systematic trend-following models dominate the managed futures industry. Of the nearly $100 billion managed by commodity trading advisors, easily a third or more is controlled by a handful of managers who describe themselves as trend followers. Even so, it is no easy thing to find the data one needs to separate the contribution of generic trend following as a trading strategy from the influence of what actual managers do when trading in practice. The most intense research is done by the managers themselves, and they are unlikely to give away any knowledge that has value to peers and competitors. Actual track records are available, of course, as well as indexes based on actual track records. But actual track records represent the combined effects of trading strategies, risk management, leverage, cash management, resizing, and any number of other things that can differentiate one manager from another.

At the same time, there is a long list of questions about trend-following trading systems that cry out for answers. Here are just a few:

- Is there an inherent return to trend following?
- Are trend-following systems all the same? And if not, how sensitive are they to incremental variation in trade signals, portfolio construction, transactions costs, contract rolls, stops, resizing, and leverage?
- How do generic trend-following results correlate with actual track records?
- Do market environments matter?
- Are there predictable give-backs?

To answer these and other questions about trend-following trading systems, we have assembled the data and written the programs necessary to determine the basic profit-and-loss characteristics of the two most widely used trend-following systems—moving average crossover and range breakout. The purpose of this chapter is to explain the steps involved in constructing a database of trend-following profits and losses. It also serves as an explanatory guide to a new performance report that shows how these two kinds of trend-following systems have worked in a wide range of futures markets.

## The Two Basic Strategies

The two most popular trend-following systems are moving average/crossover and range breakout. Each defines a trend or price pattern by comparing a current market price or recent average price with a longer history of the price and buys or sells when the recent price measure is above or below the longer price measure.

### Moving Average/Crossover

The basic moving average crossover system defines two moving averages—a fast-day average and a slow-day average—and is long if the fast-day average is higher than the slow-day average or short if the fast-day average is lower than the slow-day average. That is, if

$$F = \text{number of days in the fast moving average}$$

and

$$S = \text{number of days in the slow moving average}$$

then the rule is:

$$\text{If F-day average} > \text{S-day average, long, otherwise short}$$

For example, if $F = 20$ and $S = 80$, we would calculate the average price for the past 20 days and the past 80 days and compare the two. If the 20-day average were higher than the 80-day average, we would be long. Otherwise, we would be short. And, in the simplest kind of moving average system, we would always be in, either long or short.

An illustration of this simple "two-line" moving average system is provided in Exhibit 4.1, which traces the fast and slow averages for the S&P 500 from

**EXHIBIT 4.1** Example of a 20/80 Moving Average Crossover System

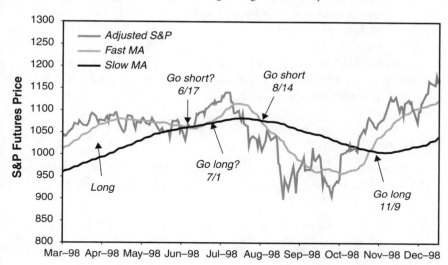

*Source:* Bloomberg, Newedge Prime Brokerage Research.

March through December 1998. During the early months, the system was long S&Ps. Then, on June 17, the fast average dipped below the slow average, and the system would go short. On July 1, the fast average crossed the slow average, and the system went long. The system later went short on August 14 and long again on November 9.

We have added question marks to the short position on June 17 and the subsequent long position on July 1. The reason for the question marks is that it is possible for a system like this to produce spurious trades if the fast average is not, in some sense, significantly different from the slow average. To prevent the possibility of spurious trading in our own calculations, we have overlaid on the system a simple statistical standard for determining whether the fast average is higher or lower than the slow average. That is, we establish a buffer zone equal to two standard deviations of daily changes in the fast moving average and then use the following modified trading rule:

If F-day average > S-day average + buffer, go long

If F-day average < S-day average − buffer, go short

When stated this way, there is a small range of prices around the slow average within which the trader can be short even if the fast average is slightly higher than the slow average or long even if the fast average is slightly lower than the slow average. And, as it happened, the buffer would have eliminated the trades on June 17 and July 1.

One source of differences in the results of applying a rule like this is in the details. In our work, we calculated moving averages using daily closing prices and transacted at the next day's opening price if the rule produced a buy or sell signal. Contract rolls (discussed below) were done at closing prices.

## Range Breakout

A range breakout system compares the current market price with the highest and lowest market prices for the past N days. That is, if

$$N = \text{number of days used to define the price range}$$

then the rule is:

$$\text{If price} > \text{N-day high, go long}$$
$$\text{If price} < \text{N-day low, go short}$$

Or, similarly, whenever the market establishes a new N-day high or N-day low, the system generates a buy or sell signal. In its simplest form, this system is always in, which results in some interesting ambiguities. That is, once you are long, you stay long as long as the price stays above the N-day low. Or, if you are short, you stay short as long as the price stays below the N-day high. As a result, when the price is trading within the N-day range (which is most of the time), whether you are long or short depends entirely on your most recent trade.

An example of a 50-day range breakout system is illustrated in Exhibit 4.2, which covers the same months as the moving average system shown in Exhibit 4.1. As it happened, this system also was long during the early months, and produced a short signal on June 17. Thereafter, it generated long and short signals at roughly, but not exactly, the same times as the 20/80 moving average system.

For the purposes of this work, we compared each day's closing price with an N-day high/low determined using daily high and low prices. If the result produced a trading signal, the resulting trades were done at the next day's

**EXHIBIT 4.2**   Fifty Day Range Breakout System

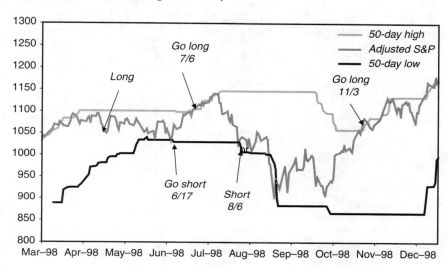

*Source:* Bloomberg, Newedge Prime Brokerage Research.

opening price. Once the initial position was taken, the system was always in the market. Contract rolls were done at daily closing prices.

## Making the Systems Work in Practice

Perhaps the hardest part of an exercise like this is the sheer volume of detail that is required to do things correctly. Once the markets are selected (perhaps the easiest job of all), there is the problem of gathering data, dealing with things like date mismatches, making sure the calculations are true to the logic of the trading systems, and checking to make sure that the results are reasonable. In this section, we outline our choice of markets, constructing the price series, and the assumptions we used when generating trading signals and calculating gains and losses.

### Choice of Markets and Portfolio Weights

For the purposes of this exercise, we chose 39 futures markets that can be grouped into the four broad classes shown in Exhibit 4.3. We chose this set

**EXHIBIT 4.3**  Market Selection and Portfolio Weights

| | | Futures Markets | Standard Deviation of Daily Changes ($/contract) | Number of Contracts | Position Standard Deviation | Sector Standard Deviation |
|---|---|---|---|---|---|---|
| Equity | 1 | S&P 500 | 3,227 | 1 | 3,227 | |
| | 2 | CAC 40 | 552 | 7 | 3,863 | |
| | 3 | DAX 30 | 1,828 | 2 | 3,656 | |
| | 4 | NIKKEI 225 | 2,029 | 2 | 4,059 | |
| | 5 | AUSSIE SPX | 422 | 9 | 3,794 | 19,707 |
| | 6 | FTSE 250 | 959 | 4 | 3,834 | |
| | 7 | SWEDISH OMX | 150 | 25 | 3,739 | |
| | 8 | NASDAQ 100 | 5,588 | 1 | 5,588 | |
| | 9 | DJ EURO STOXX | 624 | 6 | 3,747 | |
| | 10 | HANG SENG | 1,472 | 3 | 4,416 | |
| Interest Rate | 11 | US 30 YEAR | 663 | 6 | 3,976 | |
| | 12 | US 10 YEAR | 428 | 9 | 3,854 | |
| | 13 | GERMAN BUND | 417 | 9 | 3,755 | |
| | 14 | GERMAN BOBL | 264 | 14 | 3,697 | |
| | 15 | AUSSIE 10 YEAR | 434 | 9 | 3,905 | |
| | 16 | UK 10 YEAR GILT | 743 | 5 | 3,717 | 19,674 |
| | 17 | JAPAN 10 YEAR | 3,625 | 1 | 3,625 | |
| | 18 | JAPAN 3 MONTH | 54 | 71 | 3,837 | |
| | 19 | US 3 MONTH | 326 | 12 | 3,908 | |
| | 20 | EUROPE 3 MONTH | 78 | 49 | 3,806 | |
| | 21 | UK SHORT STERLING | 76 | 50 | 3,796 | |
| | 22 | AUSSIE 3 MONTH | 96 | 39 | 3,731 | |
| Foreign Currency | 23 | JAPANESE YEN | 855 | 7 | 5,987 | |
| | 24 | EURO | 684 | 8 | 5,470 | |
| | 25 | SWISS FRANC | 635 | 9 | 5,713 | |
| | 26 | BRITISH POUND | 488 | 11 | 5,372 | 20,618 |
| | 27 | AUSTRALIAN DOLLAR | 414 | 13 | 5,378 | |
| | 28 | CANADIAN DOLLAR | 254 | 22 | 5,584 | |
| | 29 | MEXICAN PESO | 395 | 14 | 5,532 | |
| Commodity | 30 | CRUDE OIL | 523 | 11 | 5,757 | |
| | 31 | NATURAL GAS | 1,487 | 4 | 5,948 | |
| | 32 | SUGAR | 193 | 31 | 5,993 | |
| | 33 | HEATING OIL | 627 | 9 | 5,643 | |
| | 34 | COTTON | 527 | 11 | 5,801 | |
| | 35 | CORN | 190 | 31 | 5,880 | 20,533 |
| | 36 | COFFEE | 1,487 | 4 | 5,950 | |
| | 37 | SOYBEANS | 404 | 14 | 5,658 | |
| | 38 | GOLD | 259 | 22 | 5,688 | |
| | 39 | COPPER | 354 | 16 | 5,662 | |
| | | | | | Portfolio | 46,414 |

*Source:* Bloomberg, Newedge Prime Brokerage Research.

of contracts for three main reasons. First, they are all comparatively liquid. Second, we have 10-year high/low/open/close price histories for all but three of them.[*] Third, they provide a good representation of four main market groupings: equities, bonds, currencies, and commodities.

Portfolio construction can vary widely in complexity and sophistication. For our purposes, we first calculated the standard deviation of daily dollar gains and losses for each of the commodities. We then chose whole numbers of each contract so that each individual futures market would exhibit about the same amount of risk within its market sector. We then scaled the numbers of contracts so that each of the broad sectors would exhibit about the same amount of risk as the others. The resulting contract weights are shown in Exhibit 4.3 along with the standard deviation of dollar changes in position value for each contract.

As a practical matter, the most volatile contracts set a rough lower limit on the size of the trading program. For example, the standard deviation of daily changes in the value of one S&P 500 contract for the 10-year period was $3,227. For the NASDAQ 100, it was $5,588, while for the 10-year JGB contract, it was $3,625 (when yen gains and losses were translated into dollar gains and losses). Strictly speaking, we could have chosen the NASDAQ 100 contract as our numeraire and scaled everything else off of that. As it was, we decided to slightly overweight this contract by using the S&P 500 and JGB contracts as our representative contracts and scale everything from there.

As the results show, each equity and interest rate contract position had daily standard deviation in the mid-to-upper-$3,000 range. Each of the currency and commodity contract positions had a standard deviation in the upper-$5,000 range. Taken together, each sector as a sub-portfolio had a standard deviation of about $20,000.

## Calculating Transactions Costs

The next step was to simulate gains and losses from the two basic trend-following systems. To do this, we had to determine when the systems would buy and sell for any given set of day parameters, the prices at which they would buy and sell, and the numbers of contracts traded in each transaction.

---

[*]The exceptions are DJ Eurostoxx (6/19/98), Nasdaq100 (4/9/96), and OMX (3/25/94). Our source for price data was Bloomberg, with the exception of Euribor, for which CQG was the source, and Aussie SPX, for which the Sydney Futures Exchange was the source. Our continuous series for the euro was the result of chaining the old Deutschemark contract with the new euro contract using the fixed conversion rate at the time the euro was introduced.

And to do this, we first had to deal with the fact that futures contracts have fixed expiration dates and that any trading system using futures has to come to grips with contract rolls. Contract rolls present three kinds of problems. First, there is the practical problem of how to calculate moving averages or price ranges when shifting from one futures price series to the next. Second, a futures trading system will trade for two reasons. The first is when the system generates a buy or sell signal. The second is when the time comes to transfer a long (or short) position from the expiring contract to the next contract month. Third, the trader has some discretion about just when to roll from one contract month to the next.

## Concatenating Futures Price Series

One practical feature of futures is the expiration cycle that governs trading in each market. In most cases, it is common practice to concentrate trading in the contract that is nearest expiration, at least until market participants reach a market consensus about shifting, or rolling, their positions and trading into the next contract month.

As shown in Exhibit 4.4, the quarterly cycle is the most common, at least for financial commodities. In this cycle, contracts expire in March, June, September, and December on dates that are specific to each contract. Some stock index contracts follow a monthly expiration cycle, as do energy futures and copper. Agricultural commodities follow various forms of an every-other-month cycle.

In most futures markets, the relationship between futures prices and their underlying spot prices is governed by arbitrage relationships. In a negative carry market, where it costs more to finance a position in the underlying commodity than the commodity provides in terms of interest or dividends, futures prices will be higher than spot prices. This kind of relationship is illustrated by the upward-sloping line in Exhibit 4.5. In positive carry markets, where the commodity generates more income than it costs to finance the position, the futures price will be lower than the spot price, and longer-dated futures prices will be lower than nearby futures prices. An example of this would be the downward-sloping line in Exhibit 4.5.

Much of the time, equity futures look like negative carry markets because dividend income tends to be less than the costs of financing. As a result, futures prices tend to be higher than spot prices, and more-distant futures prices tend to be higher than futures that expire sooner. And, much of the time, bond markets look like positive carry markets, at least when the yield curve is upward sloping. Coupon income will exceed finance expense, and

**EXHIBIT 4.4**  Contract Roll Schedule

| Instruments | Cycle |
|---|---|
| S&P 500 | HMUZ |
| DAX 30 | HMUZ |
| Nikkei 225 | HMUZ |
| CAC 40 | FGHJKMNQUVXZ |
| Aussie SPX | HMUZ |
| FTSE 250 | HMUZ |
| Swedish OMX | FGHJKMNQUVXZ |
| Nasdaq 100 | HMUZ |
| Hang Seng | FGHJKMNQUVXZ |
| DJ Euro Stoxx | HMUZ |
| US 30-Y Bond | HMUZ |
| US 10-Y Bond | HMUZ |
| German Bund | HMUZ |
| German Bobl | HMUZ |
| Aussie 10 year | HMUZ |
| UK 10 -Y Gilt | HMUZ |
| Japan 10 year | HMUZ |
| Japan 3 Month | HMUZ |
| US 3 Month | HMUZ |
| Aussie 3 Month | HMUZ |
| Euro 3 Month | HMUZ |
| UK Short Sterling | HMUZ |
| Japanese Yen | HMUZ |
| Euro | HMUZ |
| Swiss Franc | HMUZ |
| British Pound | HMUZ |
| Australian Dollar | HMUZ |
| Canadian Dollar | HMUZ |
| Mexican Peso | HMUZ |
| Crude Oil | FGHJKMNQUVXZ |
| Natural Gas | FGHJKMNQUVXZ |
| Sugar | FHKNV |
| Heating Oil | FGHJKMNQUVXZ |
| Cotton | HKNVZ |
| Corn | HKNUZ |
| Coffee | HKNUZ |
| Soybean | FHKNQUX |
| Gold | GJMQVZ |
| Copper | FGHJKMNQUVXZ |

| Explanation: | | |
|---|---|---|
| F - January | K - May | U - September |
| G - February | M - June | V - October |
| H - March | N - July | X - November |
| J - April | Q - August | Z - December |

*Source:* Newedge Prime Brokerage Research.

**EXHIBIT 4.5**   Spot and Futures Price Spreads

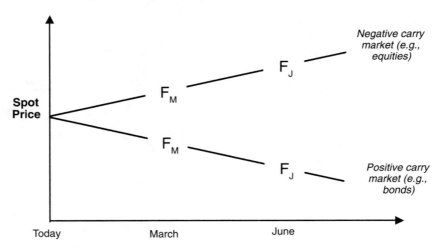

*Source:* Newedge Prime Brokerage Research.

bond futures prices will be lower than spot prices. FX markets can be either way, depending on the relationship between domestic and foreign interest rates, and commodities markets, where arbitrage is often more costly and difficult to do, exhibit patterns that reflect anticipated demands and supplies and can take any shape.

For us, these price relationships complicate the problem of calculating moving averages or high/low price ranges. Consider Exhibit 4.6, which shows the March 1994 S&P 500 futures price series as that contract approaches expiration, and the June 1994 series, which is where open positions will be held once the March contract has expired. The fact that the June contract prices are higher than the March prices is simply a result of negative carry and not because futures prices have risen in any sense.

To incorporate the June price series with the March series, we can do either of two things. First, when calculating any moving average or historical price range, we can increase all March and earlier contract prices by the difference between the June and the March prices, and recalculate everything. Or we can adjust the June futures prices down by an amount equal to the difference between the June and March prices. This second approach, which is illustrated in Exhibit 4.7, is the simpler approach and allows us to generate a continuous price series that can be used for all of our applications. In Exhibit 4.8, we compare a history of raw S&P 500 futures prices with its continuous price history. As one would expect, because we are adjusting successive futures prices

**EXHIBIT 4.6**   Raw S&P 500 Futures Price Series

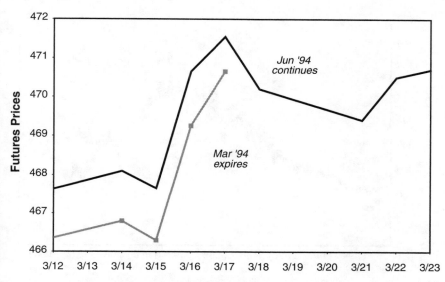

*Source:* Bloomberg, Newedge Prime Brokerage Research.

**EXHIBIT 4.7**   Constructing a Continuous Futures Price Series

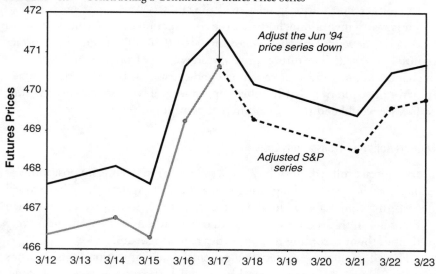

*Source:* Bloomberg, Newedge Prime Brokerage Research.

**EXHIBIT 4.8**    Raw and Continuous S&P 500 Futures Price Series

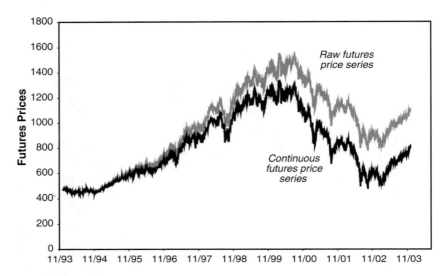

*Source:* Bloomberg, Newedge Prime Brokerage Research.

down, the continuous series tends to drift down relative to the raw series. If we were doing the same thing for a positive carry market, the continuous series would tend to drift up relative to the raw series.

It is worth mentioning here that the construction of a continuous futures price series depends on what we assume about the shift from one contract month to the next. The futures price spread will vary from day to day because of changes in carry and relative richness and cheapness. In our work, we make the shift on expiration day. In other applications, if we were making the shift earlier, we would end up with a different continuous series.

## Contract Rolls and Transactions Costs

Every contract roll requires a buy and a sell to maintain an open position. For example, if the system is long going into a contract expiration, we have to sell the expiring contract and buy the next contract. For some markets, as shown in Exhibit 4.4, this is done quarterly. In others, it is done every month, every other month, or according to some other regular schedule.

The effect of these trades on a system's total transaction costs depends on the liquidity of the spread markets in which these trades would be done. Because spread trades are less risky than outright buys and sells, the markets for spreads are tighter, and often there will be small concessions in terms of brokerage and clearing fees. Thus, in practice, the cost of rolling contracts will be less per contract than the cost of responding to buy and sell signals, which require outright purchases or sales.

## Choosing the Best Time to Roll

In this round of work, we do not deal with this problem. Rather, we have assumed that all contract rolls take place at contract expiration. In practice, this approach would not be the best approach because the best time to roll a position depends in part on the market in which you are trading and on whether you want to roll a long or short position. To use futures to your best advantage requires an understanding of how futures trading behaves around contract expirations and how spread markets respond. In some markets, contract rolls take place several weeks before the nearby contract expires. In others, the rolls take place during the last few days of the expiring contract's life. And in almost all cases, one would avoid doing anything on the last day of a contract's life.

## Transactions Costs

As a rough and liberal approximation of the effect of transactions costs on our simulated profit/loss (P/L) results, we have used $50 per contract per side to represent both market impact (bid/asked spread and slippage) and brokerage costs. With this assumption, the cost of a round turn would be $100. This is clearly more than the costs of trading in most markets, especially for the spread trades involved in contract rolls.

The number of trades generated by any given system was reckoned this way when calculating the net profit/loss for a single futures contract. The first buy or sell signal generated by the system results in the purchase or sale of a single contract. All subsequent signals require the purchase or sale of two contracts. For example, if we are already long, then a short signal requires us to sell one contract to offset our long position and to sell a second contract to establish a short position. Further, every contract roll requires us to trade two contracts, one in the expiring contract month and one in the next contract month to maintain an open long or short position.

## Other Considerations

In producing our results, we ignored stops, assumed continuous resizing, omitted interest income, and made no allowance for management fees. Each of these will be encountered in actual trading programs. Our goal, however, is to produce completely generic trend-following gains and losses, and so we have isolated these possible influences.

## Stops

Stops are used to get out of the market. In some instances, stops will be triggered by a trading loss of a predetermined size. These are known as *risk management stops*. In other instances, stops will be triggered by ambiguous trading signals. For example, a trend follower might use a three-line moving average that is long only if a fast average is greater than a medium-term average, which is in turn greater than a slow average. If any one of the three is out of order, the system would be flat, or out of the market. Range-breakout traders might use an inner range and an outer range that allows the trader to be out of the market if the price is trading within the inner range.

Our chief reason for ignoring stops—and risk management stops in particular—is that their application is so varied. That is, while there may be generally accepted risk management stops (e.g., get out if a position loses .5% of portfolio), there is very little agreement about the conditions that would cause the system to get back in the market.

## Continuous Resizing

Resizing is the problem of adjusting the scale of a trading program as it makes or loses money. Below, when we convert futures gains and losses into rates of return, we will use a denominator of $5 million. Because our gains and losses are produced by the fixed contract portfolio in Exhibit 4.3, we never vary the size of the trading program. As a result, our rates of return based on a fixed $5 million would be the same as those of a manager who returns all profits and who requires additional cash when there are losses. They would also be the same as those of a manager who scales up the size of the trading program when making money and scales it down when losing money.

Again, this is an area of managed futures trading in which there is no one standard practice. Some managers will resize regularly. Others will resize infrequently.

## Interest Income

The gains and losses reported here are pure futures gains and losses and represent, as a result, pure excess return. In an actual trading program, for which some actual cash has been invested, there would be interest income as well as futures trading income. In such cases, interest income has to be netted out before one can calculate a Sharpe ratio.

## Fees

Fees comprise some combination of an ongoing management fee and a performance fee. The ongoing management fee is fairly straightforward and usually assessed against the total amount of money invested in the program. Performance fees, however, are time dependent because under most circumstances, a manager collects a performance or incentive fee only if the fund's or account's value is higher than its most recent high-water mark. What one pays or collects in performance fees depends to a large extent on when the program starts trading. For this reason, two trading systems might make the same amount of money gross of fees in a given quarter but yield different net amounts because one was above water while the other was under water.

## Case Study: Two Models from 1994–2003

Three of our questions at the outset were: (1) Is there an inherent return to trend following?, (2) Are trend following systems all the same?, and (3) How do generic trend-following results correlate with actual track records? To answer these questions, we use the results of the two trend-following models and their respective ranges of parameter choices for the entire period from 1994 through 2003.

### A Question of Inherent Return

Ten years of data is just that—a 10-year experience. Even so, Exhibit 4.9 provides some interesting insights into the gains and losses generated by trend-following trading systems. In the upper panel, for example, we find the portfolio results by year for a 60/180-day moving average system and an 80-day breakout system.[*] For these 10 years, both the moving average system and the breakout system had one losing year. And, although the chart doesn't show it, both systems over the full 10 years produced a total gain of $5.8 million, gross of fees, once all the dust had settled.

---

[*] Actual P/L histories for each trading system begin when the first position is taken. As a result, the starting dates for the P/L histories used here begin at different times. Most models will have kicked in before the end of 1994, but in the case of a very slow moving average, the first positions might not have been taken until 1995.

**EXHIBIT 4.9**   P/L Gains and Losses From 1995–2004

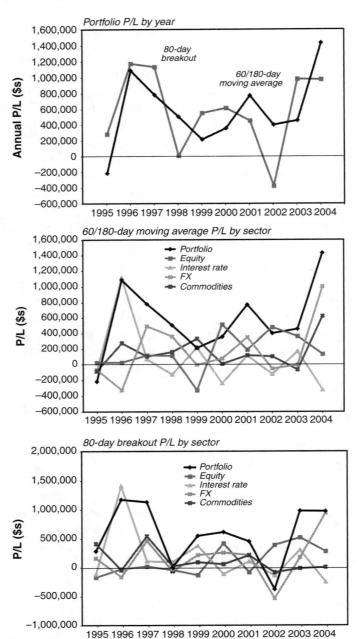

*Source:* Bloomberg, Newedge Prime Brokerage Research.

The middle and lower panels show the annual P/L results for the four broad sectors for both systems. These exhibit a great deal more variability year to year than does the portfolio, which seems like a good argument for diversification. Also, even though the chart does not show it, each sector, when all was said and done by the end of 2003, had delivered somewhere between 20 and 30 percent of the total portfolio return.

## Are All Systems the Same?

It has been suggested that there is very little difference between trend-following models, and that there is little room to improve results through a better choice of day for calculating moving averages or breakout ranges. To some extent this is true, but the evidence presented in Exhibit 4.10 for breakout systems and Exhibit 4.11 for moving average systems suggests that there can be substantial differences in trading results.

**EXHIBIT 4.10** Portfolio Trading Results for Breakout Systems (January 1994–December 2003)

| Days | Daily P/L Results | | Total Number of Half Turns |
|---|---|---|---|
| | Average | Standard Deviation | |
| 10 | −2,289 | 43,080 | 113,218 |
| 20 | −904 | 44,491 | 90,133 |
| 30 | −30 | 44,612 | 80,579 |
| 40 | 784 | 45,406 | 74,765 |
| 50 | 1,359 | 46,142 | 70,997 |
| 60 | 1,644 | 46,131 | 69,032 |
| 70 | 2,079 | 46,004 | 67,381 |
| 80 | 2,295 | 46,285 | 66,082 |
| 90 | 2,073 | 46,541 | 65,217 |
| 100 | 2,213 | 46,289 | 64,475 |
| 110 | 2,259 | 46,031 | 63,114 |
| 120 | 2,247 | 45,317 | 62,120 |

*Source:* Bloomberg, Newedge Prime Brokerage Research.

**EXHIBIT 4.11** Portfolio Trading Results for Moving Average Crossover Systems (with Buffer) (January 1994–December 2003)

*Average Daily P/L*

| Slow Days | Fast Days | | | | | | | | | |
|---|---|---|---|---|---|---|---|---|---|---|
| | 20 | 40 | 60 | 80 | 100 | 120 | 140 | 160 | 180 | 200 |
| 40 | −578 | | | | | | | | | |
| 60 | 488 | 757 | | | | | | | | |
| 80 | 838 | 1,457 | 1,268 | | | | | | | |
| 100 | 1,429 | 1,577 | 995 | 1,194 | | | | | | |
| 120 | 1,575 | 1,715 | 1,603 | 1,927 | 1,155 | | | | | |
| 140 | 1,856 | 2,068 | 1,994 | 1,871 | 1,696 | 1,501 | | | | |
| 160 | 2,100 | 2,424 | 1,891 | 2,103 | 1,694 | 1,728 | 1,614 | | | |
| 180 | 2,465 | 2,844 | 2,389 | 1,904 | 1,916 | 1,961 | 1,736 | 2,065 | | |
| 200 | 2,826 | 3,071 | 2,785 | 2,448 | 2,507 | 2,416 | 2,382 | 2,039 | 1,921 | |
| 220 | 3,039 | 3,453 | 2,898 | 2,774 | 2,598 | 2,540 | 2,500 | 2,703 | 2,137 | 2,624 |
| 240 | 3,190 | 3,579 | 3,082 | 3,029 | 3,197 | 3,096 | 2,956 | 2,700 | 2,802 | 2,975 |
| 260 | 3,334 | 3,386 | 3,305 | 3,165 | 3,091 | 3,077 | 3,165 | 2,940 | 3,008 | 3,094 |
| 280 | 3,520 | 3,616 | 3,597 | 3,455 | 3,221 | 3,335 | 3,134 | 2,751 | 2,732 | 3,305 |
| 300 | 3,222 | 3,591 | 3,394 | 3,364 | 3,042 | 2,970 | 2,776 | 2,709 | 2,934 | 3,122 |
| 320 | 3,003 | 3,500 | 3,366 | 3,233 | 2,819 | 2,636 | 2,643 | 2,678 | 2,963 | 3,035 |

*Standard Deviation of Daily P/L*

| Slow Days | Fast Days | | | | | | | | | |
|---|---|---|---|---|---|---|---|---|---|---|
| | 20 | 40 | 60 | 80 | 100 | 120 | 140 | 160 | 180 | 200 |
| 40 | 45,159 | | | | | | | | | |
| 60 | 45,207 | 43,752 | | | | | | | | |
| 80 | 45,418 | 44,688 | 43,884 | | | | | | | |
| 100 | 45,535 | 44,992 | 44,495 | 43,354 | | | | | | |
| 120 | 45,992 | 45,071 | 44,566 | 44,084 | 42,889 | | | | | |
| 140 | 45,787 | 44,985 | 44,704 | 43,940 | 43,369 | 43,506 | | | | |
| 160 | 45,838 | 45,235 | 44,796 | 44,725 | 44,246 | 44,265 | 44,000 | | | |
| 180 | 46,069 | 45,284 | 44,668 | 44,820 | 44,659 | 44,425 | 43,871 | 43,591 | | |
| 200 | 46,246 | 45,362 | 44,865 | 45,266 | 45,091 | 44,815 | 44,609 | 43,888 | 43,047 | |
| 220 | 46,239 | 45,162 | 45,347 | 45,466 | 45,198 | 45,395 | 45,218 | 44,449 | 43,529 | 43,309 |
| 240 | 46,620 | 45,498 | 45,758 | 45,582 | 45,564 | 45,727 | 45,853 | 45,119 | 44,221 | 43,771 |
| 260 | 46,855 | 45,673 | 45,565 | 45,647 | 45,606 | 45,924 | 45,731 | 45,031 | 44,461 | 44,077 |
| 280 | 47,113 | 45,949 | 46,059 | 45,919 | 46,122 | 46,509 | 46,086 | 45,470 | 45,142 | 45,386 |
| 300 | 46,596 | 45,926 | 46,187 | 46,124 | 46,317 | 46,195 | 46,152 | 45,595 | 45,279 | 45,371 |
| 320 | 47,020 | 46,361 | 46,377 | 46,358 | 46,447 | 46,319 | 46,236 | 46,192 | 45,818 | 45,998 |

*Total Number of Half Turns*

| Slow Days | Fast Days | | | | | | | | | |
|---|---|---|---|---|---|---|---|---|---|---|
| | 20 | 40 | 60 | 80 | 100 | 120 | 140 | 160 | 180 | 200 |
| 40 | 89,772 | | | | | | | | | |
| 60 | 78,912 | 78,372 | | | | | | | | |
| 80 | 74,252 | 72,220 | 73,500 | | | | | | | |
| 100 | 71,183 | 69,290 | 69,491 | 70,173 | | | | | | |
| 120 | 68,346 | 66,730 | 66,380 | 66,548 | 67,239 | | | | | |
| 140 | 66,600 | 65,007 | 64,694 | 64,521 | 65,002 | 65,599 | | | | |
| 160 | 65,735 | 63,703 | 63,403 | 63,722 | 63,690 | 64,116 | 64,339 | | | |
| 180 | 63,585 | 61,824 | 61,763 | 61,784 | 61,643 | 61,891 | 62,380 | 62,998 | | |
| 200 | 62,460 | 60,668 | 60,404 | 60,286 | 60,314 | 60,476 | 60,767 | 61,041 | 61,689 | |
| 220 | 61,489 | 60,113 | 59,707 | 59,467 | 59,424 | 59,381 | 59,491 | 59,430 | 60,203 | 60,548 |
| 240 | 60,746 | 59,192 | 58,841 | 58,570 | 58,319 | 58,318 | 58,268 | 58,318 | 58,439 | 58,963 |
| 260 | 59,268 | 57,989 | 57,482 | 57,504 | 57,143 | 57,126 | 56,921 | 56,977 | 57,013 | 57,143 |
| 280 | 58,898 | 57,290 | 56,933 | 56,803 | 56,618 | 56,381 | 56,284 | 56,231 | 56,463 | 56,558 |
| 300 | 58,017 | 56,435 | 56,125 | 55,699 | 55,634 | 55,620 | 55,490 | 55,426 | 55,337 | 55,462 |
| 320 | 57,372 | 55,543 | 55,257 | 55,006 | 54,872 | 54,767 | 54,576 | 54,575 | 54,481 | 54,444 |

*Source:* Bloomberg, Newedge Prime Brokerage Reasearch.

In particular, both exhibits suggest that relatively short-term trading programs do not do especially well. A 20/40-day moving average system, for example, lost money on average, as did 10-day, 20-day, and 30-day breakout systems. On the other hand, we can see in both exhibits that at some point, the trading systems produce roughly the same results over a fairly wide range of day assumptions. For example, in Exhibit 4.11, we have highlighted all of the fast- and slow-day combinations that produced an average daily P/L of $3,000 or more. There is a high point in the neighborhood of 40/280, but given the volatility of gains and losses, the neighboring results differ very little. And, in Exhibit 4.10, we find that once we get to a 70-day breakout, there is very little to be gained by extending the number of days out to 120.

## Generic Results versus Real Track Records

We undertook two exercises to confirm the reasonableness of our results. Our first reasonableness check was to see how our results correlated with real track records. For this exercise, we chose four managers—AHL, Aspect, Campbell, and Graham—which are self-described trend followers and which manage a very large fraction of managed futures money. We also included the Lehman total return bond index and the S&P 500 as proxies for two real asset classes. Third, we included the Barclay CTA index and both the Mt. Lucas and CISDM generic trend-following results. The correlations of monthly returns for the five years from January 1999 through December 2003 are shown in Exhibit 4.12.

**EXHIBIT 4.12** Correlations of Monthly Trend-Following Returns with Other Benchmarks (January 1999–December 2003)

| | 80-Day Breakout | 60/180-Day Moving Average | AHL | Aspect | Campbell | Graham | Lehman | S&P | Barclay CTA | MLM | CISDM |
|---|---|---|---|---|---|---|---|---|---|---|---|
| 80-Day B/O | 1.00 | | | | | | | | | | |
| 60/180 Mvg Avg | 0.90 | 1.00 | | | | | | | | | |
| AHL | 0.74 | 0.62 | 1.00 | | | | | | | | |
| Aspect | 0.66 | 0.57 | 0.90 | 1.00 | | | | | | | |
| Campbell | 0.76 | 0.62 | 0.72 | 0.71 | 1.00 | | | | | | |
| Graham | 0.71 | 0.61 | 0.70 | 0.68 | 0.77 | 1.00 | | | | | |
| Lehman | 0.37 | 0.47 | 0.35 | 0.34 | 0.41 | 0.26 | 1.00 | | | | |
| S&P | −0.38 | −0.31 | −0.40 | −0.37 | −0.38 | −0.38 | −0.30 | 1.00 | | | |
| Barclay CTA | 0.68 | 0.54 | 0.85 | 0.87 | 0.82 | 0.72 | 0.40 | −0.34 | 1.00 | | |
| MLM | 0.59 | 0.57 | 0.42 | 0.34 | 0.49 | 0.45 | 0.26 | −0.31 | 0.44 | 1.00 | |
| CISDM | 0.75 | 0.59 | 0.80 | 0.80 | 0.93 | 0.83 | 0.38 | −0.42 | 0.93 | 0.49 | 1.00 |

*Source:* Bloomberg, Barclay Hedge, Newedge Prime Brokerage Research.

Our second reasonableness check was to see how much trading our systems generated. For these purposes, round turns per million is a standard measure of a manager's trading velocity. The upper panel of Exhibit 4.13 shows the relationship between round turns per million for various moving average systems. The lower panels show how trading velocity varies with the number of days used to determine the breakout range. For the trading systems in the middle of the pack, the number of round turns per million was between 600 and 800 contracts per year, which is in line with the experience of trend-following managers.

## Rates of Return and Leverage

Because futures have no net cashing-out value, futures gains and losses are not by themselves rates of return. To translate them into rates of return, we have to overlay the trading program on some amount of cash. For the sake of illustration, Exhibit 4.14 shows what the annual rates of return and annualized volatilities of returns would have been if we assumed an investment of $5 million. For the purposes of this exhibit, we chose the 60/180 moving average results and the 80-day breakout results.

In both cases, the program trading results produced what look like reasonable rates of returns and volatilities. Rates of return varied between losses of 5–10 percent on the downside and gains of 20–30 percent on the upside. Overall, the rate of return for both programs was about 10 percent. The annualized volatility of returns ranged from a low of around 10 percent at the beginning of the period to 15–20 percent by the end of the period. And the ratio of return to risk seems to be within reasonable bounds.

Rates of return and return volatilities are inversely proportional to the amount of money we choose to attach to the trading program. If we were to double the investment to $10 million, we would have half the return and half the volatility. If we were to invest only $2.5 million in this program, we would double both returns and volatility.

## Commodities and Capacity Constraints

Commodities markets tend to be less liquid than financial markets. Many managers, to get around the constraint that illiquid commodities markets would place on their trading capacity, continue to expand by decreasing the weight that commodities have in their portfolios.

**EXHIBIT 4.13** Relationship Between Round Turns Per Million for Various Moving Average Systems

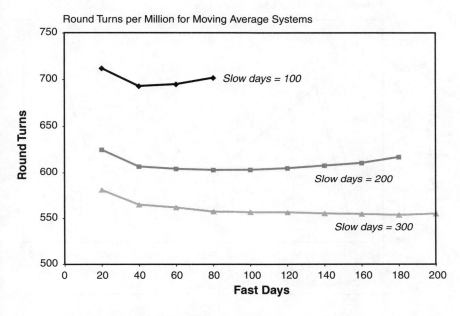

Round Turns per Million for Moving Average Systems

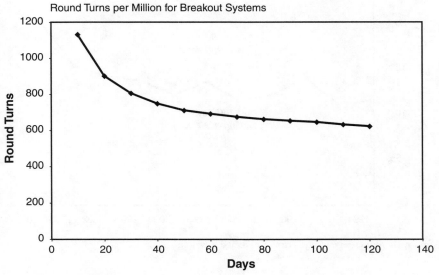

Round Turns per Million for Breakout Systems

*Source:* Bloomberg, Newedge Prime Brokerage Research.

**EXHIBIT 4.14**   60/180 Moving Average Results and the 80-day Breakout Results

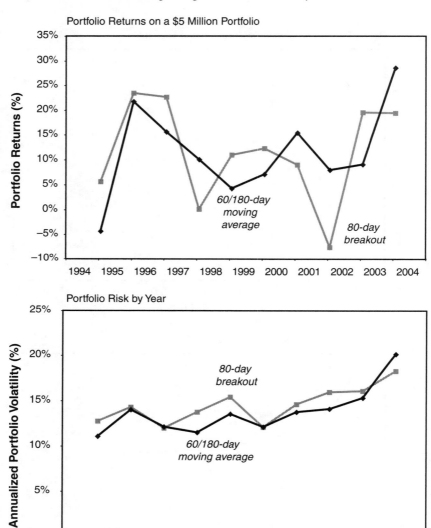

*Source:* Bloomberg, Newedge Prime Brokerage Research.

**EXHIBIT 4.15** Ratio of Return to Risk With and Without Commodities (before Fees)

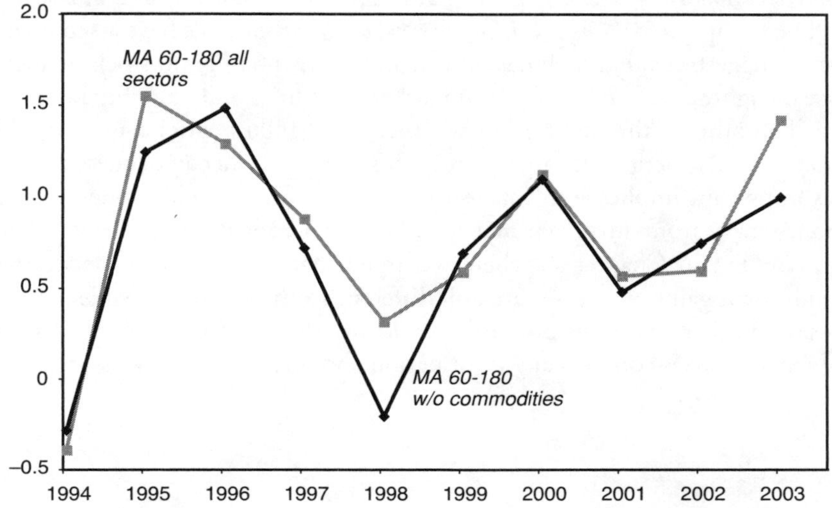

*Source:* Bloomberg, Newedge Prime Brokerage Research.

To get a sense of what is lost when commodities play a diminished role in a broader portfolio, we compare the return/risk ratios for two portfolios—one that includes all four sectors, and one that contains only the three financial sectors—using a 60/180 moving average system. Exhibit 4.15 shows the return/risk ratios (before fees) for the two portfolios by year. As the exhibit shows, the results vary from year to year. In some years the portfolio without commodities has a higher return/risk ratio, while in others the portfolio with commodities has the higher ratio.

On balance, though, the presence of commodities would have improved the performance of this portfolio. In 3 of the 10 years (1995, 1998, and 2003), the improvement afforded by commodities was substantial. Over the entire 10-year period, the return/risk ratio would have been 0.75 [= 10.6%/14.2%] with commodities and 0.65 [= 7.9%/12.1%] without commodities. This drop in the ratio is right in line with what one might expect from dropping an uncorrelated return stream from the portfolio.

## Market Environment and Give-Backs

Now that we can calculate gains and losses for generic trend-following trading systems, we intend to tackle two important questions. One is the question of whether market environment has any measurable influence on what trend followers make or lose. Perhaps the hardest part of this next round of research will be to capture what is meant by *market environment*. We have assembled a list of suggestions that includes bullish and bearish bond and stock markets, ease or tightness of Fed policy, and market volatilities and volatility ratios.

The other is the question of whether trend followers tend to give back profits after a period of large gains. This is a hotly debated question and has important implications for decisions about when to add money or take money away from any given manager. Our own contribution to this debate is presented in Chapter 7, where we argue that there is no evidence that conditional gains and losses are any different from unconditional gains and losses. In other words, we can find no evidence that the length of a CTA's run of gains or losses contains any information about subsequent gains or losses.

# CHAPTER 5

# Two Benchmarks for Momentum Trading

Returns in the CTA sector probably can be best understood as the combination of two powerful forces. One is the influence of *trend following* or *momentum trading*, which appears over long stretches of time to be profitable. The other is the presence of uncorrelated trading strategies that are also profitable and whose diversifying effects greatly improve the risk/return profiles both of individual CTAs and of portfolios of CTAs.

The influence of trend following on CTA returns can be clearly seen in Exhibit 5.1, which shows two relationships. In the upper panel is the relationship between weekly returns of the *Newedge CTA Index*, which comprises roughly equal numbers of trend followers and non–trend followers, and the *Newedge CTA Trend Sub-Index*, which captures the returns of a subset of CTAs who are widely recognized in the industry as trend followers. Here we see that the relationship is tight and that the overall correlation of returns for 2000 through 2009 was 0.97.

In the lower panel is the relationship between weekly returns on the *Newedge CTA Trend Sub-Index* and those on a basic 20/120 moving average model that employs a broadly diversified, volatility-weighted portfolio of futures on equities, interest rates, foreign exchange, and commodities. In this case, the correlation was 0.67, which is a value that looks like the correlations that the subset of trend followers' returns exhibit with one another.

Given its comparatively high and stable correlation with actual trend-following CTAs, we believe that this particular trend-following model and parameter combination—which we publish as the *Newedge Trend Indicator*—has a useful role to play for both investors and managers. Investors will have a benchmark that provides position level transparency in all of the

99

**EXHIBIT 5.1** Correlations Between Newedge CTA Index and Newedge CTA Trend Sub-Index

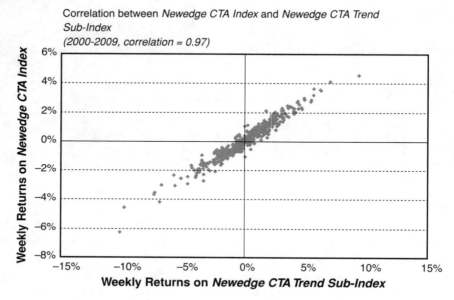

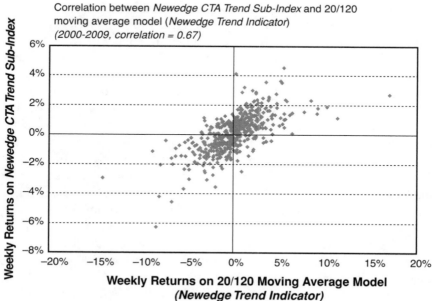

*Source:* Barclay Hedge, Newedge Prime Brokerage Research.

markets that it employs, which in turn allows ready access to information about sources of returns. For their part, managers will have an independent, no-ax-to-grind standard of comparison that they can use in conversations with their clients.

Both of these benchmarks are published daily. The main purpose of this chapter is to describe the construction of the two benchmarks, especially the work involved in building even the most basic trend-following models. These include:

- Our choices of markets to trade
- The creation of continuous futures price series
- The treatment of trade execution and transaction costs
- Our choices of position weights to create balanced, volatility-weighted portfolios
- Our choice of the 20/120 moving average model

We also review the lessons we learned along the way, including:

- The high and stable correlation that can be achieved with the simplest moving average model
- The importance of liquidity and transactions costs in building portfolios and managing contract rolls
- The challenges to managing return volatility
- Where and when trend-following models made money during the years 2000 through 2009

## Data and the Trend-Following Sub-Index

In Chapter 4, we worked with a 10-year period from 1994 through 2003. In this round of work, we focus instead on the 10-year period from 2000 through 2009, which allows us to work with the behavior of the *Newedge CTA Index*, which was first published in January 2000.

### The *Newedge CTA Index*

The *Newedge CTA Index* is nearly ideal for a case study on trend following. First, it represents the largest CTAs who were open for investment, and so we are looking at a realistic portfolio for large, institutional investors. Second, while the relative representation of trend followers in the index has varied slightly from year to year, the average number of trend-following CTAs in the index was roughly half. Third, we have daily return data, which allow us to focus almost as finely as we want on what drives CTAs' returns. Fourth, we know all of the constituents well and are able to easily and reliably identify those CTAs who have generally been recognized in the industry to be trend followers.

## The *Newedge CTA Trend Sub-Index*

For the purposes of this research, we constructed an index based on the performance of those CTAs who were generally known to be trend followers. For each of the years, the selection process included two steps. The first was to select by name the CTAs who were known to be trend followers. A headcount of trend followers and non–trend followers in the *Newedge CTA Index* is shown by year in Exhibit 5.2. On average over the full 10 years, trend followers accounted for just under half of the CTAs in the broader index, although their relative importance was as low as 41 percent in 2002 and as high as 60 percent in 2006.

The second was a reasonableness check that involved a correlation cluster analysis to see if their return correlations supported the idea that they shared something in the way they traded. An example of such a correlation cluster analysis is provided in Exhibit 5.3, which shows the results for 2009.

**EXHIBIT 5.2**   Trend Followers in the *Newedge CTA Index*

| | Trend Followers | Non–Trend Followers | Total | Trend-Following Share |
|---|---|---|---|---|
| 2000 | 10 | 8 | 18 | 0.56 |
| 2001 | 9 | 10 | 19 | 0.47 |
| 2002 | 7 | 10 | 17 | 0.41 |
| 2003 | 11 | 11 | 22 | 0.50 |
| 2004 | 10 | 12 | 22 | 0.45 |
| 2005 | 10 | 13 | 23 | 0.43 |
| 2006 | 9 | 6 | 15 | 0.60 |
| 2007 | 9 | 11 | 20 | 0.45 |
| 2008 | 10 | 10 | 20 | 0.50 |
| 2009 | 11 | 9 | 20 | 0.55 |
| | 96 | 100 | 196 | 0.49 |

*Source:* Barclay Hedge, Newedge Prime Brokerage Research.

**EXHIBIT 5.3** Correlation Cluster Results of Daily Returns for CTAs in the 2009 *Newedge CTA Index*

| Designation | CTA | Correlation | | | | | | | | | |
|---|---|---|---|---|---|---|---|---|---|---|---|
| | | 1 | 2 | 3 | 4 | 5 | 6 | 7 | 8 | 9 | 10 |
| TF | 1 Altis Partners (GFP Composite) | 1.00 | 0.72 | 0.78 | 0.78 | 0.70 | 0.54 | 0.74 | 0.66 | 0.72 | 0.63 |
| TF | 2 Campbell & Co., Inc. (FME Large) | 0.72 | 1.00 | 0.82 | 0.81 | 0.67 | 0.67 | 0.70 | 0.50 | 0.62 | 0.49 |
| TF | 3 Graham Capital (Diversified) | 0.78 | 0.82 | 1.00 | 1.00 | 0.69 | 0.79 | 0.75 | 0.43 | 0.55 | 0.49 |
| TF | 4 Graham Capital (K4) | 0.78 | 0.81 | 1.00 | 1.00 | 0.69 | 0.79 | 0.74 | 0.43 | 0.55 | 0.49 |
| | 5 IKOS Partners (Financial USD) | 0.70 | 0.67 | 0.69 | 0.69 | 1.00 | 0.55 | 0.56 | 0.38 | 0.58 | 0.34 |
| TF | 6 Sunrise Capital (Diversified) | 0.54 | 0.67 | 0.79 | 0.79 | 0.55 | 1.00 | 0.68 | 0.14 | 0.36 | 0.50 |
| TF | 7 Transtrend, B.V. (Admiralty Fund) | 0.74 | 0.70 | 0.75 | 0.74 | 0.56 | 0.68 | 1.00 | 0.53 | 0.64 | 0.53 |
| TF | 8 Aspect Capital (Diversified) | 0.66 | 0.50 | 0.43 | 0.43 | 0.38 | 0.14 | 0.53 | 1.00 | 0.79 | 0.61 |
| TF | 9 Brummer & Partners (Lynx) | 0.72 | 0.62 | 0.55 | 0.55 | 0.58 | 0.36 | 0.64 | 0.79 | 1.00 | 0.65 |
| TF | 10 Chesapeake Capital (Diversified) | 0.63 | 0.49 | 0.49 | 0.49 | 0.34 | 0.50 | 0.53 | 0.61 | 0.65 | 1.00 |
| TF | 11 Millburn Ridgefield (Diversified) | 0.71 | 0.75 | 0.59 | 0.58 | 0.55 | 0.44 | 0.66 | 0.80 | 0.78 | 0.71 |
| TF | 12 Winton Capital (Diversified) | 0.60 | 0.63 | 0.48 | 0.48 | 0.53 | 0.37 | 0.60 | 0.77 | 0.77 | 0.71 |
| | 13 Crabel Capital (Multi-Product) | 0.08 | −0.01 | −0.01 | −0.01 | −0.14 | −0.09 | 0.19 | 0.25 | 0.22 | 0.26 |
| | 14 R.G. Niederhoffer (Diversified) | 0.10 | 0.05 | 0.01 | 0.00 | −0.01 | −0.19 | 0.16 | 0.23 | 0.25 | 0.07 |
| | 15 QIM (Global) | 0.45 | 0.33 | 0.42 | 0.42 | 0.34 | 0.27 | 0.46 | 0.34 | 0.43 | 0.37 |
| | 16 Grossman Asset Mgmt. (Currency) | 0.27 | 0.30 | 0.20 | 0.20 | 0.23 | 0.20 | 0.17 | 0.36 | 0.30 | 0.37 |
| | 17 FX Concepts (Global Currency) | 0.16 | 0.36 | 0.20 | 0.20 | 0.15 | 0.13 | 0.31 | 0.34 | 0.38 | 0.27 |
| | 18 FX Concepts (Dev. Market Curr.) | 0.18 | 0.25 | 0.09 | 0.09 | 0.14 | 0.06 | 0.16 | 0.21 | 0.27 | 0.27 |
| | 19 Eagle Trading Systems (Yield) | 0.24 | 0.06 | 0.12 | 0.12 | 0.22 | −0.17 | 0.21 | 0.51 | 0.31 | −0.04 |
| | 20 Boronia Capital (Diversified) | 0.21 | 0.21 | 0.14 | 0.14 | 0.29 | 0.15 | 0.23 | 0.27 | 0.50 | 0.32 |

| Designation | CTA | Correlation | | | | | | | | | |
|---|---|---|---|---|---|---|---|---|---|---|---|
| | | 11 | 12 | 13 | 14 | 15 | 16 | 17 | 18 | 19 | 20 |
| TF | 1 Altis Partners (GFP Composite) | 0.71 | 0.60 | 0.08 | 0.10 | 0.45 | 0.27 | 0.16 | 0.18 | 0.24 | 0.21 |
| TF | 2 Campbell & Co., Inc. (FME Large) | 0.75 | 0.63 | −0.01 | 0.05 | 0.33 | 0.30 | 0.36 | 0.25 | 0.06 | 0.21 |
| TF | 3 Graham Capital (Diversified) | 0.59 | 0.48 | −0.01 | 0.01 | 0.42 | 0.20 | 0.20 | 0.09 | 0.12 | 0.14 |
| TF | 4 Graham Capital (K4) | 0.58 | 0.48 | −0.01 | 0.00 | 0.42 | 0.20 | 0.20 | 0.09 | 0.12 | 0.14 |
| | 5 IKOS Partners (Financial USD) | 0.55 | 0.53 | −0.14 | −0.01 | 0.34 | 0.23 | 0.15 | 0.14 | 0.22 | 0.29 |
| TF | 6 Sunrise Capital (Diversified) | 0.44 | 0.37 | −0.09 | −0.19 | 0.27 | 0.20 | 0.13 | 0.06 | −0.17 | 0.15 |
| TF | 7 Transtrend, B.V. (Admiralty Fund) | 0.66 | 0.60 | 0.19 | 0.16 | 0.46 | 0.17 | 0.31 | 0.16 | 0.21 | 0.23 |
| TF | 8 Aspect Capital (Diversified) | 0.80 | 0.77 | 0.25 | 0.23 | 0.34 | 0.36 | 0.34 | 0.21 | 0.51 | 0.27 |
| TF | 9 Brummer & Partners (Lynx) | 0.78 | 0.77 | 0.22 | 0.25 | 0.43 | 0.30 | 0.38 | 0.27 | 0.31 | 0.27 |
| TF | 10 Chesapeake Capital (Diversified) | 0.71 | 0.71 | 0.26 | 0.07 | 0.37 | 0.37 | 0.27 | 0.27 | −0.04 | 0.32 |
| TF | 11 Millburn Ridgefield (Diversified) | 1.00 | 0.86 | 0.23 | 0.17 | 0.40 | 0.46 | 0.41 | 0.25 | 0.18 | 0.36 |
| TF | 12 Winton Capital (Diversified) | 0.86 | 1.00 | 0.22 | 0.15 | 0.41 | 0.53 | 0.41 | 0.30 | 0.25 | 0.31 |
| | 13 Crabel Capital (Multi-Product) | 0.23 | 0.22 | 1.00 | 0.68 | 0.51 | 0.18 | 0.36 | 0.08 | 0.09 | 0.30 |
| | 14 R.G. Niederhoffer (Diversified) | 0.17 | 0.15 | 0.68 | 1.00 | 0.48 | 0.16 | 0.34 | 0.18 | 0.22 | 0.23 |
| | 15 QIM (Global) | 0.40 | 0.41 | 0.51 | 0.48 | 1.00 | 0.24 | 0.18 | 0.12 | 0.13 | 0.32 |
| | 16 Grossman Asset Mgmt. (Currency) | 0.46 | 0.53 | 0.18 | 0.16 | 0.24 | 1.00 | 0.20 | 0.18 | 0.09 | −0.09 |
| | 17 FX Concepts (Global Currency) | 0.41 | 0.41 | 0.36 | 0.34 | 0.18 | 0.20 | 1.00 | 0.44 | 0.14 | 0.32 |
| | 18 FX Concepts (Dev. Market Curr.) | 0.25 | 0.30 | 0.08 | 0.18 | 0.12 | 0.18 | 0.44 | 1.00 | 0.04 | 0.22 |
| | 19 Eagle Trading Systems (Yield) | 0.18 | 0.25 | 0.09 | 0.22 | 0.13 | 0.09 | 0.14 | 0.04 | 1.00 | −0.03 |
| | 20 Boronia Capital (Diversified) | 0.36 | 0.31 | 0.30 | 0.23 | 0.32 | −0.09 | 0.32 | 0.22 | −0.03 | 1.00 |

*Source:* Barclay Hedge, Newedge Prime Brokerage Research.

In this analysis, all CTAs in a cluster must have a minimum correlation of 0.50 with every other CTA in that cluster. As it turned out, the trend followers fell into two fairly highly correlated groups, while most of the rest formed groups of one, or at most two. The one exception in this example was IKOS Partners, which fell into the larger correlation cluster of trend followers even though IKOS does not represent itself as a trend-following manager.

## Three Correlation Questions

This new index, which will be published as the *Newedge CTA Trend Sub-Index*, is calculated the same way as the *Newedge CTA Index*. That is, it assigns equal weight to each CTA at the time it is reconstituted, which is the first business day of the year.

While we do not want to get sidetracked by anything that is not directly related to developing benchmarks for trend followers, we have in the course of our work encountered three questions about correlation that we think deserve attention. These are:

1. How is it possible for the correlation between returns on the *Newedge CTA Trend Sub-Index* and those on the broader *Newedge CTA Index* to be as high as they are when the pairwise correlations we observe are substantially lower?
2. How hard is it to build a CTA portfolio whose returns are not highly correlated to a pure trend-following CTA portfolio?
3. How is it that IKOS, which is not principally a trend-following CTA, appears in a large correlation cluster with a group of well-known trend followers?

Although we intend to deal with these questions in a separate research note, we think the key to all three questions is in the averaging of returns that one does when building an index or a portfolio.

Consider, for example, Exhibit 5.4, which shows how the correlation between returns on two indexes—a broad index that contains both correlated and uncorrelated assets and a sub-index that contains only the correlated assets—changes as the number of correlated assets in the mix increases. To construct this exhibit, we assumed that return volatility was the same for all CTAs, that the correlation of trend followers' returns with other trend followers' returns was 0.6, and that all other return correlations—trend followers with non–trend followers and non–trend followers with one another—were

**EXHIBIT 5.4** Correlation between Returns on a Sub-Index of Correlated Returns and a Broader Index (Correlation among "Trend Followers" = 0.60, All Other Correlations = 0.0, Total Number of CTAs = 20)

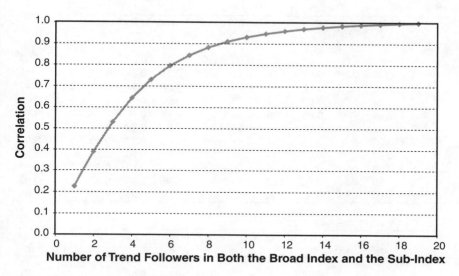

*Source:* Newedge Prime Brokerage Research.

zero. Measured along the horizontal axis is the number of trend followers in both the broader index and the trend following sub-index. For this exercise, the total number of CTAs was set at 20.

What stands out in this exhibit is just how quickly the presence of correlated returns in a broader index influences the relationship between the two. With only one or two trend followers in the broader index, the correlation of returns between the two is fairly low. But once the number of trend followers makes up half of the total, the correlation between the sub-index returns and the broader index returns exceeds 0.90. So the value of 0.97 that we see in the upper panel of Exhibit 5.1 makes sense.

As for the second question, the information provided in Exhibit 5.5 suggests that it is extraordinarily difficult to build a portfolio whose returns don't look like trend-following returns, even under the best of circumstances. In the upper panel, we have assumed that the average pairwise correlation of trend followers' returns is 0.64, and that all other correlation pairs are zero. In such a world, if one had as few as three trend-following CTAs, it would be difficult to reduce the portfolio's return correlation with the trend-following sub-index to less than 0.60.

**EXHIBIT 5.5** How Much Will a Portfolio Resemble Trend Following? (Correlation between Portfolio Returns and Returns on a 10-Asset Trend-Following Sub-Index)

($\rho_{TF}$ = 0.64, $\rho_{NTF}$ = .00, $\rho_{TF/NTF}$ = .00)

| | | Number of Non–Trend Followers in Portfolio | | | | | | | | | |
|---|---|---|---|---|---|---|---|---|---|---|---|
| | | 0 | 1 | 2 | 3 | 4 | 5 | 6 | 7 | 8 | 9 | 10 |
| Number of Trend Followers in Portfolio | 0 | | 0.00 | 0.00 | 0.00 | 0.00 | 0.00 | 0.00 | 0.00 | 0.00 | 0.00 | 0.00 |
| | 1 | 0.82 | 0.58 | 0.47 | 0.41 | 0.37 | 0.34 | 0.31 | 0.29 | 0.27 | 0.26 | 0.25 |
| | 2 | 0.91 | 0.79 | 0.72 | 0.66 | 0.61 | 0.57 | 0.54 | 0.51 | 0.49 | 0.47 | 0.45 |
| | 3 | 0.94 | 0.88 | 0.83 | 0.79 | 0.75 | 0.72 | 0.69 | 0.66 | 0.64 | 0.62 | 0.60 |
| | 4 | 0.96 | 0.92 | 0.89 | 0.86 | 0.83 | 0.81 | 0.78 | 0.76 | 0.74 | 0.72 | 0.71 |
| | 5 | 0.97 | 0.95 | 0.92 | 0.90 | 0.88 | 0.86 | 0.84 | 0.83 | 0.81 | 0.79 | 0.78 |
| | 6 | 0.98 | 0.96 | 0.95 | 0.93 | 0.91 | 0.90 | 0.88 | 0.87 | 0.86 | 0.84 | 0.83 |
| | 7 | 0.99 | 0.97 | 0.96 | 0.95 | 0.94 | 0.92 | 0.91 | 0.90 | 0.89 | 0.88 | 0.87 |
| | 8 | 0.99 | 0.98 | 0.97 | 0.96 | 0.95 | 0.94 | 0.93 | 0.92 | 0.91 | 0.90 | 0.90 |
| | 9 | 1.00 | 0.99 | 0.98 | 0.97 | 0.96 | 0.95 | 0.95 | 0.94 | 0.93 | 0.92 | 0.92 |
| | 10 | 1.00 | 0.99 | 0.99 | 0.98 | 0.97 | 0.96 | 0.96 | 0.95 | 0.95 | 0.94 | 0.93 |

($\rho_{TF}$ = 0.64, $\rho_{NTF}$ = .21, $\rho_{TF/NTF}$ = .27)

| | | Number of Non–Trend Followers in Portfolio | | | | | | | | | |
|---|---|---|---|---|---|---|---|---|---|---|---|---|
| | | 0 | 1 | 2 | 3 | 4 | 5 | 6 | 7 | 8 | 9 | 10 |
| Number of Trend Followers in Portfolio | 0 | | 0.33 | 0.42 | 0.48 | 0.51 | 0.54 | 0.56 | 0.58 | 0.59 | 0.60 | 0.61 |
| | 1 | 0.82 | 0.72 | 0.70 | 0.69 | 0.69 | 0.69 | 0.69 | 0.69 | 0.69 | 0.69 | 0.69 |
| | 2 | 0.91 | 0.85 | 0.82 | 0.80 | 0.79 | 0.78 | 0.77 | 0.76 | 0.76 | 0.75 | 0.75 |
| | 3 | 0.94 | 0.91 | 0.88 | 0.86 | 0.85 | 0.84 | 0.83 | 0.82 | 0.81 | 0.80 | 0.80 |
| | 4 | 0.96 | 0.94 | 0.92 | 0.90 | 0.89 | 0.88 | 0.87 | 0.86 | 0.85 | 0.84 | 0.83 |
| | 5 | 0.97 | 0.96 | 0.94 | 0.93 | 0.92 | 0.90 | 0.89 | 0.88 | 0.88 | 0.87 | 0.86 |
| | 6 | 0.98 | 0.97 | 0.96 | 0.95 | 0.93 | 0.92 | 0.91 | 0.91 | 0.90 | 0.89 | 0.88 |
| | 7 | 0.99 | 0.98 | 0.97 | 0.96 | 0.95 | 0.94 | 0.93 | 0.92 | 0.92 | 0.91 | 0.90 |
| | 8 | 0.99 | 0.98 | 0.98 | 0.97 | 0.96 | 0.95 | 0.94 | 0.94 | 0.93 | 0.92 | 0.92 |
| | 9 | 1.00 | 0.99 | 0.98 | 0.98 | 0.97 | 0.96 | 0.95 | 0.95 | 0.94 | 0.93 | 0.93 |
| | 10 | 1.00 | 0.99 | 0.99 | 0.98 | 0.97 | 0.97 | 0.96 | 0.96 | 0.95 | 0.94 | 0.94 |

*Source:* Newedge Prime Brokerage Research.

But if we use correlations more like those we observe in practice, the task becomes nearly impossible. The correlation values we used in the lower panel are the average values we observed for 2009. Using these values, we find the fairly shocking result that a portfolio with no trend followers at all can produce returns with a correlation of 0.60 to those on the trend-following sub-index. And if the portfolio has just one trend follower, it would be impossible to reduce the portfolio's return correlation to anything less than 0.69.

With regard to the presence of IKOS in a cluster of well-known trend followers, what we may be seeing at the individual CTA level is the influence that trend following can exhibit on one's return correlations, even if it represents a small part of one's overall portfolio of trading strategies.

## Ten Years of Net Asset Values

To complete the case for our interest in trend following, we have charted in Exhibit 5.6 the net asset values for the *Newedge CTA Index* and the *Newedge CTA Trend Sub-Index* from 2000 through 2009. Here, the eye can confirm what the scatter plots and correlation clusters suggest. That is, trend following is a major force in this industry. The fortunes of trend followers and the industry tend to rise and fall together, although with one significant difference. While the two paths follow one another closely, the total index path exhibits much lower volatility than that exhibited by the trend-following sub-index path. The lower volatility stems from the presence of low correlation returns, and the result is a higher return/risk ratio for the industry than for the trend followers by themselves.

**EXHIBIT 5.6**   Net Asset Values for *Newedge CTA Index* and *Newedge CTA Trend Sub-Index* (Net of Fees)

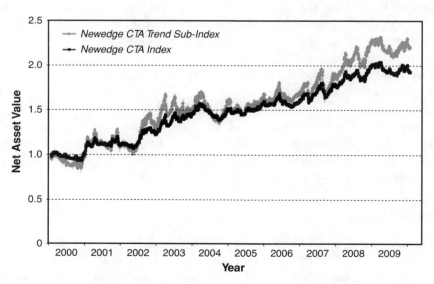

*Source:* Barlcay Hedge, Newedge Prime Brokerage Research.

## Trend-Following Models

As discussed in Chapter 4, two of the most widely recognized approaches to trend following are *range breakout* and *moving average crossover*. These are extremely simple approaches to identifying trends and we apply them in the simplest possible way.

### Range Breakout

The simplest range breakout approach uses a single parameter, which measures the length of the look-back period for calculating high and low prices. For example, a 20-day breakout model works this way. If you are short and the price rises above the 20-day high, you reverse position and go long. If you are long and the price falls below the 20-day low, you reverse position and go short. In the work that follows, we consider look-back periods from 20 to 240 days.

### Moving Average Crossover

This approach calculates two moving averages—one for a short period (the fast average or F-day average) and one for a longer period (the slow average or S-day average). In this approach, if the fast average is above the slow average, you are long. If the fast average is below the slow average, you are short. In the work that follows, we consider every combination of fast- and slow-day pairs involving fast days from 20 to 220 and slow days from 40 to 240.

## Laying the Groundwork for Analyzing Returns to Trend Following

The raw material for studying trend following includes markets, price histories, and a portfolio-weighting scheme. In the spirit of being as true as possible to the way this might have worked in real life, we began each year by selecting the markets that would have been available at the time.

### Choice of Markets

Because we had decided to use a two-year look-back period to estimate return volatilities when constructing our portfolios, we required any futures market we included to have two years of daily data as of the end of August of that year. The reason for this peculiar ending period is a production timeline that we intend to use when publishing the benchmark. That is, we plan to gather data through the end of August of each calendar year, use the month of September to reselect markets, analyze the data, and construct the portfolio that will be used from October of the current year through September of the following year. Thus, any given calendar year's returns will reflect nine months of returns from the portfolio constructed in the current year and three months of returns from the portfolio constructed from the previous year.

As it was, we had 50 futures markets at the end of August 1997. These were used to construct the portfolio we used beginning October 1999. It was this portfolio's returns for the first nine months of 2000 that we use to compare the returns of the *Newedge CTA Index* and the *Newedge CTA Trend Sub-Index*. By the end of August 2009, we had 55 markets.

When constructing our price histories, we allowed for the replacement of one market by another. One such example is the substitution of the E-mini S&P 500 contract for the "big" S&P 500 contract.

We also used futures contracts for which we had good data to serve as proxies for trades that would take place elsewhere. For example, we used foreign exchange futures to represent cash market trades in foreign exchange. Currency futures typically are not large or liquid enough for larger CTAs, but the futures markets are sufficiently well-tied to the spot and forward markets for their prices to be reliable proxies for the prices that govern trading in the cash market. We also used the COMEX copper contract in our work, although the major copper trading market is the London Metals Exchange.

## Contract Rolls

One of the single most important features of futures contracts is that they expire and must be replaced. The transaction that replaces an expiring September contract with a December contract is known as a "roll," and the way these rolls are handled by each CTA can have a substantial effect on the results of a trading program.

Although there are as many ways to achieve a roll as there are overlapping days in the two contracts' lives, what we find is that contract rolls in each market tend to be concentrated in a few days during which the "roll market" is as liquid as it is ever going to be.

For this reason, we adopted a roll rule that would tend to follow the liquidity. In particular, our rule was to roll:

- Two business days after open interest in the deferred contract exceeds open interest in the lead or expiring contract, or three business days before the lead contract expires, whichever happens first.

While not particularly sophisticated, this two-part rule should satisfy most reasonableness requirements. The first part would tend to keep us in the liquid part of the contract cycle, and the second part keeps us away from contract expirations.

## Concatenating the Price Series

Before concatenating the price series to produce a continuous futures price series for each market, we found it necessary to take care of two practical matters. One was cleaning the data to get rid of or repair obvious errors in the data series. The other was to rule out contracts in the expiration cycle that do not, for whatever reason, really attract any trading volume. Exhibit 5.7 shows the contract roll schedule for the markets included in our 2009 portfolio. Notice that most contracts follow a quarterly expiration, although four of the equity futures markets have a monthly expiration cycle.

We find the most complicated expiration cycles in the commodities markets, and it is here that we find expiration months that don't trade. In the table, these months are highlighted. Notice that "V" (which stands for October) is highlighted for Cotton #2 and Gold, "K" (May) is highlighted for Lean Hogs, and "F" (January) is highlighted for Sugar #11 and Silver.

In its own way, Exhibit 5.7 is a useful resource for those doing due diligence on CTAs because it provides an insight into where their issues with managing transaction costs might lie. Financial futures contracts typically expire only four times a year and tend to be liquid. Commodity futures, in contrast, expire with a much higher frequency and tend not to be as liquid. As a result, it is generally more difficult to control costs in commodities trading than it is in financial markets and requires a higher level of knowledge about the ways those markets work.

## Constructing a Portfolio

In choosing the numbers of contracts to hold in each market, we had two objectives. The first was to construct a portfolio for which the standard deviation of gains and losses would translate into an annualized return volatility of 15 percent on a $2 billion portfolio. We chose 15 percent because it is roughly consistent with the return volatility we observe in the industry. We chose $2 billion because it was a large enough number to force us to think about market liquidity and feasible position sizes. Thus, our objective was an annualized standard deviation of daily gains and losses of $300,000,000.

**EXHIBIT 5.7** Contract Roll Schedule

| Instruments | F | G | H | J | K | M | N | Q | U | V | X | Z |
|---|---|---|---|---|---|---|---|---|---|---|---|---|
| CAC 40 | F | G | H | J | K | M | N | Q | U | V | X | Z |
| DJIA Mini | | | H | | | M | | | U | | | Z |
| S&P 500 E-mini | | | H | | | M | | | U | | | Z |
| DAX | | | H | | | M | | | U | | | Z |
| Hang Seng | F | G | H | J | K | M | N | Q | U | V | X | Z |
| IBEX 35 | F | G | H | J | K | M | N | Q | U | V | X | Z |
| KOSPI | | | H | | | M | | | U | | | Z |
| Nikkei 225 | | | H | | | M | | | U | | | Z |
| NASDAQ 100 Mini | | | H | | | M | | | U | | | Z |
| Swedish OMX | F | G | H | J | K | M | N | Q | U | V | X | Z |
| Russell 2000 Mini | | | H | | | M | | | U | | | Z |
| MIB | | | H | | | M | | | U | | | Z |
| Euro STOXX 50 | | | H | | | M | | | U | | | Z |
| SPI 200 | | | H | | | M | | | U | | | Z |
| FTSE 100 | | | H | | | M | | | U | | | Z |
| German Schatz | | | H | | | M | | | U | | | Z |
| US 3 Month Rate (Eurodollar) | | | H | | | M | | | U | | | Z |
| Euro 3 Month Rate (Euribor) | | | H | | | M | | | U | | | Z |
| US 5 Year | | | H | | | M | | | U | | | Z |
| UK 10 Year (Gilt) | | | H | | | M | | | U | | | Z |
| Australian 3 Month | | | H | | | M | | | U | | | Z |
| Japan 10 Year (JGB) | | | H | | | M | | | U | | | Z |
| UK Short Sterling | | | H | | | M | | | U | | | Z |
| German 5 Year (BOBL) | | | H | | | M | | | U | | | Z |
| German 10 Year (BUND) | | | H | | | M | | | U | | | Z |
| US 2 Year | | | H | | | M | | | U | | | Z |
| US 10 Year | | | H | | | M | | | U | | | Z |
| US 30 Year | | | H | | | M | | | U | | | Z |
| Australian 10 Year | | | H | | | M | | | U | | | Z |
| Japan 3 Month | | | H | | | M | | | U | | | Z |
| Australian Dollar | | | H | | | M | | | U | | | Z |
| British Pound | | | H | | | M | | | U | | | Z |
| Canadian Dollar | | | H | | | M | | | U | | | Z |
| Euro | | | H | | | M | | | U | | | Z |
| Japanese Yen | | | H | | | M | | | U | | | Z |
| New Zealand Dollar | | | H | | | M | | | U | | | Z |
| Mexican Peso | | | H | | | M | | | U | | | Z |
| Swiss Franc | | | H | | | M | | | U | | | Z |
| Soybean Oil | F | | H | | K | | N | Q | U | V | | Z |
| Corn | | | H | | K | | N | | U | | | Z |
| Cocoa | | | H | | K | | N | | U | | | Z |
| Crude Oil | F | G | H | J | K | M | N | Q | U | V | X | Z |
| Cotton #2 | | | H | | K | | N | | | **V** | | Z |
| Gold | | G | | J | | M | | Q | | **V** | | Z |
| Copper | F | G | H | J | K | M | N | Q | U | V | X | Z |
| Heating Oil | F | G | H | J | K | M | N | Q | U | V | X | Z |
| Coffee | | | H | | K | | N | | U | | | Z |
| Live Cattle | | G | | J | | M | | Q | | V | | Z |
| Lean Hog | | G | | J | **K** | M | N | Q | | V | | Z |
| Natural Gas | F | G | H | J | K | M | N | Q | U | V | X | Z |
| Soybeans | F | | H | | K | | N | Q | U | | X | |
| Sugar #11 | **F** | | H | | K | | N | | | V | | |
| Silver | **F** | | H | | K | | N | | U | | | Z |
| Wheat | | | H | | K | | N | | U | | | Z |
| RBOB | F | G | H | J | K | M | N | Q | U | V | X | Z |

*Note: The months in shaded boxes are officially listed, but excluded from our study due to low activities.*

*Source:* Bloomberg.

## Volatility Weights

The second objective was to volatility weight our contract positions. In practice, we approached the problem by dividing the world into four broad market sectors—equities, interest rates, foreign exchange, and commodities—and assigning them relative volatility weights of 30 percent, 30 percent, 30 percent, and 10 percent. We chose a lower weight for commodities to reflect the fact that these markets are, in general, less liquid than the financial markets. A number of managers have suggested that we could increase the weight for commodities without incurring too great a liquidity burden, or that we should reduce the weight of a sector like equities. As it is, we chose these weights because they are plausible, and we plan to review our weighting methodology in the next round of research.

We did all we could to assign equal volatility to each contract within each broad sector. The major impediment to this objective was market size. We limited our positions to the smaller of 1 percent of average open interest or 5 percent of average daily volume, where these averages were calculated over the two years leading up to choice of portfolio weights. We did not constrain positions in foreign exchange markets because these are generally viewed as providing more than enough liquidity for the kinds of portfolios we were building.

## Volatility Estimation and Forecasting

In this round of research, we use the two previous years of data to establish contract weights for the following year. Thus, we are using a two-year look back and a one-year look forward. As a forecasting method, this approach worked fairly well, at least in 8 out of the 10 years in the study. The longish look-back period and the fairly long look-forward period allow temporary changes in volatility to wash out over time. We did find, though, that such a long look-back period did not work well during the financial crisis of late 2008 and early 2009. During these years, our portfolios exhibited volatility that was roughly twice what we had targeted. In contrast, we found that actual CTAs were more nimble in their risk management and succeeded in keeping their return volatilities under control.

## Sample Portfolio

An example of the kind of portfolio this approach produced is shown in Exhibit 5.8, where you can see all of the markets traded and the number of contracts used in each case. In this case, we used data from September 2007

**EXHIBIT 5.8** Market Selection and Portfolio Weights (as of 10/1/2009)

| | Futures Markets | Annual $ Volatility per Contract | Number of Contracts | Annual $ Volatility | Remark | Annual Sector Volatility ($) |
|---|---|---|---|---|---|---|
| Equity | 1 CAC 40 | 18,017 | 875 | 15,764,611 | | |
| | 2 DJIA Mini | 15,371 | 828 | 12,727,250 | CAPPED | |
| | 3 S&P 500 E-mini | 17,714 | 890 | 15,765,151 | | |
| | 4 DAX | 61,499 | 256 | 15,743,817 | | |
| | 5 Hang Seng | 54,459 | 290 | 15,793,123 | | |
| | 6 IBEX 35 | 49,308 | 320 | 15,778,626 | | |
| | 7 KOSPI | 27,857 | 566 | 15,767,016 | | |
| | 8 Nikkei 225 | 40,575 | 389 | 15,783,819 | | $174,495,468 |
| | 9 NASDAQ 100 Mini | 10,364 | 1521 | 15,763,842 | | |
| | 10 Swedish OMX | 4,236 | 3722 | 15,766,304 | | |
| | 11 Russell 2000 Mini | 23,004 | 685 | 15,757,883 | | |
| | 12 MIB | 54,598 | 289 | 15,778,856 | | |
| | 13 Euro STOXX 50 | 13,598 | 1159 | 15,760,337 | | |
| | 14 SPI 200 | 26,397 | 597 | 15,759,200 | | |
| | 15 FTSE 100 | 26,412 | 597 | 15,767,785 | | |
| Interest Rate | 16 German Schatz | 3,149 | 6711 | 21,133,842 | | |
| | 17 US 3 Month Rate (Eurodollar) | 3,286 | 6432 | 21,133,480 | | |
| | 18 Euro 3 Month Rate (Euribor) | 2,524 | 6475 | 16,343,672 | CAPPED | |
| | 19 US 5 Year | 7,236 | 2920 | 21,129,638 | | |
| | 20 UK 10 Year (Gilt) | 16,021 | 1319 | 21,131,914 | | |
| | 21 Australian 3 Month | 2,119 | 1083 | 2,294,895 | CAPPED | |
| | 22 Japan 10 Year (JGB) | 62,838 | 336 | 21,113,416 | | |
| | 23 UK Short Sterling | 2,503 | 3435 | 8,598,659 | CAPPED | $174,476,904 |
| | 24 German 5 Year (BOBL) | 7,460 | 2833 | 21,134,303 | | |
| | 25 German 10 Year (BUND) | 11,612 | 1820 | 21,133,381 | | |
| | 26 US 2 Year | 5,746 | 3678 | 21,134,952 | | |
| | 27 US 10 Year | 11,123 | 1900 | 21,133,191 | | |
| | 28 US 30 Year | 16,889 | 1251 | 21,127,603 | | |
| | 29 Australian 10 Year | 10,466 | 1998 | 20,910,659 | CAPPED | |
| | 30 Japan 3 Month | 554 | 990 | 548,034 | CAPPED | |
| Foreign Currency | 31 Australian Dollar | 17,280 | 1893 | 32,710,421 | | |
| | 32 British Pound | 14,296 | 2289 | 32,723,362 | | |
| | 33 Canadian Dollar | 13,645 | 2398 | 32,720,522 | | |
| | 34 Euro | 23,252 | 1407 | 32,715,734 | | |
| | 35 Japanese Yen | 17,675 | 1851 | 32,715,604 | | $174,479,868 |
| | 36 New Zealand Dollar | 13,392 | 2443 | 32,717,653 | | |
| | 37 Mexican Peso | 6,136 | 5333 | 32,721,280 | | |
| | 38 Swiss Franc | 16,506 | 1982 | 32,714,393 | | |
| Commodity | 39 Soybean Oil | 9,368 | 630 | 5,901,539 | | |
| | 40 Corn | 8,874 | 665 | 5,901,016 | | |
| | 41 Cocoa | 9,524 | 358 | 3,409,506 | CAPPED | |
| | 42 Crude Oil | 37,938 | 156 | 5,918,355 | | |
| | 43 Cotton #2 | 10,441 | 553 | 5,773,829 | CAPPED | |
| | 44 Gold | 23,029 | 256 | 5,895,316 | | |
| | 45 Copper | 27,595 | 135 | 3,725,336 | CAPPED | |
| | 46 Heating Oil | 41,632 | 142 | 5,911,758 | | |
| | 47 Coffee | 15,162 | 389 | 5,897,869 | | $58,182,485 |
| | 48 Live Cattle | 5,739 | 810 | 4,648,642 | CAPPED | |
| | 49 Lean Hog | 6,785 | 654 | 4,437,250 | CAPPED | |
| | 50 Natural Gas | 33,199 | 178 | 5,909,448 | | |
| | 51 Soybeans | 19,994 | 295 | 5,898,377 | | |
| | 52 Sugar #11 | 5,565 | 1061 | 5,904,243 | | |
| | 53 Silver | 29,944 | 197 | 5,899,057 | | |
| | 54 Wheat | 17,478 | 338 | 5,907,530 | | |
| | 55 RBOB | 41,122 | 144 | 5,921,535 | | |
| | | | | Portfolio | | $300,011,348 |

*Source:* Bloomberg, Newedge Prime Brokerage Research.

through August 2009 to estimate volatilities and market liquidity (that is, average daily volume and open interest) to construct the portfolio that we would use from October 2009 through September 2010.

The first thing to notice about this portfolio is that the contract weights reveal fairly high correlations within sectors and almost no correlation across sectors. As a result, the volatilities for each of the contracts within a sector tend to be low relative to the sector's target volatility. In contrast, if you square each sector's volatility, add the four together, and take the square root, you obtain a number that is very close to the annualized target volatility of $300,000,000. This is almost exactly what one expects from independently distributed random variables. That is, the sum of the variances is the variance of the sum.

The second thing to notice is the number of markets capped in each sector. In equity markets, only the DJIA Mini contract was capped because of its market size, and then it was capped only a little. In interest rate markets, five markets were capped, and three of these were three-month interest rate contracts. By design, we did not cap any of the foreign currency positions, arguing that these markets are amply liquid. And in fact, the cash market trades associated with these position sizes represent comparatively small trades. In the commodities sector, we found that five markets were capped.

## Simplifying Assumptions

Armed with the price data and the portfolios, we can now turn to implementing the models. Before doing any calculations, however, we need to enumerate the various simplifying assumptions and decisions we made. In particular, we used:

- Same parameters for all markets
- Same volatility look back
- Same liquidity constraints
- No stops/always in
- Same execution assumptions
- Same transaction cost per contract
- Same portfolio for a whole year with no resizing
- No subscriptions or redemptions
- No single-currency margining costs
- Seven percent of the three-month Treasury bill rate on cash (when reckoning net asset values)

Every one of these assumptions touches on some aspect of the business of trading that requires study, refinement, finesse, and flexibility. This list also provides a useful point of reference for conversations with actual traders about how they deal with these very practical problems.

## Executing Trades

In practice, our execution rules were these. For trades generated by signals from a model, we assumed that the trades were done at the next day's closing or settlement price. For trades required for rolls, we used the closing or settlement prices for the day determined by the roll rule. In both cases, we taxed the trades at $50 per side, which was probably about right on average for outright trades determined by signals but was almost certainly much too high for roll trades.

## Each Calendar Year's Results

Given the timeline for portfolio rebalancing that we used here, each calendar year's results reflect the gains and losses on two different portfolios—one for the period running from January through September and one for the period running from October through December.

## How Did the Models Do?

We turn now to the results and review the performance of the models from three different perspectives. First, we consider the correlation of each model's weekly returns with those on the *Newedge CTA Trend Sub-Index*. Second, we review the volatility performance of the models and compare them with the volatility of returns on the *Newedge CTA Trend Sub-Index*. Third, we take a look at when and where the models made money—which years and which markets.

## Correlation with the *Newedge CTA Trend Sub-Index*

The correlations of weekly returns shown in Exhibit 5.9 are the averages of 10 single-year correlation estimates from 2000 through 2009. The results for the range breakout models for look-back periods ranging from 20 to 240 days are shown at the left of the exhibit. The results of the moving average models are arrayed to the right and are grouped by the number of "fast" days

**EXHIBIT 5.9**   Correlations with Weekly Returns on *Newedge CTA Trend Sub-Index*
(Average of Single-Year Correlations from 2000 through 2009)

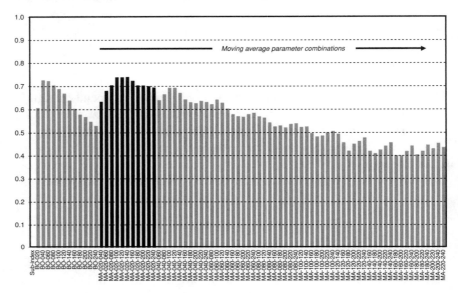

*Source:* Bloomberg, Newedge Prime Brokerage Research.

so that all results for a fast-day moving average using 20 days are grouped
together in order of increasing numbers of slow days. So the results for the
20/40 parameter choice are first on the left, followed by 20/60, 20/80, and
so on to 20/240. The very last vertical bar on the right represents the results
for 220/240 combination. With this way of ordering the results, one moves
from faster systems on the left to slower systems on the right—both within a
group with a common number of fast days, and across groups as the number
of fast days increases.

   We found that both types of models—range breakout and moving average
crossover—were capable of producing respectably high correlations. For the
range breakout model, the highest average correlations were produced by look-
back periods of 40 and 60 days. For the moving average systems, the highest
correlations were produced by the 20/100, 20/120, and 20/140 parameter
combinations. In both types of models, the correlations were generally higher
for faster models and tended to decline as the models slowed down and the
holding periods increased.

   We find these results encouraging. If we are looking for a single, basic
trend-following model and parameter combination to represent a benchmark

for an individual trend-following CTA, a correlation of 0.70 or more is perfectly adequate. For one thing, it is a value that looks like the pairwise correlations in Exhibit 5.3 for our 11 trend-following CTAs. For another, if you fast-forward to Exhibit 5.18, you will see that a 20/120 moving average model produces correlations that would cause it to fall into a correlation cluster with 6 of the 11 trend followers in 2009.

As it is, in choosing between the breakout and moving average models, we came down in favor of the moving average model partly because its average correlation performance was slightly greater than the highest breakout correlations. And within the moving average models, the eye is drawn to the 20/120 model's results because they fall between the 20/100 and 20/140 models, both of which seem to produce nearly identical results. Thus, 20/120 is in the middle of what appears to be a stable range of parameter choices.

Our choice of the 20/120 model is reinforced somewhat by the evidence provided in Exhibit 5.10, which shows how the correlations behaved by year for each choice of slow days. In this exhibit, one can see that the annual correlation estimates for the 20/120 combination are very slightly more tightly clustered than for the 20/100 and 20/140 combinations. And all three are more tightly grouped than their faster and slower neighbors.

**EXHIBIT 5.10** Correlations of Moving Average Model Returns with *Newedge CTA Trend Sub-Index* (Number of Fast Days = 20)

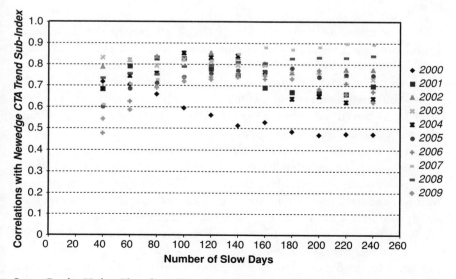

*Source:* Barclay Hedge, Bloomberg, Newedge Prime Brokerage Research.

**EXHIBIT 5.11**  Annualized Return Volatilities (Averages of Single-Year Volatilities from 2000 through 2009)

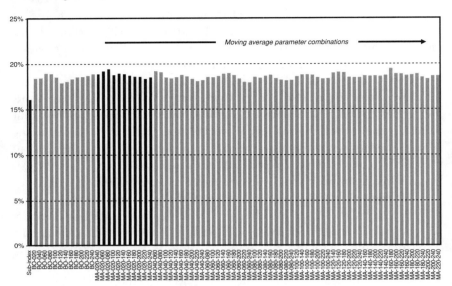

*Source:* Bloomberg, Newedge Prime Brokerage Research.

## Volatility

The average return volatilities are shown in Exhibit 5.11, in which the leftmost vertical bar represents the average return volatility for CTAs in the *Newedge CTA Trend Sub-Index* from 2000 through 2009. The other bars, which are organized in the same way as those in the correlation exhibit, show that the result of our experiment produced an average volatility of returns just slightly less than 20 percent and very close to the average return volatility that trend followers exhibited for the same period.

The similarity in the average volatilities of actual trend followers and of our trend-following models is in part accidental. Consider Exhibit 5.12, which tracks the two sets of volatilities year by year. The line with circles represents the history of average annual return volatilities for CTAs in the *Newedge CTA Trend Sub-Index.* The vertical bars with the shaded bands show the range of volatilities for the 78 different model/parameter combinations. The narrow vertical line represents the range from highest to lowest volatilities, while the gray band represents one standard deviation of the distribution of realized volatilities.

**EXHIBIT 5.12** Annualized Return Volatilities for CTAs in the *Newedge CTA Trend Sub-Index* and All Model/Parameter Combinations (Shaded Bands Contain 1 Standard Deviation, Ends of Vertical Lines Represent Minimum and Maximum Values)

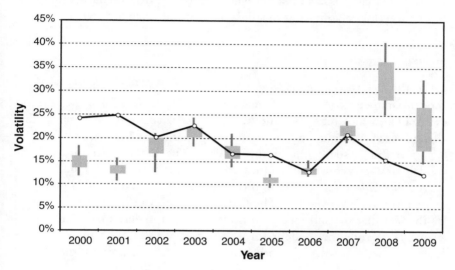

*Source:* Bloomberg, Newedge Prime Brokerage Research.

From the history of return volatilities for the trend-following CTAs, it seems that they had been reducing their volatility targets as the decade progressed. During the first four years, their return volatilities were all above 20 percent, while their average return volatility during the last six years was 15.8 percent. It is also apparent that trend-following CTAs managed to control their return volatilities during 2008 and early 2009, years that were heavily affected by the financial crisis.

From the history of return volatilities for the 78 model/parameter combinations, we see that for the first eight years of the experiment, the volatility forecasting approach we used was fairly effective and produced results that were not very different from what the industry produced. It is also apparent that the two-year look-back and one-year look-forward approach did not handle the U.S. financial crisis very well and resulted in volatilities for 2008 and 2009 that were roughly double what the industry managed to achieve.

Looking back to Exhibit 5.10, we find that the higher volatility did not hurt the correlations of the moving average model returns with those of the *Newedge CTA Trend Sub-Index.* And, since high and stable correlation is our main objective, the high volatility produced by our approach was more instructive than bothersome. On the other hand, if we find ourselves wanting to produce a benchmark that captures the volatility characteristics of the industry as well, it is clear that we would need to revisit the question of how best to forecast volatility and to adjust our portfolio weights.

## Profits and Losses

Over the 10 years, the *Newedge CTA Trend Sub-Index* and all of the model/parameter combinations made money. In Exhibit 5.13, the leftmost vertical bar, which represents the *Newedge CTA Trend Sub-Index*, shows that this subset of the industry yielded an average annualized return of 9 percent.

Two things stand out in this exhibit. The first is that most of the model/parameter combinations produced higher returns than did the *Newedge CTA Trend Sub-Index*. The second is that the faster models tended not to do as well as the slower models. The first observation can be explained mainly by the fact that the sub-index returns were net of management and performance fees, while the model returns are gross. We deal with this difference later when we construct a hypothetical net asset value history for the 20/120

**EXHIBIT 5.13** Annualized Returns (Averages of Single-Year Returns from 2000 through 2009)

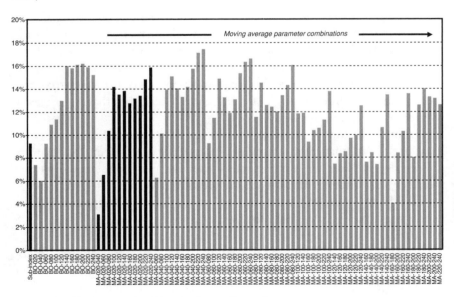

*Source:* Bloomberg, Newedge Prime Brokerage Research.

**EXHIBIT 5.14** Transaction Costs Example (2009, Moving Average Models with Fast Days = 20)

| Number of Slow Days | Number of Outright Contracts Traded | Number of Contracts Rolled | Percent Contracts Rolled | Outright Cost (at $50) | Roll Cost (at $50) | Roll Cost (at $10) | Total Cost (at $50) | Total Cost (at $10) |
|---|---|---|---|---|---|---|---|---|
| 40 | 1,396,692 | 535,557 | 28% | $69,834,600 | $53,555,700 | $10,711,140 | $123,390,300 | $80,545,740 |
| 60 | 865,718 | 535,557 | 38% | $43,285,900 | $53,555,700 | $10,711,140 | $96,841,600 | $53,997,040 |
| 80 | 581,574 | 535,557 | 48% | $29,078,700 | $53,555,700 | $10,711,140 | $82,634,400 | $39,789,840 |
| 100 | 466,700 | 535,557 | 53% | $23,335,000 | $53,555,700 | $10,711,140 | $76,890,700 | $34,046,140 |
| 120 | 392,792 | 535,557 | 58% | $19,639,600 | $53,555,700 | $10,711,140 | $73,195,300 | $30,350,740 |
| 140 | 338,792 | 535,557 | 61% | $16,939,600 | $53,555,700 | $10,711,140 | $70,495,300 | $27,650,740 |
| 160 | 303,968 | 535,557 | 64% | $15,198,400 | $53,555,700 | $10,711,140 | $68,754,100 | $25,909,540 |
| 180 | 288,078 | 535,557 | 65% | $14,403,900 | $53,555,700 | $10,711,140 | $67,959,600 | $25,115,040 |
| 200 | 298,016 | 535,557 | 64% | $14,900,800 | $53,555,700 | $10,711,140 | $68,456,500 | $25,611,940 |
| 220 | 196,628 | 535,557 | 73% | $9,831,400 | $53,555,700 | $10,711,140 | $63,387,100 | $20,542,540 |
| 240 | 200,976 | 535,557 | 73% | $10,048,800 | $53,555,700 | $10,711,140 | $63,604,500 | $20,759,940 |

*Source:* Newedge Prime Brokerage Research.

moving average model. The second observation affords us an opportunity to review the influence of trading velocity and transactions costs.

Exhibit 5.14 provides a summary of the transaction history of the moving average models that used 20 days to calculate the fast moving average in 2009. As the number of slow days increases from 40 to 240, you can see that the number of outright contracts traded falls from 1,396,692 to 200,976. You can also see that the number of contracts rolled is exactly the same for all of the parameter choices, again because the models were always in the market and the position sizes were all the same.

From the cost calculations that we have provided, it is quite clear that trading velocity can have a substantial effect on net returns. With our $50 per side assumption, the $60 million difference in outright trade costs would have amounted to a difference of 3 percent in net returns on a $2 billion portfolio. As a result, trading costs explain quite a bit, but by no means all, of the lower returns produced by the higher-velocity parameter choices.

It is also clear that the costs of rolling contracts can loom large. The difference between $50 per side and $10 per side when rolling more than half a million contracts a year is worth about 2 percent in net return.

Exhibit 5.15 is meant to provide a reasonableness check on our simulated trade experience with the moving average models. The metric here is round turns per million, which is a standard measure for comparing trading velocities among CTAs. The solid line that corresponds to "Simulation" shows how a moving average model with the fast average based on 20 days would have traded in a market in which the mean drift or change is zero and the volatility is constant. What we find is that our trend-following models when applied to

**EXHIBIT 5.15**   Round Turns per $1 Million (Indexed)

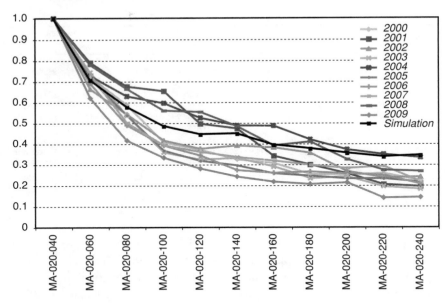

*Source:* Bloomberg, Newedge Prime Brokerage Research.

actual price data produced similar results, but in most cases tended to trade slightly fewer contracts. By itself, this is interesting because it is a result that one would expect in a world in which prices exhibit more trends—or positive serial correlation in changes—than one finds with a perfectly efficient random price process.

The higher returns can also be explained in part by the fact that our approach to targeting return volatility produced a return volatility for 2008 that was more than double the target value. And, as shown in Exhibit 5.16, 2008 was probably the strongest year of the 10 for the 20/120 moving average model, which made money in all four sectors. As a result, our models all produced gains in 2008 that were more than double what they would have been with tighter risk controls.

Another important difference between our approach and what one would find in the practices of actual trend followers is illustrated in Exhibit 5.17, which shows the average gain or loss by market. Here we find that the 20/120 model made money in nearly every market over the entire 10-year period with the notable exception of E-mini S&Ps, which is one of the most liquid and actively traded equity markets in the world. In a broadly diversified,

**EXHIBIT 5.16** Net Dollar Gains and Losses for the 20/120 Moving Average Model (*Newedge Trend Indicator*) ($2 Billion Portfolio with Realized Volatilities Shown in Exhibit 5.12)

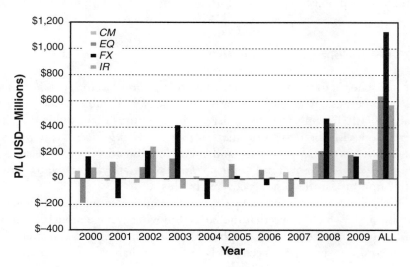

*Source:* Bloomberg, Newedge Prime Brokerage Research.

**EXHIBIT 5.17** Total Dollar Gains and Losses for the 20/120 Moving Average Model (*Newedge Trend Indicator*) (2000–2009)

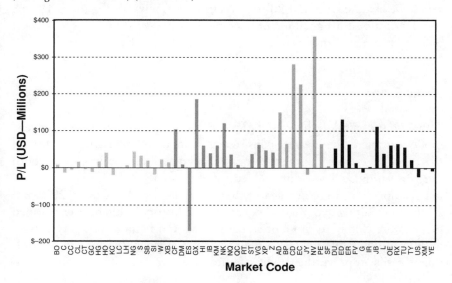

*Source:* Bloomberg, Newedge Prime Brokerage Research.

volatility-weighted portfolio, these losses would not put much drag on the overall portfolio's performance. But such a pronounced source of losses would certainly be an object of intense scrutiny by any real trading firm.

## The *Newedge Trend Indicator*

We have chosen to use a 20/120 moving average model as the *Newedge Trend Indicator* because of its solid correlative properties. In Exhibit 5.1, we showed that a 20/120 moving average model produced returns that exhibited a 0.67 correlation with the returns on the *Newedge Trend Sub-Index*. As it was, we chose that particular parameter and model combination partly because it had produced—as shown in Exhibits 5.9 and 5.10—the highest and tightest correlation fits for the 10 years covered by this study.

Our choice was reinforced by the correlation cluster analysis provided in Exhibit 5.18, which shows that the 20/120 moving average model fell into a cluster that contained Altis, Campbell, Graham, Sunrise, and Transtrend. In other words, it would have been nearly indistinguishable from CTAs who are widely recognized as trend followers.

For the sake of completeness, we have produced a hypothetical net asset value history for the *Newedge Trend Indicator* as if it were initiated on the first business day of January 2000. For the purposes of producing this hypothetical series, we assumed a 2 and 20 fee structure. As shown in Exhibit 5.19, the trend indicator did a good job of tracking the *Newedge CTA Index* and *Trend Sub-Index*, albeit with lower returns, through most of the decade.

## Next Steps

Although we found in this round of research that the 20/120 moving average model exhibited the greatest consistency in its correlation with returns on the *Trend Sub-Index*, we also recognize opportunities for improving both the correlation and volatility of returns exhibited by the *Trend Indicator*. For example, had we been able to reduce the volatility of returns in 2008 and 2009, the resulting hypothetical net asset value history would have conformed much more closely to those of actual CTAs. And because volatility plays a fairly important role in the estimation of correlations, tighter risk controls might easily improve the model's return correlations with trend followers' returns.

**EXHIBIT 5.18** Correlation Cluster Results of Daily Returns for CTAs in the 2009 *Newedge CTA Index*

| Designation | | CTA | 1 | 2 | 3 | 4 | 5 | 6 | 7 | 8 | 9 | 10 | 11 | 12 | 13 | 14 | 15 | 16 | 17 | 18 | 19 | 20 | 21 |
|---|---|---|---|---|---|---|---|---|---|---|---|---|---|---|---|---|---|---|---|---|---|---|---|
| | 1 | Crabel Capital (Multi-Product) | 1.00 | 0.67 | 0.51 | −0.16 | 0.08 | 0.00 | −0.01 | −0.01 | −0.13 | −0.09 | 0.19 | 0.25 | 0.22 | 0.26 | 0.24 | 0.22 | 0.18 | 0.36 | 0.09 | 0.09 | 0.30 |
| | 2 | R.G. Niederhoffer (Diversified) | 0.67 | 1.00 | 0.48 | −0.06 | 0.10 | 0.06 | 0.01 | 0.00 | −0.01 | −0.19 | 0.16 | 0.23 | 0.25 | 0.07 | 0.18 | 0.15 | 0.16 | 0.34 | 0.18 | 0.22 | 0.23 |
| | 3 | QIM (Global) | 0.51 | 0.48 | 1.00 | 0.34 | 0.44 | 0.33 | 0.42 | 0.42 | 0.34 | 0.27 | 0.46 | 0.34 | 0.44 | 0.37 | 0.40 | 0.41 | 0.24 | 0.19 | 0.12 | 0.13 | 0.32 |
| TF | 4 | Newedge Trend Indicator | −0.16 | −0.06 | 0.34 | 1.00 | 0.70 | 0.69 | 0.79 | 0.79 | 0.73 | 0.65 | 0.58 | 0.27 | 0.43 | 0.40 | 0.45 | 0.44 | 0.10 | 0.09 | 0.26 | 0.15 | 0.14 |
| TF | 5 | Altis Partners (GFP Composite) | 0.08 | 0.10 | 0.44 | 0.70 | 1.00 | 0.72 | 0.78 | 0.78 | 0.70 | 0.54 | 0.74 | 0.66 | 0.73 | 0.63 | 0.71 | 0.60 | 0.27 | 0.17 | 0.19 | 0.24 | 0.21 |
| TF | 6 | Campbell & Co., Inc. (FME Large) | 0.00 | 0.06 | 0.33 | 0.69 | 0.72 | 1.00 | 0.82 | 0.82 | 0.67 | 0.67 | 0.71 | 0.51 | 0.62 | 0.50 | 0.75 | 0.63 | 0.30 | 0.36 | 0.25 | 0.07 | 0.21 |
| TF | 7 | Graham Capital (Diversified) | −0.01 | 0.01 | 0.42 | 0.79 | 0.78 | 0.82 | 1.00 | 1.00 | 0.69 | 0.79 | 0.75 | 0.43 | 0.55 | 0.50 | 0.59 | 0.48 | 0.20 | 0.20 | 0.10 | 0.13 | 0.14 |
| TF | 8 | Graham Capital (K4) | −0.01 | 0.00 | 0.42 | 0.79 | 0.78 | 0.82 | 1.00 | 1.00 | 0.69 | 0.79 | 0.74 | 0.43 | 0.55 | 0.49 | 0.58 | 0.48 | 0.20 | 0.20 | 0.09 | 0.12 | 0.13 |
| | 9 | IKOS Partners (Financial USD) | −0.13 | −0.01 | 0.34 | 0.73 | 0.70 | 0.67 | 0.69 | 0.69 | 1.00 | 0.55 | 0.55 | 0.37 | 0.58 | 0.35 | 0.55 | 0.53 | 0.24 | 0.14 | 0.14 | 0.20 | 0.30 |
| TF | 10 | Sunrise Capital (Diversified) | −0.09 | −0.19 | 0.27 | 0.65 | 0.54 | 0.67 | 0.79 | 0.79 | 0.55 | 1.00 | 0.69 | 0.15 | 0.37 | 0.50 | 0.45 | 0.37 | 0.20 | 0.13 | 0.06 | −0.16 | 0.15 |
| TF | 11 | Transtrend, B.V. (Admiralty Fund) | 0.19 | 0.16 | 0.46 | 0.58 | 0.74 | 0.71 | 0.75 | 0.74 | 0.55 | 0.69 | 1.00 | 0.53 | 0.64 | 0.54 | 0.66 | 0.60 | 0.17 | 0.32 | 0.16 | 0.20 | 0.23 |
| TF | 12 | Aspect Captial (Diversified) | 0.25 | 0.23 | 0.34 | 0.27 | 0.66 | 0.51 | 0.43 | 0.43 | 0.37 | 0.25 | 0.53 | 1.00 | 0.79 | 0.62 | 0.79 | 0.77 | 0.37 | 0.35 | 0.21 | 0.52 | 0.27 |
| TF | 13 | Brummer & Partners (Lynx) | 0.22 | 0.25 | 0.44 | 0.43 | 0.73 | 0.62 | 0.55 | 0.55 | 0.58 | 0.37 | 0.64 | 0.79 | 1.00 | 0.66 | 0.78 | 0.77 | 0.30 | 0.39 | 0.27 | 0.31 | 0.50 |
| TF | 14 | Chesapeake Capital (Diversified) | 0.26 | 0.07 | 0.37 | 0.40 | 0.63 | 0.50 | 0.50 | 0.49 | 0.35 | 0.50 | 0.54 | 0.62 | 0.66 | 1.00 | 0.72 | 0.71 | 0.37 | 0.27 | 0.27 | −0.03 | 0.32 |
| TF | 15 | Millburn Ridgefield (Diversified) | 0.24 | 0.18 | 0.40 | 0.45 | 0.71 | 0.75 | 0.59 | 0.58 | 0.55 | 0.45 | 0.66 | 0.79 | 0.78 | 0.72 | 1.00 | 0.86 | 0.46 | 0.41 | 0.25 | 0.17 | 0.36 |
| TF | 16 | Winton Capital (Diversified) | 0.22 | 0.15 | 0.41 | 0.44 | 0.60 | 0.63 | 0.48 | 0.48 | 0.53 | 0.37 | 0.60 | 0.77 | 0.77 | 0.71 | 0.86 | 1.00 | 0.53 | 0.42 | 0.30 | 0.25 | 0.31 |
| | 17 | Grossman Asset Mgmt. (Currency) | 0.18 | 0.16 | 0.24 | 0.10 | 0.27 | 0.30 | 0.20 | 0.20 | 0.24 | 0.20 | 0.17 | 0.37 | 0.30 | 0.37 | 0.46 | 0.53 | 1.00 | 0.19 | 0.18 | 0.09 | −0.09 |
| | 18 | FX Concepts (Global Currency) | 0.36 | 0.34 | 0.19 | 0.09 | 0.17 | 0.36 | 0.20 | 0.20 | 0.14 | 0.13 | 0.32 | 0.35 | 0.39 | 0.27 | 0.41 | 0.42 | 0.19 | 1.00 | 0.44 | 0.16 | 0.32 |
| | 19 | FX Concepts (Dev. Market Curr.) | 0.09 | 0.18 | 0.12 | 0.26 | 0.19 | 0.25 | 0.10 | 0.09 | 0.14 | 0.06 | 0.16 | 0.21 | 0.27 | 0.27 | 0.25 | 0.30 | 0.18 | 0.44 | 1.00 | 0.04 | 0.22 |
| | 20 | Eagle Trading Systems (Yield) | 0.09 | 0.22 | 0.13 | 0.15 | 0.24 | 0.07 | 0.13 | 0.12 | 0.20 | −0.16 | 0.20 | 0.52 | 0.31 | −0.03 | 0.17 | 0.25 | 0.09 | 0.16 | 0.04 | 1.00 | −0.03 |
| | 21 | Boronia Capital (Diversified) | 0.30 | 0.23 | 0.32 | 0.14 | 0.21 | 0.21 | 0.14 | 0.13 | 0.30 | 0.15 | 0.23 | 0.27 | 0.50 | 0.32 | 0.36 | 0.31 | −0.09 | 0.32 | 0.22 | −0.03 | 1.00 |

*Source:* Barclay Hedge, Bloomberg, Newedge Prime Brokerage Research.

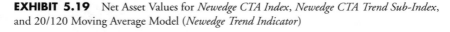

**EXHIBIT 5.19**   Net Asset Values for *Newedge CTA Index*, *Newedge CTA Trend Sub-Index*, and 20/120 Moving Average Model (*Newedge Trend Indicator*)

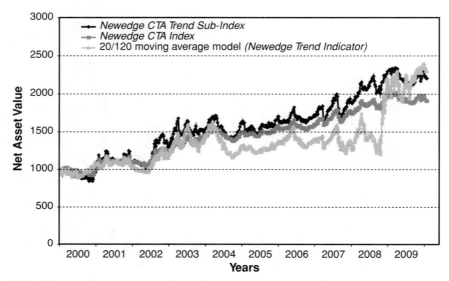

*Source:* Barclay Hedge, Bloomberg, Newedge Prime Brokerage Research.

Early comments on this research have also suggested other areas to explore when working to improve return correlations. These include:

- Sector weights
- Choice of parameters
- Blending of two or more models and/or parameter sets

For example, we have heard that a number of trend followers employed a higher weight for commodities than we did and a lower weight for equities. Also, we know that the 20/120 moving average model did not exhibit the highest return correlation in all of the 10 years. Early in the decade, faster moving average models produced higher correlations, while later in the decade, slower models did better on this measure. For us, the challenge will be to see whether we can find a way to better anticipate correlations and to adapt to them in a way that makes sense. We know, too, that actual CTAs use a blend of models, and perhaps we can improve correlations by blending two or more models.

Our guiding principles in this ongoing work to improve the *Trend Indicator*'s performance will be sense and simplicity. We will depart from the basic assumptions used in this round of research only with the greatest reluctance. Instead, we will focus on innovations that promise substantial improvements in correlation without violating the spirit of this benchmark.

# CHAPTER 6

# The Value of Daily Return Data

The question of whether investors benefit from the availability of daily return data for CTAs raises two related questions. First, are the data any good? Second, if the data are in fact clean and accurate, what can I learn from daily data that I can't learn from monthly or even quarterly data?

CTAs occupy one of the more liquid spaces in the hedge fund spectrum. Futures are among the most liquid and accurately marked financial instruments in the world and so lend themselves to clean valuation. On the other hand, CTAs may use instruments other than futures. Also, CTAs produce the return data voluntarily, and, except in limited cases, investors cannot invest or redeem on net asset values calculated from daily return estimates.

The answer to the first question appears to be *yes*. In the first part of this chapter, we examine two sets of daily returns—one used to calculate the *Newedge CTA Index* and one used to calculate the *Newedge AlternativeEdge Short-Term Traders Index*. In both cases, although for different reasons, we can conclude that daily data are for the most part reliable. Any errors that we can observe directly appear to be small and unbiased, and there appears to be no evidence of significant serial correlation.

The answer to the second question is that under the right circumstances, daily data allow you to get a better picture of the volatility of a manager's returns—both clearer and faster—than you can get from monthly data. And, since volatility is such an important ingredient in risk management and portfolio construction, it can be worth a lot to have daily returns.

Exhibit 6.1, for example, shows two distributions of estimated volatilities for a manager with a one-year track record. In one case (the wider one), we have 12 monthly returns with which to estimate the annualized volatility

129

**EXHIBIT 6.1**   One-Year Track Record

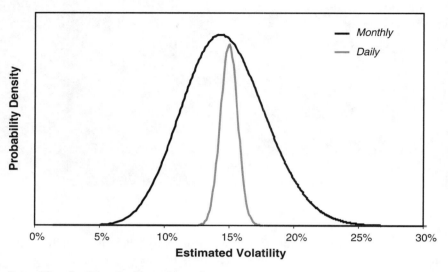

*Source:* Newedge Prime Brokerage Research.

of returns. In the other, we have 252 daily returns to work with. In this example, the true volatility of returns is 15 percent in both cases, but the range of estimated volatilities is much wider for monthly returns than for daily returns. With daily returns, most of our estimates of the manager's volatility fall somewhere between 13 and 17 percent. With monthly returns, however, the estimates look like they could plausibly fall anywhere from 6 to 24 percent. As a rule, given the difference in the number of observations, the range of estimates using monthly data would be roughly the square root of 21, or 4.6 times wider than what you would get using daily data.

## How Good Are Daily Data?

We have two data sets that allow us to take a look at the quality of daily data. One comprises the data that make up the *Newedge CTA Index*, which has been published daily since January 2000. The other comprises the daily return series that are used to calculate the *Newedge AlternativeEdge Short-Term Traders Index (STTI)*, which has been published daily since January 2008. In both cases, the daily index values are publicly available, while the individual CTAs' returns are not. We have access to the individual series as part of our working arrangement with Barclay Hedge, but we are bound not to redistribute them. We can, however, provide summary statistics that shed light on their quality, and that is what we do here.

As a practical matter, we can provide more insight into the quality of the short-term traders' data than we can for the returns that go into calculating the *Newedge CTA index*. With short-term traders, our working arrangement with Barclay Hedge entails parallel data collection and index calculation facilities that are designed to be reconciled with one another. This allows us to keep close tabs on how often and how much CTAs revise their daily numbers. It also has allowed us to work closely with the CTAs who report on improving the quality of what they submit. In contrast, the returns that are used to calculate the *Newedge CTA Index* are seen only by Barclay Hedge.

## Newedge CTA Index Data

One important hallmark of returns reported by hedge funds that trade in markets that are liquid and easily marked is the absence of any autocorrelation. For example, the smoothing of returns that one finds in the returns of hedge funds that trade in illiquid markets in which the instruments are difficult to price (e.g., mortgage-backed securities or convertible bonds) produces positive autocorrelation. And indeed, when we look at monthly returns reported for the *Newedge CTA Index*, we find a complete lack of autocorrelation.

We find a similar lack of autocorrelation in daily return data, even though the challenges are greater. While it is true, for example, that the markets that CTAs trade are liquid, they tend to be marked at different times of day. Asian markets, for example, would tend to reach the end of the most active part of their trading day earlier than would Europeans, who in turn conclude most of their business before U.S. markets finally quiet down in the middle of the U.S. afternoon. One can imagine, therefore, that one might find some relationship between one day's returns and the next day's returns—a one-day lag—while these time-of-day issues work themselves out.

Even with these challenges, however, a close look at daily returns reveals no evidence of the smoothing that might be caused by overlapping market trading periods. For our purposes here, we used a data set for 2009 that comprises daily returns for the *Newedge CTA Index* and for the 20 individual CTAs whose returns make up the index.

Our first step was to evaluate the behavior of the index. In Exhibit 6.2, we report the z-values for autocorrelations calculated for lags ranging from 1 day to 22 days, which more or less covers a trading month. The z-value is the autocorrelation estimate for each lag divided by its standard deviation. You

**EXHIBIT 6.2**   Z-values of *Newedge CTA Index* Serial Correlations

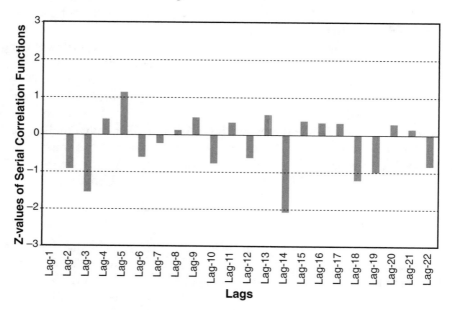

*Source:* Newedge Prime Brokerage Research.

can see that the z-value for a one-day lag, which seems like the most likely candidate for smoothing, is about as close to zero as it can be and is barely discernible. For the other lags, one sees values that are certainly not zero, but only one out of the 22 values exceeds a value of 2 (in this case –2), which is about what one would expect from pure randomness.

Our second step was to drill down on the component returns. Here, too, we find a distribution of z-values that look completely random. In Exhibit 6.3, we have overlaid the distribution of actual z-values estimated for 20 CTAs and for lags ranging from 1 to 22 days on a theoretical distribution of z-values for a world in which true autocorrelations are zero. Out of a total of 440 estimates (20 CTAs · 22 lags), we found that less than 5 percent of the estimates exceeded an absolute value of 2.0.

## Short-Term Traders Index Data

Since the beginning of 2008, we have been collecting daily data from CTAs whose returns are used in the calculation of the *Newedge AlternativeEdge Short-Term Traders Index (STTI).* Our experience with these data has provided

**EXHIBIT 6.3** Z-value Distribution of Serial Correlations for Newedge CTA Components for 2009

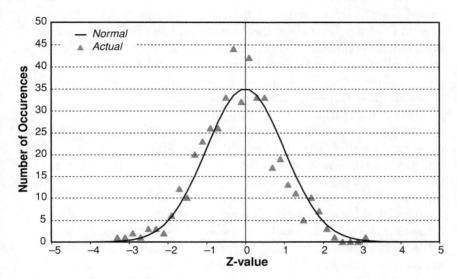

*Source:* Newedge Prime Brokerage Research.

valuable insights into the accuracy of numbers that are reported daily, why and how often they are revised, and on whether they exhibit any biases. What we have found, and what we describe here, is that daily return estimates can for the most part be considered unbiased estimates of returns that are eventually locked down.

Before taking a close look at these forces, though, a natural question to ask is why originally reported daily returns might need to be revised, or why they might not produce return calculations that conform to returns reported elsewhere. After all, to the extent that CTAs trade futures, the underlying markets are accurately marked at the close of each trading day. The short list of reasons for the need to revise daily estimates is this:

- One typically cannot subscribe or redeem on daily estimates.
- Trade breaks require reconciliation.
- The CTA is reporting for a "representative" account, which assumes specific things about currency denominations, liquidation and reinvestment, and estimates of incentive and management fees.
- Mistakes are made.

The first point suggests that there is less urgency around producing accurate numbers on a daily basis because no real money is involved. The second point reflects a reality of futures trading and the fact that even in a world of electronic trading, there can be disagreements about the details surrounding specific trades that must be reconciled. The third point reflects the complexity of the relationships that a CTA will have with investors who invest at different times, or who want their returns translated into different currencies. The final point stems from varying levels of quality control in the production and transmission of return estimates on a daily basis.

For the purposes of evaluating the component CTAs' reporting behavior, we isolated the 26 CTAs who reported returns for the second half of 2009. This gives us a consistent data set because the reporting population is fixed for the period. It also allows us to compare the accuracy of their reported returns with the values that we locked down at the end of March 2010.

The first thing we found is that revisions are common but not universal. In Exhibit 6.4, we show the number of revisions reported by the 26 component CTAs. At one extreme, we found that one CTA reported nearly 700 revisions to a maximum of 140 possible daily returns.* At the other extreme, we found that five of the constituents reported no revisions in their returns. And in between, the number of revisions ranged from over 200 down to just a few.

A natural question to ask is whether the revisions that CTAs submitted to us imparted any spin or change to the index. That is, were their initially reported return values on average higher or lower than the values that were eventually locked down. For the six months, we observed the following:

- 1,164 daily returns were revised at least once.
- 273 returns were revised at least twice.
- 29 returns were revised at least three times.
- 8 returns were revised at least four times.

The remaining daily returns were never revised. The effects of these revisions are summarized in Exhibit 6.5. The first vertical line on the left shows the distribution of daily returns as finally locked down less the initially reported return. There were 1,164 of these observations, and the average revision was –0.0047 percent with a standard deviation of 0.1175. The second

*This CTA firm's reporting practices were so unusual that we have chosen to work with them separately and to exclude their revisions from the analysis that follows. We have also excluded a number of errors in reporting that would have been captured by our new reporting procedures and that would have biased the results for the remaining CTAs.

**EXHIBIT 6.4** Number of Revisions by Constituent

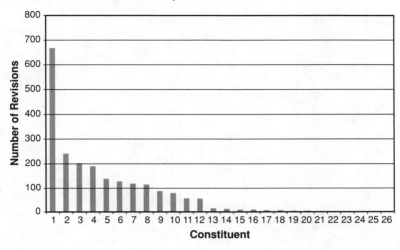

*Source:* Newedge Prime Brokerage Research.

**EXHIBIT 6.5** Difference between Lockdown and Reported Return (Excluding Constituent 1)

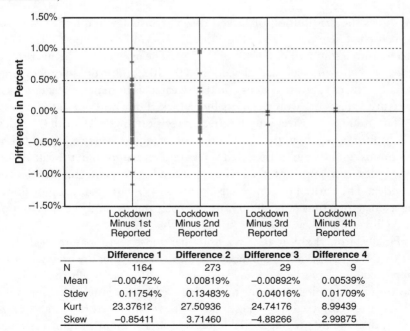

|  | Difference 1 | Difference 2 | Difference 3 | Difference 4 |
|---|---|---|---|---|
| N | 1164 | 273 | 29 | 9 |
| Mean | −0.00472% | 0.00819% | −0.00892% | 0.00539% |
| Stdev | 0.11754% | 0.13483% | 0.04016% | 0.01709% |
| Kurt | 23.37612 | 27.50936 | 24.74176 | 8.99439 |
| Skew | −0.85411 | 3.71460 | −4.88266 | 2.99875 |

*Source:* Newedge Prime Brokerage Research.

**EXHIBIT 6.6**   Distribution of Weighted Revisions

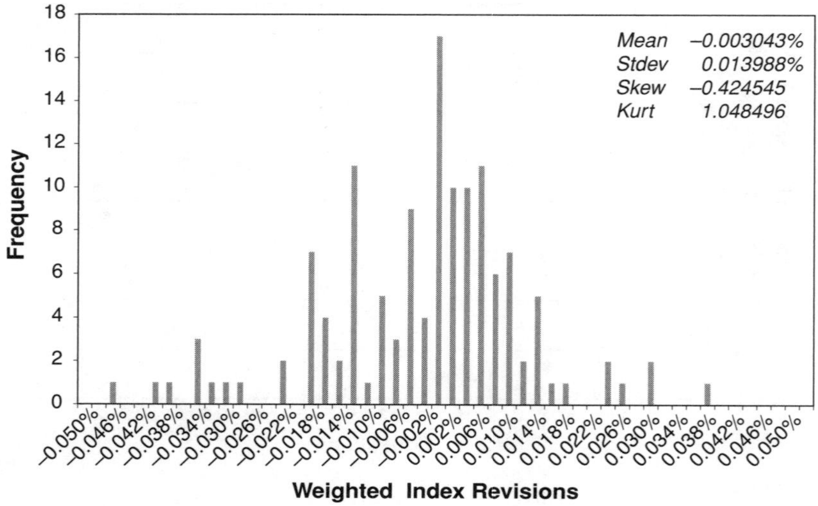

| | |
|---|---|
| Mean | −0.003043% |
| Stdev | 0.013988% |
| Skew | −0.424545 |
| Kurt | 1.048496 |

*Source:* Newedge Prime Brokerage Research.

line shows the distribution of locked down returns less the return as it was first revised. There were 273 of these differences, and the average was 0.0082 percent with a standard deviation of 0.1348. The average for the next round was −0.0089% with a standard deviation of 0.0402, and so on. In other words, the daily returns submitted to us could be treated as unbiased expectations of the return values that would eventually be locked down in our data set.

This result carries over into the effect of revisions on the value of the index. In Exhibit 6.6, we show the distribution of weighted averages of the CTAs' revisions using the weights that each CTA's returns are given in the calculation of the index. As is apparent, the revision process has only a negligible effect on the index. The entire horizontal axis covers only 5 basis points up or down. The average outcome was −0.003, or 0.3 basis points, and the distribution has no discernible skew or excess kurtosis.

Finally, from Exhibit 6.7, we find that most revisions are dealt with quickly. Nearly all revisions are made the business day after the original return is reported. As a result, we know that by the time we reach the end of a reporting month, most revisions to the daily returns leading up to that point will have been corrected and our estimate of the monthly return estimate based on daily data should provide a reliable guess about the monthly return estimate that will be reported by the CTA some days after the end of the month.

**EXHIBIT 6.7**  Number of Revisions in the First 21 Business Days after Trade Date

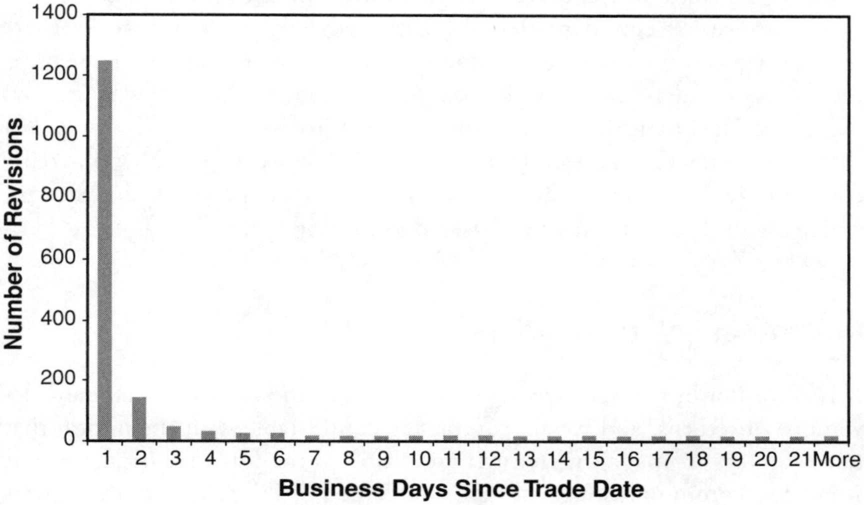

*Source:* Newedge Prime Brokerage Research.

## Lessons Learned

The results from our work with daily return data used in the calculation of the Short-term Traders Index are encouraging, but their quality was no accident. Between the beginning of 2008, when we first began collecting daily data, and now, we have had to work closely with the component CTAs to improve both the quality and the consistency of their data. By the end of 2009, the quality control steps we had taken included:

- Standard data format
- Fees net of returns, inclusive of interest
- Complete return history every day
- Explanation of any revisions to returns more than 45 days old
- Lockdown of year-end values at the end of the first quarter
- Complete revision histories (beginning mid-2009)

Quality control steps that we intend to explore include:

- Daily "fat-finger" and "no-finger" checks
- Index adjustment to reflect each manager's confirmed monthly returns

where the "no-finger" check is meant to capture those episodes in which the manager inadvertently reports a zero return when in fact the return is not zero.

Once we are confident that the data with which we are working are reliable, we can move on to the question of how daily data might help us improve our understanding of the risks in CTA returns. Most of what follows focuses on the question of estimating the volatility of returns, which is a key metric by which CTAs are evaluated. At the end, however, we show that daily data can give us a more sober assessment of a CTA's potential drawdowns, which are underestimated when based on monthly return data alone.

## Estimating Return Volatility

It is common in risk management to talk about the volatility (standard deviation) of returns, and we are completely comfortable with the notion that our estimates of managers' returns are prone to random statistical error. It seems less common, though, to talk about the possibility that our estimates of volatility are prone to random statistical error as well.

But they are. Estimated volatility is a sample statistic with a distribution of its own. And, as we show in this chapter, the distribution is skewed. Estimates can be biased, and the errors in our estimates depend hugely on how frequently we measure returns, how long a manager's track record is, and how volatile a manager's returns are.

The particular question that prompted us to take a close look at this problem involved daily and monthly data. The case in point involved two managers, both with very short track records. In one case, the estimated volatility of returns derived from monthly returns was several percentage points below the estimate derived from daily returns. In the other, the monthly volatility estimate was several percentage points above that derived from daily returns. Our initial conversation focused on serial correlations in returns, but a closer look convinced us that what the investor observed was more likely just the result of sampling error.

The purpose of this chapter is to present what we have learned from asking what errors in volatility estimates should look like. In addition to showing that volatility estimates based on daily return data are roughly 4.6 times better than those based on monthly return data, we show that estimates of volatility:

- Improve with length of track record
- Are better for managers with lower volatilities of returns

- Tend to be skewed and somewhat biased
- Depend on the skewness of underlying returns

We also consider some of the more important implications of using daily rather than monthly returns to estimate volatilities. For one thing, daily data make it much easier to detect differences between any two managers' risk profiles and to discern changes in the volatility of any given manager's returns. For another, daily data provide a truer picture of a manager's likely maximum drawdowns than do monthly data.

## Distributions of Estimated Volatility

Exhibit 6.8 adds two panels to Exhibit 6.1 and shows distributions of estimated volatilities derived from daily and monthly returns for track records of 1, 5, and 10 years. The sequence of panels provides useful insights into the breadth and shape of the distribution of estimated volatilities.[*]

### Daily versus Monthly Data

Daily data produce greater precision in our estimates of the volatility of return. Irrespective of the length of track record, the improvement is roughly the square root of 21 (the number of business days in a month). That is, the standard deviation of estimated volatility derived from monthly data is about $21^{1/2}$, or 4.6 times larger than that derived from daily data.

### Length of Track Record

The standard deviation of volatility estimates declines roughly as the square root of the length of the track record. This is apparent in Exhibit 6.9, which shows 95 percent confidence intervals for estimated volatility against the length of track record. It is also clear that it takes a lot of years of monthly

---

[*]As a matter of sheer practicality, the distributions of estimated volatilities of returns provided in this chapter have been derived from distributions of estimated variances of returns. In some cases, this is because the distribution of the variance is well known (i.e., the chi-square distribution if returns are normally distributed). In other cases, especially those where the underlying returns are skewed, this is because we have had to simulate the distributions of estimated variances. In all cases, we use these derived distributions to draw conclusions about the bias and precision of estimated volatilities.

**EXHIBIT 6.8**   Distributions of Estimated Volatilities

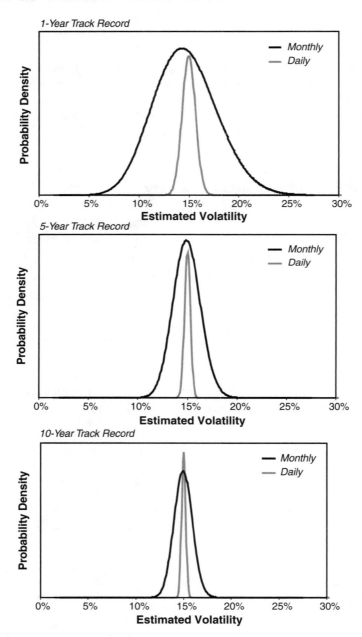

*Source:* Newedge Prime Brokerage Research.

**EXHIBIT 6.9**   Derived 95 Percent Confidence Intervals for Volatility Estimates

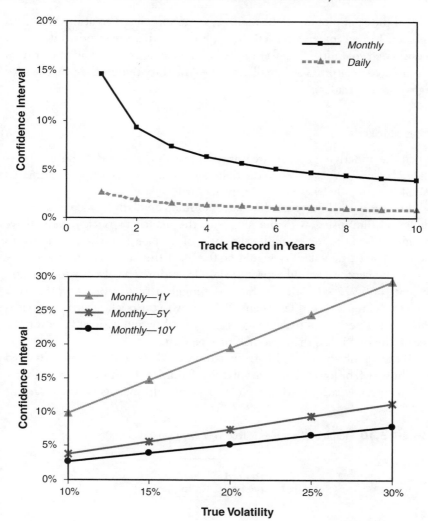

*Source:* Newedge Prime Brokerage Research.

return data to get as clear a picture as one gets using daily data. A 10-year track record, for example, affords 120 monthly observations, which would be about as many observations as one would get with 5 or 6 months of daily data. Using the same reasoning, it would take 20 or 21 years of monthly data to get the same precision that one gets with 1 year of daily data.

## The Effect of Volatility

In all of the examples so far, the manager's true annualized volatility of returns has been 15 percent. Exhibit 6.9 shows, however, that the standard deviation of estimated volatility is itself a function of the manager's true volatility. Errors in estimated volatilities are smaller for low-volatility traders than they are for high-volatility traders.

## Biases and Skews

When the underlying returns are normally distributed, the distribution of estimated volatilities is skewed to the right. Also, the expected value of estimated volatility is slightly less than the manager's true volatility.

Exhibit 6.10 shows that the bias in estimated volatility is comparatively small and diminishes with the length of the manager's track record. If we use monthly data, for example, the ratio of average estimated volatility to the manager's true volatility would be 0.978. If the manager's true volatility were 15 percent, we would expect the average estimated volatility to be 14.67 percent [= 0.978 · 15%]. You can see, though, that this bias becomes very small as the track record lengthens. With a two-year track record, the bias is only about 1 percent of the manager's true volatility, and with a five-year track record, the bias is less than one-half of 1 percent.

If the distribution of estimated volatilities is skewed, then most estimated volatilities will be lower than true volatility. Exhibit 6.11 shows the probability that any given volatility estimate will be less than the manager's true volatility.

**EXHIBIT 6.10**   Ratio of Estimates to True Volatility (Monthly Data)

| Track Record (years) | Ratio |
|---|---|
| 1 | 0.978 |
| 2 | 0.989 |
| 3 | 0.993 |
| 4 | 0.995 |
| 5 | 0.996 |
| 6 | 0.996 |
| 7 | 0.997 |
| 8 | 0.997 |
| 9 | 0.998 |
| 10 | 0.998 |

*Source:* Newedge Prime Brokerage Research.

**EXHIBIT 6.11**   Probability that Estimated Volatility Is Less than True Volatility

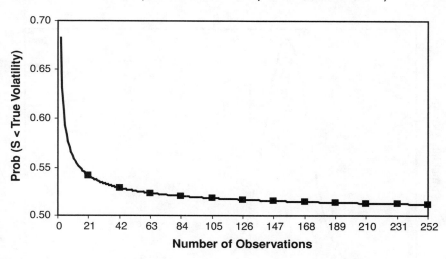

*Source:* Newedge Prime Brokerage Research.

For example, with 21 observations (about 1 month of daily data or 1 year and 8 months of monthly data), we would expect that about 54 percent of our estimated volatility would be lower than true volatility. Although this skewness in our estimates diminishes as track records lengthen, it never quite disappears.

## Is One Manager More Volatile than Another?

Consider the problem of discerning whether one manager's returns are more volatile than another's. In Exhibit 6.12, we have drawn two distributions of estimated volatilities—one centered around 15 percent, the other around 18 percent. These distributions have been drawn so that 5 percent of the lower-volatility distribution lies to the right of the crossover point and 5 percent of the higher-volatility distribution lies to the left. Thus, the overlap is small enough that we have 95 percent confidence in finding that one manager is more volatile than the other.

To draw these distributions, though, we needed 164 observed returns, which would require slightly less than 8 months of daily data, but nearly 14 years of monthly data.

The problem of detecting differences in the volatility of any two managers' returns shows up in any other comparison that depends on estimated volatility

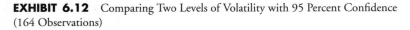

**EXHIBIT 6.12**   Comparing Two Levels of Volatility with 95 Percent Confidence
(164 Observations)

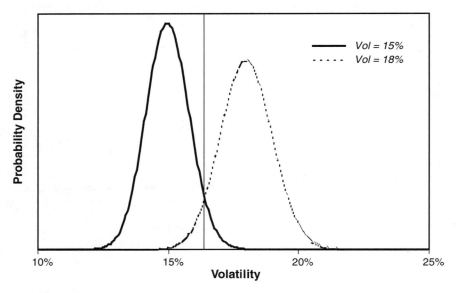

*Source:* Newedge Prime Brokerage Research.

as well. For example, a manager whose true Sharpe ratio is 1.00 (e.g., a true mean return of 20% and a true standard deviation of returns of 20%) might report an estimated Sharpe ratio anywhere from 0.67 (if estimated volatility were 30%) to 2.00 (if estimated volatility were 10%). This example also suggests that the distribution of estimated Sharpe ratios would be skewed to the right, even if the distribution of estimated volatilities were not.

### Have a Manager's Returns Become More Volatile?

Exactly the same lesson, but with a slight twist, applies to changes in a manager's risk profile. Suppose a manager whose true volatility has been 15 percent adopts a more risky strategy whose true volatility is 18 percent. What is the shortest possible span, from the time of the change, needed to detect the change with 95 percent confidence? The answer is 164 observations, which is the number of daily or monthly observations needed to allow approximately 1.6 standard deviations of estimated volatility to be 3 percent [= 18% − 15%] or less. With daily data, you would need 164 days from the time of the change in volatility to be able to detect the increase with any confidence. With

**EXHIBIT 6.13**   How Long It Takes to Discern a Change in a Manager's Volatility with 95 Percent Confidence (Original Volatility 15%)

| Manager's New Volatility | Number of Observations | Track Record Years | |
|---|---|---|---|
| | | Daily | Monthly |
| 16 | 1300 | 5.16 | 108.3 |
| 17 | 347 | 1.38 | 28.9 |
| 18 | 164 | 0.65 | 13.7 |
| 19 | 98 | 0.39 | 8.2 |
| 20 | 67 | 0.27 | 5.6 |

*Source:* Newedge Prime Brokerage Research.

monthly data, you would need that many months. As a result, a change in volatility that can be detected within 0.65 year using daily data would require 13.7 years to detect using monthly data.

Exhibit 6.13 shows how many return observations one needs to be able to detect a change in return volatility with 95 percent confidence. It is apparent that small changes (e.g., 1 percent) would be nearly impossible to detect within any reasonable amount of time. It is also apparent that if one is limited to using monthly return data, even fairly large changes in volatility (e.g., 5 percent) would require several years to detect.

## Beware a False Sense of Confidence

Perhaps the safest conclusion we can draw about the daily/monthly question is that whatever we are going to learn about a manager's volatility, we will learn the square root of 21 times faster using daily data than we will using monthly data. Having said that, there is always the danger that daily return data can contribute to a false sense of confidence.

The results presented so far depend on some basic assumptions that hold up better in some cases than in others. For example, we assume that the return measures are accurate and not clouded by measurement error. In practice, though, the ratio of noise to signal will be higher for daily data than for monthly data and so will reduce the effectiveness of daily data.

We assume, too, that returns are normally distributed and that volatility is constant over time, which are familiar assumptions in the world of option pricing. This view of the world assumes that the return generator can be sliced up into time intervals as short as you want and that any short interval provides an accurate representation of any longer period. This view would not work well for trading strategies that rely on low-frequency events. Convergence trades, for example, may blow up two or three times a decade. If so, three months of daily data would be nothing like five years of monthly data.

We also assume that there is no serial correlation, either positive or negative, in a manager's returns. If a manager's returns are either mean reverting or tend to produce trends over longish cycles, then daily return data would tend to provide a different picture of volatility than would monthly data. For that matter, something as simple as the fact that different markets around the globe close at different times during a standard 24-hour day means that there can be a small amount of day-to-day serial correlation in measured returns. And, as a result, non-synchronous marks effectively rob us of some of our daily observations.

To the extent any of these key assumptions don't hold, then dividing time up into trading days rather than trading months will not produce as much useful information as one thinks. And, in addition to providing a false sense of confidence in the precision of one's risk estimates, the use of daily data may produce skewed or biased estimates of the manager's true risk profile.

## What If Underlying Returns Are Highly Skewed?

To this point, we have worked with returns that are normally distributed. Exhibit 6.14 sheds some light on what happens to the distribution of estimated volatilities when the distribution of underlying returns is highly skewed. In this case, as shown in the upper panel, one set of returns is normally distributed and symmetrical while the other is very much skewed to the right. The middle and lower panels compare the distributions of estimated volatilities derived from the two sets of return distributions. Three lessons stand out.

First, the distribution of estimated volatilities from the skewed return distribution is itself more skewed than the distribution of estimated volatilities from the normal return distribution. This is illustrated in Exhibit 6.15 (see page 148), which compares the probability that estimated volatility will be less than true volatility for the two sets of underlying returns. Exhibit 6.15 also shows that the difference in the skewness becomes less pronounced as the track record lengthens.

Second, as can be seen most clearly in the bottom panel of Exhibit 6.14, the distribution of estimated volatilities from the skewed return distribution is more kurtotic than that for normally distributed returns. There are fewer estimates around the center of the distribution and more around the shoulders.

**EXHIBIT 6.14**   Return Distributions

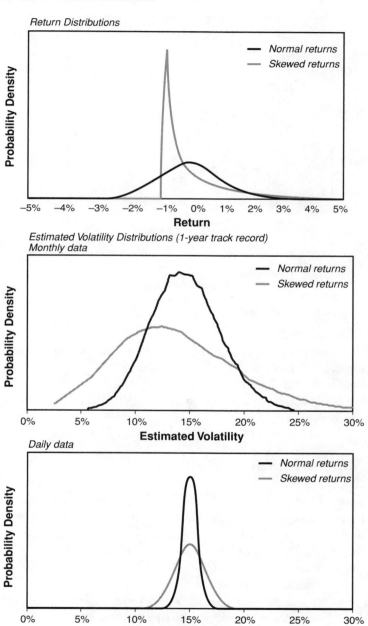

*Source:* Newedge Prime Brokerage Research.

**EXHIBIT 6.15**   Probability that Estimated Volatility Is Less than True Volatility

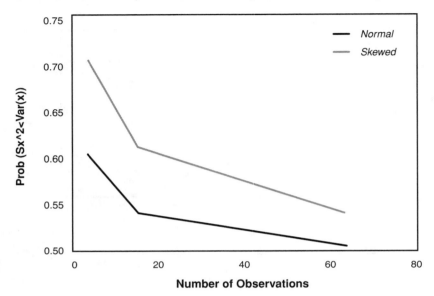

*Source:* Newedge Prime Brokerage Research.

Third, it is apparent from a comparison of the middle and bottom panels that daily data are just as productive here as they are when returns are more normally distributed. The standard deviation of estimated volatilities from daily data is still about the square root of 21 smaller than those derived from monthly return data.

## Effect on Drawdown Distributions

If we can track the daily value of a manager's portfolio and use daily values for the purpose of reckoning drawdowns, our views of what a manager's drawdown experience should look like would change quite a lot. For one thing, because daily returns are smaller than monthly returns, we would expect to see a lot more small drawdowns with daily returns. At the same time, because monthly snapshots of the true value of a manager's position almost certainly will miss the true maximums and minimums, using a daily series should produce larger expected maximum drawdowns.

Exhibit 6.16 bears out this intuition. The upper panel compares the distributions of all drawdowns that one would observe using daily and monthly

**EXHIBIT 6.16**   Drawdown Distributions

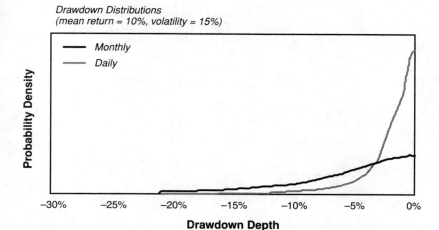

Drawdown Distributions
(mean return = 10%, volatility = 15%)

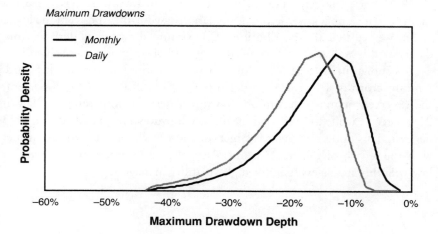

Maximum Drawdowns

*Source:* Newedge Prime Brokerage Research.

data. The lower panel compares the distribution of maximum drawdowns. In constructing these distributions, we have assumed a five-year track record, a 10 percent mean return, and a 15 percent volatility of returns.[*]

---

[*]For an explanation of how these distributions are constructed and what they mean, please see "Understanding drawdowns" (Burghardt, Duncan, and Liu, *AlternativeEdge Research Note*, September 4, 2003).

**EXHIBIT 6.17**  Average Maximum Drawdown (Mean Return = 10%)

| Volatility | Track Record (Years) | Expected Maximum Drawdown Monthly | Daily | Ratio of Daily Monthly |
|---|---|---|---|---|
| 10 | 1 | −6.0 | −8.6 | 1.42 |
| 15 | 1 | −10.4 | −14.2 | 1.36 |
| 30 | 1 | −24.3 | −31.5 | 1.30 |
| 10 | 5 | −12.2 | −14.7 | 1.20 |
| 15 | 5 | −22.4 | −26.3 | 1.17 |
| 30 | 5 | −56.5 | −64.7 | 1.15 |
| 10 | 10 | −15.2 | −17.8 | 1.17 |
| 15 | 10 | −28.7 | −32.7 | 1.14 |
| 30 | 10 | −76.3 | −84.3 | 1.11 |

*Source:* Newedge Prime Brokerage Research.

From the upper panel, we find that using daily data would produce a much higher frequency of small drawdowns than we would observe using monthly data, and a lower frequency of large drawdowns. And from the lower panel, we see that the distribution of maximum drawdowns derived from daily data lies well to the left of what we would observe using monthly data.

As shown in Exhibit 6.17, for a manager with a five-year track record, a mean return of 10 percent, and a true volatility of returns of 15 percent, the expected or mean maximum drawdown derived from monthly data is 22.4 percent, while the expected maximum drawdown from daily data is 26.3 percent. This understatement is larger for short track records and diminishes with the length of the track record. Also, the understatement is larger for low-volatility managers than for high-volatility managers.

# CHAPTER 7

# Every Drought Ends in a Rainstorm

## Mean Reversion, Momentum, or Serial Independence?

When is the best time to give your money to a manager? And when is the best time to take it back? Although the most common statement on marketing collateral is "Past returns may not be indicative of future results," the most common metric for manager selection and portfolio construction remains past returns. And of past returns, a manager's most recent returns bear the most weight.

The temptation to use a manager's recent track record to determine the best time to invest is almost as powerful as the pull of the sun on the earth. For some, this temptation takes the form of a belief in *mean reversion*, which suggests that a manager who has experienced a string of extraordinary gains is due to give some back, or that a manager who has experienced a string of unusually large losses is due for a recovery. For others, this temptation takes the form of a belief in momentum or *persistence*, which suggests that a manager who is "hot" will continue to be hot, while a manager who is on a losing streak will continue to lose money.

Investors in the first camp will resist investing in a manager who is on a winning streak and will find themselves drawn to investing in a manager who is in drawdown. Investors in the second camp will be inclined to follow the winning managers and shun the losers. Of the two camps, the second may well be larger because it always seems easier for a manager to raise money after a run of good performance.

There is a third camp, however, that works with the belief that a manager's returns are *serially independent*—that they do not depend on recent performance. In this view of the world, a manager's expected returns are the same at the end of a long winning streak as they are at the end of a long losing streak.

The difference between the first two camps and the third is potentially huge. Investors who try to time investments when returns exhibit neither mean reversion nor persistence leave a lot of money on the table and move money around unnecessarily. Also, we think that the evidence that draws people to either of these camps is anecdotal at best. Statements such as "All I know is, during LTCM, *blah, blah, blah*...," or "If you believe this manager will survive, you are better off investing on drawdowns," are common. And, though these views are comfortingly intuitive and seemingly obvious, they lack the rigor of thorough and objective analysis.

Our own research suggests that the third camp is closer to the truth. That is, all of the work we report on in this chapter suggests that future returns do not depend on past returns. For some readers, this may smack of the nettlesome "no black swan" problem, but given the data we have assembled, we find no compelling evidence that returns are anything but independent of past returns.

## A Focus on Conditional Returns

At the heart of this problem is the question of whether any aspect of a manager's future returns—mean, volatility, or correlation with other managers' returns—depends in any way on past returns. The main focus of this chapter is on whether there is any evidence that returns are anything other than serially independent. We describe the data we assembled for this project and report on the various ways we have tried to test for conditional returns.

## The Costs of Being Wrong about Timing Investments Can Be Substantial

The null hypothesis here is that returns are serially independent. And, although we use standard kinds of significance levels to evaluate our results, we should keep in mind that the cost of rejecting this null when it is true can be really big.

**EXHIBIT 7.1**  Cost of Timing Investments when Returns Are Serially Independent

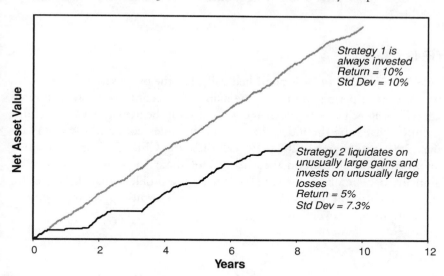

*Source:* Newedge Prime Brokerage Research.

Exhibit 7.1 shows the results of two different strategies for investing in a manager whose true return is 10 percent annualized, whose true volatility is 10 percent annualized, and whose returns from one period to the next are independent. In one case, you simply invest $1 at the outset and stay invested. In the other, you employ a rule that takes you out if the manager has an unusually high return and that puts you back in if the manager has had an unusually large loss.

As the exhibit shows, two things happen when you employ the second rule because the rule leaves you uninvested (or invested only in cash) for roughly half the time. The first is that you realize roughly half the return of the *always-in* strategy. The second is that your Sharpe ratio goes down because your volatility of returns falls, but by less than half.

It is important, then, to take a close look at the evidence on managers' returns and see whether we can unearth any evidence that returns are not independently random from one period to the next.

## The Data

For these exercises, we assembled two data sets comprising the returns of actual managers (CTAs) and one data set comprising the returns of

Newedge's generic trend-following models. These are listed in the headers of Exhibit 7.2.

## CFB 13

The *Newedge CTA Index* is published daily. For the purposes of this research, we were given permission to use the daily track records for individual managers if we agreed to preserve their anonymity. Of the managers whose returns go into calculating the index, 13 were in the index continuously from January 2001 to December 2004. We call these the CFB 13. To preserve their anonymity, we normalized the volatility of these 13 return streams to an annualized value of 15 percent. We discuss the problem that this poses for this research in the section that examines the relationship between returns, volatilities, and drawdowns.

## Barclay 43

Barclay maintains data on monthly returns for a broad set of CTAs, many of whose track records extend back to the 1970s. For the purpose of this work, we limited our focus to those managers who had at least $100 million under management as of March 2005, who had a minimum of 10 years of reported returns, and had data gaps of no more than three consecutive months. This left us with 43 managers. Of these 43, 41 had track records that extended back as far as January 1994.

## CF Generic

Newedge USA, LLC, maintains a daily record of returns to six generic trend-following trading models. These include three moving average crossover models (for day combinations of 20/40, 80/160, and 120/240) and three range breakout models (for 20, 80, and 240 days). For a description of how these models work, see Chapter 4. These return series begin with January 1994.

## Daily versus Monthly

When working with daily returns, we worked within the constraint set by the CFB 13 set, which begins with January 2001, even though we have daily returns for the generic model dating back to 1994. When working with monthly returns, we worked within the constraint set by the CF generic set, which begins with January 1994, even though we have actual return data for real managers going back further. In both cases, the data series run through the end of 2004. Thus, we have four years of daily returns and, for all but two managers, 11 years of monthly returns with which to work.

## The Test Tally

Exhibit 7.2 provides an overview of the kinds of tests we have done so far and of the tests we plan to do. In particular, we have tested directly for the absence of randomness in returns by looking at the distributions of autocorrelation estimates and runs. We have constructed return distributions for which the conditioning variable is past returns, the number of consecutive gains or losses, or the length and depth of drawdown. And we have constructed a very limited set of volatility distributions for which these were the conditioning variables.

The tally includes tests for the following:

1. *Serial dependence:* If returns are serially independent, then knowing a manager's net asset value history sheds no light on what that manager is expected to make, or how volatile a manager's returns will be, in the days or months ahead. An unusually large string of gains or losses augurs nothing about what the manager is expected to make going forward.

   Serial dependence, on the other hand, will show up in track records in two ways. First, returns across months will be correlated, either positively or negatively. For example, if an unusually large gain tends to be followed by

**EXHIBIT 7.2**  Test Tally

| Condition | Response | Data Sets | | | |
|---|---|---|---|---|---|
| | | Daily | | Monthly | |
| | | CFB 13 | CF Generic | Barclay 43 | CF Generic |
| Serial dependence | Autocorrelation | x | x | x | x |
| | Abnormal runs | x | x | x | x |
| Past returns | Return | no | no | x | x |
| | Volatility | planned | planned | no | no |
| Consecutive gains/ | Return | no | no | x | x |
| losses | Volatility | planned | planned | no | no |
| Drawdown length/ | Return | no | no | x | x |
| depth | Volatility | planned | planned | no | no |

*Source:* Barclay Hedge, Newedge Prime Brokerage Research.

another unusually large gain, returns will be positively serially correlated. In contrast, if an unusually large gain tends to be followed by a loss, or by a below-average gain, returns would be negatively serially correlated.

Second, strings of unusually large gains or losses will be either longer and fewer, or shorter and more plentiful, than we would expect to find if returns across months are independent. Sequences of gains and losses (or sequences of above-average and below-average returns) are known as *runs*. In a string of coin tosses, for example, we might observe

$$H\ H\ T\ T\ H\ T\ H\ H\ H\ T$$

if we were to toss the coin 10 times. In this sequence there are six runs. The shortest of these are the H, T, and T. The longest is the string of three H's toward the end of the sequence. The number of runs in a sequence is a statistic with a well-known distribution. It is possible, therefore, to test for unusually large or small numbers of runs.

2. *Past returns:* We have constructed distributions of returns and return volatilities for which the conditioning variable is past returns over known horizons. We have done the return distributions for both the daily and monthly data sets. We have done the volatility distributions only for the daily data set because we cannot get enough reliable volatility observations from the monthly data set to produce any kind of interesting comparisons.

3. *Consecutive gains and losses:* In these tests, we constructed distributions of returns and volatilities for which the conditioning variable is the number of gains or losses in a row. As with the tests on past returns, we did returns for both the daily and monthly data sets, and volatilities only for the daily data set.

4. *Drawdown length and depth:* Here the conditioning variable is how long and how deep the manager has been in drawdown.

## Test for Serial Dependence: Autocorrelation

For these tests, we estimated correlations between returns for lags ranging from 1 to 24 days when using the daily data sets and from 1 to 24 months when using the monthly data sets. The 24 days is slightly more than a trading month, which seems adequate for detecting relationships whose frequencies are a month or less. The 24 months allows us to detect lags as long as two years (see Exhibits 7.19 and 7.20 in the Empirical Update feature at the end of the chapter for more detail).

## Sample Size and Statistical Significance

To interpret these results, we need an idea of what constitutes statistical significance. In general, if the null hypothesis is that correlation is zero, the standard deviation of the estimate converges to $1/N^{.5}$ (1 over the square root of the sample size) as the sample size grows.

Consider the autocorrelation estimates shown in Exhibit 7.3, which are those for the first manager in the daily data set. For these calculations, we had 1,042 daily returns, which would give us 1,041 observations for calculating the correlation between daily returns lagged one day (e.g., today's and tomorrow's). When calculating autocorrelations between returns lagged 24 days, we had 1,018 observations. Thus, one standard deviation for the 1-day lag estimates was .03099, while one standard deviation for the 24-day lag estimates was .03134. In Exhibit 7.3, the roughly horizontal lines represent two standard deviations about zero. In this case, the estimate for the 8-day lag was more than two standard deviations away from zero, while the estimates for 4-day and 24-day lags were just inside of the two-standard-deviation line.

A similar effect is perhaps even more evident in the lower panel of Exhibit 7.3, which shows autocorrelation estimates for the same manager but for monthly returns. The effect of reducing the sample size as one extends the length of the lag is to increase the standard deviation of the estimate from about 0.17 to something closer to 0.20. And, in this case, 1 out of the 24 estimates was greater than two standard deviations, which is quite consistent with randomness.

## Autocorrelation Distributions

The distributions of autocorrelation estimates based on daily return data are shown in Exhibit 7.4. The upper panel shows how the estimates for the CFB 13 were distributed. The lower panel shows how the estimates for the CF generic strategies were distributed. We have not differentiated between estimates for different lags, so these are the distributions for all managers (or strategies) and all lags.

The distributions of autocorrelation estimates based on monthly return data are shown in Exhibit 7.5 (see page 160). The upper panel shows how the estimates for the Barclay 43 were distributed. The lower panel shows how the estimates for the CF generic strategies were distributed.

The main conclusion that we draw from these distributions is that it would be difficult to reject the null hypothesis that returns are serially independent. Except for the rather odd shape of the distribution for daily returns generated

**EXHIBIT 7.3**  Autocorrelation Estimates

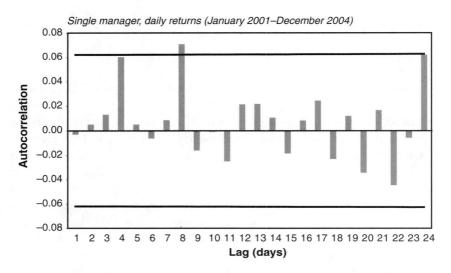

Single manager, daily returns (January 2001–December 2004)

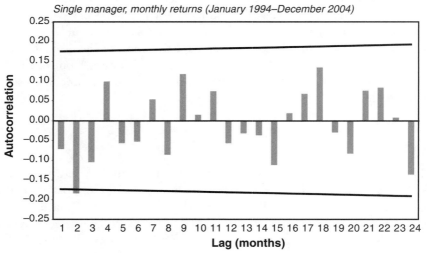

Single manager, monthly returns (January 1994–December 2004)

*Source:* Barclay Hedge, Newedge Prime Brokerage Research.

by our generic models (it has almost no tails at all), the distributions are roughly what one would expect if serial correlations were zero. The narrower distributions obtained from the daily return data are consistent with the much larger sample size. For daily data, two standard deviations of error is slightly more than .06. For the monthly data, two standard deviations of error is just over .17. Given these values, we find that 7.7 percent of the estimates for the

**EXHIBIT 7.4**   Distribution of Autocorrelation Estimates

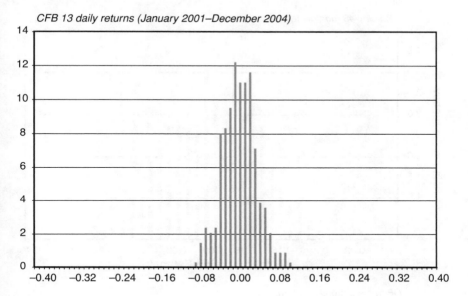

*CFB 13 daily returns (January 2001–December 2004)*

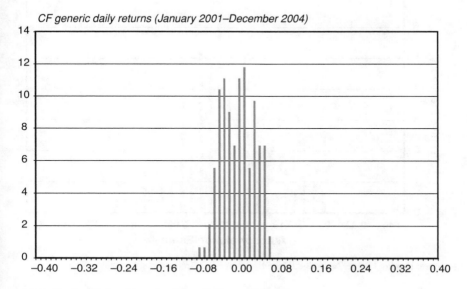

*CF generic daily returns (January 2001–December 2004)*

*Source:* Barclay Hedge, Newedge Prime Brokerage Research.

**EXHIBIT 7.5**   Distribution of Autocorrelation Estimates

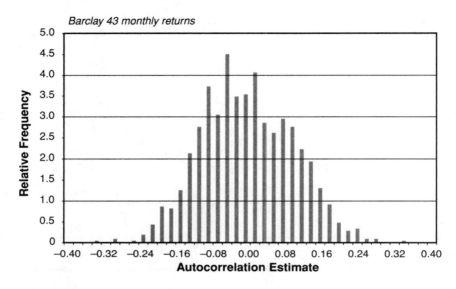

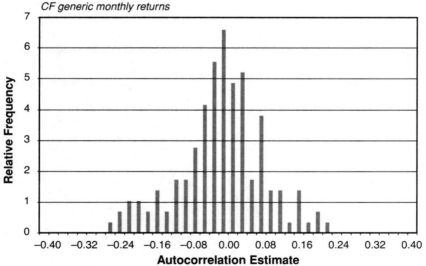

*Source:* Barclay Hedge, Newedge Prime Brokerage Research.

CFB 13 managers' daily returns were outside of two standard deviations, while only 1.4 percent of the estimates for the CF generic returns were more than two standard deviations away from zero. For the monthly returns, 5.4 percent of the actual managers' estimates and 6.3 percent of the generic strategies estimates were outside of two standard deviations.

## Autocorrelation Estimates for Compound Returns

It is our thinking that if single-period returns seem to be serially uncorrelated, then compound returns—that is, multi-period returns—are likely to be serially uncorrelated as well. Our results on this point are shown in Exhibits 7.6 through 7.8.

Exhibit 7.6, which shows the autocorrelation of monthly returns for a single manager, was chosen for its apparent lack of randomness. If anything, the wave-like appearance of these estimates looks almost artificial. Even so, if we look at relationships between combinations of returns, we come up empty handed. The top panel of Exhibit 7.7 shows the autocorrelations between returns over various periods. For example, the top row shows the correlation

**EXHIBIT 7.6** Autocorrelation Estimates for Manager 24 Monthly Returns (January 1994–December 2004)

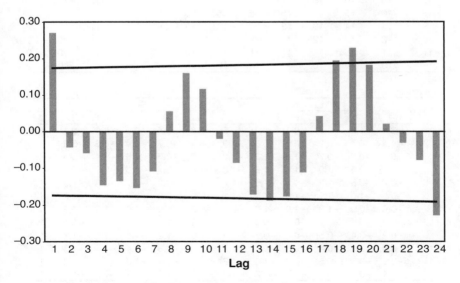

*Source:* Barclay Hedge, Newedge Prime Brokerage Research.

**EXHIBIT 7.7**   Autocorrelations and Z-Values (Manager 24, January 1994–
December 2004)

*Autocorrelation Estimates*

| Lead | Lag | | | | | | | | | | | |
|---|---|---|---|---|---|---|---|---|---|---|---|---|
| | 1 | 2 | 3 | 4 | 5 | 6 | 7 | 8 | 9 | 10 | 11 | 12 |
| 1 | 0.27 | 0.14 | 0.08 | 0.01 | −0.04 | −0.10 | −0.14 | −0.11 | −0.05 | −0.01 | −0.02 | −0.04 |
| 2 | 0.14 | 0.05 | −0.02 | −0.10 | −0.16 | −0.21 | −0.22 | −0.17 | −0.10 | −0.08 | −0.09 | −0.14 |
| 3 | 0.08 | −0.02 | −0.10 | −0.18 | −0.25 | −0.27 | −0.24 | −0.18 | −0.13 | −0.12 | −0.16 | −0.22 |
| 4 | 0.01 | −0.10 | −0.18 | −0.26 | −0.30 | −0.29 | −0.24 | −0.19 | −0.16 | −0.18 | −0.23 | −0.30 |
| 5 | −0.04 | −0.16 | −0.25 | −0.30 | −0.30 | −0.27 | −0.23 | −0.20 | −0.19 | −0.23 | −0.30 | −0.38 |
| 6 | −0.10 | −0.21 | −0.27 | −0.29 | −0.27 | −0.25 | −0.23 | −0.21 | −0.23 | −0.29 | −0.37 | −0.43 |
| 7 | −0.14 | −0.22 | −0.24 | −0.24 | −0.23 | −0.23 | −0.23 | −0.24 | −0.28 | −0.34 | −0.41 | −0.45 |
| 8 | −0.11 | −0.17 | −0.18 | −0.19 | −0.20 | −0.21 | −0.24 | −0.27 | −0.33 | −0.38 | −0.42 | −0.43 |
| 9 | −0.05 | −0.10 | −0.13 | −0.16 | −0.19 | −0.23 | −0.28 | −0.33 | −0.37 | −0.40 | −0.41 | −0.41 |
| 10 | −0.01 | −0.08 | −0.12 | −0.18 | −0.23 | −0.29 | −0.34 | −0.38 | −0.40 | −0.40 | −0.40 | −0.39 |
| 11 | −0.02 | −0.09 | −0.16 | −0.23 | −0.30 | −0.37 | −0.41 | −0.42 | −0.41 | −0.40 | −0.39 | −0.38 |
| 12 | −0.04 | −0.14 | −0.22 | −0.30 | −0.38 | −0.43 | −0.45 | −0.43 | −0.41 | −0.39 | −0.38 | −0.38 |

*Number of Independent Observations*

| Lead | Lag | | | | | | | | | | | |
|---|---|---|---|---|---|---|---|---|---|---|---|---|
| | 1 | 2 | 3 | 4 | 5 | 6 | 7 | 8 | 9 | 10 | 11 | 12 |
| 1 | 131 | 65 | 43 | 32 | 25 | 21 | 18 | 16 | 14 | 12 | 11 | 10 |
| 2 | 65 | 65 | 43 | 32 | 25 | 21 | 18 | 15 | 14 | 12 | 11 | 10 |
| 3 | 43 | 43 | 42 | 32 | 25 | 21 | 18 | 15 | 13 | 12 | 11 | 10 |
| 4 | 32 | 32 | 32 | 31 | 25 | 21 | 17 | 15 | 13 | 12 | 11 | 10 |
| 5 | 25 | 25 | 25 | 25 | 25 | 20 | 17 | 15 | 13 | 12 | 11 | 10 |
| 6 | 21 | 21 | 21 | 21 | 20 | 20 | 17 | 15 | 13 | 12 | 11 | 10 |
| 7 | 18 | 18 | 18 | 17 | 17 | 17 | 17 | 15 | 13 | 12 | 10 | 10 |
| 8 | 16 | 15 | 15 | 15 | 15 | 15 | 15 | 15 | 13 | 12 | 10 | 9 |
| 9 | 14 | 14 | 13 | 13 | 13 | 13 | 13 | 13 | 13 | 11 | 10 | 9 |
| 10 | 12 | 12 | 12 | 12 | 12 | 12 | 12 | 12 | 11 | 11 | 10 | 9 |
| 11 | 11 | 11 | 11 | 11 | 11 | 11 | 10 | 10 | 10 | 10 | 10 | 9 |
| 12 | 10 | 10 | 10 | 10 | 10 | 10 | 10 | 9 | 9 | 9 | 9 | 9 |

*Z-values*

| Lead | Lag | | | | | | | | | | | |
|---|---|---|---|---|---|---|---|---|---|---|---|---|
| | 1 | 2 | 3 | 4 | 5 | 6 | 7 | 8 | 9 | 10 | 11 | 12 |
| 1 | 3.1 | 1.2 | 0.6 | 0.1 | −0.2 | −0.5 | −0.6 | −0.4 | −0.2 | 0.0 | −0.1 | −0.1 |
| 2 | 1.2 | 0.4 | −0.2 | −0.5 | −0.8 | −1.0 | −0.9 | −0.7 | −0.4 | −0.3 | −0.3 | −0.4 |
| 3 | 0.6 | −0.2 | −0.7 | −1.0 | −1.2 | −1.2 | −1.0 | −0.7 | −0.5 | −0.4 | −0.5 | −0.7 |
| 4 | 0.1 | −0.5 | −1.0 | −1.5 | −1.5 | −1.3 | −1.0 | −0.7 | −0.6 | −0.6 | −0.8 | −1.0 |
| 5 | −0.2 | −0.8 | −1.2 | −1.5 | −1.5 | −1.2 | −1.0 | −0.8 | −0.7 | −0.8 | −1.0 | −1.2 |
| 6 | −0.5 | −1.0 | −1.2 | −1.3 | −1.2 | −1.1 | −0.9 | −0.8 | −0.8 | −1.0 | −1.2 | −1.3 |
| 7 | −0.6 | −0.9 | −1.0 | −1.0 | −1.0 | −0.9 | −0.9 | −0.9 | −1.0 | −1.2 | −1.3 | −1.4 |
| 8 | −0.4 | −0.7 | −0.7 | −0.7 | −0.8 | −0.8 | −0.9 | −1.0 | −1.2 | −1.3 | −1.4 | −1.3 |
| 9 | −0.2 | −0.4 | −0.5 | −0.6 | −0.7 | −0.8 | −1.0 | −1.2 | −1.3 | −1.4 | −1.3 | −1.2 |
| 10 | 0.0 | −0.3 | −0.4 | −0.6 | −0.8 | −1.0 | −1.2 | −1.3 | −1.4 | −1.4 | −1.3 | −1.2 |
| 11 | −0.1 | −0.3 | −0.5 | −0.8 | −1.0 | −1.2 | −1.3 | −1.4 | −1.3 | −1.3 | −1.2 | −1.1 |
| 12 | −0.1 | −0.4 | −0.7 | −1.0 | −1.2 | −1.3 | −1.4 | −1.3 | −1.2 | −1.2 | −1.1 | −1.1 |

*Source:* Barclay Hedge, Newedge Prime Brokerage Research.

between 1-month returns and returns for following periods ranging from 1 month to 12 months. The second row shows the correlations between 2-month returns and subsequent returns for periods ranging from 1 month to 12 months.

Some of these correlation values seem large enough to be worth considering. For example, the correlation estimates in the lower-right-hand corner of the table are often larger than –0.40. The correlation between 7-month returns and the following 12-month returns is –0.45.

The middle panel, however, shows how many independent observations we have to work with for each of these estimates. For example, given 132 monthly observations, we have 131 non-overlapping estimates for single-period correlations. Once we consider 2-month returns, however, the number of independent observations is cut in half. In the case of the correlation between 7-month returns and 12-month returns, we have only 10 observations.

As a result, as shown in the bottom panel of Exhibit 7.7, we are left with only one estimate that is statistically significant, and that is the estimate for the correlation between consecutive monthly returns, which was 0.27 and had a z-value of 3.1.

It is worth noting, too, that this one instance of statistical significance may be of no practical value for an investor given the time required to increase or decrease the amount of money invested with a manager. The full month's return is not known until the month is over.

The two panels of Exhibit 7.8 summarize the results for the 13 managers' daily returns and the 43 managers' monthly returns. Each panel shows the fraction of total managers for which the z-value of the correlation estimate was greater than 2.0. In the upper panel, .07 represents one manager. In the lower panel, .02 represents one manager. While a value greater than .05 suggests that the result might not have happened by chance, the preponderance of zeros combined with the fact that z-values greater than 2.0 for more than one manager appear in so few cases (3 in the case of daily returns, and 16 in the case of monthly returns) suggests that these are random occurrences.

## Test for Serial Dependence: Runs

In this exercise, we are interested in whether the number of runs in a manager's gains or losses is unusually large or small. And for our purposes, the null hypothesis is that each month's return is drawn from a distribution that is independent of whatever has gone before. If this is true, then if we have a

**EXHIBIT 7.8**   Autocorrelations of Compound Monthly Returns (Fraction of Z-Values Greater Than 2.0)

Daily for CFB 13 Managers (January 2001–December 2004)

| Lead | Lag 1 | 2 | 3 | 4 | 5 | 6 | 7 | 8 | 9 | 10 | 11 | 12 |
|---|---|---|---|---|---|---|---|---|---|---|---|---|
| 1 | 0.29 | 0.14 | 0 | 0 | 0 | 0 | 0 | 0 | 0 | 0 | 0 | 0 |
| 2 | 0.14 | 0.07 | 0 | 0 | 0 | 0 | 0 | 0 | 0 | 0 | 0 | 0 |
| 3 | 0 | 0 | 0 | 0 | 0 | 0 | 0 | 0 | 0 | 0 | 0 | 0 |
| 4 | 0 | 0 | 0 | 0 | 0 | 0 | 0 | 0 | 0 | 0 | 0 | 0 |
| 5 | 0 | 0 | 0 | 0 | 0 | 0 | 0 | 0 | 0 | 0 | 0 | 0 |
| 6 | 0 | 0 | 0 | 0 | 0 | 0.07 | 0.07 | 0.07 | 0 | 0 | 0 | 0 |
| 7 | 0 | 0 | 0 | 0 | 0 | 0.07 | 0.07 | 0.07 | 0 | 0 | 0 | 0 |
| 8 | 0 | 0 | 0 | 0 | 0 | 0.07 | 0.07 | 0.07 | 0 | 0 | 0 | 0 |
| 9 | 0 | 0 | 0 | 0 | 0 | 0 | 0 | 0 | 0 | 0 | 0 | 0 |
| 10 | 0 | 0 | 0 | 0 | 0 | 0 | 0 | 0 | 0 | 0 | 0 | 0 |
| 11 | 0 | 0 | 0 | 0 | 0 | 0 | 0 | 0 | 0 | 0 | 0 | 0 |
| 12 | 0 | 0 | 0 | 0 | 0 | 0 | 0 | 0 | 0 | 0 | 0 | 0 |

Monthly for Barclay 43 Managers (January 1994–December 2004)

| Lead | Lag 1 | 2 | 3 | 4 | 5 | 6 | 7 | 8 | 9 | 10 | 11 | 12 |
|---|---|---|---|---|---|---|---|---|---|---|---|---|
| 1 | 0.02 | 0 | 0 | 0 | 0 | 0 | 0 | 0 | 0 | 0 | 0 | 0 |
| 2 | 0 | 0.09 | 0.05 | 0 | 0 | 0 | 0 | 0 | 0 | 0 | 0 | 0 |
| 3 | 0 | 0.05 | 0 | 0.05 | 0.05 | 0.05 | 0 | 0 | 0 | 0 | 0 | 0 |
| 4 | 0 | 0 | 0.05 | 0.09 | 0.05 | 0.07 | 0.02 | 0.02 | 0 | 0 | 0 | 0 |
| 5 | 0 | 0 | 0.05 | 0.05 | 0.09 | 0.07 | 0.02 | 0.02 | 0.02 | 0 | 0 | 0 |
| 6 | 0 | 0 | 0.05 | 0.07 | 0.07 | 0.02 | 0.02 | 0.02 | 0.02 | 0 | 0 | 0 |
| 7 | 0 | 0 | 0 | 0.02 | 0.02 | 0.02 | 0.02 | 0.02 | 0.02 | 0 | 0.02 | 0.02 |
| 8 | 0 | 0 | 0 | 0.02 | 0.02 | 0.02 | 0.02 | 0.02 | 0 | 0.02 | 0.02 | 0.02 |
| 9 | 0 | 0 | 0 | 0 | 0.02 | 0.02 | 0.02 | 0 | 0.02 | 0.02 | 0.02 | 0.02 |
| 10 | 0 | 0 | 0 | 0 | 0 | 0 | 0 | 0.02 | 0.02 | 0.02 | 0.02 | 0 |
| 11 | 0 | 0 | 0 | 0 | 0 | 0 | 0.02 | 0.02 | 0.02 | 0.02 | 0.02 | 0 |
| 12 | 0 | 0 | 0 | 0 | 0 | 0 | 0.02 | 0.02 | 0.02 | 0 | 0 | 0 |

*Source:* Barclay Hedge, Newedge Prime Brokerage Research.

manager who has produced a total of $n_1$ gains and $n_2$ losses, the expected number of runs (consecutive gains or losses) would be[*]

$$E\left(runs\right) = \frac{2n_1 n_2}{n_1 + n_2} + 1$$

The sample variance of the number of runs would be

$$V\left(runs\right) = \frac{2n_1 n_2 \left(2n_1 n_2 - n_1 - n_2\right)}{\left(n_1 + n_2\right)^2 \left(n_1 + n_2 - 1\right)}$$

---

[*]See Annie Dudley, SAS Institute Inc., "The Runs Test, Nonparametric Testing for Randomness in a Series of Runs," (http://www.jmp.com/news/jmpercable/04_spring1997/runs_test.html), who in turn cites Siegal, *Nonparametric Statistics* (McGraw-Hill, 1956), and Mendenhall, Scheaffer, and Wackerly, *Mathematical Statistics with Applications*, 3rd ed. (Duxbury Press, CA, 1986).

The results of our runs tests are shown in Exhibit 7.9, which borrows a graphing technique from the world of technical traders. Each vertical bar summarizes information about a particular manager or portfolio. The clear circle in the middle represents the expected number of runs, while the shaded bar represents two standard deviations on either side of the mean. The diamond represents the observed number of runs.

## Runs in Daily Returns

The upper panel shows how runs were distributed for daily returns from January 2001 through December 2004. The first bar on the left summarizes the results for the *Newedge CTA Index*. The next 13 (numbers 2–14) are the results for the 13 managers who were in the index through the entire four years. The last six bars on the right are the results for the six Newedge USA, LLC, generic strategies.

What stands out in these results is a suggestion of slightly fewer and longer runs than one would expect at random. While most of the estimates are within two standard deviations of the mean, the number of runs was less than expected in all but two cases, and in four instances (three for the actual managers and once for the generic strategies), the observed number of runs is outside the two-standard-deviation range. Overall, the average number of runs was 15 to 20 less than the expected number of 520.

## Runs in Monthly Returns

Here there is almost no suggestion of abnormal numbers of runs. The observed number of runs was outside the two-standard-deviation range in only one case. Overall, the average observed number of runs was 64, while the expected number of runs was 65.

## Conditional Return Distributions

Given the absence of any compelling evidence of serially correlated returns, at least in our monthly return data, we expect to find little evidence that managers' return distributions depend on anything having to do with past returns. Even so, for the sake of completeness, we provide examples of what conditional return distributions look like from three different angles. First, we consider past return as the conditioning variable. Second, we use the number of consecutive gains or losses as the conditioning variable. Third, we use the length and depth of the manager's drawdown.

**EXHIBIT 7.9**   Runs of Gains and Losses

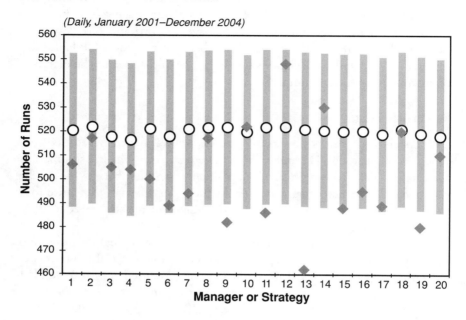

(Daily, January 2001–December 2004)

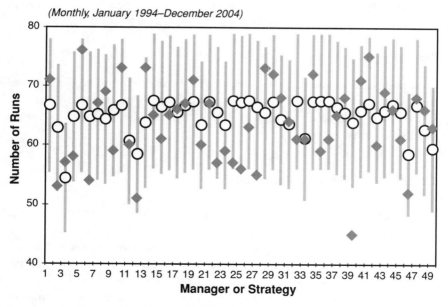

(Monthly, January 1994–December 2004)

*Source:* Barclay Hedge, Newedge Prime Brokerage Research.

In these exercises, we use the monthly data for the Barclay 43 managers and have normalized the volatility of each manager's returns to an annualized value of 15 percent. This was not to preserve anonymity because these managers' monthly returns are publicly available. Rather, the chief advantage of normalizing return volatilities is that our results are not distorted by the presence of highly volatile return streams. Leverage is somewhat arbitrary and something that can be increased at will by the investor by varying the amount of risk allocated to each manager.

We have chosen to use non-overlapping observations on returns. We have two reasons for this decision. First, the use of overlapping data tends to overstate the apparent statistical significance of one's results. We provide an example of this effect in the next subsection, which shows how return distributions are conditioned on past returns.

Second, the use of overlapping data carries with it an implicit lag structure that might better be isolated and studied directly. Consider Exhibit 7.10, which illustrates this point well. The shaded times series is the manager's net asset value relative to his most recent high-water mark. When the series is above zero, the manager is setting new highs. When the series is below zero, the manager is in drawdown. In this setting, consider the two drawdown points $DD_1$ and $DD_2$ and their corresponding lagged returns $R_1$ and $R_2$. From this

**EXHIBIT 7.10** The Problem with Overlapping Observations (Drawdown and Lagged Returns)

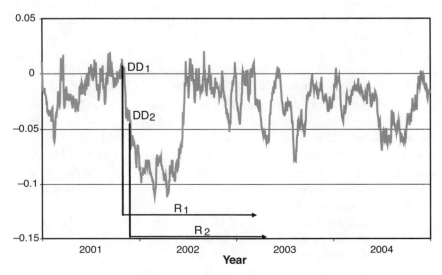

*Source:* Barclay Hedge, Newedge Prime Brokerage Research.

picture it is easy to see that $R_1$ and $R_2$ share much of the same experience and are different only because $R_1$ contains a small amount of return information for the period between our observations of $DD_1$ and $DD_2$, while $R_2$ contains a small amount of return information at the end of its span. Thus, if we think there is a relationship between drawdowns and lagged returns like these, such a relationship would have to manifest itself in the difference between that part of the return in $R_1$ that is not in $R_2$ and that part of the return in $R_2$ that is not in $R_1$.

Third, we have decided to focus on the monthly data series mainly because months are the basic unit of time for this business.

## Past Returns

Exhibit 7.11 provides different perspectives on whether return distributions are conditional in any way on past returns. The three panels in Exhibit 7.11 show how the distributions of six-month returns were related to the previous six-month returns. In this exhibit, managers' past returns are shown on the horizontal axis. Each vertical bar provides a thumbnail description of the distributions that managers made in the next six months. The clear circle shows the average return. The narrow black line shows the range of six-month returns so that the bottom of the line is the lowest return while the top of the line is the maximum return. The wider shaded bar represents either a two-standard-deviation or two-standard-error range of return outcomes. The horizontal line represents the unconditional mean six-month return for the entire data set.

The three panels differ in the following respects. The upper and middle panels differ in their perspective on statistical significance. The shaded gray band in the upper panels shows two standard deviations of variability in returns while the shaded gray band in the middle panel (and again in the bottom panel) shows two standard errors of variability in the mean return. Because the standard error is the standard deviation divided by the square root of the sample size, a visual comparison of the upper and middle panels shows how the sample size thins out as we look at the extremes. As we look at higher and lower past returns, the number of observations decreases, and the width of the two-standard-error band increases.

The middle and bottom panels differ in the choice of data. In the middle panel, we use overlapping six-month returns. That is, we look at the previous and subsequent six-month returns for every single month in the data set. In the bottom panel, we do not allow the data to overlap.

**EXHIBIT 7.11**   Six-Month Lead/Six-Month Lag

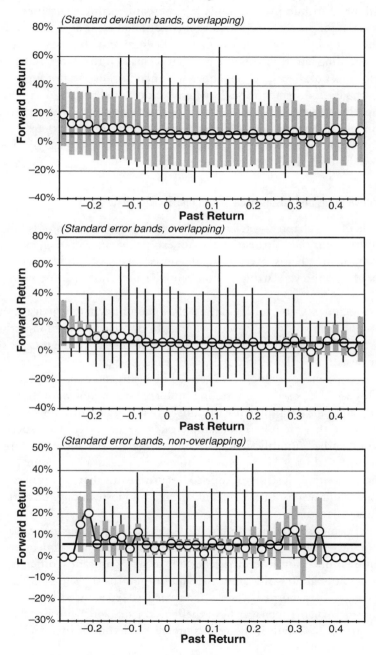

*Source:* Barclay Hedge, Newedge Prime Brokerage Research.

The effect of using non-overlapping data on the appearance of these conditional distributions is striking. We chose this example because when we used overlapping data, it appeared as if conditional six-month returns might actually be significantly greater than zero. Beginning with losses of 6 percent and proceeding left in the middle panel, it seems as if the two-standard-error band for most of these cases lies above the unconditional return line.

In the bottom panel, though, where we do not allow the data points to overlap, this apparently significant relationship disappears. There are still two cases in which the outcomes look statistically significant (one at –6% and one at +10%), but otherwise the conditional distributions appear much more random than when we used overlapping data.

## Consecutive Gains and Losses (One-Month and Six-Month Returns)

The title of this chapter—"Every drought ends in a rainstorm"—is based on a feature of runs that is true of every run except the one you happen to be in at the moment. That is, every string of consecutive losses ends at some point with a gain, and every string of consecutive gains ends at some point with a loss.

We include Exhibit 7.12 because it shows conditional return distributions for loss and gain strings of various lengths. In our data set, the longest string of losses experienced by any manager was 9 months, while the longest string of gains was 17. By definition, these were runs of –9 and +17 and, as shown in the upper panel of Exhibit 7.12, ended in a gain and a loss respectively.

This exercise posed an interesting problem. We do not want to use over-lapping data, but the problem with runs is that you do not know when they are over until they are over. For example, suppose a manager has experienced four consecutive monthly gains. Without knowing the subsequent history of returns, we do not know whether this constitutes a run of four gains or whether it is simply a string of four consecutive gains that is part of a longer run. As a result, we measure consecutive gains and losses along the horizontal axis rather than runs.

The results shown in Exhibit 7.12 suggest that strings of consecutive gains or losses convey little useful information about subsequent returns. Conditional one-month returns seem not to be significantly different from zero. Conditional non-overlapping six-month returns show a weak tendency to be greater than normal when a manager has experienced losses and less than normal when a manager has experienced gains, but with the exception of loss strings of 2 and 3, the results are all borderline if they tend toward significance at all.

**EXHIBIT 7.12**   Conditional Return Distributions for Loss and Gain Strings

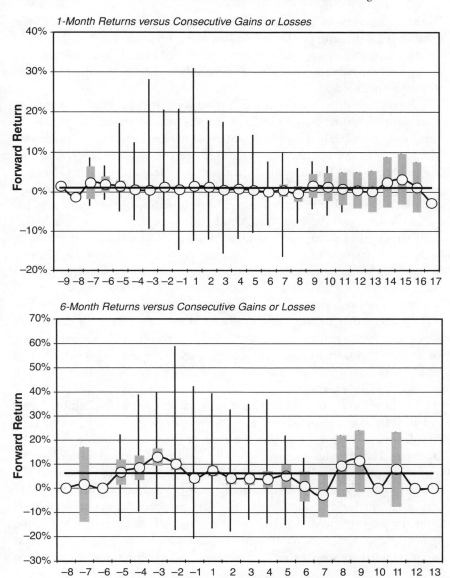

*Source:* Barclay Hedge, Newedge Prime Brokerage Research.

## Drawdown

In these exercises, we reckoned each manager's drawdown using net asset value series beginning at 100 at the beginning of January 1994. The main shortcoming of this approach is that our drawdown calculations will not correspond to a manager's true drawdown until the series we are using produces true high-water marks.

We organized the data in the following way. At the end of each month, we recorded both the amount of the manager's drawdown and the number of months the manager had been in drawdown. (We also kept track of months for which the manager was above water and lumped those observations together in a single bucket.) We then allocated the data to drawdown bucket sizes of 5 percentage points (e.g., 0–5%, 5–10%, etc.). Given these classifications and sortings, we were able to construct conditional return distributions in which the conditions were the length and depth of drawdown.

Exhibit 7.13 provides two examples of return distributions for drawdowns of 20 to 25 percent. The length of drawdown in months is measured along the horizontal axis so that one can see how the distribution of returns changes as the managers' time spent in drawdown increases. From the upper panel of Exhibit 7.13, which shows the distribution of subsequent one-month returns, it is apparent that for drawdowns of this depth, the length of drawdown does not seem to matter. The lower panel of Exhibit 7.13 provides similar information for non-overlapping six-month returns, but also provides a vivid reminder of how thinly we have to slice the data set whenever we try to look at longer-period returns.

Just how thinly the data may have to be sliced is shown in Exhibit 7.14A and B. The upper panel shows how many observations we have for each drawdown classification when we limit our look at one-month returns. The lower panel shows what happens when we limit our look at non-overlapping six-month returns. In both cases, we have highlighted certain areas of the table to show where most of the data lie and to remind us of the difference between normal and unusual events. The dark-gray area, for example, includes approximately 65 percent of the total number of observations, while the light-gray area adds another 30 percent. Taken together, the grayed-in areas comprise what we might think of as two standard deviations of experience

**EXHIBIT 7.13** Return Distributions for Drawdowns of 20 to 25 Percent

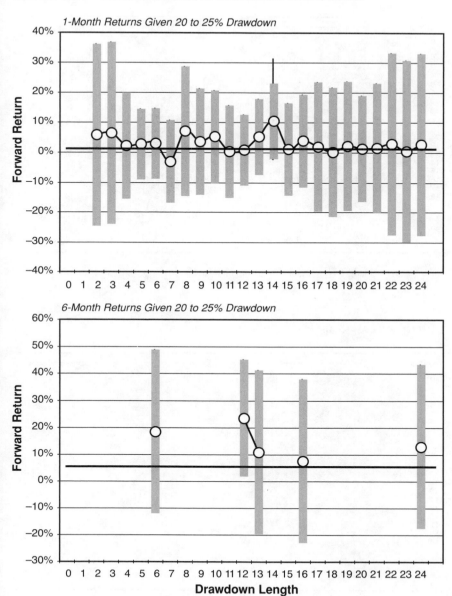

*Source:* Barclay Hedge, Newedge Prime Brokerage Research.

**EXHIBIT 7.14A**   Number of One-Month Return Observations

| Months | Drawdown Depth | | | | | | | | | | | | |
|---|---|---|---|---|---|---|---|---|---|---|---|---|---|
| | 0 | −0.05 | −0.10 | −0.15 | −0.20 | −0.25 | −0.30 | −0.35 | −0.40 | −0.45 | −0.50 | −0.55 | −0.60 |
| 0 | 1644 | | | | | | | | | | | | |
| 1 | | 585 | 138 | 10 | 3 | | | | | | | | |
| 2 | | 347 | 174 | 29 | 3 | 1 | | | | | | | |
| 3 | | 230 | 147 | 42 | 4 | 1 | | | | | | | |
| 4 | | 136 | 133 | 53 | 14 | 3 | | | | | | | |
| 5 | | 100 | 100 | 46 | 19 | 7 | | | | | | | |
| 6 | | 82 | 67 | 45 | 22 | 7 | | | | | | | |
| 7 | | 64 | 58 | 44 | 16 | 5 | 1 | | | | | | |
| 8 | | 50 | 49 | 41 | 13 | 2 | 2 | 1 | | | | | |
| 9 | | 29 | 44 | 27 | 13 | 3 | 1 | 1 | | | | | |
| 10 | | 20 | 37 | 19 | 18 | 4 | | | | | | | |
| 11 | | 22 | 25 | 24 | 15 | 4 | | | | | | | |
| 12 | | 18 | 23 | 18 | 15 | 7 | 1 | | | | | | |
| 13 | | 16 | 20 | 18 | 14 | 6 | 3 | | | | | | |
| 14 | | 10 | 21 | 19 | 10 | 6 | 2 | | | | | | |
| 15 | | 11 | 22 | 15 | 6 | 4 | 2 | | | | | | |
| 16 | | 14 | 17 | 14 | 6 | 4 | 1 | | 1 | | | | |
| 17 | | 11 | 11 | 20 | 5 | 2 | | | 2 | | | | |
| 18 | | 7 | 16 | 15 | 4 | 2 | 2 | | | | | | |
| 19 | | 8 | 12 | 16 | 4 | 2 | 1 | | | | | | |
| 20 | | 14 | 12 | 8 | 3 | 3 | | | | | | | |
| 21 | | 11 | 12 | 5 | 5 | 2 | | | | | | | |
| 22 | | 4 | 12 | 4 | 2 | 1 | | | | | | | |
| 23 | | 5 | 10 | 3 | 2 | 1 | | | | | | | |
| 24 | | 37 | 72 | 52 | 10 | 1 | | | | | | | |

*Source:* Barclay Hedge, Newedge Prime Brokerage Research.

**EXHIBIT 7.14B**   Number of Six-Month Return Observations

| Months | Depth | | | | | | | | | | | | |
|---|---|---|---|---|---|---|---|---|---|---|---|---|---|
| | 0 | −0.05 | −0.10 | −0.15 | −0.20 | −0.25 | −0.30 | −0.35 | −0.40 | −0.45 | −0.50 | −0.55 | −0.60 |
| 0 | 281 | | | | | | | | | | | | |
| 1 | | 121 | 13 | 2 | | | | | | | | | |
| 2 | | 38 | 27 | 2 | | | | | | | | | |
| 3 | | 67 | 34 | 7 | | | | | | | | | |
| 4 | | 24 | 19 | 9 | 5 | | | | | | | | |
| 5 | | 17 | 17 | 4 | 1 | | | | | | | | |
| 6 | | 20 | 7 | 7 | 7 | 1 | | | | | | | |
| 7 | | 9 | 5 | 3 | 2 | | | | | | | | |
| 8 | | 9 | 6 | 3 | | | | | | | | | |
| 9 | | 3 | 10 | 5 | 3 | | | | 1 | | | | |
| 10 | | 4 | 5 | 5 | 3 | | | | | | | | |
| 11 | | 3 | 4 | 3 | | | | | | | | | |
| 12 | | 4 | 5 | 5 | 7 | 2 | | | | | | | |
| 13 | | 3 | 2 | 2 | 4 | 1 | | | | | | | |
| 14 | | 1 | | | | | | | | | | | |
| 15 | | 3 | 7 | 5 | | | | | | | | | |
| 16 | | 1 | 5 | 3 | 1 | 1 | 1 | | | | | | |
| 17 | | | | 1 | | | | | | | | | |
| 18 | | 2 | 5 | 4 | 2 | | 1 | | | | | | |
| 19 | | 1 | 2 | 1 | 1 | | | | | | | | |
| 20 | | 1 | | | | | | | | | | | |
| 21 | | 4 | 2 | | 2 | | | | | | | | |
| 22 | | 1 | 2 | 1 | | | | | | | | | |
| 23 | | 1 | | | | | | | | | | | |
| 24 | | 8 | 12 | 7 | 2 | 1 | | | | | | | |

*Source:* Barclay Hedge, Newedge Prime Brokerage Research.

with returns and drawdowns and so would fall within the range of normal business experience. Once we are outside of the 95 percent region, we are dealing with just a very few data points, and in some cases, with returns that were generated by only one or perhaps two managers.

## Conclusion

The question we have tackled here is whether there is any evidence that managers' returns are conditional on past performance. So far, everything we have done suggests that they are not. Autocorrelations of returns seem to be randomly distributed around zero. Runs of gains and losses seem to be roughly what one would expect from serially independent returns. And this apparent randomness carried through into those exercises in which we looked at actual return distributions that were conditioned on past returns, on strings of consecutive gains and losses, and on depth and length of drawdown. Even though we have organized the data systematically, those instances in which we find results that appear to be statistically significant are so few that they are nearly anecdotal.

We did not come away completely empty handed, though. We learned something useful about the dangers of using overlapping data. And with this lesson came the insight that we really have very little data with which to work, even with 11 years of monthly return data. As a result, some of the questions that people have posed, especially those that entail long investment horizons, almost certainly cannot be answered with the data we have at hand.

We do plan to tackle the questions of how volatility and correlation might be related to past performance, although the data challenges are more severe with volatility and correlation than they are with returns. At the same time, gaining insights into volatility and correlation is at least as important to portfolio construction as insight into returns, so the effort should be rewarding.

### Empirical Update

The exhibits in this chapter were prepared using a data set that covered the years from 2001 through 2004. The purpose of this empirical update is to see how some of the more important results held up when tested against a longer and more up-to-date set of data. In particular, the data we used for these updated exhibits include monthly returns for 54 managers who, as of December 2009, had a 10-year track record, $100 M in AUM, and used futures as their primary investment instrument. For these exhibits we use the 10 years of returns from January 2000 through December 2009.

Exhibit 7.15 is an updated version of the lower panel of Exhibit 7.8 and is the result of a lead/lag exercise in order to detect the presence of serial correlation in a manager's return series. The table displays the fraction of z-values greater than 2.0, which would indicate a level of statistical significance. When compared to the original set of results, we find the evidence of autocorrelation has decreased. The number of lead/lag combinations with fractional z-value scores greater than 2.0 has decreased as has their magnitude.

In Exhibit 7.16, which is an updated version of the lower panel of Exhibit 7.9, we display the results from an updated runs test to detect evidence of serial independence. In this exhibit, the white circle represents the expected number of runs given the manager's number of gains and losses. The gray line represents two standard deviations on either side of the mean while the diamond symbolizes the observed number of runs. When compared with the original results, nothing much has changed. The number of observed runs is greater than expected in some cases and less in others. Furthermore, only 2 of the 54 observations are outside of the two-standard-deviation band.

Exhibit 7.17 is an updated version of the bottom panel of Exhibit 7.11 and shows the results of a six-month lead/lag exercise where we compare six-month manager returns to their returns over the previous six-months. In this exhibit, the past six months' return is displayed on the x-axis and the forward six months' return is shown on the y-axis. The circle represents the average forward return conditional on the past return. The solid black line displays the minimum and maximum returns while the shaded bar represents a two-standard-deviation band around the mean. The red line indicates the unconditional mean over the entire period. When compared to the original work, we continue to see a lack of relationship between past and future six-month returns. The conditional observations fall slightly above/below the unconditional mean with no regularity.

Finally, in Exhibit 7.18, which is an updated version of Exhibit 7.12, we display forward returns conditional on a series of consecutive gains or losses. The upper panel shows one-month returns while the lower panel shows six-month returns. As in the previous work, the patterns of randomness still hold true. It is difficult to find anything in these charts that would lead investors to believe they had a higher probability of achieving a return in excess of the unconditional mean return. (See Exhibits 7.19 on page 179 and 7.20 on page 180).

**EXHIBIT 7.15** Autocorrelations of Compound Monthly Returns (Fraction of Z-Values Greater Than 2.0)

Monthly for Barclay 54 Managers (2000–2009)

| Lead | 1 | 2 | 3 | 4 | 5 | 6 | 7 | 8 | 9 | 10 | 11 | 12 |
|---|---|---|---|---|---|---|---|---|---|---|---|---|
| 1 | 0.11 | 0.02 | 0 | 0 | 0 | 0 | 0 | 0 | 0 | 0 | 0 | 0 |
| 2 | 0.02 | 0.04 | 0 | 0 | 0 | 0.02 | 0 | 0 | 0 | 0 | 0 | 0 |
| 3 | 0 | 0 | 0 | 0 | 0.04 | 0.04 | 0.02 | 0 | 0 | 0 | 0 | 0 |
| 4 | 0 | 0 | 0 | 0.07 | 0.05 | 0.04 | 0.02 | 0 | 0 | 0 | 0 | 0 |
| 5 | 0 | 0 | 0.04 | 0.05 | 0.04 | 0.04 | 0.02 | 0.02 | 0 | 0 | 0 | 0 |
| 6 | 0 | 0.02 | 0.04 | 0.04 | 0.04 | 0.04 | 0.02 | 0 | 0 | 0 | 0 | 0 |
| 7 | 0 | 0 | 0.02 | 0.02 | 0.02 | 0.02 | 0.02 | 0 | 0 | 0 | 0 | 0 |
| 8 | 0 | 0 | 0 | 0 | 0.02 | 0 | 0 | 0 | 0 | 0 | 0 | 0 |
| 9 | 0 | 0 | 0 | 0 | 0 | 0 | 0 | 0 | 0 | 0 | 0 | 0 |
| 10 | 0 | 0 | 0 | 0 | 0 | 0 | 0 | 0 | 0 | 0 | 0 | 0 |
| 11 | 0 | 0 | 0 | 0 | 0 | 0 | 0 | 0 | 0 | 0 | 0 | 0 |
| 12 | 0 | 0 | 0 | 0 | 0 | 0 | 0 | 0 | 0 | 0 | 0 | 0 |

*Source:* Barclay Hedge.

**EXHIBIT 7.16** Runs of Gains and Losses (Monthly, January 2000–December 2009)

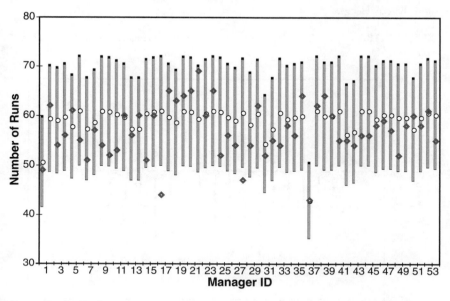

*Source:* Barclay Hedge.

**EXHIBIT 7.17** Six-Month Lead/Six-Month Lag (54 Managers, 2000–2009; Standard Error Bands, Non-Overlapping)

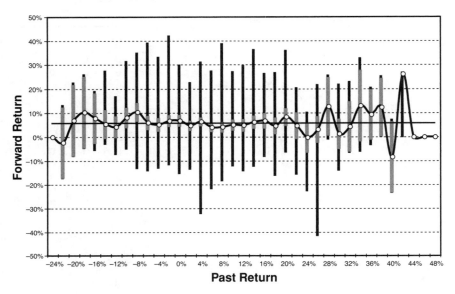

*Source:* Barclay Hedge.

**EXHIBIT 7.18A** One-Month Returns versus Consecutive Gains or Losses (54 Managers, 2000–2009)

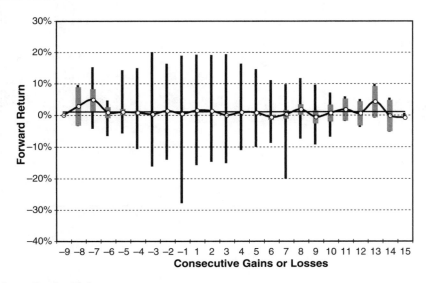

*Source:* Barclay Hedge.

**EXHIBIT 7.18B**   Six-Month Returns versus Consecutive Gains or Losses (54 Managers, 2000–2009)

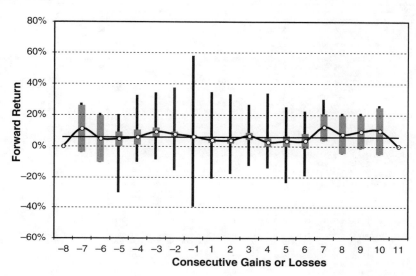

*Source:* Barclay Hedge.

**EXHIBIT 7.19**   Autocorrelation of Daily Returns (January 2001–December 2004)

| Manager or Strategy | | 1 | 2 | 3 | 4 | 5 | 6 | 7 | 8 | 9 | 10 | 11 | 12 | 13 | 14 | 15 | 16 | 17 | 18 | 19 | 20 | 21 | 22 | 23 | 24 |
|---|---|---|---|---|---|---|---|---|---|---|---|---|---|---|---|---|---|---|---|---|---|---|---|---|---|
| | CFB Composite | 0.01 | 0.01 | 0.00 | 0.05 | 0.02 | -0.03 | 0.02 | 0.02 | 0.00 | -0.03 | -0.05 | 0.03 | 0.01 | 0.04 | -0.04 | 0.01 | 0.03 | 0.00 | -0.03 | -0.03 | 0.01 | -0.02 | -0.01 | 0.06 |
| | 1 | 0.00 | 0.01 | 0.01 | 0.06 | 0.01 | -0.01 | 0.01 | 0.07 | -0.02 | 0.00 | -0.02 | 0.02 | 0.02 | 0.01 | -0.02 | 0.01 | 0.02 | -0.02 | 0.01 | -0.03 | 0.02 | -0.04 | -0.01 | 0.06 |
| | 2 | -0.06 | -0.07 | 0.03 | 0.02 | 0.01 | 0.02 | 0.01 | -0.05 | 0.04 | 0.03 | -0.05 | 0.08 | 0.03 | -0.04 | -0.06 | 0.06 | -0.02 | -0.04 | -0.01 | -0.08 | -0.03 | 0.04 | -0.03 | 0.00 |
| | 3 | -0.02 | -0.02 | -0.01 | 0.01 | -0.02 | -0.02 | -0.02 | 0.07 | -0.01 | 0.00 | -0.08 | 0.01 | 0.02 | 0.06 | -0.05 | 0.07 | 0.04 | -0.01 | -0.05 | -0.03 | -0.03 | -0.03 | 0.06 | 0.07 |
| | 4 | 0.05 | 0.02 | 0.01 | 0.04 | -0.02 | 0.01 | 0.03 | 0.01 | 0.02 | -0.07 | -0.04 | -0.01 | -0.01 | -0.01 | 0.00 | 0.05 | -0.01 | 0.03 | -0.05 | -0.07 | -0.03 | 0.00 | 0.02 | 0.03 |
| CFB 13 and Composite | 5 | 0.09 | 0.02 | -0.01 | 0.00 | 0.03 | 0.06 | 0.05 | -0.01 | 0.10 | 0.02 | 0.03 | 0.01 | -0.03 | -0.04 | 0.01 | 0.03 | -0.03 | 0.01 | 0.01 | 0.00 | 0.00 | 0.03 | -0.03 | 0.02 |
| | 6 | 0.09 | -0.01 | 0.01 | 0.03 | -0.02 | -0.03 | -0.01 | -0.01 | 0.01 | -0.02 | -0.07 | -0.03 | 0.05 | 0.02 | -0.04 | -0.04 | 0.04 | 0.02 | -0.01 | -0.06 | -0.01 | 0.00 | -0.02 | 0.03 |
| | 7 | -0.05 | -0.02 | 0.00 | 0.01 | 0.02 | 0.02 | -0.02 | 0.01 | 0.00 | 0.01 | -0.03 | 0.07 | -0.02 | 0.01 | -0.01 | -0.04 | 0.03 | -0.02 | -0.02 | 0.01 | 0.01 | -0.03 | -0.06 | 0.04 |
| | 8 | 0.09 | 0.04 | 0.03 | 0.00 | 0.00 | 0.04 | -0.02 | 0.01 | 0.03 | -0.07 | -0.03 | -0.08 | 0.02 | 0.07 | 0.00 | -0.04 | 0.04 | -0.03 | -0.03 | -0.03 | 0.02 | 0.04 | -0.03 | 0.03 |
| | 9 | -0.04 | -0.03 | 0.03 | 0.04 | 0.04 | -0.01 | -0.01 | 0.05 | 0.00 | 0.00 | -0.05 | -0.01 | 0.00 | 0.03 | -0.02 | 0.06 | -0.01 | -0.01 | 0.02 | 0.03 | -0.02 | -0.01 | 0.05 | 0.00 |
| | 10 | -0.03 | -0.03 | 0.02 | 0.04 | -0.04 | 0.04 | 0.00 | 0.03 | 0.01 | 0.01 | -0.06 | 0.03 | 0.00 | -0.01 | -0.01 | 0.01 | 0.00 | -0.02 | 0.03 | 0.02 | 0.03 | 0.01 | 0.01 | 0.09 |
| | 11 | 0.00 | -0.02 | -0.02 | 0.03 | 0.03 | 0.01 | -0.01 | -0.01 | -0.01 | -0.02 | -0.04 | 0.06 | -0.01 | -0.01 | -0.03 | 0.02 | 0.04 | -0.02 | -0.02 | 0.05 | 0.03 | 0.01 | -0.01 | 0.05 |
| | 12 | 0.04 | -0.03 | -0.07 | 0.03 | 0.02 | -0.01 | 0.01 | 0.08 | 0.04 | -0.03 | -0.07 | 0.00 | 0.01 | 0.00 | -0.06 | 0.02 | 0.05 | 0.00 | 0.00 | -0.02 | -0.01 | 0.01 | 0.00 | 0.10 |
| | 13 | -0.02 | 0.01 | 0.01 | 0.05 | 0.01 | 0.03 | 0.01 | -0.01 | 0.00 | -0.04 | 0.00 | 0.04 | 0.03 | 0.02 | -0.02 | 0.01 | -0.04 | -0.02 | -0.05 | -0.01 | -0.04 | 0.01 | -0.01 | 0.06 |
| | 15 | 0.04 | 0.00 | -0.03 | 0.03 | -0.04 | -0.01 | 0.02 | 0.05 | -0.01 | 0.01 | -0.01 | 0.00 | -0.03 | -0.03 | 0.02 | 0.01 | -0.02 | -0.02 | 0.02 | 0.06 | 0.03 | 0.04 | -0.04 | 0.06 |
| | 16 | 0.01 | 0.03 | -0.01 | 0.05 | -0.02 | -0.02 | 0.02 | 0.05 | -0.05 | -0.04 | -0.03 | 0.03 | 0.01 | 0.02 | 0.05 | 0.04 | -0.01 | 0.00 | -0.04 | -0.06 | -0.01 | -0.02 | 0.04 | 0.05 |
| CF Generic | 17 | 0.01 | -0.03 | 0.01 | 0.05 | 0.01 | -0.03 | 0.01 | 0.06 | -0.03 | -0.05 | -0.04 | 0.05 | 0.01 | 0.02 | -0.04 | 0.04 | 0.02 | -0.03 | -0.01 | -0.04 | -0.03 | 0.01 | 0.04 | 0.05 |
| | 18 | 0.02 | 0.04 | -0.01 | 0.06 | 0.01 | -0.05 | -0.02 | 0.02 | 0.02 | -0.03 | -0.02 | -0.04 | 0.00 | -0.02 | 0.01 | -0.04 | -0.02 | 0.00 | -0.02 | -0.01 | 0.03 | 0.00 | 0.06 | |
| | 19 | 0.03 | 0.03 | 0.00 | 0.05 | -0.03 | -0.01 | 0.03 | 0.04 | -0.04 | -0.06 | -0.02 | 0.05 | 0.04 | 0.02 | 0.02 | 0.03 | 0.00 | 0.00 | -0.02 | -0.04 | -0.02 | -0.02 | 0.05 | 0.05 |
| | 20 | 0.01 | -0.03 | 0.03 | 0.04 | 0.01 | -0.01 | 0.01 | 0.01 | -0.04 | -0.07 | -0.03 | 0.04 | 0.05 | 0.02 | -0.05 | 0.00 | 0.02 | -0.03 | 0.00 | -0.05 | -0.03 | 0.00 | 0.04 | 0.03 |
| | Mean | 0.00 | 0.00 | 0.00 | 0.00 | 0.00 | 0.00 | 0.00 | 0.00 | 0.00 | 0.00 | 0.00 | 0.00 | 0.00 | 0.00 | 0.00 | 0.00 | 0.00 | 0.00 | 0.00 | 0.00 | 0.00 | 0.00 | 0.00 | 0.00 |
| | StDev | 0.04 | 0.03 | 0.02 | 0.02 | 0.02 | 0.03 | 0.02 | 0.03 | 0.03 | 0.03 | 0.03 | 0.04 | 0.02 | 0.03 | 0.03 | 0.03 | 0.02 | 0.02 | 0.02 | 0.04 | 0.02 | 0.03 | 0.03 | 0.03 |

*Source:* Barclay Hedge, Newedge Prime Brokerage Research.

**EXHIBIT 7.20**   Autocorrelation of Monthly Returns (January 1994–December 2004)

| Manager or Strategy | 1 | 2 | 3 | 4 | 5 | 6 | 7 | 8 | 9 | 10 | 11 | 12 | 13 | 14 | 15 | 16 | 17 | 18 | 19 | 20 | 21 | 22 | 23 | 24 |
|---|---|---|---|---|---|---|---|---|---|---|---|---|---|---|---|---|---|---|---|---|---|---|---|---|
| 1 | -0.07 | -0.18 | -0.10 | 0.01 | -0.06 | -0.05 | 0.05 | -0.09 | 0.12 | 0.02 | 0.07 | -0.06 | -0.03 | -0.04 | -0.11 | 0.02 | 0.07 | 0.14 | -0.03 | -0.08 | 0.08 | 0.08 | 0.01 | -0.14 |
| 2 | 0.12 | 0.01 | 0.18 | 0.06 | 0.10 | -0.09 | 0.09 | 0.19 | -0.04 | 0.01 | -0.02 | 0.08 | 0.11 | -0.08 | 0.09 | 0.08 | -0.21 | 0.06 | 0.00 | 0.12 | -0.09 | -0.08 | 0.08 | 0.04 |
| 3 | -0.12 | -0.09 | 0.15 | -0.15 | -0.14 | 0.12 | -0.05 | 0.07 | -0.02 | -0.11 | -0.02 | 0.24 | 0.02 | -0.08 | 0.22 | -0.18 | -0.07 | 0.19 | 0.02 | 0.01 | 0.03 | -0.06 | -0.06 | -0.02 |
| 4 | 0.00 | -0.05 | -0.09 | -0.01 | -0.09 | -0.10 | -0.06 | 0.00 | 0.28 | 0.07 | -0.06 | -0.03 | 0.01 | -0.13 | -0.06 | 0.01 | 0.17 | 0.03 | 0.17 | -0.04 | 0.01 | -0.04 | -0.01 | -0.20 |
| 5 | -0.12 | 0.02 | 0.14 | -0.01 | -0.06 | 0.13 | -0.08 | -0.10 | 0.02 | -0.12 | 0.10 | -0.14 | -0.06 | -0.14 | -0.07 | -0.04 | -0.01 | -0.02 | -0.01 | -0.00 | -0.09 | 0.10 | 0.06 | 0.01 |
| 6 | 0.04 | 0.11 | -0.07 | -0.14 | 0.03 | 0.00 | 0.13 | 0.05 | -0.02 | 0.14 | 0.09 | 0.01 | -0.04 | 0.07 | 0.04 | 0.13 | 0.06 | 0.08 | -0.05 | -0.19 | -0.11 | -0.00 | -0.05 | 0.02 |
| 7 | -0.03 | -0.01 | -0.02 | -0.15 | -0.03 | -0.03 | -0.03 | 0.02 | 0.01 | 0.18 | 0.15 | -0.12 | -0.04 | -0.04 | -0.03 | -0.03 | -0.10 | 0.13 | 0.16 | 0.03 | 0.11 | -0.17 | -0.08 | -0.10 |
| 8 | -0.05 | -0.10 | -0.03 | -0.14 | -0.11 | -0.10 | -0.02 | 0.00 | 0.12 | 0.12 | 0.14 | -0.18 | -0.04 | -0.02 | -0.09 | -0.04 | -0.06 | 0.16 | 0.13 | 0.02 | 0.07 | -0.12 | -0.06 | -0.04 |
| 9 | 0.04 | -0.05 | 0.08 | -0.08 | -0.06 | -0.04 | 0.05 | 0.08 | 0.14 | 0.04 | 0.15 | 0.01 | -0.20 | -0.09 | -0.11 | -0.09 | 0.07 | 0.10 | -0.03 | 0.11 | 0.02 | -0.09 | 0.02 | -0.16 |
| 10 | -0.08 | -0.10 | -0.04 | -0.09 | -0.00 | -0.05 | -0.11 | -0.06 | 0.02 | 0.06 | 0.06 | 0.01 | 0.08 | -0.14 | -0.01 | 0.04 | -0.05 | 0.14 | 0.15 | -0.19 | 0.06 | 0.05 | -0.00 | -0.01 |
| 11 | 0.06 | -0.05 | 0.09 | 0.09 | -0.01 | -0.02 | -0.06 | 0.01 | 0.11 | 0.07 | -0.11 | -0.09 | 0.11 | -0.03 | -0.04 | -0.03 | -0.05 | 0.01 | 0.21 | -0.03 | -0.01 | 0.09 | 0.15 | -0.01 |
| 12 | 0.07 | -0.15 | 0.07 | -0.02 | -0.16 | -0.02 | 0.09 | -0.04 | -0.04 | 0.17 | 0.09 | -0.07 | 0.16 | 0.04 | -0.01 | 0.08 | 0.01 | -0.01 | 0.06 | 0.04 | -0.02 | -0.07 | 0.08 | 0.11 |
| 13 | -0.09 | -0.07 | -0.07 | 0.15 | -0.01 | 0.01 | -0.03 | 0.09 | -0.13 | 0.10 | 0.11 | -0.02 | -0.06 | 0.17 | 0.11 | 0.05 | 0.15 | 0.06 | -0.09 | -0.02 | 0.16 | -0.04 | 0.02 | -0.01 |
| 14 | -0.01 | -0.05 | -0.11 | -0.11 | -0.05 | -0.01 | -0.14 | 0.09 | 0.08 | 0.11 | -0.02 | 0.04 | -0.09 | -0.05 | -0.11 | -0.14 | -0.13 | 0.14 | 0.08 | 0.16 | 0.09 | -0.06 | 0.01 | -0.09 |
| 15 | 0.15 | 0.02 | -0.10 | -0.16 | 0.00 | -0.07 | -0.10 | 0.01 | 0.02 | 0.07 | -0.01 | -0.03 | -0.04 | 0.07 | -0.06 | -0.12 | -0.06 | 0.05 | 0.16 | 0.16 | 0.02 | 0.02 | 0.05 | -0.10 |
| 16 | 0.02 | -0.00 | -0.07 | -0.11 | -0.11 | 0.09 | -0.04 | 0.03 | 0.05 | 0.12 | 0.22 | -0.06 | -0.07 | -0.08 | -0.16 | -0.13 | 0.01 | 0.01 | 0.17 | 0.00 | 0.10 | 0.01 | -0.04 | -0.05 |
| 17 | 0.06 | -0.04 | 0.02 | -0.15 | -0.13 | 0.04 | -0.01 | 0.05 | 0.08 | 0.03 | -0.01 | -0.04 | -0.11 | -0.12 | -0.00 | -0.04 | 0.02 | 0.06 | 0.14 | 0.03 | 0.05 | -0.17 | -0.16 | -0.08 |
| 18 | 0.11 | -0.14 | -0.06 | -0.21 | -0.15 | 0.08 | -0.01 | -0.03 | 0.01 | -0.02 | -0.06 | 0.00 | 0.04 | -0.19 | -0.11 | -0.10 | -0.01 | 0.20 | 0.15 | -0.02 | 0.11 | -0.05 | -0.02 | -0.01 |
| 19 | 0.00 | -0.05 | -0.01 | -0.13 | -0.12 | -0.17 | -0.08 | 0.15 | 0.08 | 0.10 | -0.02 | -0.08 | 0.00 | -0.10 | 0.02 | 0.00 | -0.14 | 0.16 | 0.06 | -0.05 | 0.04 | -0.07 | 0.03 | -0.09 |
| 20 | 0.04 | -0.14 | -0.02 | -0.01 | -0.01 | -0.09 | -0.21 | -0.05 | -0.09 | -0.01 | 0.09 | 0.12 | -0.07 | 0.07 | 0.17 | -0.03 | -0.06 | 0.07 | 0.01 | -0.19 | -0.00 | 0.04 | -0.00 | -0.03 |
| 21 | -0.08 | -0.13 | -0.23 | 0.06 | 0.22 | -0.05 | 0.00 | -0.11 | 0.12 | 0.08 | -0.18 | -0.09 | -0.02 | 0.01 | 0.00 | 0.06 | 0.01 | -0.02 | -0.17 | -0.01 | 0.00 | 0.13 | 0.02 | -0.07 |
| 22 | -0.11 | -0.00 | 0.12 | -0.06 | -0.16 | 0.18 | -0.19 | -0.05 | 0.03 | -0.07 | 0.10 | -0.02 | 0.10 | -0.01 | -0.06 | 0.24 | 0.06 | -0.03 | 0.03 | 0.08 | -0.01 | 0.02 | -0.03 |  |
| 23 | 0.08 | 0.04 | 0.02 | 0.13 | -0.05 | -0.11 | -0.07 | 0.12 | -0.07 | -0.16 | 0.05 | -0.20 | -0.07 | -0.10 | -0.01 | -0.08 | 0.01 | -0.11 | -0.01 | -0.05 | -0.13 | 0.12 | 0.05 | 0.04 |
| 24 | 0.27 | -0.04 | -0.06 | -0.15 | -0.13 | -0.15 | -0.11 | 0.06 | 0.16 | 0.12 | -0.02 | -0.09 | -0.17 | -0.19 | -0.18 | -0.11 | 0.04 | 0.19 | 0.23 | 0.18 | 0.02 | -0.03 | -0.08 | -0.23 |
| 25 | 0.17 | -0.13 | -0.22 | -0.17 | 0.12 | 0.09 | -0.09 | 0.02 | 0.04 | 0.12 | 0.06 | -0.01 | -0.04 | 0.01 | -0.09 | -0.12 | -0.21 | 0.01 | 0.09 | 0.09 | -0.07 | -0.14 | -0.02 | 0.11 |
| 26 | 0.14 | -0.08 | -0.09 | -0.03 | -0.07 | -0.13 | -0.07 | -0.03 | 0.09 | 0.08 | -0.02 | -0.03 | -0.12 | -0.15 | -0.12 | 0.03 | 0.01 | 0.01 | 0.09 | 0.05 | -0.03 | 0.01 | 0.02 | -0.09 |
| 27 | 0.13 | -0.05 | -0.05 | -0.01 | -0.05 | -0.19 | -0.09 | 0.07 | 0.12 | -0.01 | -0.04 | -0.01 | -0.06 | -0.01 | -0.04 | -0.08 | 0.08 | 0.14 | 0.11 | 0.05 | 0.08 | -0.03 | 0.03 | -0.14 |
| 28 | 0.00 | -0.11 | 0.08 | -0.13 | 0.02 | -0.06 | -0.01 | -0.02 | 0.03 | 0.02 | -0.07 | -0.03 | -0.02 | -0.19 | -0.02 | -0.03 | -0.14 | 0.24 | 0.11 | 0.06 | 0.16 | -0.12 | 0.10 | -0.18 |
| 29 | 0.03 | -0.02 | -0.04 | -0.16 | -0.10 | -0.06 | -0.05 | -0.01 | 0.03 | 0.16 | -0.07 | -0.00 | -0.04 | -0.24 | 0.00 | -0.01 | 0.20 | 0.09 | 0.00 | -0.01 | -0.14 | -0.02 | -0.11 |  |
| 30 | 0.06 | -0.08 | 0.09 | 0.03 | -0.00 | 0.03 | -0.08 | -0.15 | -0.05 | -0.05 | -0.05 | 0.09 | -0.01 | -0.06 | -0.01 | 0.06 | 0.02 | 0.01 | -0.18 | 0.00 | 0.00 | -0.10 | 0.01 | -0.16 |
| 31 | 0.08 | -0.13 | -0.09 | -0.12 | 0.02 | 0.15 | -0.03 | 0.02 | 0.04 | 0.04 | -0.01 | 0.03 | 0.09 | 0.08 | 0.05 | -0.06 | -0.01 | 0.03 | -0.01 | 0.01 | 0.04 | -0.07 | 0.24 | 0.00 |
| 32 | 0.12 | -0.11 | -0.01 | -0.24 | -0.01 | -0.02 | -0.13 | 0.10 | 0.11 | 0.06 | 0.11 | -0.03 | 0.01 | -0.11 | -0.21 | -0.19 | -0.09 | 0.16 | 0.33 | -0.08 | 0.07 | -0.01 | -0.07 | -0.07 |
| 33 | 0.15 | 0.02 | 0.06 | -0.17 | 0.06 | -0.04 | 0.03 | -0.02 | -0.08 | 0.01 | 0.06 | 0.16 | 0.05 | 0.13 | 0.06 | 0.03 | -0.06 | -0.19 | -0.04 | -0.14 | -0.00 | 0.06 | 0.05 | 0.10 |
| 34 | -0.07 | -0.05 | 0.04 | -0.16 | 0.04 | 0.00 | 0.05 | -0.04 | 0.06 | 0.02 | 0.09 | -0.04 | -0.07 | -0.03 | -0.10 | -0.02 | -0.14 | 0.26 | 0.08 | 0.01 | 0.11 | -0.01 | -0.12 | -0.01 |
| 35 | 0.01 | -0.15 | -0.04 | -0.09 | -0.08 | -0.14 | -0.00 | -0.05 | 0.12 | 0.03 | -0.08 | 0.04 | -0.03 | -0.12 | -0.12 | 0.08 | 0.06 | 0.14 | 0.06 | 0.12 | 0.01 | -0.14 | -0.22 |  |
| 36 | 0.09 | -0.32 | -0.13 | 0.03 | 0.13 | 0.01 | -0.01 | -0.09 | 0.16 | -0.02 | -0.13 | 0.06 | 0.01 | -0.06 | -0.09 | -0.09 | -0.02 | 0.07 | 0.21 | -0.05 | -0.06 | 0.14 | 0.03 | -0.08 |
| 37 | 0.05 | -0.28 | -0.14 | 0.10 | 0.08 | -0.11 | -0.13 | -0.09 | 0.23 | 0.07 | -0.14 | -0.03 | 0.07 | -0.06 | -0.09 | 0.03 | -0.01 | 0.13 | 0.18 | -0.16 | 0.04 | 0.12 | 0.08 | -0.13 |
| 38 | -0.01 | -0.19 | -0.03 | -0.04 | 0.00 | 0.12 | -0.16 | -0.04 | 0.13 | 0.13 | -0.00 | -0.14 | 0.15 | -0.07 | -0.02 | 0.03 | 0.01 | -0.03 | 0.19 | 0.02 | -0.05 | -0.01 | 0.06 | -0.04 |
| 39 | 0.13 | 0.03 | -0.02 | -0.15 | -0.29 | -0.04 | -0.04 | 0.13 | 0.12 | 0.11 | -0.06 | 0.01 | -0.09 | 0.00 | 0.00 | -0.08 | -0.02 | -0.08 | 0.01 | -0.07 | 0.08 | 0.16 | 0.16 |  |
| 40 | -0.01 | -0.14 | -0.04 | -0.04 | -0.02 | -0.12 | -0.06 | 0.04 | 0.16 | -0.06 | -0.12 | -0.03 | 0.04 | -0.09 | -0.17 | -0.01 | -0.08 | 0.13 | 0.09 | 0.08 | 0.12 | 0.04 | -0.04 | 0.01 |
| 41 | -0.08 | -0.03 | 0.03 | -0.19 | 0.06 | -0.18 | -0.03 | 0.06 | 0.09 | 0.03 | -0.01 | -0.12 | -0.09 | -0.14 | 0.07 | -0.06 | 0.12 | 0.20 | -0.09 | 0.12 | -0.00 | -0.05 | 0.00 |  |
| 42 | 0.06 | -0.04 | 0.13 | -0.19 | -0.08 | 0.03 | -0.01 | 0.11 | 0.12 | 0.14 | 0.00 | 0.01 | -0.05 | -0.17 | 0.06 | 0.02 | -0.01 | 0.14 | 0.07 | 0.08 | 0.21 | 0.01 | -0.01 | -0.10 |
| 43 | 0.03 | -0.10 | -0.03 | -0.08 | 0.06 | -0.07 | -0.08 | 0.03 | 0.08 | 0.12 | 0.13 | -0.04 | 0.05 | -0.14 | 0.01 | -0.02 | 0.08 | 0.07 | 0.10 | 0.07 | 0.00 | -0.06 | -0.02 | -0.03 |
| CF Generic 1 | 0.02 | -0.05 | -0.06 | -0.25 | 0.00 | -0.08 | -0.01 | -0.02 | 0.03 | 0.10 | -0.07 | 0.04 | 0.05 | -0.13 | 0.11 | -0.08 | -0.03 | 0.09 | 0.04 | -0.02 | 0.01 | 0.04 | -0.03 | -0.09 |
| CF Generic 2 | -0.02 | -0.12 | -0.04 | -0.04 | -0.09 | -0.16 | -0.11 | 0.06 | 0.04 | 0.08 | 0.03 | 0.00 | -0.04 | -0.22 | -0.03 | 0.01 | 0.04 | 0.05 | 0.00 | -0.01 | 0.10 | -0.03 | 0.06 | -0.01 |
| CF Generic 3 | 0.02 | -0.14 | -0.03 | -0.02 | -0.09 | -0.20 | -0.05 | 0.15 | -0.06 | 0.01 | 0.04 | 0.15 | 0.02 | -0.22 | 0.01 | 0.09 | -0.04 | 0.01 | -0.02 | 0.06 | 0.03 | -0.01 | 0.07 | -0.12 |
| CF Generic 4 | 0.02 | 0.00 | -0.01 | -0.22 | -0.00 | -0.06 | -0.10 | 0.02 | 0.06 | 0.21 | -0.02 | 0.05 | 0.07 | -0.19 | -0.05 | -0.05 | -0.14 | 0.18 | -0.03 | 0.04 | 0.10 | -0.08 | 0.19 | -0.21 |
| CF Generic 5 | -0.02 | -0.07 | -0.03 | 0.07 | -0.10 | -0.24 | -0.08 | 0.07 | -0.06 | 0.02 | 0.07 | 0.04 | 0.13 | -0.15 | 0.01 | -0.06 | -0.02 | 0.00 | -0.02 | -0.06 | -0.02 | -0.03 | -0.02 | -0.03 |
| CF Generic 6 | -0.02 | -0.15 | -0.04 | 0.09 | -0.12 | -0.17 | -0.03 | 0.17 | 0.00 | -0.05 | -0.00 | 0.14 | -0.05 | -0.19 | 0.07 | -0.03 | -0.01 | 0.14 | 0.06 | 0.00 | -0.02 | -0.05 | -0.00 | -0.06 |
| Mean | 0.03 | -0.08 | -0.02 | -0.07 | -0.04 | -0.04 | -0.05 | 0.02 | 0.06 | 0.05 | 0.01 | -0.01 | -0.03 | -0.08 | -0.03 | -0.02 | -0.02 | 0.09 | 0.07 | 0.00 | 0.03 | -0.02 | 0.01 | -0.06 |
| StDev | 0.08 | 0.08 | 0.09 | 0.11 | 0.09 | 0.10 | 0.07 | 0.08 | 0.08 | 0.08 | 0.09 | 0.09 | 0.08 | 0.01 | 0.09 | 0.07 | 0.09 | 0.09 | 0.11 | 0.09 | 0.07 | 0.08 | 0.08 | 0.09 |

Rows 1–43 are grouped under *Barclay 43*; the final six rows are grouped under *CF Generic*.

*Source:* Barclay Hedge, Newedge Prime Brokerage Research.

# CHAPTER 8

# Understanding Drawdowns

Within the universe of hedge funds and CTAs, one of the most widely quoted measures of risk is *peak-to-trough drawdown*. Our experience suggests, however, that investors do not have a widely accepted way of forming expectations about just how much managers who are in business over long periods of time might be expected to lose. Rather, we find that investors tend to monitor a manager's worst or maximum drawdown with only informal or anecdotal information about the manager's average annual or previous year's returns. Drawdown as a measure of risk has failed to attract the same kind of research and attention that is devoted to other common measures such as return volatility, VaR, or Sharpe ratios.

Our purpose here is to show that it is possible to get a reasonable fix on what drawdown distributions should look like. This is no trivial problem. Any manager for whom the standard deviation of returns is large enough to produce a loss in any given investment period will experience drawdowns. Most managers are in drawdown most of the time. And managers who have been in business a long time may well have experienced more and bigger drawdowns than those with short track records.

If it is possible to predict how drawdowns should behave, then we can address two important kinds of questions.

1. Looking back over a manager's track record, does his drawdown history make sense? That is, do the frequency and size of his drawdowns look reasonable, and does his maximum drawdown accord with what we would expect?

2. Looking forward, what kinds of drawdowns should we expect over any given investment horizon? How many drawdowns should he experience? How big? How likely is it that his largest drawdown going forward will be greater than his maximum drawdown so far? And, if it is bigger, how much bigger?

What we show here is that the three most important determinants of drawdowns are length of track record, mean return, and volatility of returns. The acid test, we think, is that our simulated drawdown distributions do a very good job of explaining the kinds of drawdown patterns that CTAs have exhibited over the past 10 years.

### *Drawdown* Defined

Drawdown measures the change in the value of a portfolio from any newly established *peak* (or high-water mark) to a subsequent *trough* (or low-water mark).

One of the things that makes drawdowns interesting is that they depend so much on the sequence of a manager's returns. The usual summary statistics such as mean and volatility of returns reflect nothing of the sequence in which the returns occur. The sequence is critical, however, for drawdowns. Two managers with identical means and volatilities of returns can experience very different drawdowns.

In practice, a drawdown is defined as the percent change in a manager's net asset value from a high-water mark to the next low-water mark. A net asset value qualifies as a high-water mark if it is higher than any previous net asset value *and* if it is followed by a loss. Thus, points A and D in Exhibit 8.1 are high-water marks, but point C is not, even though net asset value at that point is higher than it has ever been. Point C is not a high-water mark because it is followed by a gain.

A net asset value qualifies as a low-water mark if it is the lowest net asset value between two high-water marks. Point B qualifies as a low-water mark. Or, if one is at the end of a data series, a low-water mark is simply the lowest net asset value following the last high-water mark. For example, point F, which follows the newly established high-water mark at E, would be a low-water mark for the purpose of calculating drawdowns even though the manager's net asset value has not yet reached a new high-water mark.

A manager's maximum drawdown is simply the largest of these drawdowns.

**EXHIBIT 8.1**   Net Asset Value History with Sample High- and Low-Water Marks

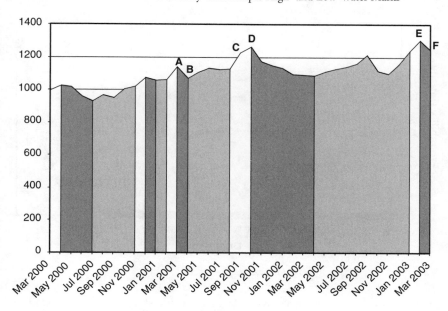

*Source:* Barclay Hedge, Newedge Prime Brokerage Research.

## What Should They Look Like?

Because realized drawdowns are the result of sequences of returns and depend entirely on the paths that a manager's net asset value can follow, the only practical way to discover what drawdowns should look like is to simulate as many net asset value paths as one needs to produce reasonable-looking distributions. In what follows, we have used Monte Carlo simulations in which we have controlled for the length of track record, the distribution of returns, deleveraging when in a drawdown, and survival. The resulting drawdown distributions have two basic shapes.

For a given return distribution and length of track record, the frequency and size of a manager's entire collection of drawdowns will look like the distribution shown in Exhibit 8.2. In this exhibit (and in all of our drawdown exhibits), we show drawdowns as negative percent changes, and so we see in Exhibit 8.2 a high frequency of small drawdowns and a small frequency of large drawdowns.

Also, even though any given manager can only have one worst drawdown, it still makes sense to think of the distribution from which that worst or

**EXHIBIT 8.2**   Distribution of All Drawdowns

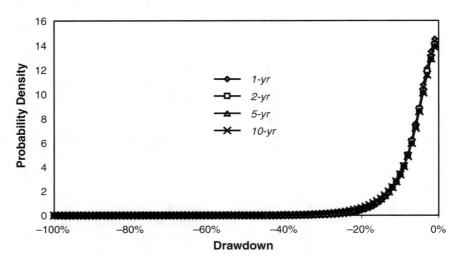

*Source:* Newedge Prime Brokerage Research.

maximum drawdown was drawn. Or, if we think of several managers, all of whom have the same or very similar track records and return characteristics, we can think about what the distribution of their various worst drawdowns should look like. An example of what the distribution of maximum drawdowns should look like is provided in Exhibit 8.3.

## What Forces Shape the Distributions?

In our simulations, we were able to control the return-generating process for most of the things that would seem to make sense. In particular, we controlled for:

- Length of track record
- Mean return
- Volatility of returns
- Skewness
- Kurtosis
- Deleveraging when in drawdown

Of these, the only three that have any empirical importance seem to be length of track record, mean return, and the volatility of returns. The rest

**EXHIBIT 8.3** Distribution of Maximum Drawdowns

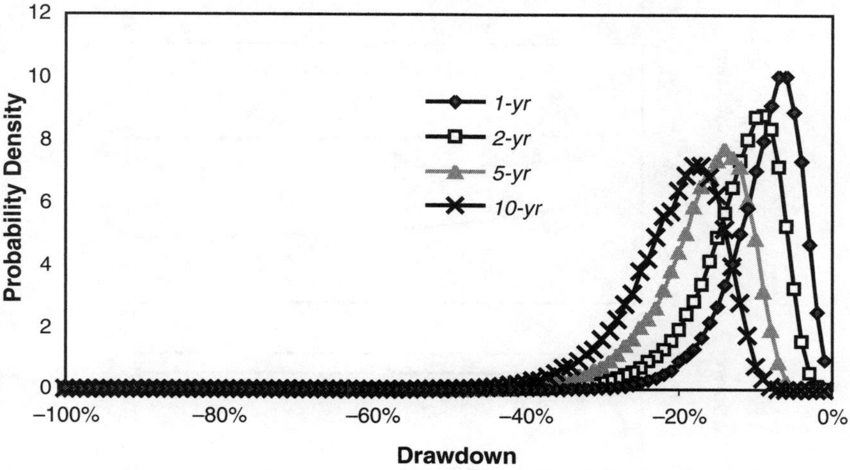

*Source:* Newedge Prime Brokerage Research.

tend not to matter much, in some cases because the effect of a change in the variable is small and in others because the range of the variable is small.

## The Distribution of All Drawdowns

From Exhibit 8.2, we can see that length of track record matters very little to the distribution of all drawdowns. In other words, the likelihood of experiencing a drawdown of any given size is largely independent of how long a manager is in business.

Mean return and the volatility of returns, however, matter a lot. Exhibit 8.4 shows a manager's average or expected drawdown versus length of track record for different values of the four key moments of the return distribution. In the top panel, for example, we have varied the manager's mean return while holding volatility, skewness, and excess kurtosis (xk) constant. And, as one would expect, higher mean returns lead to smaller expected drawdowns.

From the second panel in Exhibit 8.4, it is also apparent that the volatility of returns has a large influence over a manager's drawdowns. Higher volatility leads to larger expected drawdowns.

Skewness and kurtosis, on the other hand, matter very little, at least given the range of values for skewness and kurtosis that we have observed in CTA returns over the past 10 years. The most plausible reason for this seems to

**EXHIBIT 8.4**   Track Record, Mean Return, and Volatility of Returns Have the Greatest Effect on Expected Drawdowns

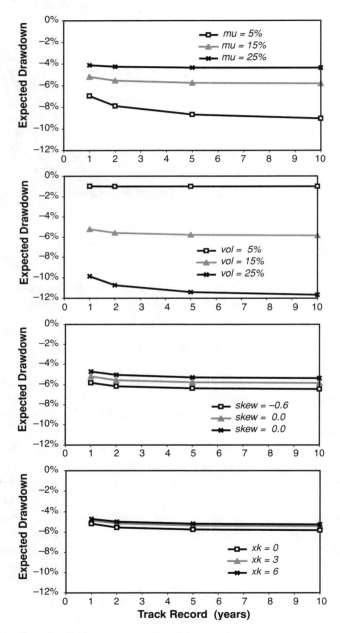

*Source:* Newedge Prime Brokerage Research.

be that drawdowns are the result of adding together sequences of returns. As a result, even though the distribution from which any given return is drawn may be higher skewed or exhibit fat tails, the result of adding returns together produces a random variable that tends (à la the central limit theorem) to be more normally distributed.

## The Distribution of Maximum Drawdowns

A manager's worst drawdown is taken from a distribution that is highly sensitive to length of track, mean return, and volatility of returns. Skewness and kurtosis, on the other hand, tend not to matter much.

The likelihood of any given drawdown is independent of how long a manager is in business. But the likelihood of experiencing a drawdown that is bigger than anything experienced so far increases with every passing day. As a result, as shown in Exhibit 8.3, increases in the length of track record shift the entire maximum drawdown distribution to the left.

Exhibit 8.5 shows how the distribution is affected by mean returns and the standard deviation of returns. The values we have chosen here correspond roughly to the range of values we observe in our database of CTA returns. As the upper panel shows, high returns tend to produce smaller maximum drawdowns, while the lower panel shows how increases in the volatility of returns increase the likelihood of large maximum drawdowns.

### How to Simulate Drawdowns: A Sample of 10,000

To simulate net asset value series where skewness and kurtosis are zero, we draw sample returns from a lognormal return distribution. To capture skewness and kurtosis, we sample returns from a generalized lambda distribution. The values of skewness and excess kurtosis used in this chapter were roughly consistent with the range of values we observed for CTAs in our database. From the return series, we construct net asset value series. And from these, we derive the simulated drawdowns that are used to produce the theoretical drawdown distributions. A typical run usually requires 10,000 iterations to produce a smooth distribution.

Exhibit 8.6 compares the effects of changing each of the four return characteristics on a manager's expected maximum drawdown. In each panel, it is apparent that length of track record matters more than it did with the expected value of all drawdowns. Each of these curves is considerably steeper

**EXHIBIT 8.5**   Effects of Returns and Volatility on Maximum Drawdowns

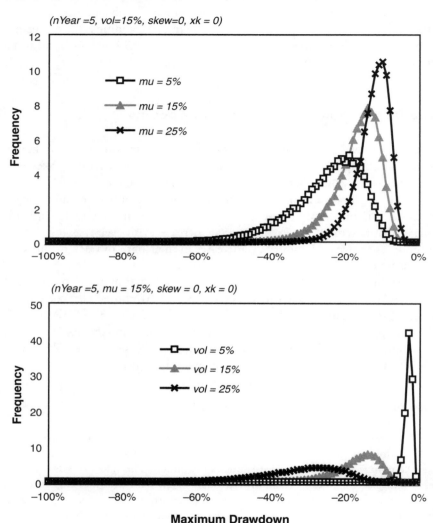

*Source:* Newedge Prime Brokerage Research.

here than those in Exhibit 8.4. It is also apparent that mean return and volatility of returns matter a lot, while skewness and kurtosis matter hardly at all.

To put the importance of these things in perspective, we calculated the partial effect of each moment on expected maximum drawdown and

**EXHIBIT 8.6**   The Three Most Important Variables for Maximum Drawdown Are Length of Track Record, Mean Return, and Volatility

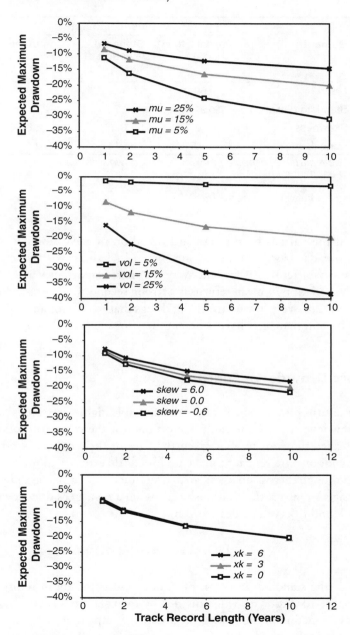

*Source:* Newedge Prime Brokerage Research.

**EXHIBIT 8.7**    How Important Are the Four Moments for Expected Maximum
Drawdowns?

| Moment | Potential Effect | | |
|---|---|---|---|
| | Partial Effect* (%) | Standard Deviation of Moment | Combined Effect (%) |
| Mean | 68.0 | 0.139 | 9.5 |
| Standard deviation | −191.0 | 0.133 | −25.4 |
| Skewness | 2.7 | 1.035 | 2.8 |
| Kurtosis | 0.1 | 5.914 | 0.4 |

\* Local partial of expected maximum drawdown with respect
to each moment.

*Source:* Newedge Prime Brokerage Research.

multiplied the partials by the standard deviation of each moment as measured in our database. The results are shown in Exhibit 8.7, which shows
that volatility of returns is far and away the most important variable across
managers. Variation in mean returns is a strong second. In contrast, skewness
and kurtosis rank very low on the list of things that matter for an explanation
of why different managers have different drawdowns.

## The Core Drawdown Function

If higher returns produce smaller drawdowns while higher volatilities produce
larger drawdowns, then one can trade off one for the other to produce the
same expected drawdowns. But given the sizes of their respective effects, it
can take a lot of extra return to make up for a little extra volatility.

Even though there is no clean, analytical function that relates drawdowns
to a manager's returns, the relationship between a manager's drawdowns and
his returns and risks can be described by

$$DD/\sigma = f(\mu/\sigma)$$

where $\sigma$ is the standard deviation of returns and is the mean return. That
is, a manager's drawdowns, when divided by the volatility of returns, can be
written as a function of the manager's modified Sharpe ratio (i.e., the ratio of
mean return to the standard deviation of returns).

**EXHIBIT 8.8** Shape of the Relationship between Expected Maximum Drawdowns and Returns when Both Are Normalized for Volatility

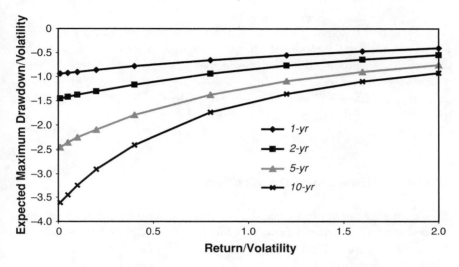

*Source:* Newedge Prime Brokerage Research.

The shape of this function is illustrated in Exhibit 8.8 for track records ranging from 1 to 10 years. The curvature bears out our sense that volatility matters more than mean return. A doubling of a manager's mean return while holding return volatility constant will reduce expected drawdown per unit of volatility but by less than half. In turn, a doubling of volatility while holding mean return constant will more than double expected maximum drawdown per unit of volatility.

If we are concerned only about the sizes of drawdowns, as opposed to drawdowns per unit of volatility, this relationship can be rewritten as

$$DD = \sigma f(\mu/\sigma)$$

which suggests the following:

- A doubling of both mean return and volatility (which would leave the modified Sharpe ratio unchanged) will exactly double expected maximum drawdowns.
- A doubling of volatility alone will more than double expected maximum drawdowns.

- One would have to more than double mean return to compensate for a doubling of volatility.

These points help to illustrate the differences between drawdown, volatility of returns, and a modified Sharpe ratio as measures of risk. All three are related but provide different perspectives. Two managers with the same volatility of returns will have different expected drawdowns if their mean returns are different. Two managers with identical modified Sharpe ratios will have different expected drawdowns if their return volatilities are different.

## Empirical Drawdown Distributions

To see whether this approach could be used to explain the drawdown patterns we observe, we constructed drawdown histories for 1, 2, 5, and 10 years in the following way using CTA returns from the Barclay's database. Using return histories for all managers with a 1-year track record as of November 2002, we determined what their drawdowns would have been had they all started from scratch at the end of November 2001. Then, for all managers who had a 2-year track record as of November 2002, we determined what their drawdowns would have been had they all started fresh at the end of November 2000. And so forth for 5-year and 10-year track records. By design, this approach produces different drawdown histories than those actually reported by the CTAs in our database. It has the advantage, however, of putting all managers up against the same market conditions.

The results of these efforts are shown in Exhibit 8.9. The distributions of all drawdowns are shown in the upper panel, while the distributions of maximum drawdowns are shown in the lower panel.

## Reconciling Theoretical and Empirical Distributions

The distribution of all drawdowns shown in Exhibit 8.9 looks about the way we would expect. The distributions of maximum drawdowns, on the other hand, posed a real challenge. First, they are irregularly shaped. Second, as shown in Exhibit 8.10, where we focus on the distribution of maximum drawdowns for 10-year track records, the observed distribution does not fit well with the theoretical distribution (labeled "Discrete") derived from the actual distribution of returns for all CTAs with a 10-year track record.

**EXHIBIT 8.9** Observed Drawdown Distributions (1993–2002)

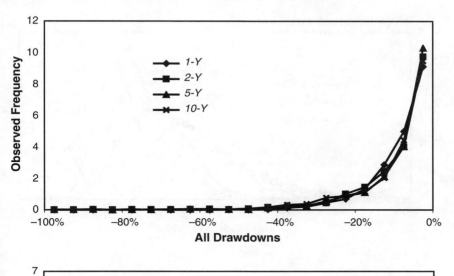

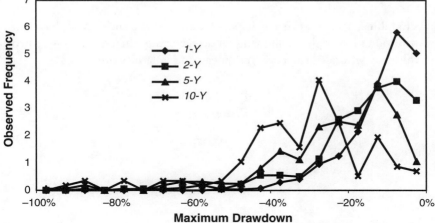

*Source:* Barclay Hedge, Newedge Prime Brokerage Research.

The problem is that the observed drawdown distribution peaks at a much lower level of drawdowns than does the theoretical. One plausible explanation for the difference in the shapes of the two distributions is that managers may deleverage when they are in drawdown—that is, scale back the risk they take—and thereby avoid the larger drawdowns they would experience if they were to keep the volatility of returns constant.

**EXHIBIT 8.10**   First Cut at Explaining Observed Maximum Drawdowns

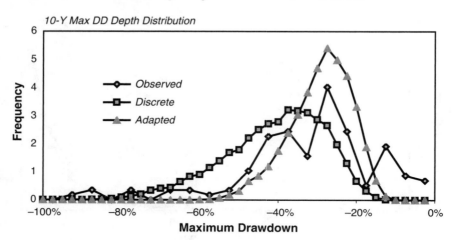

*Source:* Barclay Hedge, Newedge Prime Brokerage Research.

Exhibit 8.10 shows that it is possible to pull the theoretical drawdown distribution to the right by allowing for deleveraging when simulating returns. In this case, we scaled the manager's mean and volatility of returns as

$$\mu' = f \times \mu$$
$$\sigma' = f \times \sigma$$

where

$$f = 1 - [\text{abs}(\text{drawdown})]^{1/2}$$

so that if a manager's current drawdown were 50 percent, the scaling factor would be .29 [$= 1 - .5^{1/2}$]. The new distribution of maximum drawdowns that results is labeled "Adapted" in Exhibit 8.10 and peaks just about where it should.

One main drawback to this approach is that the evidence on deleveraging is largely anecdotal. We know managers who attest to the fact that they scale back risk when in drawdown. We know other managers, however, who say that they do not. And we have not yet been able to find any evidence in the volatilities of managers' returns that suggests that they deleverage when in drawdown.

**EXHIBIT 8.11**   Range of Returns and Volatilities for Managers with a 10-Year Track Record

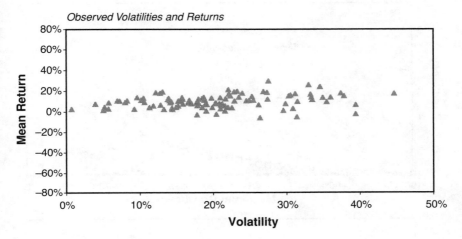

Managers Grouped by Volatility

| Volatility Range | Number of Managers | Group Return | Group Volatility |
|---|---|---|---|
| 0.0%–12.5% | 19 | 8.3% | 8.6% |
| 12.5%–25.0% | 64 | 9.4% | 18.8% |
| 25.0%–50.0% | 9 | 12.3% | 32.4% |

*Source:* Barclay Hedge, Newedge Prime Brokerage Research.

Another main drawback to this approach is that while it produces a mass of probabilities that looks like what we observe, it greatly underpredicts the several large drawdowns that we observe in the data.

A better solution seems to lie in the fact that managers exhibit very different volatilities of returns. This is borne out in Exhibit 8.11, which shows a scatter plot of mean returns and their corresponding volatilities for those managers for whom we have 10 years of performance data. For the purposes of this exercise, we grouped the managers into three broad volatility groups: low (0–12.5%), medium (12.5–25%), and high (25–50%).

Using the group returns and group volatilities, we simulated the three maximum drawdown distributions shown in the upper panel of Exhibit 8.12. Then, using the numbers of managers in each of the three groups, we produced a composite distribution that is a weighted average of the three separate distributions.

**EXHIBIT 8.12**   Composite Maximum Drawdown Distribution

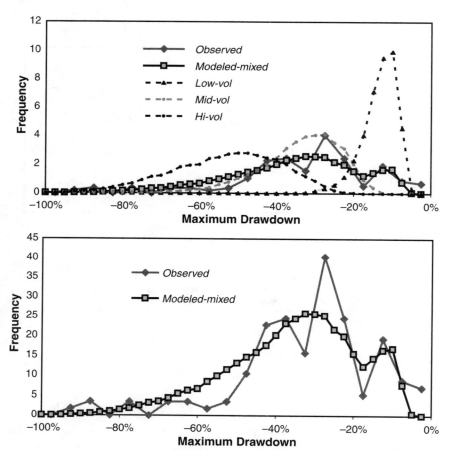

*Source:* Barclay Hedge, Newedge Prime Brokerage Research.

The resulting composite distribution has some attractive features. First, because of the presence of the low-volatility group, the composite distribution peaks about where it should. Second, because of the presence of the high-volatility group, the composite distribution allows for a sufficiently high probability of large drawdowns. And third, as shown in the lower panel of Exhibit 8.12, the composite even exhibits some of the irregular shape that we see in the observed distribution of drawdowns.

## Putting a Manager's Experience in Perspective

At this point, we think it is reasonable to draw two theoretical drawdown distributions for any given manager, both based on length of track record and the mean and volatility of returns. We have done this in Exhibit 8.13 for a manager with a 10-year track record, a mean return of just over 12 percent, and a standard deviation of returns of 20 percent. Over this, we have superimposed the manager's actual drawdowns, which are represented by the horizontal lines stemming from the vertical axis on the right. This particular manager has experienced 17 drawdowns over the 10 years, most of them less than 10 percent. The maximum drawdown was just over 40 percent.

Overall, this manager's actual drawdown experience is roughly in line with what we would expect. The maximum drawdown is in the upper end of the theoretical distribution, but appears to be only about one standard deviation above the mean.

**EXHIBIT 8.13**   Assessing a Manager's Drawdown Experience

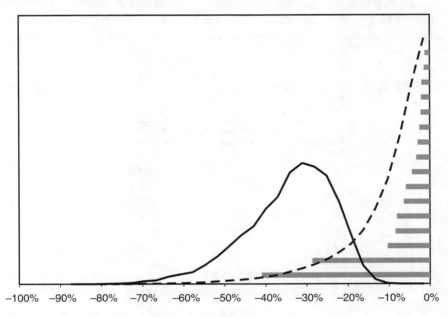

*Source:* Barclay Hedge, Newedge Prime Brokerage Research.

## What about Future Drawdowns?

What kinds of drawdowns might an investor expect going forward? This work
suggests that we can form reasonable expectations about the size and frequency
of drawdowns for any given investment horizon. We can also say something
useful about the possibility that a manager will experience a larger drawdown
than the maximum drawdown to date. In particular, for a given investment
horizon and assumptions about the mean and volatility of returns, we can
calculate the likelihood that a manager will experience a worse drawdown and
a conditional maximum drawdown to go with it.

For example, how likely is it that a manager whose worst drawdown to
date is 41 percent will have a worse drawdown over any given investment
horizon? If we are willing to assume a mean return and volatility (e.g., 12%
and 20%), we find in Exhibit 8.14 that the probability of experiencing a
drawdown greater than 41 percent is only 0.1 percent over the next year but
would be 23.4 percent if the investment horizon is extended to 10 years.
We also find that the expected value of this worse drawdown would be 44.1
percent if it occurs in the next year but would be 49.0 percent if experienced
over a 10-year horizon.

In practice, we can use any target drawdown, not just the worst or
maximum drawdown to date. And we can, if need be, modify the assumptions
about the manager's returns to produce more realistic theoretical distributions.

**EXHIBIT 8.14**   How Much Worse Can It Get?

*(Mean Return = 12%, Volatility = 20%)*

| Investment Horizon (years) | Probability of a Drawdown > 41% | Expected Drawdown if > 41% |
|---|---|---|
| 1 | 0.1% | −44.1% |
| 2 | 1.7% | −45.8% |
| 3 | 4.3% | −47.1% |
| 4 | 6.8% | −47.3% |
| 5 | 9.5% | −47.8% |
| 6 | 12.9% | −48.2% |
| 7 | 15.3% | −48.4% |
| 8 | 17.8% | −48.8% |
| 9 | 20.5% | −49.1% |
| 10 | 23.4% | −49.0% |

*Source:* Barclay Hedge, Newedge Prime Brokerage Research.

This would be especially useful if we think that a manager's trading strategy is likely to produce a mix of volatilities over time. The drawdown distributions for high and low return volatilities have very different shapes and could produce very different probabilities of large losses than one would get using an assumption of constant volatility.

## Further Questions

Our conversations with clients and colleagues about this work have generated several questions that deserve a closer look. How important, for example, are serially correlated returns? How reliable are our estimates of return volatilities? Would the analysis be better if one had daily rather than monthly return data? Would this analysis work as well for hedge funds as it does for commodity trading advisors? What happens if a manager's return volatility changes in response to drawdowns?

First, serially correlated returns could have a measurable effect on draw-down distributions, but we have found no evidence of serial correlation in CTA returns. Volatility estimates based on monthly return data can be subject to very large statistical errors and would be much improved, at least in the case of CTAs, if we had daily return data. To the extent one can get reliable return and volatility information about hedge funds, the analysis should work well. It is much harder, though, to get the same quality information about hedge funds as one can get for CTAs. And, while we know that some managers deleverage when in drawdown, the evidence on CTAs as a class is ambiguous.

# CHAPTER 9

# How Stock Price Volatility Affects Returns

It is, by now, widely known that stocks do not do well when stock volatility is high. Or perhaps stock price volatility is high when stocks are not doing well. Either way, we find that stock price volatility—and the volatility of the S&P 500 in particular—looms large in stock portfolio returns. The question we want to tackle here is whether stock volatility plays a similar role in CTA returns. That is, do CTA returns, or their correlations with stock returns, depend on stock price volatility?

Among the most important of our findings—based on the data shown in Exhibit 9.1—are these:

- S&P 500 returns are negatively correlated with S&P 500 price volatility.
- CTA returns are largely unrelated to S&P 500 price volatility.
- The correlation of S&P 500 returns with CTA returns, which is slightly positive when stock price volatility is normal or low, becomes negative when stock price volatility is high.

We also learned that:

- S&P 500 price volatility may be the single most important source of market volatility globally.

Taken together, these findings seem to be at odds with at least one widely held notion about CTAs—that is, that CTAs are in some sense long volatility. Their returns do not exhibit the kind of straddle shape that one would expect

201

**EXHIBIT 9.1**   S&P 500 Net Asset Value versus Price Volatility

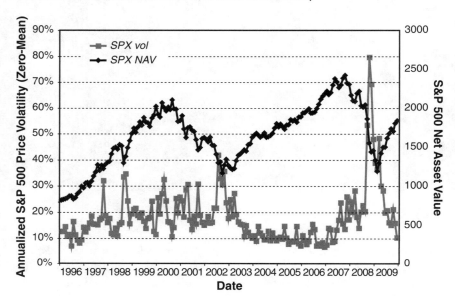

*Source:* Bloomberg, Barclay Hedge, Newedge Prime Brokerage Research.

of a long-volatility position. CTAs might, on the other hand, be considered a volatility hedge for a stock portfolio. But the sense in which they are has more to do with the shift from positive to negative correlation in returns as volatility goes from low or normal to high than it does with overall CTA returns.

## A Look at Historical Returns

For the purposes of this work, we look at the 12-year period from January 1996 through December 2007. This gives us a good look at two bull markets and one bear market in the U.S. stock market. We have monthly return data for 51 CTAs from which we construct an equally weighted index. And we chose daily price data for 39 futures markets that allow us to drill down on price volatility over fairly short periods of time.

Perhaps the best measure of CTA returns, especially those of large CTAs, is the *Newedge CTA Index*. This index—originally published as the *Carr Barclay CTA Index* and then as the *Calyon Barclay CTA Index*—is based on the returns of the 20 largest CTAs that are open to investment and willing to provide daily data. The index is reconstituted annually, in January, and is free of survivorship bias.

**EXHIBIT 9.2** Net Asset Values for Stocks and CTAs (Indexed in US$, January 1996–December 2009)

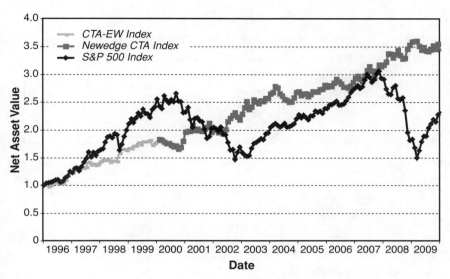

*Source:* Bloomberg, Barclay Hedge, Newedge Prime Brokerage Research.

Its history, however, begins in January 2000. To extend our look back, we turned to a set of 51 CTAs with $50 million under management and for which we had monthly return data from January 1996. We used these histories to construct an equally weighted index of returns and net asset values. This allowed us to add another four years to the data set and to include one more bull market in stocks.

The substitute index is a good proxy for the *Newedge CTA Index* with one caveat. As shown in Exhibit 9.2, the two indexes tracked one another well from 2000 through 2007. The correlation of monthly returns for the two indexes was 97 percent. The caveat is that the average returns for the substitute index were higher than for the *Newedge CTA Index*, which could be due in part to survivorship bias. But since our research interest is not in average CTA returns by themselves, but rather in whether CTA returns depend on stock price volatility, any upward bias likely disappears when comparing any two means.

## Stock Price Volatility and Returns on the S&P 500

The fact that stock returns are negatively correlated with stock price volatility is a phenomenon that has been observed for decades. It is consistent with

**EXHIBIT 9.3**  Monthly CTA Returns versus Monthly S&P 500 Returns in High-Volatility
Months (January 1996–December 2009)

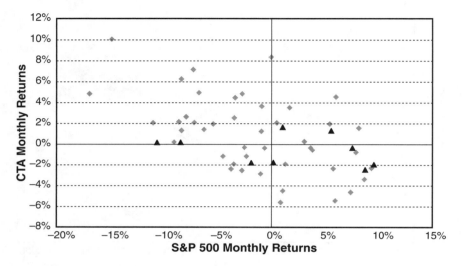

*Source:* Bloomberg, Newedge Prime Brokerage Research.

the idea that overall leverage in equities increases as stock prices fall. It is
consistent with the fact that implied volatilities for the equity options with
lower strike prices (e.g., out-of-the-money puts) are higher than those for
equity options with higher strike prices (e.g., out-of-the-money calls), as lower
strikes correspond to lower returns and correspondingly higher volatilities over
the life of the option. And it is borne out in experience with equity index
returns.

Exhibit 9.3 shows monthly net asset values plotted against an annualized
measure of historical monthly volatility in the S&P 500 in the top panel.
Throughout this chapter, we measure volatility as the annualized square root
of the average of squared returns. This way of calculating volatility assumes a
mean return of zero, which is not conventional, but which is approximately
correct for daily returns and allows us to avoid understating volatility when
a market or CTA is on a run, either positive or negative. In the middle
panel is a scatter of monthly S&P 500 returns against monthly values of
the level of stock price volatility. The correlation between the two is –0.25.
The negative correlation is more pronounced if one uses quarterly returns
versus quarterly measures of price volatility, as shown in the bottom panel.
Here the correlation between the two is –0.43. In both cases, the negative
correlations are influenced by one particular occurrence in July 2002. This is

more apparent in the bottom panel, where you can see one observation in the upper-left-hand corner that corresponds to a loss of more than 17 percent. Without this quarter, the correlation of quarterly returns would have been −0.33. Without that month, the correlation of monthly returns would have been −0.21.

While the correlation seems weakly negative in monthly returns, the relationship seems strong enough to merit our attention. To get another perspective on the relationship, we divided the 144 months in our data set into periods of low-, normal-, and high-volatility months. The distinction is a little arbitrary, but in this exercise, we divided up the sample period into 36 least-volatile months, the 36 most-volatile months, and the 72 months in between. These are illustrated in Exhibit 9.4, in which the calm months are those with volatility less than 10.98 percent and the volatile months are those with volatility greater than 18.75 percent.

The statistical significance of the relationship between monthly volatility and returns is illustrated in Exhibit 9.5, which shows, using a candlestick kind of chart, the mean return (the dot inside of each band) and a two-standard-deviation band of returns around the mean for each level of volatility. As is apparent, there is a lot of overlap. For example, it would be hard to say that stock returns are significantly lower when stocks are volatile than when stock

**EXHIBIT 9.4** Stock Price Volatility by Month

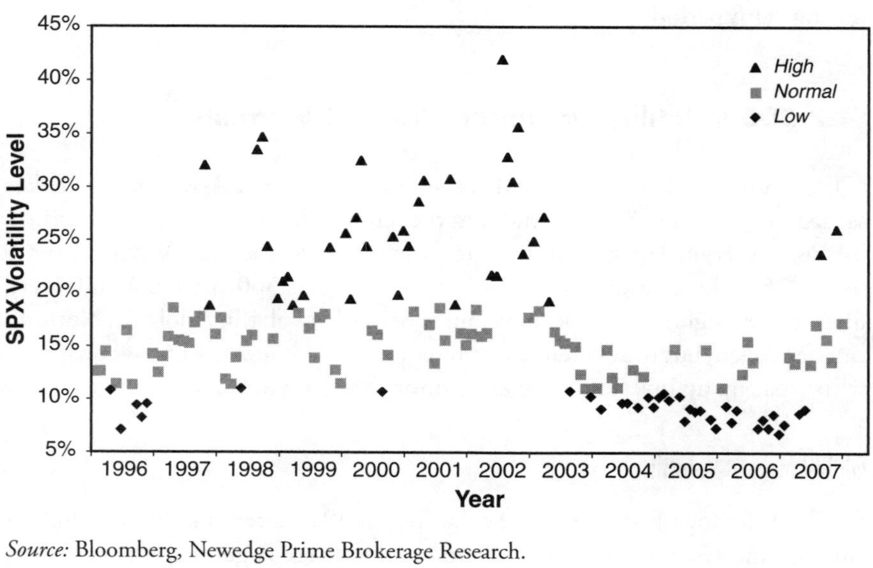

*Source:* Bloomberg, Newedge Prime Brokerage Research.

**EXHIBIT 9.5**   Stock Returns by Volatility Level

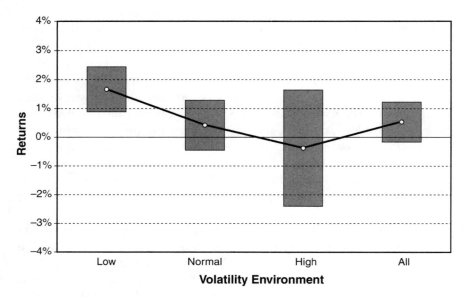

*Source:* Bloomberg, Newedge Prime Brokerage Research.

volatility is "normal." It is apparent, though, at least in this data set, that stock returns are significantly lower during normal or volatile periods than they are during calm periods.

## S&P 500 Volatility Dominates Market Volatility

CTAs trade a wide range of markets, so it is natural to ask whether it makes sense to expend much effort studying the relationship between price volatility in the U.S. equity market and the returns that CTAs realize. What we show here is that the answer is probably yes—that S&P 500 price volatility very likely is the single most important source of market volatility globally. Nothing can be proven, but the evidence we present here is compelling and is consistent with what many investors have known for years, anyway.

### Global Market Volatility

Exhibit 9.6 shows historical price volatility for 39 different markets, including equities, interest rates, currencies, and commodities. A guide to the contracts

**EXHIBIT 9.6**   Volatilities in 39 Markets

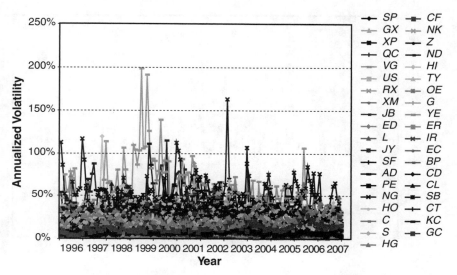

| | | | | |
|---|---|---|---|---|
| | **SP** | S&P 500 | | |
| | CF | CAC 40 | | |
| | GX | DAX 30 | | |
| **Equity** | NK | NIKKEI 225 | | |
| | XP | AUSSIE SPX | | |
| | Z | FTSE 250 | | |
| | QC | SWEDISH OMX | | |
| | ND | NAS DAQ 100 | | |
| | VG | DJ EURO STOXX | | |
| | HI | HANG SENG | | |
| | US | US 30 YEAR | | |
| | TY | US 10 YEAR | | |
| | RX | GERMAN BUND | | |
| | OE | GERMAN BOBL | | |
| | XM | AUSSIE 10 YEAR | | |
| **Interest Rates** | G | UK 10 YEAR GILT | | |
| | JB | JAPAN 10 YEAR | | |
| | YE | JAPAN 3 MONTH | | |
| | ED | US 3 MONTH | | |
| | ER | EUROPE 3 MONTH | | |
| | L | UK SHORT STERLING | | |
| | IR | AUSSIE 3 MONTH | | |

| | | |
|---|---|---|
| | JY | JAPANESE YEN |
| | EC | EURO |
| **Foreign Exchange** | SF | SWISS FRANC |
| | BP | BRITISH POUND |
| | AD | AUSTRALIAN DOLLAR |
| | CD | CANADIAN DOLLAR |
| | PE | MEXICAN PESO |
| | CL | CRUDE OIL |
| | NG | NATURAL GAS |
| | SB | SUGAR |
| | HO | HEATING OIL |
| **Commodity** | CT | COTTON |
| | C | CORN |
| | KC | COFFEE |
| | S | SOYBEANS |
| | GC | GOLD |
| | HG | COPPER |

*Source:* Bloomberg, Newedge Prime Brokerage Research.

**EXHIBIT 9.7**  S&P 500 and Average Market Volatility

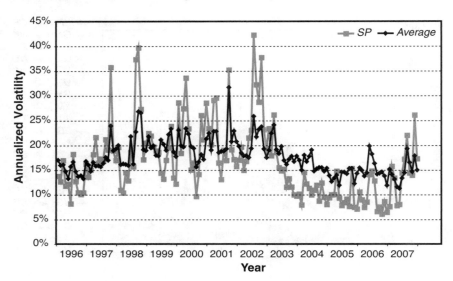

*Source:* Bloomberg, Newedge Prime Brokerage Research.

listed in the legend is provided at the end of this chapter. The exhibit is a visual mess, but can be untangled in a couple of ways.

One is shown in Exhibit 9.7, which compares a simple average of the volatilities in Exhibit 9.6 with S&P 500 volatility. The two series seem to rise and fall reasonably well with one another, and the correlation between the two series is +0.81. In other words, in a simple regression of average market volatility against S&P 500 volatility, the R-squared would be somewhere around 0.64.

## Eigen Analysis

Another way to disentangle the forces that are behind market volatility is to calculate the eigenvalues of the 39 independent vectors needed to explain the volatility we see in these markets. These values are shown in Exhibit 9.8 where we find that one eigenvector alone explains $\frac{11}{39}$ of the variance in all of the series.

To interpret what is shown in Exhibit 9.8, one needs to know this about eigenvectors and eigenvalues. First, the eigenvectors themselves are the result of a computational method that finds the 39 uncorrelated or independent

**EXHIBIT 9.8** Eigenvalues for 39 Market Volatilities

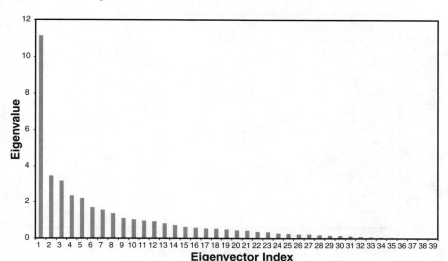

*Source:* Bloomberg, Newedge Prime Brokerage Research.

series that explain 100 percent of the variation in the 39 volatility series we have here. The raw materials for this kind of analysis are 39 volatility series that have been normalized so that the variance of each of the series is 1.0. In practice, then, this means that eigenvalues shed useful light on the values one sees in a correlation matrix, not in the covariance matrix. And the sum of the eigenvalues is 39, which is the sum of the variances of 39 independent time series.

For example, if all 39 of our volatility series were completely uncorrelated with one another, all 39 eigenvalues would be 1.0, and all of the off-diagonal elements of the correlation matrix would be zero. That is, each series would explain itself and nothing else. On the other hand, if all 39 of our volatility series were perfectly correlated, the first eigenvalue would be 39, all the rest would be zero, and the off-diagonal elements of the correlation matrix would be 1.0.

Here, the fact that the highest eigenvalue is 11 means that there is enough overall correlation among the 39 volatility series that more than 25 percent of their variability can be explained by a single force (whatever that force may be). After the first eigenvalue, things drop off pretty quickly. The next four values are greater than 2, and the five after that are greater than 1, so it is apparent that there are other forces at work, but not as influential.

**EXHIBIT 9.9**   First Eigenvector versus SPX Volatility (Rho = 84%)

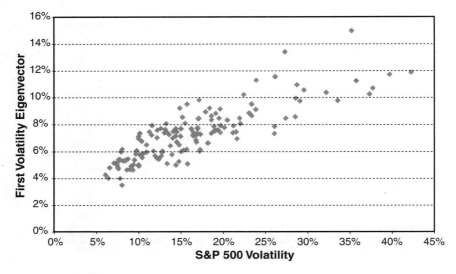

*Source:* Bloomberg, Newedge Prime Brokerage Research.

Finally, because eigenvectors are simply the result of a computational technique, there is no guarantee that the vectors themselves represent anything that we observe in the markets. In this case, though, our inclination is to think that it might be related to stock price volatility. And, as we see in Exhibit 9.9, the correlation between the 144 values that make up the first eigenvector and the 144 monthly observations of S&P 500 price volatility line up remarkably well. The correlation between the two series is 0.84, which reinforces our notion that volatility in the U.S. stock market is probably the most compelling force driving global market volatility.

## CTA Returns, Correlations, and Volatility

Against this backdrop, we turn now to the question of whether CTA returns or their correlations with S&P 500 returns are related to volatility.

The relationship between CTA returns and S&P 500 return volatility is shown in Exhibit 9.10. What we find there is that CTA returns tend to be slightly higher both when stocks exhibit low and high volatility than when stock price volatility falls in the normal range. This seems at odds with the notion that CTAs are in some sense long volatility. At least it appears that CTA returns are largely independent of stock price volatility.

**EXHIBIT 9.10** CTA Returns by Stock Price Volatility Level

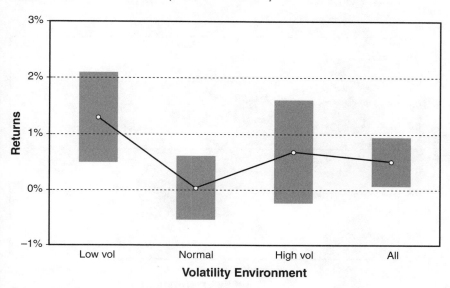

*Source:* Bloomberg, Newedge Prime Brokerage Research.

The more interesting relationship is found in Exhibit 9.11, which shows how the correlation between CTA and S&P returns behaved during low-, normal-, and high-volatility periods. Overall, if we did not differentiate between low-, normal-, and high-volatility periods, we would find that the correlation of CTA and S&P returns was very slightly negative and very close to zero. During low-volatility and normal periods, however, the correlation of the two return series was slightly positive: 0.52 on average during low-volatility months and 0.25 on average during normal months. In contrast, during high-volatility months, the average correlation of the two returns was −0.55.

Is there any value in these findings for a portfolio manager? The answer is most likely *no* if the manager's hope or intent is to use the knowledge to improve portfolio performance. Unless the results were persistent and reliable, and unless the different volatility states could be anticipated reliably and in time to do something useful in response, the fact that correlations or returns might depend on stock price volatility does not affect the overall performance of a portfolio. Our own work on transition probabilities suggests that the volatility states are hard to predict and that even if we knew what they would be, very little could be gained by adjusting asset mixes through time. And,

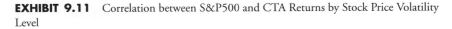

**EXHIBIT 9.11**   Correlation between S&P500 and CTA Returns by Stock Price Volatility Level

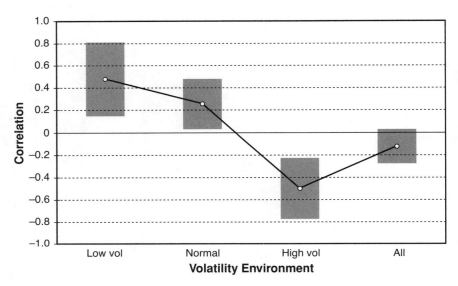

*Source:* Bloomberg, Newedge Prime Brokerage Research.

as a practical matter, the mix of assets in institutional portfolios is influenced by a host of constraints and cost considerations that tend to retard the speed with which investment reallocations take place.

A more valuable application of these findings likely is in the way managers evaluate the performance of alternative investments against the performance of their other assets. Exhibit 9.12 provides scatter plots of S&P and CTA returns for the three volatility levels and illustrates the practical differences between fairly positive (low-volatility), slightly positive (normal-volatility), and fairly negative (high-volatility) correlations.

The return data in these scatters are organized slightly differently in Exhibit 9.13, which shows the numbers of months that the S&P and CTAs were making or losing money in the three volatility environments. In the bottom panel, which shows gains and losses for all conditions, one can see that both assets made money during most months in the sample period. The stock portfolio made money in 86 out of 144 months. The CTA portfolio made money in 81 out of 144 months. Also, the likelihood that CTAs would make money during those months when stocks were making money was only slightly higher [63% = 54/86] than the overall probability

**EXHIBIT 9.12**   CTA Returns versus Stock Returns—Low Volatility

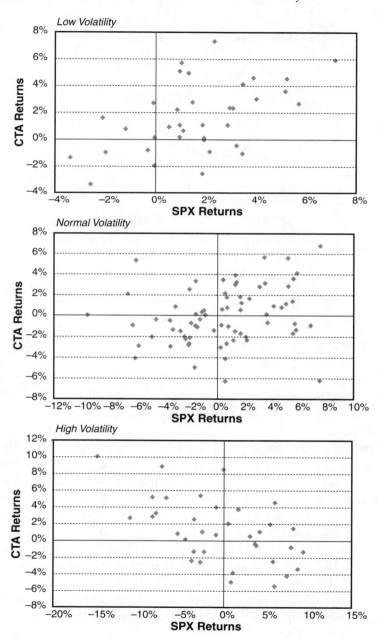

Source: Bloomberg, Newedge Prime Brokerage Research.

**EXHIBIT 9.13**  Distributions of Monthly Gains and Losses (Number of Months, January 1996–December 2007)

| Low Volatility | | Loss | S&P500 Gain | Total |
|---|---|---|---|---|
| | Gain | 4 | 22 | 26 |
| CTAs | Loss | 5 | 5 | 10 |
| | Total | 9 | 27 | 36 |
| **Normal Volatility** | | Loss | **S&P500** Gain | Total |
| | Gain | 8 | 25 | 33 |
| CTAs | Loss | 22 | 17 | 39 |
| | Total | 30 | 42 | 72 |
| **High Volatility** | | Loss | **S&P500** Gain | Total |
| | Gain | 15 | 7 | 22 |
| CTAs | Loss | 4 | 10 | 14 |
| | Total | 19 | 17 | 36 |
| **All Settings** | | Loss | **S&P500** Gain | Total |
| | Gain | 27 | 54 | 81 |
| CTAs | Loss | 31 | 32 | 63 |
| | Total | 58 | 86 | 144 |

*Source:* Bloomberg, Newedge Prime Brokerage Research.

[56% = 81/144]. The number of months in which S&P and CTA returns were in the same direction was also 85 out of 144. So, for the sample period as a whole, the conditional probability that CTAs would make money in any given month was not really different from the overall probability that they would make money. That is, the two return series appear to be uncorrelated.

But the conditional probabilities for CTAs making or losing money change dramatically when one subdivides the sample period according to stock volatility levels. As shown in the top panel, which covers the low-volatility month, stocks made money in 27 out of 36 months, and during these months, CTAs made money 22 times, or 81 percent [= 22/27] of the time. Also, S&P and CTA returns were in the same direction 27 times out of 36, or 75 percent [= 27/36] of the time.

During high-volatility months, though, the picture is very different. Here, stock and CTA returns went in opposite directions in 25 of the 36 months. We also see that CTAs were less likely (7 times out of 17) to make money when stocks were up than they were (15 times out of 19) to make money were stocks were down.

## Conclusion

The research for this chapter began in a search for market regimes that might help us understand the circumstances under which different assets make and lose money and to use this understanding to help us improve the mix of assets in broadly diversified portfolios. Most of what we found in that work was inconclusive, but the results reported here seem to stand out from the rest.

Among other things, our findings support the idea that the U.S. stock market is a major force in market volatility globally. It is the kind of thing that many people know or suspect, but it was interesting for us to find the prejudice borne out in the data. We suspect the same is true for the finding that returns in the stock market are negatively correlated with the level of stock price volatility.

The more surprising results are that CTA returns seem to be unrelated to market volatility—at least to stock market volatility—and that the correlation of stock and CTA returns is very different in high- and low-volatility markets. The first of these is at odds with the idea that CTAs are, in some sense, long volatility. The second suggests that the expectations that investors have for CTA returns should be conditioned on the level of market volatility.

# CHAPTER 10

# The Costs of Active Management

In Chapter 15, we take a serious look at what an investor might reasonably expect to gain by actively weighting the assets or managers in a portfolio. We did not, however, look at the costs of active money management. The purpose of this chapter is to evaluate some of the obvious costs and to put them in perspective. In particular, we examine foregone loss carry-forward, dormant cash, opportunity losses, and slippage from transactions costs from the perspectives of those who invest in funds and those who invest in managed accounts.

## Forgone Loss Carry-Forward

This is a cost borne by every investor. It arises from the asymmetric fee structure that is typical in the alternative investment world of hedge funds and commodity trading advisors. That is, the manager collects performance fees only when net asset value is above the most recent high-water mark at the end of the relevant accounting period. For a manager who is under water—that is, whose net asset value is below the most recent high-water mark—all gains are free from performance fees until a new high-water mark is achieved.

Exhibit 10.1 shows what effect a policy of firing managers in drawdown could have on expected returns net of fees. For the purposes of this exercise, we assumed that all managers had 15 percent annual expected returns and 15 percent annualized return volatility. The drawdown at which a manager would

**EXHIBIT 10.1**   Value of Loss Carry-Forward

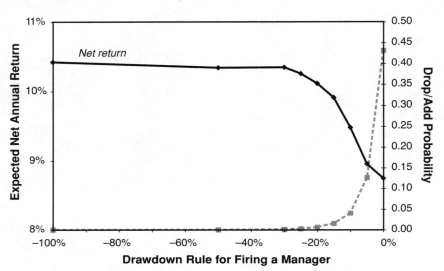

*Source:* Newedge Prime Brokerage Research.

be replaced by another manager with an identical distribution of returns is measured on the horizontal axis. The expected return net of fees is measured on the left-hand vertical axis, while the probability of firing a manager is measured on the right-hand vertical axis.

By replacing one manager with another with an identical return distribution, we know we are gaining nothing and that we are isolating the cost of loss carry-forward. In this example, the highest expected return is achieved by never firing anyone. As the drawdown percentage becomes less forgiving, the expected return net of fees falls because we have given up the "free" returns of managers who are under water. For large drawdowns, the cost is small because the probability of firing a manager is small. For smaller drawdowns, though, the cost can be substantial. For example, a 20 percent drawdown rule would decrease expected returns by 31 basis points (from 10.42–10.11%). A 10 percent drawdown rule would decrease expected returns by 94 basis points (from 10.42–9.48%).

## The Importance of Loss Carry-Forward

Just how important loss carry-forward may be depends chiefly on how likely it is that a manager's future net asset value will lie between his current net

**EXHIBIT 10.2**   Relative Importance of Loss Carry-Forward (Net Asset Value Distributions)

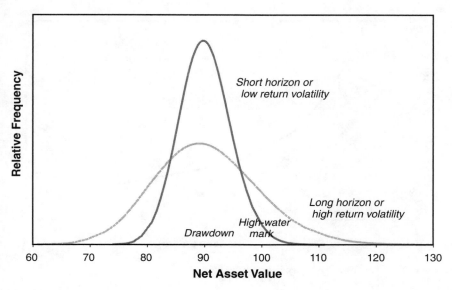

*Source:* Newedge Prime Brokerage Research.

asset value and his high-water mark. Consider Exhibit 10.2, which shows two possible distributions of future net asset values. The narrower of the two distributions might correspond either to a manager with low return volatility or, for a given level of return volatility, to a relatively short time horizon. The wider of the two might correspond either to a manager with high return volatility or to a relatively long time horizon.

For a manager in drawdown with a net asset value equal to 90 and a high-water mark of 100, it is easy to see that this range, over which returns are free of incentive fees, accounts for a relatively large fraction of the outcomes for the low-volatility or short-time-horizon distribution. As a result, the value of loss carry-forward can be expected to be a relatively more important cost when return volatilities are low or expected holding periods are short.

## How Big Is the Return Hurdle?

This intuition is borne out in Exhibit 10.3, which shows how much extra annualized return we would need from a new manager to make up for the cost of loss carry-forward incurred by firing a manager in drawdown. In all cases,

**EXHIBIT 10.3**   Required Mean Return Improvement to Make Up the Loss Carry-Forward
(15% Mean Return)

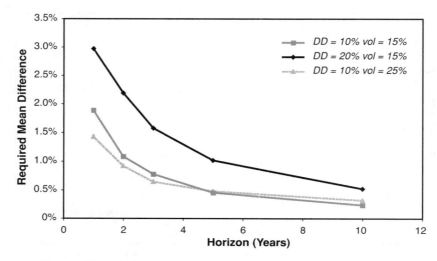

*Source:* Newedge Prime Brokerage Research.

the expected return of the manager who is fired is 15 percent. We have varied,
though, the drawdown threshold and the volatility of returns. The length of
our breakeven horizon is measured in years along the horizontal axis.

What we find accords roughly with what we would expect. First, we need
a larger incremental return from our new manager if the manager we've fired
is 20 percent under water than if the manager we've fired is 10 percent under
water. Second, at least for horizons of three years or less, we need a larger
incremental return from our new manager if return volatilities are 15 percent
rather than 25 percent.

For a one-year horizon, the extra expected returns we need are substantial.
For example, with a 20 percent drawdown rule, the new manager must
promise nearly 3 percent a year more than we expected from the manager
we've replaced. Even with a 10 percent drawdown rule, we would need an
extra 2 percent a year, although with 25 percent return volatilities, this hurdle
would be reduced to 1.5 percent.

## Liquidation and Reinvestment

In addition to giving up the benefits of loss carry-forward, the process of
liquidating and reinvesting is one that incurs three additional costs, two of

**EXHIBIT 10.4** Liquidation/Reinvestment Process

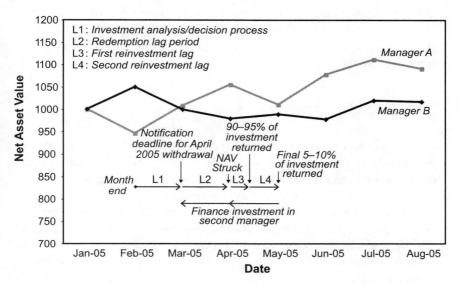

*Source:* Newedge Prime Brokerage Research.

which might go unexamined unless benchmarks and investment opportunities are well defined. These include foregone interest on dormant cash, foregone excess returns on uncommitted cash, and the market impact costs of closing out one position and opening another.

Exhibit 10.4 provides a rough schematic of the steps involved in redeeming from one manager and investing in another. The key lesson from this exhibit is that one has to deal with several leads and lags when making a decision to take money from one manager and to give it to another.

The first lag is identified as L1 and represents the time it takes to review a manager's results and make a decision about redemption. This might be anywhere from a few days to, in some complex cases, several months. The second is identified as L2 and represents the time between the notification deadline for a withdrawal and the time when a net asset value is struck. This can take several weeks. The third, L3, is the time between the striking of net asset value and the receipt of the first round of cash. And the fourth, L4, is the time that passes between the receipt of the first round of cash and the final round of cash.

The two net asset value series in Exhibit 10.4 are there to serve as a reminder that while we are gathering information, making decisions, redeeming cash, and reinvesting the proceeds of any cash received from an existing manager, things are in motion. The net asset value of the manager who now has our money (i.e., Manager A) is changing with each passing month, as is the net asset value of a manager to whom we might direct our money (i.e., Manager B).

## Foregone Interest on Dormant Cash

This is a cost that is borne chiefly by investors in funds and depends entirely on funds' practices with regard to interest payments on cash balances. Industry practices vary a great deal, but it is not uncommon to find that funds do not pay interest on the value of cash balances. In these cases, the cost of foregone interest depends on how quickly cash is returned to you.

While the mix of possible arrangements is too complex to capture in a simple way, a couple of examples illustrate just how costly foregone interest might be. Assume, for example, that you receive 95 percent of your cash in 10 calendar days with the remaining 5 percent in 30 days. In this case, if the money market rate were 5 percent, the total cost to you would be 0.153 percent [= 5% (.95 (10/360) + .05 (30/360))], or 15.3 annualized basis points.

Or suppose that you receive 90 percent of your cash in 15 days and the remaining 10 percent in 45 days. At the same market interest rate of 5 percent, your foregone interest would be 0.25 percent [= 5% (.90 (15/360) + .10 (45/360))], or 25 annualized basis points.

## Opportunity Losses

A more serious drag on performance stems from the intervals during which your investments are not committed to enterprises that promise returns in excess of market interest rates. These costs, which can be described as opportunity losses, are borne by all investors.

Exhibit 10.5 provides some sample calculations based on very simple assumptions about excess returns and investment lapses. Suppose, for example, that the expected excess return of the new manager is 5 percent (over and above money market interest rates). Suppose, too, that one month passes between the end of L2, when your net asset value is struck, and the time your new investment with another manager is effective. In this case, the one-month lapse would cost you 0.42 percent or 42 annualized basis points. That is, during the month your cash is earning money market rates, you are not involved in an enterprise that promises to pay 5 percent a year more than

**EXHIBIT 10.5**  Foregone Returns (Percent per Year)

| Excess Return (%) | Investment Lapse (Months) | | |
|:---:|:---:|:---:|:---:|
| | 1 | 2 | 3 |
| 5 | 0.42 | 0.83 | 1.25 |
| 10 | 0.83 | 1.67 | 2.50 |

*Source:* Newedge Prime Brokerage Research.

money market rates. And, as Exhibit 10.5 shows, this cost is proportional both to the manager's expected excess return and to the length of the investment lapse.

## Transactions Costs

Closing out old positions and opening new positions entails transactions costs in the form of bid/ask spreads and brokerage commissions. This is a cost borne most obviously by investors in managed accounts. It is also borne, but in a more diluted way, by investors in funds that incur transactions costs as a normal part of doing business and who, as a result, share these costs with all other investors in funds.

To get a sense of how much these costs might be, we considered an exercise in which a broadly diversified futures portfolio like those described in Chapters 4 and 5 was closed and reopened on May 8, 2007. The values of the bid/ask spreads used in this exercise were derived from Newedge's market depth database, which allows us to calculate the sweep-to-fill cost of trading futures in a wide range of futures markets.*

Exhibit 10.6 summarizes these costs for the four broad components of our trend-following portfolio. The portfolio holds 60 equity futures contracts in various markets. Given the values of the bid/ask spreads for these contracts, converted back to U.S. dollars in the case of non-dollar contracts, the average value of this cost per contract would have been $15.32, for a total cost of $919.19. The portfolio holds 274 interest rate contracts for which the average value of the bid/ask spread was $13.94, for a total cost of $3,818.60. The foreign exchange futures positions would have cost $1,050.75, while the commodities contracts—the most costly to trade by a large margin—would

---

*Our research into market liquidity and transactions costs in futures markets is detailed in Chapter 11. Sweeping the limit order book to fill an order captures the costs of immediate liquidity and so is the most costly way to accomplish a trade.

**EXHIBIT 10.6**   Cost of Trading a Diversified Futures Portfolio (Market Impact Only, in U.S. Dollars)

| Market | Number of Contracts | Average Cost per Contract* | Total Cost |
|---|---|---|---|
| Equity index | 60 | 15.32 | 919.19 |
| Interest rate | 274 | 13.94 | 3,818.60 |
| Foreign exchange | 84 | 12.51 | 1,050.75 |
| Commodities | 153 | 28.38 | 4,342.34 |
| *Portfolio* | *571* | *17.74* | *10,130.88* |

*Based on bid/ask spread for 8 May 07.*

*Source:* Newedge Prime Brokerage Research.

have cost $4,342.34. In all, the bid/ask cost of closing and reopening a position of this size would have been $10,130.88.

To turn this cost into basis points requires us to assume a notional invested amount. For example, if we associate this portfolio with a notional amount of $5 million, as we did in Chapter 4, these costs would have represented 0.20 percent, or 20 annualized basis points.

Two comments have been made about this estimate. First, it represents a comparatively small position and, as such, understates what the cost might be if a substantially larger position had to be liquidated and then reopened. Second, it does not include brokerage commissions. Because brokerage commissions vary widely from investor to investor and broker to broker, we make no effort here to correct that omission. At the same time, you will find that brokerage commissions for professional investors and money managers tend to be small relative to what you face in bid/ask spreads.

## Other Costs

Active management implies an active commitment to scouring the landscape for possible investments and ongoing study and evaluation of those managers who are in your current basket of possibilities. The costs of such an effort, however, are incurred no matter how many managers you employ or how much or how often you reallocate. A cost like this might lend itself to some kind of option analysis, but that analysis wouldn't be easy. At the very least, it would require the investor to piece together some reasonable estimates of the likelihood a successful manager will be closed to new investment and of just how much access one might gain by investing early and generously.

Relationship allocations also imply a cost. That is, you may invest more in a manager now, or not take money away from a manager now, because you have to think ahead to the day when the manager may be closed to additional or new investments.

## Conclusion

The costs of actively managing your investments are not small. By itself, a policy of replacing managers in drawdown with new managers might cost anywhere from 30–90 annualized basis points. This cost applies to the whole portfolio and applies to all investors. To overcome this cost may require new managers to promise 150–300 basis points in additional annualized returns for the same level of volatility.

The costs of dormant cash, opportunity losses, and slippage from transactions costs apply only to money that is moved from one manager to another and so works only at the margins. Even so, they can add up. Dormant cash might cost you 15–25 basis points depending on the level of money market interest rates and the time required to get your cash out of a fund. Opportunity losses might easily be 250 basis points if money is not quickly transferred from one manager to another. And slippage from transactions costs likely would be at least 20 basis points for a round turn from one manager to another.

For good or ill, these costs rarely show up as hardcopy invoices. Rather, they show up in the form of reduced returns that, in the absence of a program designed to track and measure costs, are hard to control.

# CHAPTER 11

# Measuring Market Impact and Liquidity

Poor execution can turn a good idea into a losing trade. Skilled traders (and their brokers) use their knowledge and experience to balance the immediacy of a transaction with the liquidity available in the market. This chapter reports on the work we have done to estimate the market impact of one-off trades in electronically traded futures markets.

We have invested heavily in gathering a continuous-time *market-depth* database that allows us to observe the limit order book in nearly continuous time and to track the flow of actual trades. In the case of the limit order book, we are tracking the best five bids and best five offers. This data set is exceptionally valuable for studying market liquidity and the impact of trades of various sizes. For example, it allows us to calculate a *sweep-to-fill* measure of market impact—the effect on the price of instantaneously trading as far into the book as necessary to fill an order of a given size, that is, the cost of sweeping the book to fill an order.

Exhibit 11.1 shows what the resulting sweep-to-fill market impact profiles looked like for the E-mini S&P 500 futures market during the first quarter of 2006. Information like this can be very useful to a trader. For one thing, the trader can identify the most liquid times of the trading day. For another, the trader can determine the effect of speeding up or slowing down on total transactions costs and make informed choices between tracking error and the costs of trading.

In fact, these data sets allow us to delve much more deeply into the question of market impact and liquidity and to formulate measures of market impact that take advantage of knowledge about predictable patterns of trading

227

**EXHIBIT 11.1**   Sweep-to-Fill Cost (E-mini S&Ps, 1/3/06–3/31/06)

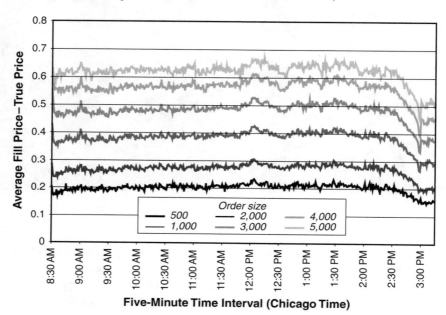

*Source:* Reuters, Newedge Prime Brokerage Research.

volume and price volatility, the risk aversion of market makers, and hidden liquidity.

The purpose of this chapter is to show the steps we have taken in using these data sets to produce useable market-impact profiles for use in designing cost-efficient trading programs. In the process, we will:

- Describe the data set we have assembled.
- Show some of the things that can be learned from the limit order book.
- Define sweep-to-fill market impact.
- Describe the risks faced by a market maker.
- Show how a simple risk-aversion model can capture the shape of the limit order book.
- Estimate the effects of hidden liquidity.
- Show our model estimates for four key futures markets.
- Show how we can allow for significant economic announcements.

We also provide, in the appendix at the end of this chapter, a derivation of the risk-averse market-maker model that we use to describe the limit order book.

## A Very Fat Data Set

To do this kind of work, we have assembled a very rich dataset for electronically traded futures that comprises price and sizes for all trades as well as the best five bids and best five asks. In assembling these data, we have recorded every instance of a change in the limit order book as well as every trade. In this way we can produce a snapshot of what the limit order book looked like at any instant. We can track additions to and withdrawals from the book, and we can infer from the status of the book the moment before each trade whether the trade occurred at the bid or the ask. From the trades themselves, we can learn about patterns of trading volume, both frequency and size, and of price volatility. The table in the appendix at the end of the chapter provides a list of the markets for which we are gathering these data.

These data lend themselves to insights into liquidity in several ways. For one thing, at the simplest level, they can tell you how much it would cost to fill an order of any given size immediately. Exhibit 11.2, for example, shows what the E-mini S&P 500 book looked like at 8:40:00 A.M. on February 21, 2006. It is worth noting that there would have been several limit order books published during the single second from 8:40:00 to 8:40:01, and that this was the first of those books.

**EXHIBIT 11.2**   Limit Order Book for E-mini S&P 500 Futures (2/21/2006, 8:40:00 A.M.)

| Price | Bid | | | Ask | | |
|---|---|---|---|---|---|---|
| | Average Price* | Total | Contracts | Contracts | Total | Average Price* |
| 1293.75 | | | | 1,361 | 5,973 | 1293.29 |
| 1293.50 | | | | 1,089 | 4,612 | 1293.16 |
| 1293.25 | | | | 1,434 | 3,523 | 1293.05 |
| 1293.00 | | | | 1,372 | 2,089 | 1292.91 |
| 1292.75 | | | | 717 | 717 | 1292.75 |
| 1292.50 | 1292.50 | 361 | 361 | | | |
| 1292.25 | 1292.35 | 870 | 509 | | | |
| 1292.00 | 1292.15 | 2,105 | 1,235 | | | |
| 1291.75 | 1292.06 | 2,686 | 581 | | | |
| 1291.50 | 1291.92 | 3,578 | 892 | | | |

*Average sweep to fill price.*

*Source:* Reuters, Newedge Prime Brokerage Research.

## Sweep to Fill

In this case, the best bid was 1292.50 with 361 contracts and the best ask was 1292.75 with 717 contracts. Thus, you could immediately sell 361 contracts at a price of 1292.50, or you could immediately buy 717 contracts at the price of 1292.75. If you wanted to sell more than 361 contracts or buy more than 717 contracts, and to do either immediately, you would have to sell at the next best bid of 1292.25 or to buy at the next best ask of 1293.00. Since there were 509 contracts at the second-best bid, you could sell as many as 870 without going deeper into the book, and if you were to sell 361 at the best bid and 509 at the next-best bid, your average trade price would be 1292.35 [= (361/870) · 1292.50 + (509/870) · 1202.25]. If you were to buy 2,089 contracts immediately, your average price would be 1292.91 [= (717/2,089) · 1292.75 + (1,372/2,089) · 1293.00].

A practice like this is known *as sweeping the book*, and the resulting average price one realizes is known as a *sweep to fill*. The immediate market impact of sweeping the book can be calculated by taking the difference between the sweep-to-fill price and some measure of the mid-market price. The market-impact profiles shown in Exhibit 11.1, for example, provide an example of how this measure of market impact looked for trades of various sizes in E-mini S&P 500 futures for the first quarter of 2006 on those days when there were no scheduled economic announcements of particular importance. For this illustration, the measure of mid-market we have used is *true market price*, which we will explain in the next section.

Profiles like these are useful guides to finding market liquidity. Notice, for example, that the market impact of a trade is higher right at the market open of 8:30 A.M. (Chicago time) than it would be even a few minutes into the trading day. You can see that market impact tends to rise as the trading day progresses and tends to be highest right around noon, when trading is slowest. It is also apparent that the market is most liquid (impact is smallest) as the market reaches the cash close time of 3:00 P.M. and remains relatively liquid until the futures close at 3:15 P.M.

## True Market Price

In the academic literature, one finds the very sensible notion that there is a true market price that lies between the best bid and the best ask. Evidence gleaned from the limit order book tends to bear this out, and those who trade or execute trades for a living will recognize the idea immediately.

Consider again the order book in Exhibit 11.2. There are 717 contracts offered at the best ask price of 1292.75, but only 361 contracts at the best bid price of 1292.50. From this information, traders and their brokers are likely to observe that the market is more heavily offered than bid and that the next trade is more likely to take place at the bid than at the offer.

To lend concreteness to this idea, we define order imbalance as ln(Bid size/Ask size). If the numbers of contracts at the bid and ask are equal, the ratio would be 1, and this measure of order imbalance would be 0. This measure of order imbalance will be negative if the number of contracts bid is less than the number offered, and will be positive if the number of contracts bid is more than the number offered. Moreover, it will be symmetrical, so that if the number of contracts bid is twice the number offered, the measure would be $\ln(2) = 0.693$. If the number of contracts bid is half the number offered, the measure would be $\ln(0.5) = -0.693$.

Now consider Exhibit 11.3, which shows the relationship between order imbalance and the time to next trade for E-mini S&Ps. When order imbalance is close to zero—that is, when the number of contracts at the bid and ask are

**EXHIBIT 11.3** Time to Next Trade versus Order Imbalance (E-mini S&P Futures, 2/4/06–2/23/06)

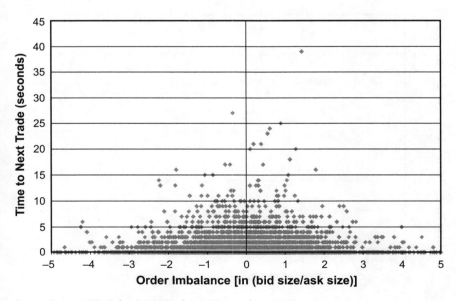

*Source:* Reuters, Newedge Prime Brokerage Research.

roughly equal—the time to next trade tends to be high. In contrast, when the order imbalance is large in either direction, the time between trades tends to be small. This seems reasonable enough if a balanced order book means that the price at which people would really like to trade is equally far from both the bid price and the ask price.

Also consider Exhibit 11.4, which shows the relationship between the next trade price and order imbalance. On the vertical axis is the difference between the next trade price and mid-market (halfway between the best bid and ask). Most of the dots in this exhibit occur at a difference of +0.125 or −0.125, which in E-mini S&Ps represents half a tick. These cases represent instances of the price trading either at the ask or at the bid when the market was 1 tick wide. There are a few cases where the price change was a full tick (either +0.25 or −0.25) or zero. These outcomes correspond to times when the market was two ticks wide.

What we find in this exhibit is that trades are more likely to take place at the ask when the order imbalance is positive and more likely to take place

**EXHIBIT 11.4**  Next Trade Price versus Order Imbalance (E-mini S&P Futures, 2/4/06–2/23/06)

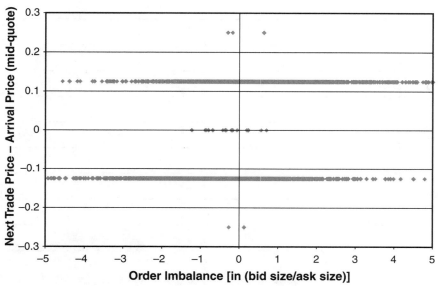

*Source:* Reuters, Newedge Prime Brokerage Research.

**EXHIBIT 11.5** Average Price Change versus Bid/Ask Imbalance (E-mini S&P Futures, 2/4/06–2/24/06)

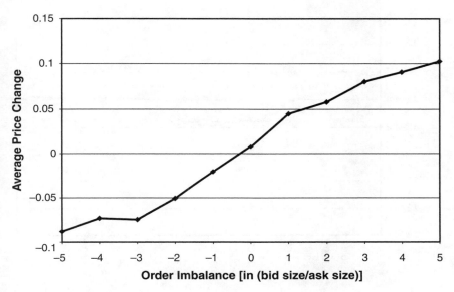

*Source:* Reuters, Newedge Prime Brokerage Research.

at the bid when the order imbalance is negative. Again, this is just what experienced traders or brokers would expect.

A slightly different representation of this feature of the market is shown in Exhibit 11.5, which shows the average price change for various order imbalance values. The effect of averaging the price changes produces a fairly well-shaped curve that confirms the idea that the "true market price" can be tied reliably to imbalances in the limit order book.

Exhibit 11.6 provides a sample of how the idea of a true market price might be used in practice. The exhibit shows a bid/ask channel for E-mini S&Ps for the 10 seconds from 8:30:00 A.M. to 8:30:10 A.M. It also shows a running calculation of the true market price, which was calculated as:

$$Trueprice = \left( \frac{Q_A}{Q_A + Q_B} \right) P_B + \left( \frac{Q_B}{Q_A + Q_B} \right) P_A$$

To be sure, the true price has to lie between the bid and ask prices, but there does seem to be some useful information about where the market is

**EXHIBIT 11.6**  Bid, Ask, and True Market Prices (E-mini S&P 500 Futures, 4/12/06, 8:30:00–8:30:10 A.M.

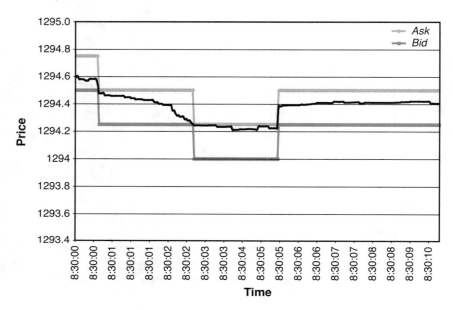

*Source:* Reuters, Newedge Prime Brokerage Research.

going based on the relationship between the true price and the surrounding bid and ask prices.

## A Representative Market Maker

For the purposes of bringing some order to the data, we will treat the great pool of traders whose business it is to provide liquidity as a single, representative, risk-averse market maker. This fairly simple approach is surprisingly effective in explaining the shape of the limit order book.

### The Market Maker's Risk

To illustrate the market maker's risk, we use a simple two-period example that allows us to consider both the speed with which the market maker's inventory can be worked off and the price risk that comes with holding the inventory.

**EXHIBIT 11.7** Market Maker's Timeline

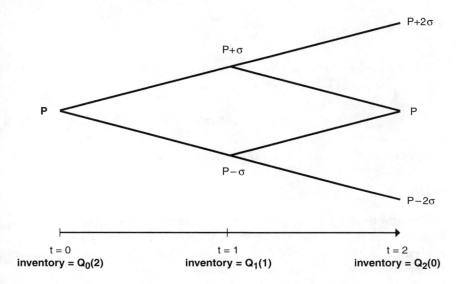

*Source:* Newedge Prime Brokerage Research.

For this example, we assume that the market maker is asked to take on an order size of two contracts, that the volume of trading in the market will allow the market maker to get rid of one contract per period, and that during each period the price can either rise or fall by an amount equal to $\sigma$. The initial price is $P_0$.

In this setting, as shown in Exhibit 11.7, the market maker's initial inventory at $t_0$ is two contracts. At $t_1$, he can get rid of one contract at $P_1$. He now has a remaining inventory of one contract, which he holds for one more period. Then, at $t_2$, he gets rid of this contract at $P_2$. Given this sequence of events, we can write the market maker's P/L as

$$P/L = Q_0(P_1 - P_0) + Q_1(P_2 - P_1)$$

If the price changes are uncorrelated from one period to the next, the variance of this P/L can be written as

$$V(P/L) = Q_0^2(P_1 - P_0)^2 + Q_1^2(P_2 - P_1)^2$$

and the standard deviation as

$$SD(P/L) = \sqrt{Q_0^2(P_1 - P_0)^2 + Q_1^2(P_2 - P_1)^2}$$

Using a price change of plus or minus $\sigma$, the market maker's total risk in our example would be

$$Totalrisk = \sqrt{2^2\sigma^2 + 1^2\sigma^2}$$

which can be divided by the initial order size to find risk per contract.

## The Market Maker's Risk Aversion

To explain the shape of the limit order book, we can assume that the market maker is risk averse. Further, as we will show, we can do a good job of explaining the shape of actual limit order books by assuming that the market maker requires an amount $\alpha$ for each unit of risk taken on.

With this assumption, and using a continuous-time expression for the market maker's risk, we can express the market maker's required compensation for taking on an order size of $Q$ as

$$TotalComp(Q) = \frac{\alpha\sigma}{\sqrt{3cv}} Q^{3/2}$$

where $\alpha$ is the market maker's required compensation per unit of risk, $\sigma$ is the standard deviation of arithmetic changes in the price, $v$ is the rate of volume traded in the market, $c$ is the fraction of that volume available to the market maker, and $Q$ is the total order size. Average market-maker compensation per contract would simply be

$$AverageComp(Q) = \alpha \frac{\sigma}{\sqrt{3cv}} Q^{1/2}$$

The intuition behind this expression is fairly straightforward. For one thing, an increase in risk aversion translates directly into an increase in the spread. For another, increases in price risk translate directly into an increase in what the market maker requires to take on a position. And third, while time does not seem to enter directly, it does indirectly. A quadrupling of the order size, for example, would quadruple the amount of time the market maker requires to unwind the position at whatever speed the flow of trading in the market allows. The effect on the spread, however, is proportional to the square root of the order size. Thus, a quadrupling of the order size only doubles the size of the spread. Trading volume, the square root of which appears in the denominator, works in the same way as order size but in the opposite direction. A quadrupling of useable trading volume in the market would cut the spread in half.

As a practical matter, compensation per contract in this exercise would be one half the bid/ask spread for orders of any given size since the market maker has to be willing to either buy or sell.

## Fitting the Curve to the Data

The usefulness of this way of thinking about market making is illustrated in Exhibits 11.8 and 11.9, which show actual and fitted values of sweep to fill impact values for two different times of day in E-mini S&P 500 trading. Exhibit 11.8 corresponds to 8:40 A.M., when the market is very active. Exhibit 11.9 corresponds to 12:40 P.M., when the market is comparatively quiet.

**EXHIBIT 11.8**   Sweep-to-Fill Costs versus Order Size (EMINISP, 8:40 A.M., Alpha = 1.94, 1/3/06–3/31/06)

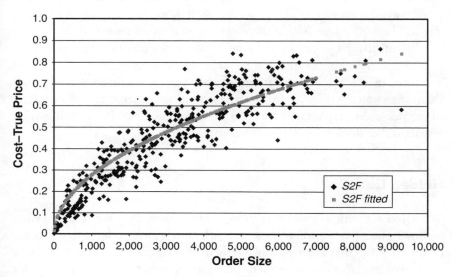

*Source:* Reuters, Newedge Prime Brokerage Research.

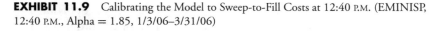

**EXHIBIT 11.9**   Calibrating the Model to Sweep-to-Fill Costs at 12:40 P.M. (EMINISP, 12:40 P.M., Alpha = 1.85, 1/3/06–3/31/06)

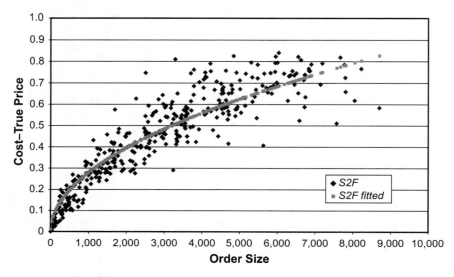

*Source:* Reuters, Newedge Prime Brokerage Research.

Using specific times of day for curve fitting is a way of controlling for trading volume and price volatility. As we will see, volume and volatility profiles exhibit a lot of regularity, so that 8:40 in the morning on one trading day will look a lot like 8:40 in the morning on another trading day.

When fitting the curves, we sought values of alpha that minimized the sum of squared errors in total trading cost. The difference between observed and fitted market impact is worth more when you are trading 5,000 contracts than when you are trading 500 contracts. So it makes sense to find estimates of the risk-aversion parameter that do the best job of explaining total market impact rather than market impact per contract.

## Hidden Liquidity

What you see with a limit order book is not necessarily what you get. First, it shows phantom liquidity—bids and offers to which traders are not really committed and that are withdrawn either for no apparent reason or because the market begins to move in their direction. Whether these are available for sweep-to-fill orders is to some extent a matter of timing and fast action. Also, the limit order book does not reveal hidden liquidity—all of those potential bids and offers controlled by traders who don't want to show their hands.

Of the two, it seems that hidden liquidity is the more important consideration when analyzing market impact. As have others, we find that the apparent impact of trades tends to be smaller than sweep-to-fill measures of market impact would suggest.

## Seconds per Half-Tick

To get a handle on hidden liquidity, we conducted the following exercise. First, we defined spans of time that could reasonably be considered instantaneous for the purposes of measuring the flow of traffic through a market. While it certainly stretches the concept of *instantaneous*, it does make sense to define a span of time over which one might reasonably expect the market not to tick up or down. This kind of span depends on two things—tick size and price volatility.

For our purposes, we define this as the interval of time for which a one-standard-deviation price move is equal to half of a tick in each market. If price changes are normally distributed, this means that roughly 68 percent of the price changes over the interval would be within plus or minus one-half of a tick.

Using realized price volatility for the six months leading up to April 11, 2006, we translated annualized price volatility to volatility per second based on the number of trading seconds in a day (using normal open and close times) and assuming 252 trading days per year. Given volatility per second, one standard deviation over $t$ seconds would be

$$\sigma_t = \sigma_s t^{1/2}$$

Setting this equal to one-half a tick and solving for $t$, we get

$$t = \frac{1}{4} \left( \frac{tick}{\sigma_s} \right)^2$$

The resulting calculations for our four markets are shown in Exhibit 11.10.

## Estimates of Hidden Liquidity

Our first step was to determine how many contracts actually traded during intervals of these lengths (five seconds in the case of E-mini S&Ps) during the

**EXHIBIT 11.10**  How Fast Is Instantaneous?

| Market | Seconds per Half Tick |
|--------|-----------------------|
| E-mini S&Ps | 6 |
| 10-year Treasury notes | 21 |
| EuroStoxx | 10 |
| EuroBunds | 10 |

*Source:* Reuters, Newedge Prime Brokerage Research.

first quarter of 2006. In practice, we started at the beginning of each trading minute during regular trading hours. For each snapshot, we classified all trades that took place at a price above the true market price at the beginning of the interval as "buys" and all trades that took place at a price below the true market price as "sells." This was an imperfect distinction, but plausible. Suppose, for example, that the true market price is 1380 at 8:40 A.M. and that we observe the following E-mini S&P trades take place during the next five seconds:

| Quantity | Price |
|----------|-------|
| 20 | 1380.50 |
| 9 | 1379.50 |
| 17 | 1379.75 |
| 6 | 1380.25 |
| 25 | 1379.75 |

We would treat the first and fourth trades of 20 and 6 contracts respectively as "buys" and the second, third, and fifth trades, or 9, 17, and 25, as "sells." The total number bought would be 26 and the total number sold would be 51.

We would then calculate volume-weighted average prices—vwaps—for the "buys" and for the "sells." In this example, the average buy vwap is 1380.44 $[= (20 \cdot 1380.50 + 6 \cdot 1380.25) / 26]$, while the average sell vwap is 1379.71 $[= (9 \cdot 1379.50 + 17 \cdot 1379.75 + 25 \cdot 1379.75) / 51]$.

**EXHIBIT 11.11**   Vwap Market Impacts (E-mini S&Ps, 1/3/06–3/31/06)

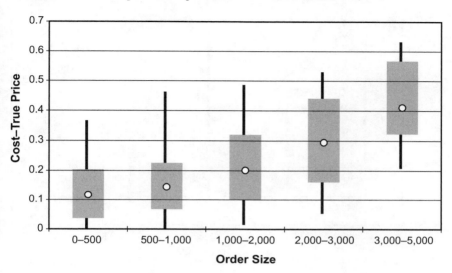

*Source:* Reuters, Newedge Prime Brokerage Research.

Given the true market price of 100, the vwap impact of buying 26 contracts would be 0.44 [= 1380.44 − 1380.00], while the vwap impact of selling 51 contracts would be 0.29 [= Absolute value (1379.71 − 1380)].

The resulting distributions of these vwap impact estimates for E-mini S&Ps are shown in Exhibit 11.11. For the sake of simplicity, we have grouped the trades by lot sizes with the 0–500 bucket containing the smallest trades and 3,000–5,000 containing the largest trades. The dot in each figure represents the average value of the impact. The box represents 80 percent of the observations, from 10 percent to 90 percent. The top and bottom of each "whisker" represents the maximum and minimum values of each distribution.

The second step was to determine what the sweep-to-fill impacts would have been for trades whose sizes were equal to the total buys and total sells in each interval. In the above example, we would have calculated the sweep-to-fill impact of buying 26 contracts given the limit order book observed at exactly 8:40:00. Similarly, we would have calculated the sweep-to-fill impact of selling 51 contracts given the same limit order book. The distributions of these sweep-to-fill impacts for various order size buckets are shown in Exhibit 11.12.

**EXHIBIT 11.12**   Sweep-to-Fill Market Impacts (E-mini S&Ps, 1/3/06–3/31/06)

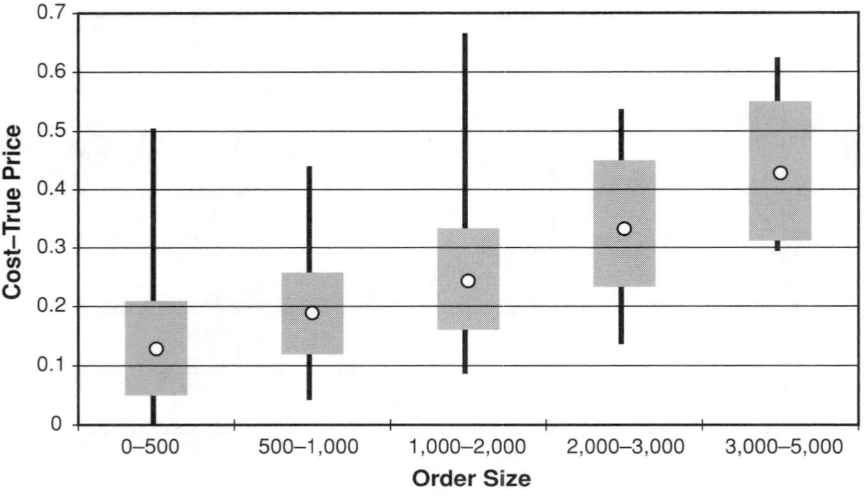

*Source:* Reuters, Newedge Prime Brokerage Research.

Comparing the two distributions, we find that actual trade prices reveal more liquidity than is apparent in the limit order book. As shown in Exhibit 11.13, the effect of hidden liquidity was worth slightly more than a cent for small orders and just under 2 cents for fairly large trade sizes. For intermediate-sized trades, though, the presence of hidden liquidity was worth considerably more. For trades between 500 and 1,000 contracts, hidden liquidity was worth 4.4 cents, while for trades between 2,000 and 3,000 contracts, hidden liquidity was worth about 3.8 cents per contract.

**EXHIBIT 11.13**   Hidden Liquidity Summary for E-mini S&Ps (1/3/06–3/31/06)

| Order Size | Average Impact | | |
|---|---|---|---|
| | Sweep to Fill | Vwap | Difference |
| 0–500 | 0.129 | 0.117 | 0.011 |
| 500–1000 | 0.189 | 0.145 | 0.044 |
| 1000–2000 | 0.243 | 0.202 | 0.042 |
| 2000–3000 | 0.332 | 0.295 | 0.038 |
| 3000–5000 | 0.428 | 0.411 | 0.017 |

*Source:* Reuters, Newedge Prime Brokerage Research.

**EXHIBIT 11.14** Risk-Aversion Parameter (Alpha) Estimates (Non-Event Days, January–March 2006)

| Market | Estimation Times | | | | Average Alpha | Hidden Liquidity Adjustment | Adjusted Alpha |
|---|---|---|---|---|---|---|---|
| E-mini S&Ps | 8:40 A.M. | 10:40 A.M. | 12:40 P.M. | 2:50 P.M. | 1.85 | 0.87 | 1.61 |
| 10-year Treasury notes | 7:50 A.M. | 9:50 A.M. | 11:50 A.M. | 1:50 P.M. | 1.79 | 0.72 | 1.29 |
| EuroStoxx | 2:10 A.M. | 5:10 A.M. | 8:40 A.M. | 10:20 A.M. | 2.13 | 0.93 | 1.98 |
| EuroBunds | 1:10 A.M. | 4:10 A.M. | 7:50 A.M. | 11:50 A.M. | 2.04 | 0.85 | 1.73 |

*Source:* Reuters, Newedge Prime Brokerage Research.

## Calibrating for Hidden Liquidity

The next-to-last step in this process required us to fit the market maker's required compensation curve to the two sets of data described here. To do this, we used sweep-to-fill and vwap impact values irrespective of the time of day for which they were calibrated. As a result, the estimates of the risk-aversion parameter are of no direct use, but we use the relative values of the estimated alphas to recalibrate the curve's fit for specific times of day.

## Estimating the Risk-Aversion Parameter

Exhibit 11.14 provides a summary of our estimates of the risk-aversion parameter (alpha) for four highly active and liquid futures markets—two equity markets and two 10-year-note markets. In all four cases, we chose four times of day for fitting the curve to sweep-to-fill impact data—a time shortly after each market's open, two times in the middle of each market's trading day, and one time shortly before the close of each market. The average unadjusted alphas for the two U.S. markets were around 1.8, while the average unadjusted European markets were slightly more than 2.0. The hidden liquidity adjustment was greatest for 10-year Treasury note futures and smallest for EuroStoxx futures.

## Volume, Volatility, and Market Impact Profiles

We have now reached the point where we can pull all of the pieces together to produce reliable market-impact profiles. Our model of market impact requires three pieces of information: trading volume, price volatility, and an estimate

**EXHIBIT 11.15** Trading Volume for E-mini S&P Futures (Thousands of Contracts per Interval, 3/23/05–3/23/06)

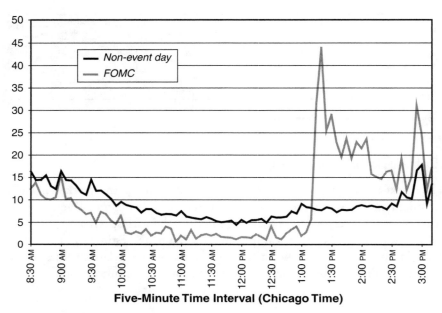

**Five-Minute Time Interval (Chicago Time)**

*Source:* Reuters, Newedge Prime Brokerage Research.

of market makers' risk aversion. An example of how it all fits together is provided in Exhibits 11.15 through 11.18.

Exhibit 11.15 shows two volume profiles for E-mini S&P futures. One is for a typical trading day for which there are no scheduled economic announcements of any particular importance. The other is for a trading day on which an FOMC announcement is scheduled. As is apparent, the presence of the FOMC announcement predictably changes the shape of the trading day and the amount of trading done at any given time during the day.

Exhibit 11.16 shows two price volatility profiles for E-mini S&P futures. Again, one is for a typical trading day, while the other is for an FOMC announcement day.

Using these profiles, we can calculate market-impact profiles for orders of various sizes for the two kinds of days. For example, Exhibit 11.17 shows what market-impact profiles would look like for order sizes ranging from 100 to 10,000 contracts at a time on a typical trading day. Exhibit 11.18 (see page 247) shows what the profiles should look like on an FOMC announcement day.

**EXHIBIT 11.16** Price Volatility for E-mini S&P Futures (Points per Interval, 3/23/05–3/23/06)

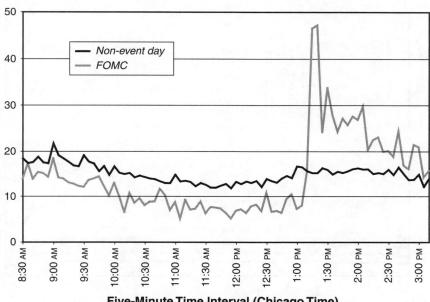

**Five-Minute Time Interval (Chicago Time)**

*Source:* Reuters, Newedge Prime Brokerage Research.

The combined effect on volume and volatility of an FOMC announcement makes the market predictably less liquid right around the announcement. The effects of the announcement on volume and volatility seem to be roughly the same orders of magnitude. But volatility matters more than volume for market impact, so the liquidity of the market falls at announcement time.

We find it encouraging that these theoretical profiles make sense. For one thing, the impact profiles for a typical trading day look like the sweep-to-fill profiles shown at the outset in Exhibit 11.1. The market tends to become less liquid as the trading day progresses until shortly before the close. The theoretical impact estimates are lowest at the cash close—another feature of the observed sweep-to-fill profiles. Also, the theoretical impact profiles, which have been reckoned using estimates of alpha adjusted for hidden liquidity, are slightly lower than the sweep-to-fill profiles.

**EXHIBIT 11.17**   Market Impact for E-mini S&P Futures on a Typical Day (Projected Spread to "True" Price)

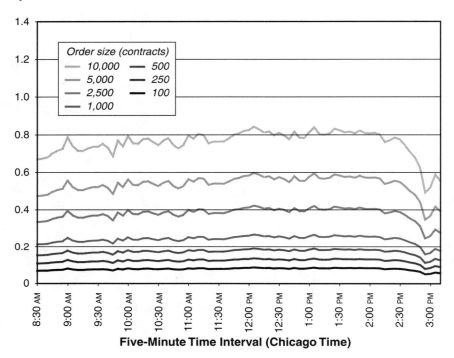

*Source:* Reuters, Newedge Prime Brokerage Research.

## Where Do We Go from Here?

At this point, we have enough confidence in this approach to measuring market impact that we will extend the analysis to cover all electronically traded markets that are active enough to provide us with enough data. Also, we plan to extend the analysis to cover sequential trades so that we can say something useful about very large trades.

Our market impact estimates will be useful in at least three trading applications. These include optimal trading strategies—that is, those that are designed to minimize market impact or produce the best tradeoff between market impact and tracking error. A second is the design of tactical execution rules for working orders. Our insights into liquidity and the possibility of using the limit order book to determine the likelihood of being filled at the

**EXHIBIT 11.18** Market Impact for E-mini S&P Futures on an FOMC Announcement Day (Projected Spread to "True" Price)

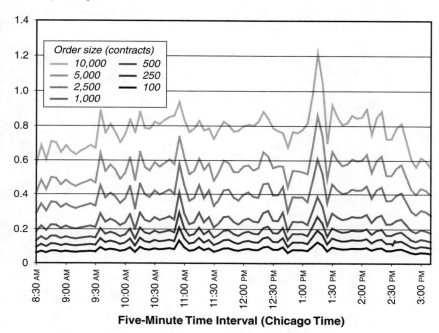

*Source:* Reuters, Newedge Prime Brokerage Research.

bid or the offer will be a natural fit for such tools. A third is the analysis of benchmarks, tracking error, and execution costs.

## Appendix

### Market Data Sets

| Contract | | Outrights | Spreads |
|---|---|---|---|
| Equities | Emini SP | 12/14/05 | 12/14/05 |
| | Emini Nasdaq | 12/14/05 | 12/14/05 |
| | Emini Russell | 12/14/05 | 12/14/05 |
| | Canada S&P60 | 5/4/06 | |

## Market Data Sets (*Continued*)

| Contract | | Outrights | Spreads |
|---|---|---|---|
| | DAX | 7/5/05 | 11/16/05 |
| | Eurostoxx 50 | 7/12/05 | 11/16/05 |
| | CAC40 | 1/10/06 | 3/23/06 |
| | AEX | 2/16/06 | |
| | FTSE100 | 7/28/05 | 4/25/06 |
| | IBEX35 | 5/5/06 | |
| | Mini Dow | 3/28/06 | 12/14/05 |
| | SPI 200 | 5/4/06 | |
| | TOPIX Index | 8/30/05 | |
| | Nikkei 225 | 5/3/06 | |
| | Hang Seng | | |
| | MSCI-Taiwan | | |
| | MSCI-SG | | |
| Bonds | US 30-year | 12/14/05 | 3/29/06 |
| | US 10-year | 12/14/05 | 12/14/05 |
| | US 5-year | 12/14/05 | 3/29/06 |
| | US 2-year | 12/14/05 | 3/29/06 |
| | Canada 10-year | 5/4/06 | |
| | Bund | 7/12/05 | 9/20/05 |
| | Bobl | 7/28/05 | |
| | Schatz | 7/28/05 | |
| | Liffe Gilt | 7/27/05 | 4/25/06 |
| | Australian 10-year | 5/4/06 | |
| | CONF | 5/5/06 | 11/16/05 |
| | JGB 10-year | 8/30/05 | |
| Money Market | Eurodollar | 12/14/05 | 12/14/05 |
| | Liffe Euribor | 7/28/05 | |
| | Fed Funds | 5/5/06 | |
| | Three-Month Canadian BAs | | |
| | Euroyen | | |
| | Short Sterling | | |
| Currencies | British Pound | 12/14/05 | |
| | Euro | 12/14/05 | |
| | Japanese Yen | 12/14/05 | |
| Energy | Brent Crude (ICE) | 4/3/06 | |
| | Gas Oil (ICE) | 4/3/06 | |
| | WTCL (ICE) | 4/14/06 | |

*Source:* Reuters, Newedge Prime Brokerage Research.

## Derivation of the Market-Depth Model

Consider an order of size $Q$ arrives at the market maker at time $a$. We assume the market maker can liquidate the position at the mid-price in proportion to the average volume over time. Specifically, the market maker will liquidate the entire position by time $T$, where $T$ solves the equation:

$$c \int_a^T dV(t) = Q$$

where $dV(t)$ is the instantaneous rate of market volume traded at time $t$, and $c$ is a constant of proportionality representing the relative speed at which the market maker can liquidate inventory: $c = 1$ implies the market maker liquidates at the average rate of trading in the market. Following this notation, let $Q(t)$ be the quantity remaining to be liquidated at time $t$:

$$Q(t) = Q(a) - c \int_a^t dV(s) = c \int_t^T dV(s) = c[V(T) - V(t)]$$

Let $p(t)$ represent the mid-price at time $t$.

Suppose the mid-price evolves according to an arithmetic Brownian motion:

$$p(t) = p(a) + \int_a^t \sigma(s) dZ(s)$$

where $\sigma(s)$ denotes the instantaneous price volatility at time $s$. Then the gain (or loss) experienced by the market maker in liquidating according to the above schedule is:

$$\prod(T) = c \int_a^T [p(t) - p(a)] dV(t)$$

$$= c \int_a^T \left( \int_a^t \sigma(s) dZ(s) \right) dV(t)$$

$$= \int_a^T \left( c \int_s^T dV(t) \right) \sigma(s) dV(s)$$

$$= \int_s^T Q(s) \sigma(s) dZ(s).$$

The variance of the market maker's profit is therefore:

$$\text{var}\left[\prod(T)\right] = \text{var}\left[\int_a^T Q(s)\sigma(s)dZ(s)\right]$$

$$= \int_a^T \text{var}[Q(s)\sigma(s)dZ(s)]$$

$$= \int_a^T Q^2(s)\sigma^2(s)\text{var}[dZ(s)]$$

$$= \int_a^T Q^2(s)\sigma^2(s)ds.$$

Suppose the market maker demands a constant price of risk, $\alpha$. Then the spread-to-mid that the market maker will charge for quantity $Q$ is:

$$\text{spread} = \alpha\sqrt{\text{var}\left[\prod(T)\right]}/Q = \alpha\sqrt{\int_\alpha^T Q^2(s)\sigma^2(s)ds}\Bigg/Q$$

# PART III

# Portfolio Construction

# CHAPTER 12

# Superstars versus Teamwork

One of the greatest tensions in the world of money management is in the pull between assets that perform well on their own and portfolios that perform well. Even the most casual students of finance know about the importance of diversification. But as soon as any one asset turns in a bad performance, the temptation to dump that asset and replace it with something that performed better is nearly irresistible.

What we found in this research is that team players outperformed superstars. We found that the difference was statistically significant. We found that in most cases replacing "underperforming" managers with someone who would have been better did little or nothing to improve overall portfolio performance. We did find, though, that firing team players for poor individual performance and replacing them with managers with higher Sharpe ratios seriously degraded the performance of the portfolio.

We ran a contest—pitting portfolios of superstars against portfolios that were chosen for the way the managers fit together—and report the findings in this chapter. We started with a set of 42 managers for whom we had monthly return data from 1995 through 2005. We then formed portfolios of 10 managers with the highest Sharpe ratios (the superstars) and compared their combined performance with that of portfolios that were formed with managers that played well together—that is, managers whose low correlations with one another produced the best possible Sharpe ratio.

The first finding was that the original portfolio of team players formed at the end of 1997 and kept together for the eight years from 1998 through 2005 turned in a cumulative Sharpe ratio of 0.85. This value can be found in

**EXHIBIT 12.1**   Team Players Outperform Superstars (8-Year Sharpe Ratios, 1998–2005)

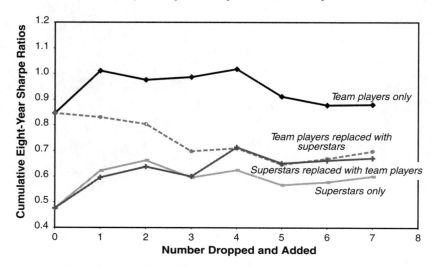

*Source:* Barclay Hedge, Newedge Prime Brokerage Research.

Exhibit 12.1 as the leftmost value of the two lines identified as "Team players only" and "Team players replaced with superstars." In contrast, the original portfolio of superstars turned in a cumulative Sharpe ratio of 0.48. This value can be found as the leftmost value of the two lines identified as "Superstars only" and "Superstars replaced with team players."

The second finding was that dropping managers for poor individual performance did little to improve things and, in one prominent case, made things a lot worse. If we stuck with team players only or if we stuck with superstars only, the final outcome was very little different from what we realized with the original managers in each case. Replacing underperformers in the Superstar portfolio with team players (Superstars replaced with team players) seemed to improve things very slightly.

But firing managers simply for losing money and replacing them with managers with better individual track records (Team players replaced with superstars) dragged the Teamwork portfolio down to the point where its eight-year record was barely better than the original Superstar portfolio.

This project took us through a number of questions related to correlation and diversification, including:

- How much diversification does low correlation allow?
- How reliable are correlation estimates?

- How do superstars stack up against teamwork?
- Were the resulting differences statistically significant?
- What do you gain by firing and replacing underperforming managers?
- What expectations should you have for individual performance?
- What is the incremental value of knowledge about returns, volatilities, and correlations?
- What are the costs of dropping and adding managers?

Throughout the chapter, we used monthly return data for 42 CTAs who had $100 million or more under management in 2005. We chose these managers for two reasons. First, their return series had no gaps in them. Second, they were all successful in raising money and running their businesses. By definition, then, we are working with successful managers who survived the period. All had good track records, and all were still open for investment. This means that we are ignoring various biases, including those from losing sight of managers who go out of business or those that arise when successful managers stop accepting money.

Our focus, though, is on the question of whether teamwork matters when forming portfolios. And for this question, the data set we have works well.

## The Contribution of Low Correlation to Portfolio Performance

The main objective of diversification is to reduce the risk for any given level of expected return. Throughout this chapter, we will refer to a diversification ratio, which we define as

$$Diversification\ Ratio = \frac{\sigma_{portfolio}}{\Sigma w_i \sigma_i} \left( = \frac{PortfolioStdDev}{AverageStdDev} \right)$$

Exhibit 12.2 shows how the diversification ratio falls as you add managers (or assets) whose true correlations range anywhere from 0.0 (most diversification) to 1.0 (no diversification).

Exhibit 12.2 reminds us of two things about correlation and diversification. First, for correlations above 0.5, the possibilities for reducing risk for any given level of return are limited—not nothing, but limited. Combining 5 managers with correlations of 0.5 with one another can reduce risk by a little more than 20 percent, but adding any more does not reduce risk much.

**EXHIBIT 12.2** Risk Reduction through Diversification

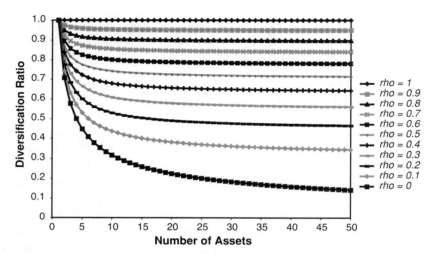

*Source:* Newedge Prime Brokerage Research.

Second, the marginal risk reduction from adding managers drops off fairly quickly, even for very low-correlation managers. By the time you have combined 10 managers with correlations of 0.0 with one another, you have milked diversification for most of what it is worth.

## How Reliable Are Correlation Estimates?

If we plan to use correlation as an organizing device for building our portfolios, we need answers to two questions. First, how good are correlation estimates? This is a sampling question that focuses on how our estimates of correlation are distributed around their true values. Second, how stable are correlation estimates over time? This focuses on the question of whether we can use correlation estimates based on historical returns to forecast the correlations we expect to observe going forward.

In answering these questions, we learned two satisfying lessons. First, it appears that the past correlations do an adequate job of forecasting future correlations. Second, and this was most surprising, our estimates of overall correlation among assets in a portfolio are more reliable for a large enough number of low-correlation managers or assets than they are for high- or medium-correlation assets.

## Estimating the Correlation between Two Assets

The mean and variance of estimates of correlation between the returns on two assets are:

$$mean(r) = \rho - \frac{\rho(1 - \rho)}{2n}$$

and

$$variance(r) = \frac{(1 - \rho^2)^2}{n} \left(1 + \frac{11\rho^2}{2n} + \cdots\right)$$

where $r$ is the estimate of $\rho$.

From the expression for the mean, we can see that estimates of correlation tend to be biased except when the true correlation is 0. From the expression for the variance, we can see that the distribution of our estimates depends both on the true value of correlation and on the sample size.

Exhibits 12.3 and 12.4 illustrate the effect of true correlation and sample size on the distribution of sample estimates. Exhibit 12.3 shows two

**EXHIBIT 12.3**  Distributions of Estimated Correlation ($N = 12$)

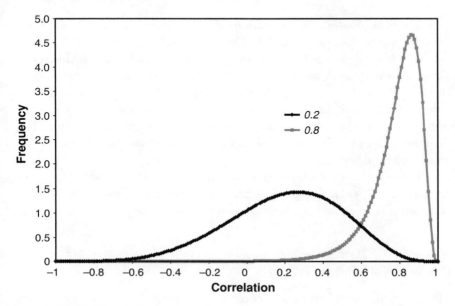

*Source:* Newedge Prime Brokerage Research.

**EXHIBIT 12.4**   Distributions of Estimated Correlation ($N = 24$)

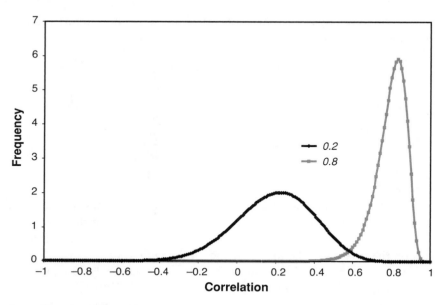

*Source:* Newedge Prime Brokerage Research.

distributions of estimated correlation—one for a true correlation of 0.8 and one for a true correlation of 0.2. The sample size in this case is 12 observations. It is hard to see the bias in these distributions, but the differences in shape and breadth are clear. When correlation is high, the distribution is both tight and skewed to the left. When correlation is low, the distribution is broad and looks more symmetrical. Notice, too, that when you have only a few observations, the overlap between the two distributions is fairly big. This suggests that it can be hard to detect differences in correlation, even if the differences are large.

Exhibit 12.4 shows how the distributions tighten up as the sample size increases. In this case the sample size is 24 rather than 12. The overlap between the two is smaller, and the high-correlation distribution has lost some of its skew.

## The Stability of Correlation Estimates

To see whether past correlations could be used as reliable predictors of future correlations, we conducted the following experiment. First, using the returns of our 42 managers, we formed portfolios of 10 randomly selected managers and did this 10,000 times for each four-year set beginning with 1995 through 1998, and continued on through 2002 through 2005. For each portfolio and for each set of years, we calculated two implied or aggregate correlations for the managers in the portfolio, one for the first three years (the past) and one for the fourth year in the set (the future).

For the purposes of this exercise, we define implied correlation as the single correlation value among all managers that sets the theoretical diversification ratio equal to the observed diversification ratio. Therefore, even though the correlations between any two managers in our 10-manager portfolios could be different from one another, our implied correlation is the average pairwise correlation that explains the diversification that we observe in the actual portfolios. Exhibit 12.5 shows the relationship between implied correlation in 1998 (the vertical axis) and the portfolios' implied correlations from 1995 through 1997.

There are two bits of good news in Exhibit 12.5. First, the relationship is tight enough to afford some discernment. For example, Exhibit 12.6 shows the distributions of implied correlations in 1998 for portfolios whose implied

**EXHIBIT 12.5** Historical and Realized Implied Correlations for Portfolios of 10 Managers (Historical, 1995–1997; Realized 1998)

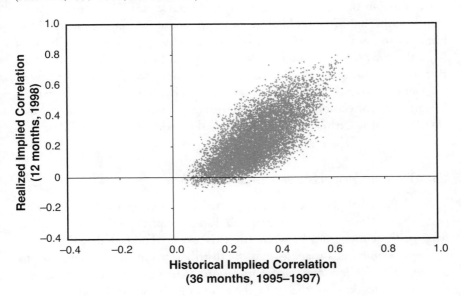

*Source:* Barclay Hedge, Newedge Prime Brokerage Research.

**EXHIBIT 12.6**   Overlapping Correlation Distributions (Historical, 1995–1997; Realized, 1998)

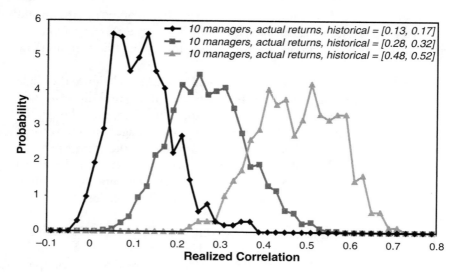

*Source:* Barclay Hedge, Newedge Prime Brokerage Research.

correlations in the previous three years had been around 0.15 (the leftmost distribution), 0.30 (the middle distribution), and 0.50 (the rightmost distribution). To be sure, there is a lot of overlap between adjacent distributions (e.g., those whose past correlations were 0.15 and 0.30, or 0.30 and 0.50). But there is almost no overlap in the distributions for past correlations of 0.15 and 0.50. In this case, there is almost no chance that a portfolio with a past implied correlation of 0.15 would turn out to be higher than the implied correlation of a portfolio whose past implied correlation had been 0.50.

## Why Is the Scatter Shaped Like an American Football?

The second bit of good news was a surprise because it seemed to be at odds with what we know about the sampling distributions of pairwise correlations (that is, the correlations between any two assets). The fact that the scatter narrows at both ends suggests that the distributions of implied correlations are narrower for low and high correlations than for medium correlations. This led us to delve further into the sampling characteristics of estimated correlations when working with more than two assets.

**EXHIBIT 12.7** Improvement in Estimates of Implied Correlation as the Number of Assets Increases

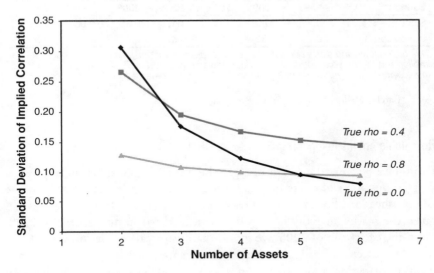

*Source:* Newedge Prime Brokerage Research.

The result is illustrated in Exhibit 12.7. The number of correlated assets is shown on the horizontal axis. The standard deviation of the implied or aggregate correlation is shown on the vertical axis. For two assets, the ranking is just what we expect to find. The standard deviation of the estimate for a true correlation of 0.0 is larger than that for a true correlation of 0.4, which in turn is larger than that for a true correlation of 0.8. As the number of assets increases, however, these standard deviations fall. But the faster the standard deviation falls, the lower is the true correlation between assets. For the assets with 0.0 correlation, by the time we get to 6 assets, the standard deviation of our estimate of implied correlation is actually lower than it is for assets with a true correlation of 0.8.

The intuition behind this result is somewhat like that behind diversification. By increasing the number of assets, we are increasing the sample size, which in turn increases the accuracy of our estimates. We get more independent information from low-correlation assets, though, than from high-correlation assets. Thus, we gain precision faster with low-correlation assets.

The results in these exhibits are mainly encouraging. It seems that past correlations do provide information about future correlations. Thus, estimated correlations can be a reliably productive tool when constructing portfolios.

**EXHIBIT 12.8** Regression Summaries (Realized and Historical Implied Correlations)

| Estimate | 1998 | 1999 | 2000 | 2001 | 2002 | 2003 | 2004 | 2005 |
|---|---|---|---|---|---|---|---|---|
| Slope | 1.04 | 0.77 | 0.83 | 1.02 | 1.19 | 0.89 | 0.90 | 0.45 |
| Correlation | 0.78 | 0.78 | 0.80 | 0.80 | 0.80 | 0.72 | 0.79 | 0.64 |

*This table shows the slope coefficient and correlation for regressions in which realized implied rho for the year in the column header was regressed on historical implied rho for the previous three years. Squaring the correlation approximates the R2 of the regression.*

*Source:* Barclay Hedge, Newedge Prime Brokerage Research.

## How Stable Are the Relationships?

Exhibit 12.8 shows the results of regressing realized against historical implied correlations for eight sets of years, each ending in the year shown in the column headers. For example, the slope and correlation from the regression given the scatter in Exhibit 12.5 is shown in the column headed by 1998. With the exception of 2005, we found that historical correlation was a fairly reliable predictor of realized correlation. This means that during these years, using information about past correlations would have been a valuable tool when forming the portfolios of team players.

Exhibit 12.9 provides a slightly different perspective on the relationship between past and future. One distribution shows realized implied correlations for portfolios whose historical correlation had been 0.30 (i.e., from 0.28 to 0.32). These were drawn from actual returns. The other distribution shows the same thing but for simulated returns using correlations estimates for the entire period from 1995 through 2005. The comforting finding here is that both distributions are centered around 0.3 and that both have about the same shape and spread. To this extent, the real world looked like the simulated world.

## The Contest

This section describes how we prepared the data, formed the initial portfolios, and explored the consequences of dropping and adding managers over time.

## Preparing the Data

Before beginning with the exercise of forming portfolios, we first netted interest income from the monthly return data. This allows us to work

**EXHIBIT 12.9** Conditional Correlations with Actual and Simulated Data
(Actual = 1995–2005)

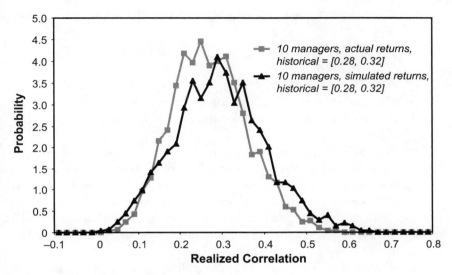

*Source:* Barclay Hedge, Newedge Prime Brokerage Research.

strictly with the managers' excess returns, which can be leveraged up or down as needed and which provide better indications of risk-adjusted excess returns.

We then normalized the return series so that all managers exhibited 15 percent annualized return volatility. This step has two practical consequences. For one thing, it disguises the identities of the managers even though the return data are publicly available. For another, and more important, it removes any possible biases in portfolio weights that stem only from differences in return volatilities.

## Looking Back and Looking Forward

In these exercises, we used three years of historical returns to make our decisions about managers to include in the portfolios and then tracked the results for the following year. For example, we used return data for 1995 through 1997 (the first three years for which we had complete monthly return data for the 42 managers) and then observed the results for 1998. In those exercises in which we dropped underperforming managers and replaced them with someone else, we would use the most recent year (e.g., 1998) to detect underperformance and then three years of data (e.g., 1996–1998) to determine the replacement. Similarly, we always used the most recent three years of data for normalizing volatilities and reweighting the managers in our portfolios.

## Finding the Players

Finding the superstars was easy, entailing nothing more than calculating the managers' annualized Sharpe ratios for the three-year look-back period and ranking them.

Finding the team players, however, promised to be much harder than it turned out to be. To find the best combination of 10 managers in a set of 42 managers would require computing the Sharpe ratio for every possible combination of 10 managers. Exhibit 12.10 shows how the number of combinations increases with the number of managers. The number of combinations for 10 managers is about 1.5 billion, and the computing required is proportional to the number of combinations.

To get around the enormity of the computing challenge, researchers seek out shortcuts that will produce approximately the right answer. In our work, we established the initial portfolio of 10 by first calculating the optimal weights

**EXHIBIT 12.10**   Computing Required to Find the Best Portfolio

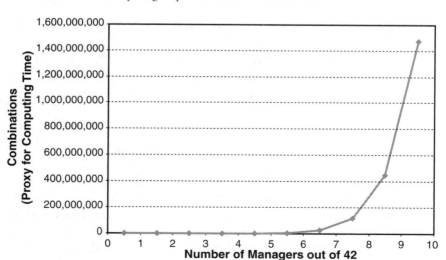

*Source:* Barclay Hedge, Newedge Prime Brokerage Research.

**EXHIBIT 12.11** Optimal Weights for 42 Managers (1995–1997)

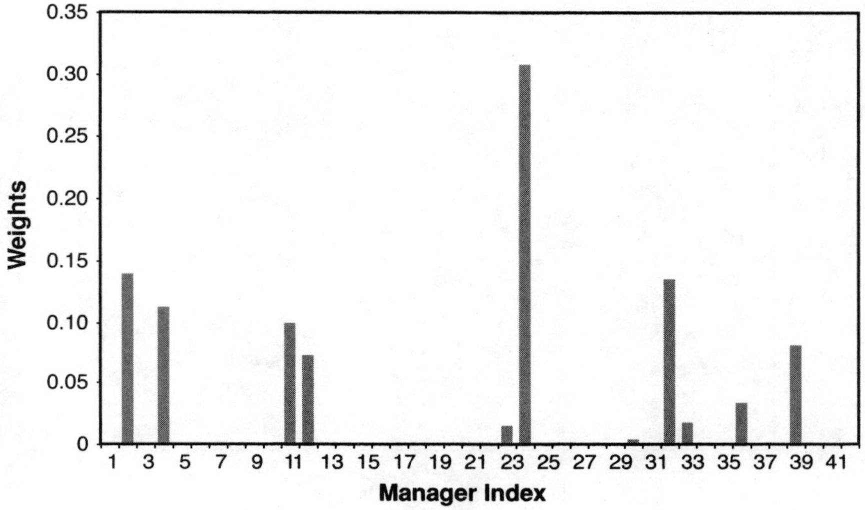

*Source:* Barclay Hedge, Newedge Prime Brokerage Research.

that we would assign each of the 42 managers if we allowed them all in the running. The resulting weights for the years 1995 through 1997 are shown in Exhibit 12.11. In this exhibit, the weight is shown on the vertical axis and the manager's index number, which is a proxy for the manager's name, is shown on the horizontal axis.

As it happened, only 11 of the managers had weights that were noticeably greater than zero, and of these, manager number 30's weight was fairly close to zero. (See Exhibit 12.11.) Given these results, we chose the 10 managers with the highest weights to make up the initial group of team players.

## How Different Were the Portfolios?

The circles and letters in Exhibit 12.12 represent the Sharpe ratios for all 42 managers for the years 1995 through 1997. The letters are used to identify managers who were selected for one of the initial portfolios. The letter *S* indicates a manager who was added to the Superstar portfolio based on her high Sharpe ratio. The letter *T* identifies managers whose weights included them in the optimal portfolio. The letter *B* was used to display those managers whose performance qualified them for both portfolios. A close inspection reveals that five managers (2, 4, 11, 24, and 32) were in both portfolios.

**EXHIBIT 12.12**   Manager Selection (Based on Data for 1995–1997)

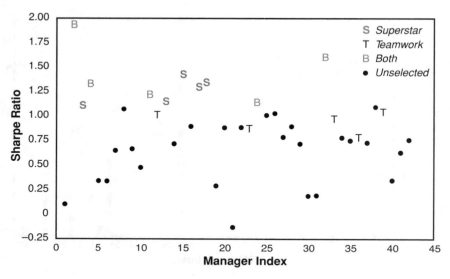

*Source:* Barclay Hedge, Newedge Prime Brokerage Research.

Five managers (3, 13, 15, 17, and 18) were only in the Superstar portfolio. And five managers (12, 23, 33, 36, and 39) were only in the Teamwork portfolio.

## Forming the Portfolios

Once we identified the managers to be included in each portfolio, we gave them equal weights in the portfolio. Given that we have scaled their return data to produce a normalized 15 percent volatility for the three years looking back, this was the same as giving each manager an equal volatility weight. This choice of a weighting scheme—in contrast to using a set of optimized weights based on historical return data—made sense in this work for a number of reasons. For one thing, we wanted to explore the effects of dropping and adding managers, and by giving equal weight to each manager, the results of dropping and adding do not depend on possibly large differences in the weights of the managers dropped and added. For another, it is a scheme that represents a kind of compromise when dealing with two different approaches to forming the portfolios in the first place.

## Comparing Performance

Exhibit 12.13 shows the outcomes of eight competing approaches to forming and managing portfolios. These include the four shown in Exhibit 12.1 plus another four. The numbers along the horizontal axis indicate the number of times a manager was dropped from the group and replaced by another. The numbers along the vertical axis show the annualized Sharpe ratios for the portfolios over the entire period of eight years for which we could analyze the portfolios' risks and returns.

For example, 0 indicates that no one was dropped from or added to either portfolio. This portfolio comprised the original 10 managers and management of this portfolio consisted of nothing more than resetting the weights using the previous three years' volatility estimates. The 1 indicates that we dropped and added managers at the end of 1998 and then stopped; the 2 indicates that we dropped and added managers again at the end of 1999 and then stopped, and so on. In all cases, the Sharpe ratio is the cumulative Sharpe ratio for the entire eight years. Thus, the 7 indicates the results of dropping and adding managers at the end of each year from 1998 through 2004.

Note that this way of keeping track of our experiments allows us to look back and compare our final results with what we would have realized if we

**EXHIBIT 12.13** Cumulative Sharpe Ratio Effects of Dropping and Adding Managers

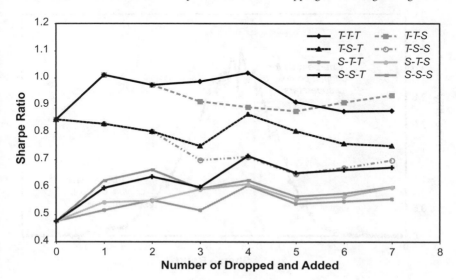

*Source:* Barclay Hedge, Newedge Prime Brokerage Research.

had done nothing or had stopped changing the portfolios anywhere along the line.

## The Original Portfolios

There are two sets of four lines in Exhibit 12.13. The upper set corresponds to portfolios that began with the original portfolio of 10 team players. As shown on the vertical axis, this portfolio, with annual reweightings but no drops or adds, achieved a Sharpe ratio of 0.85. The lower set corresponds to portfolios that began with the original portfolio of 10 superstars. This team, also with annual reweightings but no drops or adds, achieved a Sharpe ratio of 0.48.

To put these results in perspective, we conducted a separate experiment in which we formed portfolios of 10 managers drawn at random from the larger set of 42. We managed these sets exactly the same way we managed the original portfolios of team players and superstars. That is, we annually reweighted them to reflect changes in estimated volatility, but otherwise left the compositions unchanged. The resulting distribution of Sharpe ratios is shown in Exhibit 12.14.

**EXHIBIT 12.14**    Distribution of Sharpe Ratios for Randomly Selected Portfolios

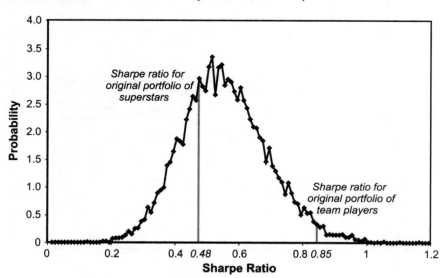

*Source:* Barclay Hedge, Newedge Prime Brokerage Research.

Because we were dealing with 42 managers who were demonstrably successful because of their comparatively long track records and assets under management, all of these portfolios produced annualized Sharpe ratios greater than 0. In other words, there wasn't a loser in the bunch. The average Sharpe ratio for the randomly formed portfolios was 0.56. The lowest was around 0.2 and the highest was around 1.0.

In this light, we see that the original team of superstars performed no better than one could have achieved by forming portfolios at random. This is a result one often finds in the finance literature that studies "hot hands" and the results of chasing those assets or managers whose most recent returns were higher than average.

As it was, historical Sharpe ratios provided no real useful information about future Sharpe ratios. Consider Exhibit 12.15, which shows the relationship between one-year realized Sharpe ratios and three-year historical

**EXHIBIT 12.15**   Historical and Realized Sharpe Ratios for Portfolios of 10 Managers (Historical, 1995–1997; Realized, 1998)

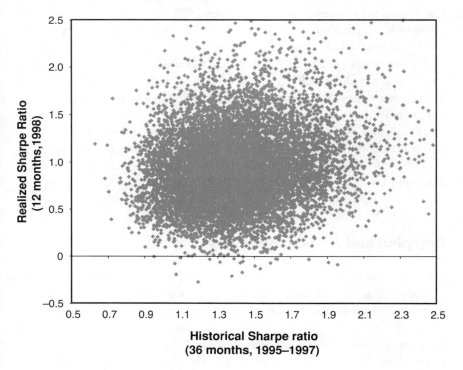

*Source:* Barclay Hedge, Newedge Prime Brokerage Research.

**EXHIBIT 12.16**   Regression Summaries (Realized and Historical Sharpe Ratios)

| Estimate | 1998 | 1999 | 2000 | 2001 | 2002 | 2003 | 2004 | 2005 |
|---|---|---|---|---|---|---|---|---|
| Slope | 0.26 | −0.46 | −0.13 | 0.16 | −0.40 | −0.17 | 0.22 | 0.06 |
| Correlation | 0.18 | −0.26 | −0.13 | 0.14 | −0.27 | −0.05 | 0.15 | 0.04 |

*This table shows the slope coefficient and correlation for regressions in which the realized Sharpe ratio for the year in the column header was regressed on the historical Sharpe ratio for the previous three years. Squaring the correlation approximates the R2 of the regression.*

*Source:* Barclay Hedge, Newedge Prime Brokerage Research.

Sharpe ratios for portfolios of 10 randomly chosen managers. Unlike the scatter in Exhibit 12.5, which has an elongated shape that suggests a useable relationship between past and future correlations, this scatter is basically a ball. Knowing what the portfolio's Sharpe ratio was over the period 1995 through 1997 tells you nothing useful about what the Sharpe ratio proved to be in 1998. This is borne out in Exhibit 12.16, which summarizes the regression results for realized Sharpe ratios from 1998 through 2005. Overall, the average slope coefficient was about 0.0, and so was the average correlation. This is in marked contrast to the results for implied correlations (Exhibit 12.8), where the average slope coefficient was slightly less than 1.0, and the correlation was fairly high. In a nutshell, past correlations helped to predict future correlations, while past Sharpe ratios did nothing to predict future Sharpe ratios.

In contrast, the original portfolio of team players achieved a Sharpe ratio that was near the upper end of the distribution. This suggests that selecting managers for their correlative properties can produce results that are better than random.

## Dropping and Adding Managers

We now turn to the question of whether portfolio performance can be improved by dropping and replacing managers. In practice, at least in this business, investors or funds of funds will tackle this problem at the margin. That is, rather than starting from scratch every year—finding what would have been the best portfolio for the year ahead and then dropping and adding as many managers as necessary—investors will keep all but the worst performers and replace only the managers they fire.

While in practice the number of managers an investor might drop will vary from year to year, we approached the problem using a strict rule. That is, if we dropped a manager at all, we dropped one and added one.

## The Eight Drop/Add Rules

For the sake of completeness, we tried eight different drop/add rules, which can be summarized as:

1. Teamwork/teamwork/teamwork (TTT)
2. Teamwork/teamwork/superstar (TTS)
3. Teamwork/superstar/teamwork (TST)
4. Teamwork/superstar/superstar (TSS)
5. Superstar/superstar/superstar (SSS)
6. Superstar/superstar/teamwork (SST)
7. Superstar/teamwork/superstar (STS)
8. Superstar/teamwork/teamwork (STT)

Each sequence represents the rule used to form the initial portfolio of 10, the criterion used to drop a manager, and the rule used to replace the manager who was dropped. For example, TTT means that all decisions were based on a manager's contribution to the overall portfolio's performance. TST, on the other hand, means that we used portfolio criteria to form the portfolio, and individual performance to drop a manager, but then reverted to portfolio contributions to find the manager's replacement. Exhibit 12.1 contains the sequences TTT, TSS, SST, and SSS.

## Defining Worst Performance

For the superstars, we simply chose the manager with the largest loss for the year. Although we are selecting and adding managers using Sharpe ratios, we found that this measure of performance had serious shortcomings when we were dealing with losses. Exhibit 12.17 shows why. In 1999, five of the managers in the Superstar portfolio experienced losses. You can see, however, that the manager with the lowest Sharpe ratio is not the manager with the worst performance. The lowest Sharpe ratio was −1.21, but both the loss and the volatility of this manager's returns were lower than those for another manager whose Sharpe ratio was −1.06. This manager's loss was nearly 14 percent with 14 percent volatility, in contrast to a 7 percent loss with 6 percent volatility.

**EXHIBIT 12.17**   The Problem with Negative Sharpe Ratios (Risks and Returns in 1999)

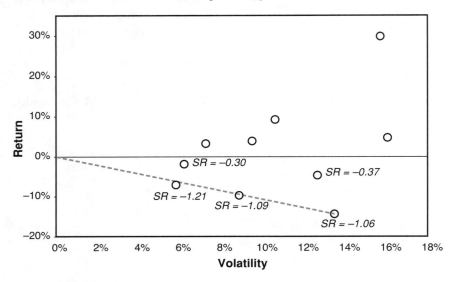

*Source:* Barclay Hedge, Newedge Prime Brokerage Research.

Identifying the worst performer in the Teamwork portfolio required considerably more computing. For this exercise, we removed each manager in turn and recomputed the Sharpe ratio of the remaining 9 managers. This left us with 10 Sharpe ratios, each corresponding to the removal of one manager. The manager we dropped was the manager whose removal left us with the highest Sharpe ratio. That is, we dropped the manager whose removal reduced the Sharpe ratio by the least. We then added a manager from the remaining set whose inclusion increased the portfolio's Sharpe ratio by the most.

## How Bad Is Bad?

Evaluating performance once you already have the results is more nuanced than the typical test for statistical significance. We have portfolios of 10 managers and, during any given year, we expect half of them to perform below average. Furthermore, we know that one of them will be the worst performer of the lot, typically posting a sizeable loss. Knowing this, how can we tell whether the managers who lose money are losing more than their past performance would suggest? The impetus for asking this question came from

**EXHIBIT 12.18**   How Bad Were They?

| Dropped at the End of | Z-Value |
|---|---|
| 1998 | −2.14 |
| 1999 | −2.14 |
| 2000 | −1.28 |
| 2001 | −0.52 |
| 2002 | −1.70 |
| 2003 | −0.72 |
| 2004 | −1.93 |

*Source:* Barclay Hedge, Newedge Prime Brokerage.

an intriguing article by Alan Marcus, who posed the question in terms of winners rather than losers.[*]

Consider the z-scores of the managers who were dropped, as shown in Exhibit 12.18. We calculated these values by dividing the differences between the most recent year's return and the preceding three years' annualized return by the standard deviation of the difference. As such, these z-scores show whether the most recent year's return was significantly less than one would have expected in light of the manager's historical performance. Two of them were greater than −2, and one was nearly −2, which looks like the kinds of numbers one uses to reject the null hypothesis of no worse than average.

To see why these z-scores are misleading, though, consider the two distributions shown in Exhibit 12.19. The one centered around zero is the standard normal, with a mean of 0.0 and a standard deviation of 1.0. The skinnier distribution, whose center is roughly halfway between −2 and −3, is the distribution of the minimum value in a sample of 10 random draws from the standard normal. That is, it is the result of drawing 10 numbers from the standard normal and looking at the smallest algebraic outcome, which typically would be the largest negative number.

Notice that when you have a sample of 10 random draws from the standard normal, you expect some losses, and one of those draws has to be the minimum. If we focus on the distribution of the minimum value in a sample of 10 random draws, we can expect the minimum value to be roughly −2.5 with a standard deviation around that value of almost 0.5. Thus,

---

[*]Alan J. Marcus, "The Magellan Fund and Market Efficiency," *Journal of Portfolio Management*, Fall 1990.

**EXHIBIT 12.19** Standard Normal Distribution and Distribution of the Minimum (with Sample Size = 10)

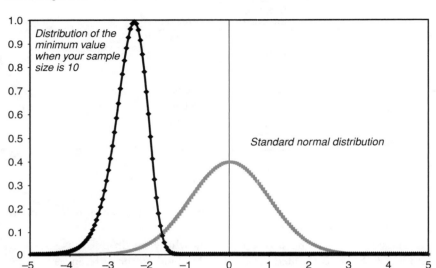

*Source:* Newedge Prime Brokerage Research.

we would expect the worst performer in our portfolios to exhibit a z-score anywhere from –1.5 to –3.5, even if the manager is doing the job for which he was hired.

This means that the standard for identifying a manager who is delivering substandard performance is a much tougher test than we thought. In this example, we would need a z-score of –3.5 or more before we might conclude that a manager was doing worse than we should expect in light of what we believe to be true about his distribution of returns, including both the mean return and the standard deviation of returns.

## The Effect of Dropping and Adding

Given the results displayed in Exhibit 12.13, the conclusions we draw are these. First, we see that the two best-performing portfolios were those that began with the original set of team players and then used the portfolio criterion when deciding whom to drop. These two are identified as TTT and TTS. At least in this set of results, it did not seem to matter much whether we then used a portfolio rule or a Sharpe ratio rule to find the replacement.

The next two were portfolios that began with the original set of team players but then used individual performance to drop a manager. These are identified as TST and TSS. Firing the manager with the largest loss in each year seems to have dragged down the performance of these portfolios.

The bottom four are almost indistinguishable, although the worst of the four was the straight Superstar portfolio (SSS). The next two from the bottom were those in which managers were dropped for portfolio considerations (STS and STT). These two suggest that when you start with a group of superstars, using portfolio reasoning to drop someone accomplishes little. This shouldn't be surprising since the group was not formed with portfolio characteristics in mind in the first place.

The only one in this set that stands out somewhat is the portfolio identified as SST, which began with the original set of superstars, fired the manager with the largest loss each year, and then used portfolio standards for finding the replacement. The improvement does not appear to have been statistically significant, but it was not nothing, either.

## The Value of Incremental Knowledge about Return Distributions

The purpose of this section is to look into the question of how much one stands to gain from improvement estimates of the key moments of managers' return distributions: mean, standard deviation, and correlation. This particular question is raised by de Santis, Litterman, Vesval, and Winkelmann, who show that knowing correlation can be worth more than knowing the mean return—an astonishing result.[*]

We find the same thing. That is, in the experiments we ran, not knowing correlations was more costly than not knowing mean returns. In turn, both were quite a bit more important than knowing the volatility of returns. We also found that longer estimation periods contributed more when estimating correlations than when estimating mean returns or their volatilities.

In this part of our research, we went through the following drill. First, we normalized the 11-year excess returns of our 42 managers to produce 15 percent volatility. Second, we calculated the means, volatilities, and correlations for the 42 managers for the full 11 years. Third, we used these estimated moments as if they were the true moments to generate sequences of returns

---

[*]Giorgio de Santis, Bob Litterman, Adrien Vesval, and Kurt Winkelmann, "Covariance Matrix Estimation," *Modern Investment Management*, Wiley Finance, 2003.

from which we could estimate one or more of the parameters. Fourth, we used these estimated parameters to determine optimal portfolio weights for the 42 managers. Finally, we used these weights, together with the true parameters, to find the Sharpe ratio that one could expect from the portfolio.

Exhibit 12.20 compares the Sharpe ratios one could expect when using one or more estimated return parameters with the Sharpe ratio that one would expect when using the true return parameters. The horizontal line at a value of 1.88 is labeled "Maximum possible," which refers to the expected Sharpe ratio one would realize from using the true values of means, standard deviations, and correlations of returns.

The curves in Exhibit 12.20 show the Sharpe ratios one would expect if one used one or more estimated parameters. The lowest curve, which is labeled "Estimating all three," shows what one would expect to achieve when using sample periods ranging from 12 to 120 observations to estimate all three parameters. The other three curves show what one would expect to achieve if it were possible to combine the estimated value of one parameter with the true values of the other two. For example, the curve labeled "Estimating volatilities" is the result of combining estimated standard deviations with the true values of the means and correlations.

**EXHIBIT 12.20**   Value of Better Estimates of Return Moments

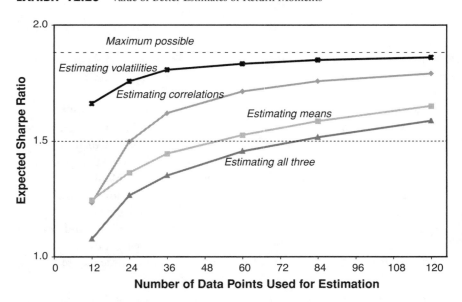

*Source:* Newedge Prime Brokerage Research.

Several interesting lessons emerge from Exhibit 12.20. First, it is clear that having to use estimated return parameters is a serious handicap on performance. By using parameter estimates that are distributed around their true values, we derive portfolio weights that are distributed around their own true values. And since the best possible weights are those that we would derive from knowing the true values of the return parameters, any other set of weights produces a less desirable outcome.

Second, we see that for small sample sizes, de Santis and his colleagues were absolutely right. We lose as much or more performance not knowing the true values of correlations as we lose not knowing the true means of the return distributions. It is interesting to note, too, that we lose comparatively little when using estimated volatilities.

Third, the incremental improvement from getting better correlation estimates is larger than it is from getting better estimates of the means. Notice that the slope of the curve labeled "Estimating correlations" is steeper than that labeled "Estimating means," at least for sample sizes ranging from 12 to 36.

## The Costs of Dropping and Adding Managers

Dropping and adding managers is not free. For one thing, given the asymmetric fee structure in this business, the firing of a manager who has lost money and is under water means giving up a loss carry-forward. For another, there are the costs associated with finding a replacement. These include at the very least due diligence and legal expenses. Third, dropping a manager today may preclude the possibility of investing in that same manager at a later date.

These costs, which we have not taken into account, produce a worse picture than those shown in Exhibits 12.1 and 12.13. There we find little or no improvement from dropping and adding managers in the best cases, and a marked deterioration in performance in one case. If we had reckoned with the kinds of costs that one would incur, all the outcomes would have deteriorated over time.

These costs also suggest that a better approach than the one we have taken here to dropping and adding managers would be to find a way to balance the possibilities of improving the portfolio against the costs of making your way from your current portfolio to what you think will be a better one. Doing this would allow you to consider a full range of possible portfolios. It would allow you to include as many assets or managers as make sense. It would allow you to drop as many as you want and add as many as you want. The challenge to doing this well is in characterizing your adjustment costs correctly.

# CHAPTER 13

# A New Look at Constructing Teamwork Portfolios

The best way to build portfolios of CTAs is to look for low correlation and place your bets there. Correlations appeared to be predictable, especially for portfolios, while Sharpe ratios did not. We found that choosing managers to maximize the portfolio's Sharpe ratio yielded better results than did choosing managers based on their individual Sharpe ratios, and the difference was statistically significant.

The Teamwork portfolios discussed in Chapter 12 were constructed, however, using conventional mean/variance analysis that was based on estimated means, volatilities, and correlations. And, when we applied it to the construction of a teamwork index, we found out, quite by accident, that it was unusually sensitive to minor changes in the eligible set. It was too sensitive, for that matter, which led us back to the question of the best approach to selecting managers for a Teamwork portfolio.

The flaw, we found, was not in giving past correlations a role in shaping our Teamwork portfolios, but in allowing past returns to have any effect at all. As you will see in Exhibit 13.3, past correlations for large-enough portfolios of CTAs can be highly predictable while past returns and, by extension, past Sharpe ratios are not.

In this new look at that research, we changed two things. First, we formed Teamwork portfolios using three different rules. Second, we allowed ourselves to construct new portfolios each year without regard to the costs of dropping and adding managers.

279

**EXHIBIT 13.1**   Probability of Inclusion in a Low-Correlation Portfolio

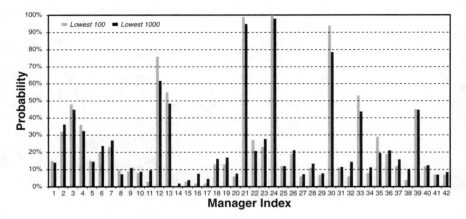

*Source:* Newedge Prime Brokerage Research.

The three teamwork rules were these. One used the conventional mean/variance approach to maximize the Sharpe ratio of the portfolio. The other two used only correlations and gave no weight at all to past returns. The first of these, which is illustrated in Exhibit 13.1, simply calculated the probability that a CTA would have been in a low-average correlation portfolio and chose those with the highest probabilities of inclusion. The second ranked CTAs using each CTA's average return correlation with all other CTAs in the eligible set and chose those with the lowest average correlations.

The Superstar portfolios were formed by identifying those CTAs who had, over the previous three years, produced the highest individual Sharpe ratios.

In a nutshell, we found the following: First, the Teamwork portfolios gave us an edge over the Superstar portfolios. While the Superstar portfolios delivered the highest Sharpe ratio in two of the eight years, they came in dead last the other six years. In contrast, the correlation-only Teamwork portfolios came in first or second in five of the eight years, and came in last only once.

Second, the correlation-only approaches gave us two benefits over the conventional mean/variance approach. For one thing, they are more robust. The removal of one or more managers from the eligible set does not materially affect the probability that the remaining low-correlation CTAs will end up in the low-correlation portfolio. For another, they are more economical and use the eligible CTA set far more sparingly. While the mean/variance portfolios performed almost as well as the correlation-only portfolios, they used 21 of the 42 CTAs over the eight years, while the correlation-only portfolios used only 14. Thus, the mean/variance approach would have dropped and added

11 CTAs; the correlation-only rules would have dropped and added only four. Given the high costs of dropping and adding CTAs, this kind of stability in one's choice of CTAs can be worth a great deal.

In the remainder of this chapter, we review this reworking of our research and conclude with a discussion of how we have applied what we've learned to the construction and management of the AlternativeEdge Teamwork Index. In particular, we

- Take a more complete look at which return statistics are persistent or predictable (volatilities and correlations) and which are not (means and Sharpe ratios).
- Explore two empirical approaches to constructing low-correlation portfolios.
- Explain why we volatility weight the CTAs in the AlternativeEdge indices.

## Why Look Back?

The main reason we have taken a fresh look at the original data set was a surprising lesson we learned when we decided to apply the teamwork methodology we used to construct a teamwork index of CTAs (Chapter 12). In a nutshell, our approach was to use estimated moments (that is, means, volatilities, and correlations) from CTAs' return distributions to solve for what would have been the nonnegative weights that produced the highest Sharpe ratio. Many of the resulting weights would be zero, and these CTAs were set aside. Our objective was to end up with 20 CTAs for the index. If we had more than this, which we did, we had to thin the herd. To do this, we simply removed, one at a time, those CTAs whose absence left us with the highest Sharpe ratio for the remaining CTAs. For example, if we had 30 CTAs, we would look at all possible 29-CTA portfolios and choose the one with the highest Sharpe ratio. Then, we would look at all possible 28-CTA portfolios, and so on.

While this approach made sense to us, we had not expected it to be quite as sensitive as it proved to be to the actual CTAs in the eligible set. This we learned in January 2008, when one of the 20 CTAs in the original index closed down and returned the money to their investors. When we went back to find a replacement for the newly missing CTA, we found that our process of elimination did not simply reach back into the eligible set and choose what had been the last runner-up. Instead, we found that our sequential optimization routine required us to actually drop three more CTAs from the set of 20 and replace them.

A new and harder look at what we had done showed us why. The kind of mean/variance approach we used still allowed past returns to affect the selection of CTAs for the Teamwork portfolio, even though we had already persuaded ourselves that past returns exhibit little or no persistence or predictability.

This prompted us to rethink the formation of Teamwork portfolios. And, while we were at it, we decided to see what would happen if we allowed each portfolio to be reconstituted each year, rather than constraining ourselves to drop and add no more than one CTA each year. While the drop/add rule we used in the original research conformed somewhat to normal business practices, it meant that the results of the research were highly sensitive to whatever luck might have been involved in the selection of the initial portfolios.

## A Fresh Look at the Original Research

Taking a fresh look at an old problem allows us to ask questions that we should have asked before. For example, in the original work, we showed that for large-enough portfolios of CTAs (we used 10), past correlations could be used to predict future correlations, while past Sharpe ratios could not be used to predict future Sharpe ratios. This time, we provide results for mean returns and volatilities of return, and show what these relationships look like for individual managers.

Also, we compared the results of portfolios that were constructed from scratch using data from 1995 through 1997 and then updated each year by dropping and adding one CTA each year. This made sense from a practical perspective in that it conformed to the sense that drops and adds are costly, and we wanted the exercise to look something like what one might encounter in the real world of portfolio management. At the same time, it gave a lot of weight to the initial draws for the Superstar and Teamwork portfolios. This time, we allow the portfolios to be reconstituted completely at the end of each year. While this is not what one would observe in practice, this approach gives a better sense of the odds that our competing approaches would outperform or underperform one another.

### The Original Data Set

The original data set comprised the returns of 42 CTAs who had $100 million or more under management in 2005. We chose these managers for two reasons. First, their returns series were continuous from 1995 through

2005. Second, they were all successful in raising money and running their businesses. By definition, then, we were working with successful managers who survived the period. All had good track records, and all were still open for investment. This meant that we ignored various biases, including those from losing sight of managers who go out of business and those that arise when successful managers stop taking new money.

## What's Predictable and What's Not?

Exhibits 13.2 and 13.3 provide the foundation for everything we have come to believe about constructing indexes of CTA performance. These particular scatters are the results of looking back three years (2002 through 2004) and forward one (2005). Exhibit 13.2 shows results for individual managers. Exhibit 13.3 shows results for randomly formed portfolios of 10 CTAs. The visual impressions they give are compelling. It is apparent that, both for individuals and for portfolios:

• Past returns *cannot* be used to predict future returns.
• Past volatilities *can* be used to predict future volatilities.
• Past Sharpe ratios *cannot* be used to predict future Sharpe ratios.
• Past correlations *can* be used to predict future correlations.

## Persistence in These Relationships

To drive home the point that these scatters are also typical and not just flukes of a particular set of years, we have provided Exhibits 13.4 and 13.5, which report the correlations of past and future values for all four measures and for two different look-back periods.

It is apparent that the correlations between past and forward values of mean returns and Sharpe ratios are variable and, on average, low. In contrast, the correlations between past and future values of return volatilities and correlations are consistently fairly high. Moreover, the relationship between past and future volatilities and correlations are somewhat higher for the 10-CTA portfolios than they are for individual managers.

## One Striking Difference

The most striking difference between the two sets of scatters is in the shapes of the scatters for past and future correlations for individual managers in Exhibit 13.2 and the 10-CTA portfolios in Exhibit 13.3. In particular, what we see

**EXHIBIT 13.2**   Conditional Predictions: Individual Managers (Look-back, 2002–2004; Look-forward, 2005)

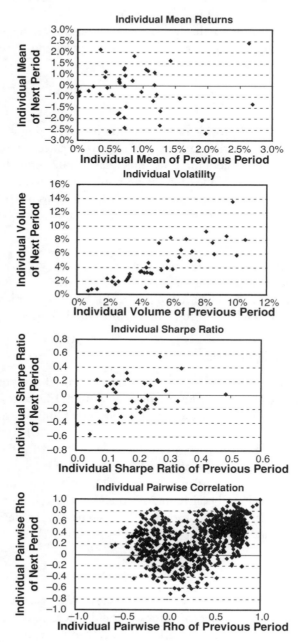

*Source:* Newedge Prime Brokerage Research, Barclay Hedge.

**EXHIBIT 13.3** Conditional Predictions: Portfolios of 10 Managers (Look-back, 2002–2004; Look-forward, 2005)

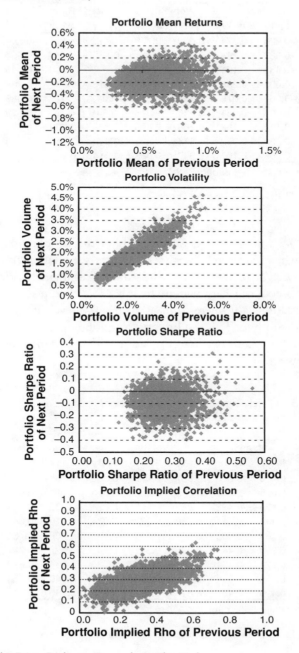

*Source:* Newedge Prime Brokerage Research, Barclay Hedge.

**EXHIBIT 13.4**  Correlation Coefficients for Individual Managers

| Fwd | Mean | | Volatility | | Sharpe Ratio | | Pairwise Rho | |
|-----|------|------|------|------|------|------|------|------|
| Year | 1y-1y | 3y-1y | 1y-1y | 3y-1y | 1y-1y | 3y-1y | 1y-1y | 3y-1y |
| 1998 | 0.226 | 0.374 | 0.630 | 0.729 | −0.022 | −0.035 | 0.584 | 0.646 |
| 1999 | −0.387 | −0.244 | 0.688 | 0.661 | 0.132 | −0.092 | 0.501 | 0.627 |
| 2000 | −0.467 | −0.191 | 0.629 | 0.778 | −0.070 | −0.171 | 0.445 | 0.682 |
| 2001 | 0.035 | 0.258 | 0.767 | 0.784 | 0.216 | 0.235 | 0.489 | 0.691 |
| 2002 | −0.054 | 0.076 | 0.887 | 0.817 | −0.017 | −0.144 | 0.688 | 0.707 |
| 2003 | −0.205 | −0.081 | 0.736 | 0.818 | −0.341 | −0.365 | 0.629 | 0.645 |
| 2004 | 0.154 | 0.165 | 0.760 | 0.805 | 0.302 | 0.069 | 0.776 | 0.712 |
| 2005 | 0.123 | −0.052 | 0.874 | 0.828 | 0.419 | 0.345 | 0.395 | 0.442 |
| 2008* | 0.155 | 0.107 | 0.657 | 0.698 | 0.314 | 0.240 | 0.435 | 0.459 |

*New data set for 2005 through 2008.

*Source:* Barclay Hedge, Newedge Prime Brokerage Research.

in Exhibit 13.2 confirms what we know about the sampling distribution of correlations when true correlations are zero. That is, even if the true correlation between two CTAs' returns is zero, the values of estimated correlations that one might observe can vary widely. In this case, we can expect to observe realized correlations anywhere from −0.8 to +0.8, even if past correlations have been close to zero. This can be very frustrating for a single manager who is trying to stake a claim to a low correlation with the returns on other CTAs or on other assets.

**EXHIBIT 13.5**  Correlation Coefficients for Randomly Formed Portfolios of 10 CTAs (2,000 Portfolios Generated Each Year)

| Fwd | Mean | | | Volatility | Sharpe Ratio | | Implied Rho | |
|-----|------|------|------|------|------|------|------|------|
| Year | 1y-1y | 3y-1y | 1y-1y | 3y-1y | 1y-1y | 3y-1y | 1y-1y | 3y-1y |
| 1998 | 0.470 | 0.517 | 0.887 | 0.866 | 0.193 | 0.187 | 0.733 | 0.778 |
| 1999 | 0.015 | −0.134 | 0.875 | 0.888 | 0.053 | −0.281 | 0.682 | 0.788 |
| 2000 | −0.128 | 0.422 | 0.842 | 0.905 | 0.024 | −0.142 | 0.596 | 0.786 |
| 2001 | 0.441 | 0.541 | 0.888 | 0.928 | 0.074 | 0.170 | 0.646 | 0.780 |
| 2002 | 0.486 | 0.505 | 0.947 | 0.944 | 0.139 | −0.266 | 0.765 | 0.800 |
| 2003 | 0.203 | 0.443 | 0.903 | 0.941 | 0.142 | −0.078 | 0.711 | 0.705 |
| 2004 | 0.221 | 0.161 | 0.943 | 0.947 | 0.333 | 0.134 | 0.872 | 0.783 |
| 2005 | 0.455 | 0.134 | 0.930 | 0.923 | 0.409 | 0.049 | 0.634 | 0.635 |
| 2008* | 0.499 | 0.464 | 0.818 | 0.811 | 0.271 | 0.140 | 0.619 | 0.622 |

*New data set for 2005 through 2008.

*Source:* Barclay Hedge, Newedge Prime Brokerage Research.

In contrast, the scatter in the bottom panel of Exhibit 13.3 suggests that if we are dealing with a portfolio of CTAs, then the range of expected outcomes for low-correlation portfolios is fairly tightly bounded. As we showed in "Superstars versus teamwork," this result can be explained by the traction one gets from expanding the sample size when true correlation is low.

## A Different and Newer Data Set

We could not update the original data set because a number of the CTAs are no longer reporting. Still, to see whether the same kinds of relationships would hold up for a newer data set, we selected from the Barclay Hedge database all CTAs who had $100 million under management as of January 2008 and had four years of returns without gaps. After filtering out duplicates and those managers we knew should not be classified as CTAs or Macro, we were left with 142.

The bottom rows of Exhibits 13.4 and 13.5 show how the correlations for this set compare with the correlations we observed for the original data set. In all cases, the values for the newer and larger data set seem to be consistent with those observed for the original set.

## Two New Approaches

If past returns tell us nothing about future returns, then we have to focus our attention on correlations and find a reliable way to determine which CTAs are likely, as a group, to exhibit a low average pairwise correlation. We describe two approaches here. Both are imperfect but serviceable ways to solve a problem that cannot be solved deterministically. That is, it is computationally out of reach to find those 10 CTAs out of 42 who exhibited the lowest average pairwise correlation with one another. The number of calculations is simply too great.

- *Highest relative frequency:* The first approach is to determine which CTAs tend to appear in the low average correlation portfolios and to choose those CTAs with the highest relative frequency of appearance.
- *Lowest average rho:* One gets nearly the same results by calculating the average correlation of each CTA's returns with the returns of all other CTAs in the eligible set, and then choosing those CTAs with the lowest averages. We found this a little surprising because the average includes correlations both with CTAs who end up in the Teamwork portfolio as well as with CTAs who do not.

## The Highest Relative Frequency Approach

The scatter plots in Exhibit 13.3 are the results of forming a large number of 10-CTA portfolios randomly and measuring the characteristics of the resulting portfolios. This is comparatively cheap and easy to do. Then, once one has the randomly formed portfolios, the next step is to choose those portfolios for which the average pairwise correlations were the lowest and find out which CTAs tend to appear most often in them. In this example, out of one million randomly formed portfolios, we ranked them from lowest to highest average correlation and chose the bottom 100 and the bottom 1,000.

Exhibit 13.6 shows the fraction of the time that each of the 42 CTAs appeared in each set. Two things stand out. First, because we are forming the portfolios at random, any of the 42 CTAs can appear in one of these low-correlation portfolios. Second, while the relative frequency of appearance tends to change for each CTA as the size of the slice increases, the rankings are fairly stable. We can easily identify 10 CTAs who are more likely than the other 32 to appear in one of these portfolios.

Increasing the size of the slice of low-correlation portfolios does not affect the outcomes much, although one can see that the likelihood of the high-probability managers tends to fall while the likelihood of the low-probability managers tends to rise. This tendency makes sense because increasing the size of the slice is a bit like relaxing the standards for admission to the portfolio.

**EXHIBIT 13.6**   Probability of Inclusion in a Low-Correlation Portfolio

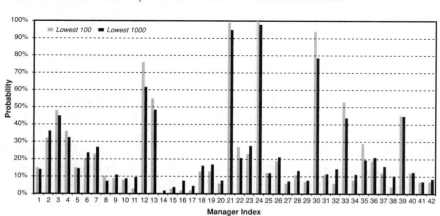

*Source:* Newedge Prime Brokerage Research.

## The "Low-Rho" Approach

An approach that is both simpler to execute and requires even less computing is to calculate the average of each CTA's correlation with all other CTAs in the eligible set—even with those of CTAs who tend not to be in the low-correlation portfolios. We define this average rho as

$$AverageRho(i) = \frac{\sum\limits_{j \neq i} \rho_{ij}}{n^*(n-1)}$$

where $\rho_{ij}$ is the correlation of the $i$th manager's returns with those of the $j$th manager.

In this work, we have averaged the pairwise correlation of each manager's returns with the returns of each of the 41 other managers' returns. The approach has an intuitive appeal, and it seems to produce outcomes that are highly consistent with those produced by the relative frequency approach.

Exhibit 13.7 plots these average correlations on the vertical axis against each CTA's probability of being included in the 1,000 lowest correlation portfolios on the horizontal axis. It is easy to see that the two approaches provide nearly the same rankings. The consistency makes intuitive sense. A

**EXHIBIT 13.7**   Average Rho versus Probability of Inclusion

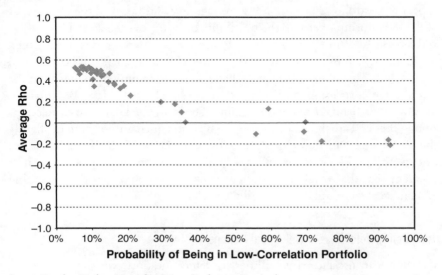

*Source:* Barclay Hedge, Newedge Prime Brokerage Research.

**EXHIBIT 13.8**   Correlation Heat Map

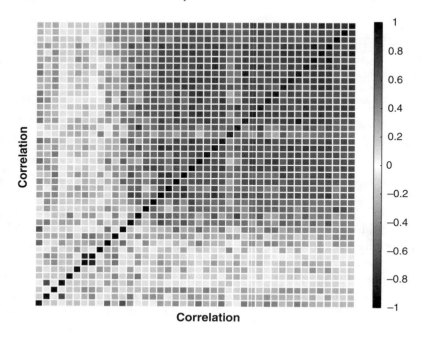

manager who is highly correlated with other managers on average is unlikely to appear in portfolios that exhibit low average correlations. And the consistency of the relationship opens up the possibility of using low rho as an inexpensive and reliable selection criterion when building a teamwork index or portfolio.

Exhibit 13.8 uses a heat map to provide a broader perspective on the two approaches. The 10 managers with the highest probability of inclusion in the low average correlation portfolios are represented by the 10 · 10 square at the lower-left-hand corner of the exhibit. The individual pairwise correlations among these 10 are mixed but appear to be distributed around zero or slightly above. They also exhibit slightly negative correlation with the 32 managers who were less likely to be in these low-correlation portfolios. And, it is apparent that the correlation gradient is fairly steep and that the remaining 32 managers seem to be fairly highly correlated with one another.

## Using Return Volatilities to Weight the Managers

We choose to use return volatilities to determine portfolio weights for the component managers. Volatilities appear to be highly predictable while returns, even though we expect them to be positive, are not. As a result, setting weights so that the volatilities of each manager's return exert the same influence on the volatility of the portfolio's returns is an optimal thing to do.

As a practical matter, to avoid any undue influence from sampling error, we place upper and lower bounds on these weights. In this case, with 10 managers in a portfolio, we allow a weight no less than 5 percent and no greater than 20 percent.

## Comparing the Four Approaches

At this point, we can ask how these two new ways of building portfolios—ways that rely only on correlation for choosing managers—compare with the approaches that were influenced in one way or another by past returns. The superstar approach, by choosing managers whose individual Sharpe ratios were higher than those of their competitors, places the greatest weight on past returns. The original teamwork approach, which combines past returns, volatilities, and correlations to identify the managers, also permits past returns to exert an influence.

To evaluate the outcomes, we consider two things. One is risk-adjusted returns, or Sharpe ratios. The other is turnover in the number of managers. We also comment on the resilience of the correlation-only portfolios in the face of changes in the eligible set.

### Sharpe Ratios Year by Year

Exhibit 13.9 provides a year-by-year summary of returns, volatilities, and Sharpe ratios for each of the four portfolios. The numbers in the rightmost column of the exhibit are the simple numerical rankings of the Sharpe ratios for the four approaches, with 1 the best, and 4 the worst. The bottom row of the exhibit shows the overall results for the full eight years, including the average ranking.

The reason for focusing on Sharpe ratio is apparent if you run your finger down the mean return column and then down the return volatility column. You will find that the Superstar portfolios turned in the highest overall returns in six of the eight years. But the return volatilities were often multiples higher than those of the Teamwork portfolios. If one allowed the Teamwork portfolio returns to be as volatile as those of the superstars' returns, the return rankings would change dramatically.

**EXHIBIT 13.9**    Year-by-Year Performance Comparisons

| Year | Portfolio | Results | | | |
| | | Mean | Volatility | SR | Rank |
|---|---|---|---|---|---|
| 1998 | Teamwork (max rel freq) | 3.53% | 2.42% | 1.458 | 3 |
| | Teamwork (low rho) | 5.15% | 2.43% | 2.116 | 1 |
| | Teamwork (mean/variance) | 5.57% | 3.64% | 1.530 | 2 |
| | Superstar | 8.61% | 7.82% | 1.101 | 4 |
| 1999 | Teamwork (max rel freq) | −3.89% | 2.44% | −1.595 | 3 |
| | Teamwork (low rho) | −3.89% | 2.44% | −1.595 | 3 |
| | Teamwork (mean/variance) | −1.29% | 2.21% | −0.583 | 2 |
| | Superstar | −0.76% | 3.94% | −0.192 | 1 |
| 2000 | Teamwork (max rel freq) | 1.09% | 6.04% | 0.181 | 2 |
| | Teamwork (low rho) | 1.62% | 4.56% | 0.355 | 1 |
| | Teamwork (mean/variance) | −0.57% | 5.42% | −0.106 | 4 |
| | Superstar | 1.42% | 8.07% | 0.176 | 3 |
| 2001 | Teamwork (max rel freq) | 4.65% | 4.00% | 1.163 | 1 |
| | Teamwork (low rho) | 5.38% | 5.01% | 1.074 | 2 |
| | Teamwork (mean/variance) | 4.23% | 5.53% | 0.764 | 3 |
| | Superstar | 8.61% | 16.25% | 0.530 | 4 |
| 2002 | Teamwork (max rel freq) | 5.61% | 2.77% | 2.027 | 2 |
| | Teamwork (low rho) | 5.73% | 2.62% | 2.185 | 1 |
| | Teamwork (mean/variance) | 7.01% | 5.68% | 1.233 | 3 |
| | Superstar | 9.96% | 12.15% | 0.820 | 4 |
| 2003 | Teamwork (max rel freq) | 12.04% | 3.13% | 3.845 | 1 |
| | Teamwork (low rho) | 12.04% | 3.13% | 3.845 | 1 |
| | Teamwork (mean/variance) | 11.17% | 4.06% | 2.750 | 3 |
| | Superstar | 7.89% | 6.39% | 1.235 | 4 |
| 2004 | Teamwork (max rel freq) | 2.13% | 2.25% | 0.946 | 2 |
| | Teamwork (low rho) | 1.33% | 2.05% | 0.649 | 3 |
| | Teamwork (mean/variance) | 3.69% | 2.29% | 1.613 | 1 |
| | Superstar | 2.94% | 5.12% | 0.575 | 4 |
| 2005 | Teamwork (max rel freq) | −0.20% | 1.42% | −0.139 | 2 |
| | Teamwork (low rho) | −0.20% | 1.42% | −0.139 | 2 |
| | Teamwork (mean/variance) | −0.70% | 2.74% | −0.254 | 4 |
| | Superstar | 3.17% | 5.41% | 0.586 | 1 |
| 98-05 | Teamwork (max rel freq) | 3.12% | 3.45% | 0.904 | 2.00 |
| | Teamwork (low rho) | 3.40% | 3.32% | 1.022 | 1.75 |
| | Teamwork (mean/variance) | 3.64% | 4.19% | 0.868 | 2.75 |
| | Superstar | 5.23% | 8.74% | 0.599 | 3.13 |

*Source:* Barclay Hedge, Newedge Prime Brokerage Research.

A number of interesting comparisons stand out. First, the Superstar portfolio came in first in two of the eight years, but dead last in five. The mean/variance approach came in best in one of the eight years, and last in two. The maximum relative frequency and low-rho portfolios tied for last in one year, but otherwise placed first or second in five of the eight years. If we simply average the rankings, we find the low-rho approach produced 1.75, and the maximum relative frequency's average ranking was 2.00. The average mean/variance ranking was 2.75, while the average superstar ranking was 3.13.

From this we conclude that the odds favor the two correlation-only approaches. We also find that the rankings are consistent with the overall Sharpe ratio rankings. The two correlation-only approaches were slightly, but not hugely, better overall than the mean/variance, but they were clearly better than the superstar approach.

## Statistical Perspective

We noted at the outset that it would have been impossible to form a bad portfolio given this data set. We knew already that all of the CTAs were successful, and that there was not a loser in the bunch. Consequently, what we would like to know is whether the differences in the Sharpe ratios produced by the four approaches were worth the trouble.

The answer is provided by Exhibit 13.10, which shows the distribution of Sharpe ratios that would have resulted from randomly selecting portfolios of 10 CTAs in which their returns were weighted the way we have weighted them in our competing portfolios. The mean of this distribution is 0.54, and its standard deviation is 0.11. With this as our standard of comparison, we can see that the superstar Sharpe ratio of 0.6 for the full eight years is only slightly above average and within one standard deviation of the mean. In contrast, all of the teamwork Sharpe ratios were well up in the distribution—all of them three standard deviations or more above the mean.

## Turnover in the Number of Funds

The final piece of evidence, which also favors the two correlation-only approaches, deals with robustness. These two approaches to building portfolios were far more parsimonious in their use of managers than either the mean/variance or the superstar approaches. This point seems important because of the costs of dropping and adding managers.

In the original round of research, we began with a portfolio of 10 managers chosen at the end of 1997 and then, each year, dropped and replaced the worst

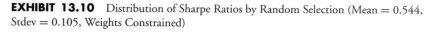

**EXHIBIT 13.10**   Distribution of Sharpe Ratios by Random Selection (Mean = 0.544, Stdev = 0.105, Weights Constrained)

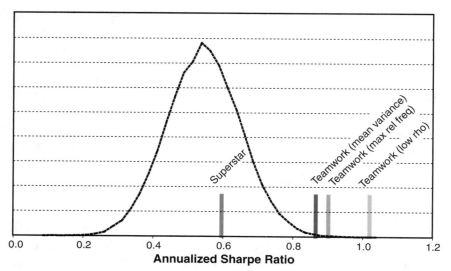

*Source:* Barclay Hedge, Newedge Prime Brokerage Research.

performer. We did this as a way to capture what might happen in a real business setting, where there is always pressure to drop underperforming assets and where, at the same time, wholesale drops and adds likely would be too costly. A possible drawback to this approach, however, is that it imparts an unduly heavy influence to the initial portfolio of 10, which changes very slowly over the years that follow.

In this round of work, we get around this by allowing ourselves to construct the portfolios from scratch for each new year. This way of working removes the element of luck in the initial draw. It allows us to examine in greater detail how each selection rule works going into a fresh period. And it allows us to learn something about the robustness or sensitivity of the selection rules to changes in the data.

Exhibit 13.11 shows how many managers, out of 42, would have been chosen over the entire eight-year period by each of the four rules. As it turned out, the two best-performing portfolios also were the most parsimonious in choosing managers. Over the eight years, the maximum relative frequency rule chose a total of 13 managers. (To be fair, because this approach uses simulated portfolios to determine the probabilities, it would occasionally choose 14

**EXHIBIT 13.11** Number of Managers Chosen out of 42

| Selection Rule | Number Chosen |
|---|---|
| Teamwork (max rel freq) | 13 |
| Teamwork (low rho) | 14 |
| Teamwork (mean/variance) | 21 |
| Superstar | 30 |

managers.) The low-rho approach chose 14. In other words, neither of these approaches found it necessary to make many replacements.

The mean/variance approach to building Teamwork portfolios was less robust. Over the eight years, it would have chosen a total of 21 managers. The higher number of drops and adds can be explained, of course, by its dependence in part on past returns as well as past correlations and volatilities.

It is at this point that the mean/variance rule seems most heavily handicapped. Its overall Sharpe ratio for the eight years was clearly better than that of the Superstar portfolio, and only slightly less good than those produced by the correlation-only approaches. To achieve this outcome, though, it required a higher turnover rate than might be practicable.

Finally, the superstar approach to portfolio building would have chosen 30 of the 42 managers at one time or another during the eight years. The high number of drops and adds is a clear reflection of the year-to-year noise in the relationship between past and future returns. So, not only did it underperform the Teamwork portfolios by a significant amount, it fired and hired managers at a very high rate, which would have produced an additional set of costs that we have not considered here.

## Resilience in the Face of Changes in the Eligible Set

Although we don't provide any evidence on this point in this chapter, one of the things we were looking for was an approach to building portfolios that was less sensitive to changes in the eligible set of CTAs. We already knew that the disappearance of a single manager from the eligible set could cause the mean/variance approach to make major changes in the composition of the optimal portfolio.

What we found with the correlation-only approaches was nearly complete resilience in the face of changes in the eligible set. Removing any one of the lowest-rho CTAs from the eligible set rarely had any effect on the rankings of the remaining CTAs. Most of the time, the replacement would simply be the next CTA on the list.

## Reviewing the Results

When building portfolios by focusing only on correlation and volatility, we run the risk of giving the impression that we are ignoring returns altogether. In fact, we have finessed this problem by choosing a data set of managers who were already successful. All of the 42 managers were good and we were confining our attention to the question of how best to optimize our choices of managers when building portfolios. We could take it for granted that each manager promised a positive expected return.

In practice, one cannot completely sidestep the question of returns. Nor can one ignore other questions that arise when doing due diligence on managers. Investors must comb through a large number of potential candidates to arrive at a set who meet well-defined minimum standards. At least one of these standards is the promise of a positive expected return.

Once the investor has identified an eligible set of possible managers, however, this is when we think our research has relevance. The investor must now decide which ones will go in the portfolio and how they should be weighted. It is at this point that we think the correlation-only rules make sense. Returns, and hence Sharpe ratios, are so dominated by noise that they appear to have no predictive power. In contrast, we find that past correlations and past volatilities can be used reliably to predict future correlations and volatilities. As a result, they appear to be able to do a better job of guiding the investor in building a portfolio. And they hold out the promise of doing so at a lower cost in terms of keeping managers in portfolios longer.

# CHAPTER 14

# Correlations and Holding Periods

## The Research Basis for the *Newedge AlternativeEdge Short-Term Traders Index*

The work we describe in Chapters 13 and 15 has persuaded us that the most reliable tool for improving a portfolio is diversification when correlations are low. It is, in short, the only reliably free lunch available in the world of investments. For one thing, correlations seem to be predictable while Sharpe ratios are not. For another, uncertainty about the true values of return distributions seriously hampers efforts to improve on a simple volatility-weighted portfolio of low-correlation assets.

At the same time, our ongoing conversations with managers and investors have produced a mountain of anecdotal evidence that short-term traders' returns should exhibit low correlations—not only with the returns of nearly any other investment alternative but with one another's returns.

For these reasons, we decided to tackle the problem of constructing an index of short-term traders' performance. We were confident that the effort would be rewarded by highlighting an investment space with very desirable correlative properties. (See Exhibit 14.1.)

**EXHIBIT 14.1** Distribution of Pairwise Correlations among 21 STTI Components (Daily returns, 6/1/07–5/30/08, Mean = 0.104)

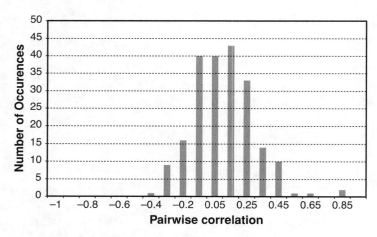

*Source:* Newedge Prime Brokerage Research.

The purpose of this chapter is to discuss the properties of the index and various strategies for replicating the index. In the process, we briefly describe:

- Key findings of "Superstars versus teamwork" and "There are known unknowns"
- Construction of the index (STTI)
- Correlations of STTI returns among themselves and with others'
- Why the correlations are low
- Why there are not more investors in this space
- Some challenges in replicating the index

## Review of Previous Research

Our confidence in correlation as an organizing principle for constructing an index stems mainly from the research we reported in Chapter 13. Everyone knows, as shown in Exhibit 14.2, that low correlation is valuable because it allows for substantial risk reduction for any given level of expected returns. What is more important, though, is that correlation appeared to be predictable while past performance as measured by Sharpe ratios was not. Exhibit 14.3 provides an example of the relationship between historical and realized implied correlations within 10-manager CTA portfolios for a look-back period of three

**EXHIBIT 14.2** Risk Reduction through Diversification

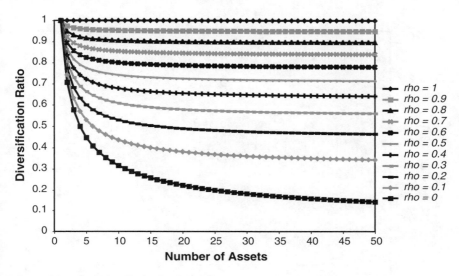

*Source:* Newedge Prime Brokerage Research.

**EXHIBIT 14.3** Historical and Realized Implied Correlations for Portfolios of 10 Managers (Historical, 1995–1997; Realized, 1998)

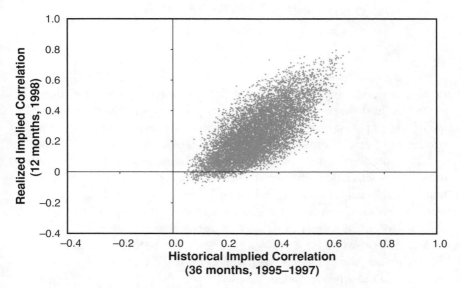

*Source:* Newedge Prime Brokerage Research.

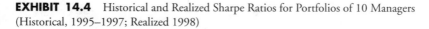

**EXHIBIT 14.4**   Historical and Realized Sharpe Ratios for Portfolios of 10 Managers (Historical, 1995–1997; Realized 1998)

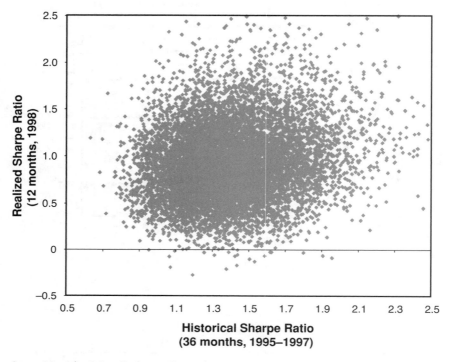

*Source:* Newedge Prime Brokerage Research.

years and a look-forward period of one year. In contrast, Exhibit 14.4 shows no relationship at all between historical and realized Sharpe ratios for the same portfolios. In these examples, the look-back period was 1995–1997, while the look-forward period was 1998. We conducted the same experiment for every similar set of years through 2005 and found roughly similar results.

The upshot of all this was that when we ran a horserace between portfolios of managers selected for their contributions to the portfolio and portfolios of managers selected for their individual performance, we found that the Teamwork portfolios significantly outperformed the Superstar portfolios. In fact, what we found, as shown in Exhibit 14.5, was that the Superstar portfolios turned in what would have been average performance for the set of managers from which we were drawing portfolios, while the Teamwork portfolios produced overall Sharpe ratios that were well up in the distribution of what one could have achieved by constructing portfolios at random.

**EXHIBIT 14.5**   Distribution of Sharpe Ratios for Randomly Selected Portfolios

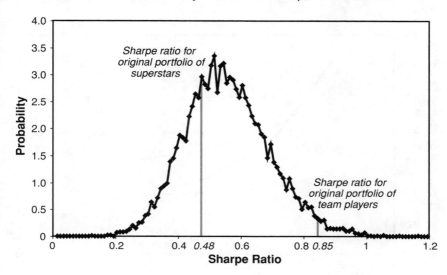

*Source:* Newedge Prime Brokerage Research.

The peculiar shape of the scatter in Exhibit 14.3 also produced a surprising insight into the difference between estimates of implied or average correlations within a portfolio and what one expects to find when estimating pairwise correlations. In particular, when correlations are truly low, the distribution of correlation estimates around the true mean is very wide. In contrast, when estimating the implied correlation of a group of assets, the distribution of the estimate can be actually smaller than it is for more highly correlated assets. As shown in Exhibit 14.6, the standard deviation of the implied correlation estimate is actually smaller for six assets when correlation is zero than when it is higher. This then explains the shape of the (American) football scatter one sees in Exhibit 14.3.

The work we did for Chapter 15 convinced us of the need for real humility when working with real portfolios. For one thing, the distributions of Sharpe ratios for reasonably short holding periods can be very wide. Exhibit 14.7 shows a one-standard-deviation band around the Sharpe ratios one might expect from volatility-weighted portfolios (at the left) and fully optimized portfolios (on the right). The lesson we took from this exhibit is that while there are things we can do to improve a portfolio's expected performance, we cannot seriously expect to detect the results of our work in track records as short as a year.

**EXHIBIT 14.6** Improvement in Estimates of Implied Correlation as the Number of Assets Increases

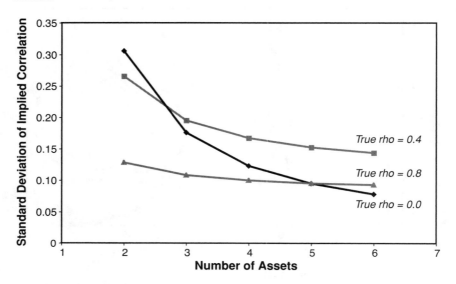

*Source:* Newedge Prime Brokerage Research.

**EXHIBIT 14.7** One-Standard-Deviation Bands for the Sharpe Ratio (12 Monthly Returns)

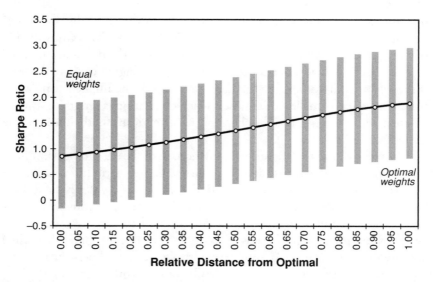

*Source:* Newedge Prime Brokerage Research.

**EXHIBIT 14.8** Sharpe Ratio as a Function of Distance from Optimal Weights (versus Number of Observations Used to Estimate Moments of Return Distributions)

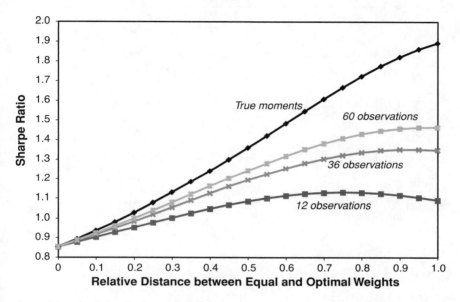

*Source:* Newedge Prime Brokerage Research.

Furthermore, we are hampered in any effort we make to optimize portfolios by the fact that we are always working with estimates of the parameters of return distributions rather than with the truth. Exhibit 14.8 provides some insight into just how much of a drag imperfect knowledge places on what we hope to do. This exhibit was the result of assuming that what we had estimated for these assets was in fact the truth, using those values to produce several thousand return paths that were consistent with those values, and then estimating over look-back periods ranging from 12 to 60 months. Given the way we've constructed the experiment, the estimates using 12 months would have the biggest errors. The curves drawn for 36 and 60 observations show how the expected results improve as the quality of the estimates improves.

The apparent drag of having to work with imperfect knowledge is huge. Moreover, if the estimation errors are large enough, the so-called "optimized" portfolio might not even be better than a compromise solution. With a 12-month look-back, for example, the highest expected Sharpe ratio comes from a portfolio that is about halfway between a simple volatility-weighted portfolio and a portfolio optimized using estimated returns, volatilities, and correlations.

**EXHIBIT 14.9**  *Newedge AlternativeEdge Short-Term Traders Index*

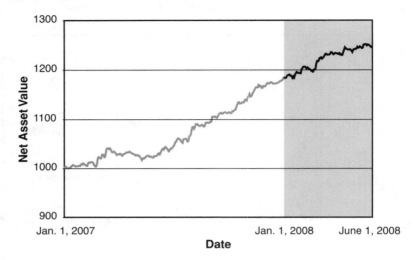

*Source:* Newedge Prime Brokerage Research.

## Index Methodology and Construction

Considering this research, the *Short-Term Traders Index* was constructed with three things in mind. It had to be simple. It had to be robust. And it had to reflect a minimum of curve fitting. To be included, a manager's trades must have an average holding period of 10 days or less. Further, the manager must trade in two or more broad market sectors—equities, fixed income, foreign currency, and commodities—be open to investment, and be willing to report daily returns.

In its current form, 90 percent of the weight is given to managers who have $100 million or more under management at the time the index is reconstituted. These managers' returns are equally volatility weighted—giving higher weight to low-volatility managers and lower weight to high-volatility managers—using estimates based on the previous year's daily returns. These weights are subject to minimum and maximum constraints to avoid serious distortions from errors in volatility estimates. At this writing, this part of the index comprises 14 programs whose combined assets under management equal $6.9 billion.

The remaining 10 percent of the index is assigned at the Index Committee's discretion to managers who are representative of the short-term space and meet all criteria except the $100 million minimum. At this writing, this part of the index comprises seven programs whose returns are equally weighted.

## How Low Are the Correlations?

Going into this exercise, we expected the correlations of returns among the managers to be low, and we expected the correlations of their returns with those for longer-term CTAs and for other investments to be low. The exhibits in this section bear this out.

### Pairwise Correlations

Exhibit 14.10 shows the distribution of pairwise correlations for the 21 programs, estimated using daily returns, for the period June 2007 through May 2008. The average of these correlations was 0.104. To put this distribution in perspective, we have overlaid the theoretical distribution of estimates one would get if the true pairwise correlation for all managers were in fact 0.104. To us, the interesting lesson in comparing the two is that the observed distribution is wider than it would be if all of the CTAs actually had the same low correlation with one another. At the same time, it seems that one could

**EXHIBIT 14.10** Actual and Theoretical Distributions of Pairwise Correlations among 21 STTI Components (Daily Returns, 6/1/07–5/30/08, Mean = 0.104)

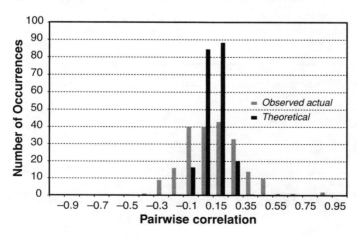

*Source:* Newedge Prime Brokerage Research.

construct the observed distribution, with the exception of the 0.85 outlier, from a blend of distributions with a fairly small range of true (and low) correlations.

## Time Series of Implied Correlations

While Exhibit 14.10 used the entire year of returns to estimate pairwise correlations, Exhibit 14.11 shows how the average or implied correlation estimates varied over the year. Each point is the average pairwise correlation estimated using that month's daily returns. Overlaid on this series are two lines that represent a two-standard-deviation band around the average of 0.116. This band was reckoned assuming that the true pairwise correlation for all managers was the sample mean. In reality, the actual two-standard-deviation band is wider than this because some of the true correlations are less than the mean used here, while some are greater. In any case, a time series like this is a useful diagnostic for monitoring the overall correlation among managers in the index.

**EXHIBIT 14.11**    Implied Correlation for 21 STTI Components (Average = 0.116)

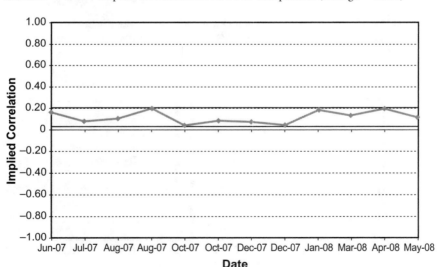

*Source:* Newedge Prime Brokerage Research.

**EXHIBIT 14.12** June 2007–May 2008

| | STTI | Newedge CTA Index | S&P 500 Index | Lehman Composite Bond Index | HFR Equity Hedge Index |
|---|---|---|---|---|---|
| STTI | 1.000 | | | | |
| Newedge CTA | 0.235 | 1.000 | | | |
| S&P 500 | −0.246 | 0.031 | 1.000 | | |
| Lehman Composite Bond Index | 0.104 | 0.068 | −0.395 | 1.000 | |
| HFR Equity Hedge | −0.131 | 0.299 | 0.771 | −0.365 | 1.000 |

*Source:* Newedge Prime Brokerage Research.

## Correlations with Returns of Other Investments

Exhibit 14.12 reports the correlation of daily returns with those on other investment vehicles including the *Newedge CTA Index*, the S&P 500, the Lehman Composite Bond Index, and the HFR Equity Hedge index. As one would expect, the correlations of STTI returns with those of other investment vehicles are all fairly low—some slightly positive, others slightly negative. Even its correlation with the *Newedge CTA Index*, which comprises the 20 largest CTAs, is only 0.235.

## Correlations of Returns Calculated over Longer Periods

Correlation estimates can be sensitive to the choice of period over which returns are calculated. For example, the use of daily data may introduce noise because of different settlement times throughout the day. To see whether the appearance of low correlation might be a result of using daily data, we calculated correlations of STTI and Newedge CTA returns for non-overlapping periods of 5, 10, and 20 days, corresponding roughly to weekly, biweekly, and monthly returns. Exhibit 14.13 shows that nothing much changes as we lengthen the period used to calculate returns. The correlations appear to

**EXHIBIT 14.13** Correlation and Sample Size

| Interval in Days | Count | Correlation | Stdev |
|---|---|---|---|
| 1 | 264 | 0.233 | 0.058 |
| 5 | 52 | 0.242 | 0.131 |
| 10 | 26 | 0.310 | 0.179 |
| 20 | 13 | −0.083 | 0.276 |

Source: Newedge Prime Brokerage Research.

increase slightly as we go from 1 to 5 to 10 days, but nothing that is inconsistent with sampling error. And then, when we go to 20 days, the estimated correlation is actually slightly negative. But again, the change is well within the range of sampling error one would expect.

## Why Are the Correlations Low?

The most obvious place to look for an explanation for the low correlations we observe is the ultimate source of all returns—the markets to which all traders have access. Two traders' returns at any moment and during any particular period can be written as:

$$R_{it} = \sum_{m=1}^{M} w_{imt} R_{mt} \qquad R_{jt} = \sum_{m=1}^{M} w_{jmt} R_{mt}$$

where $i$ and $j$ are different traders taking positions in any or all of $M$ markets.

Since both traders have access to the same markets, their returns can be different only if the weights they assign to each of the markets are different, either in size or sign.

What we suspect, of course, is that short-term traders' trades overlap very little with those of longer-term traders. Either they are not in the market at the same time or the directions they take in the markets may be independent of the directions taken by longer-term traders.

## Holding Period and Return Correlation

A simple experiment bore this out. Using five years of real-time data for S&P 500 futures from 2003–2007, we compared the results of a simple M-day/N-day breakout model implemented for various look-back periods. In particular, we implemented the rule as follows:

Entrance:     If price > M-day high, go long;
              If price < M-day low, go short
Exit:         If price < N-day high, exit long;
              If price > N-day low, exit short

**EXHIBIT 14.14**   Correlations with 80/40 Breakout Model

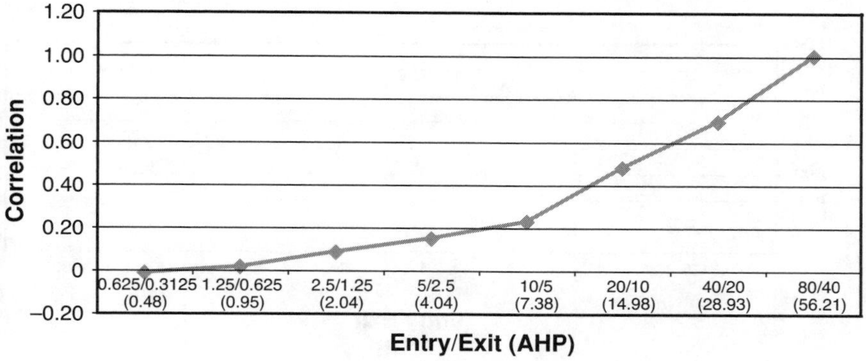

*Source:* Newedge Prime Brokerage Research.

for eight look-back periods—80/40, 40/20, and so on—reducing the times by half until we got to 0.625/0.3125. In implementing these rules, we assumed that once a trade is initiated, a new position cannot be taken until the older trade is closed out.

The effect of shortening the breakout period can be seen in Exhibit 14.14, which shows the correlation of each strategy's returns with those generated by the 80/40 breakout rule. (The resulting average holding period for each is shown in parentheses.) We see that the correlation falls as we shorten the holding period until, by the time the average holding period is under 10 days, the correlation is in the neighborhood of 0.20. By the time the holding period is less than a day, the correlation with 80/40 returns is about zero.

What we see in Exhibit 14.14 is consistent with a sense we have that there are far more ways to slice up a time series if our holding period is short than if our horizons are long. This is borne out in Exhibit 14.15, which shows how many S&P 500 trades each rule generated during the five-year period. The 80/40 rule produced a total of eight trades with an average holding period of 56 days. The 0.625/0.3125 rule, in contrast, produced almost 1,400 trades with an average holding period of less than half a day.

As a result, the amount of time that traders spend in the market at the same time and in the same direction falls as the holding period is reduced. Exhibit 14.16 bears this out by showing the fraction of the time each rule is both in the market and in the same direction as the 80/40 rule. The first number indicates that the 80/40 rule was in the market 53.8 percent of the time. As it was, each rule was in the market roughly the same percent of the

**EXHIBIT 14.15**   Number of Trades during the Five-Year Period for Different Breakout Models

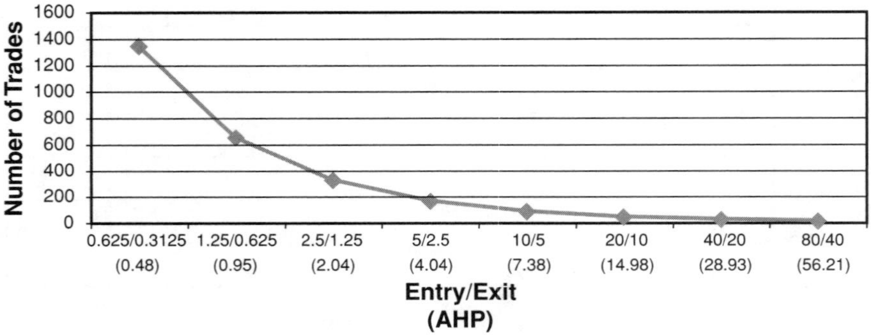

*Source:* Newedge Prime Brokerage Research.

time as the 80/40 rule, but the overlaps tended to shrink as the holding period was reduced. The shortest holding periods were in the market and in the same direction as the 80/40 rule only about 20 percent of the time.

## More Evidence on Correlation

Pierre Villeneuve, managing director of Mapleridge, offered further insights into why short-term strategies exhibit such low correlation. In a research presentation at our research forum in Bordeaux, he compared short-term and long-term trading strategies that were purely random on the one hand and that had trend-following features on the other. He also isolated the profitable

**EXHIBIT 14.16**   Fraction of the Time in the Market with the Same Position as the 80/40 Breakout Rule

| Lookback | Fraction |
|---|---|
| 80/40 | 53.8 |
| 40/20 | 42.0 |
| 20/10 | 28.9 |
| 10./5 | 22.3 |
| 5/2.5 | 23.4 |
| 2.5/1.25 | 21.3 |
| 1.25/0.625 | 19.1 |
| 0.625/0.3125 | 19.8 |

*Source:* Newedge Prime Brokerage Research.

strategies in both cases to see how focusing on "successful" trading programs might affect the results.

His purely random model was described as:

Start with a random position long/short (+1/–1)
Each day change position with probability p

In his examples:

Short-term p = 0.5
Long-term p = 0.008

So the average holding period for the short-term model was 2 days [= 1/0.5], while the average holding period for the long-term model was 125 days [= 1/0.008].

His trend-following model was described as:

Start with a random position long/short (+1/–1)
Each day if:
50-day moving average of returns is against current position, then change position with probability p (more likely to change position)
50-day moving average of returns is with current position, then change position with probability $p^2$ (less likely to change)

In his example:

Short-term p = 0.5
Long-term p = 0.02

In both cases, and for both short-term and long-term models, he generated 2,000 trials using a continuous S&P 500 futures series from 2005–2008.

The distributions of pairwise correlations for the random and trend-following short-term strategies are compared in Exhibit 14.17. It is apparent that the introduction of a trend-following component to the model increased the average correlation from 0.0 to about 0.1. In Exhibit 14.18, however, we find that the distributions of pairwise correlations for the trend-following models were independent of whether they made money or not. The distribution of correlations for those runs that produced gains in the top 25 percent was no different than the distribution of correlations for returns from all runs.

**EXHIBIT 14.17**    Short-Term Strategies Correlations

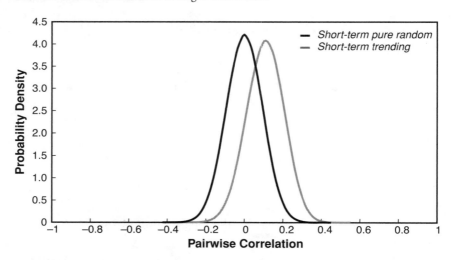

*Source:* Mapleridge Capital Corporation.

**EXHIBIT 14.18**    Short-Term Trending Strategies Correlations

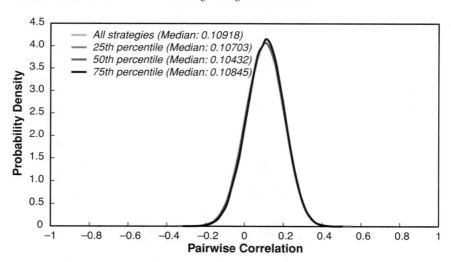

*Source:* Mapleridge Capital Corporation.

**EXHIBIT 14.19** Long-Term Strategies Correlations

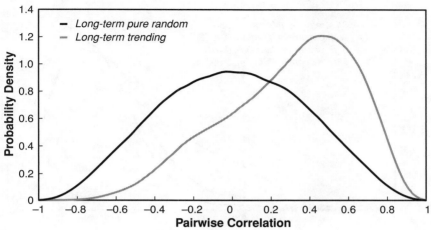

*Source:* Mapleridge Capital Corporation.

In Exhibit 14.19, we find a similar result, although the effect of introducing a trend-following component to the long-term strategies was more pronounced. The average pairwise correlation increased from 0.0 for the long-term random strategies to 0.34 for the long-term trend-following strategies. Further, in Exhibit 14.20, we see that isolating the profitable trend-following strategies—represented here by the top 25 percent of the distribution of returns—has an additional effect on the distribution of correlations. The average correlation for the 75th percentile (the top 25 percent) was 0.59.

His explanation for the differences in the short-term and long-term results agreed with our suggestion that the possible overlaps for short-term strategies are much fewer and much smaller than what one finds with long-term strategies. There are simply a lot more ways to trade markets in the short-term than in the long-term. As a result, even the successful short-term outcomes tend not to overlap with one another. With long-term strategies, however, there are comparatively few profitable trades, which suggests that overlapping positions are highly likely.

## Why Are There Not More Short-Term Traders?

If short-term trading has such desirable properties for portfolio management, why have more traders not been attracted to the space? The most obvious

**EXHIBIT 14.20**   Long-Term Trending Strategies Correlations

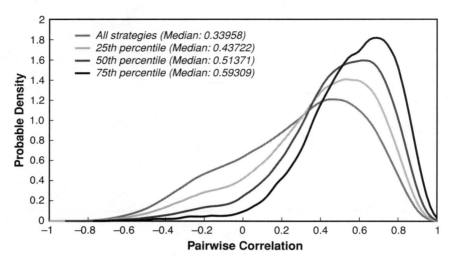

*Source:* Mapleridge Capital Corporation.

answer seems to be that the barriers to entry are high. For one thing, results are highly sensitive to transactions costs and market impacts. As a result, the amount of care and research required to ferret out profitable strategies and to keep transaction costs at an absolute minimum tend to be much greater than for longer-term trading strategies.

Although the number of possible strategies is very large, the capacity of any given strategy is questionable. At the same time, the electronic revolution in futures trading has been hugely effective in reducing transaction costs. Liquidity has improved immensely in many markets and the drag of market impact has been brought down substantially. As a result, strategies that might not have been profitable in the past may well be profitable now.

## Replicating the Index

Investors attracted to the idea of investing in this space may find it either impractical or impossible to invest in all 21 programs in the index. While all 21 are open for investment, not all take managed accounts. This increases the cost of investing because the leads and lags that are part of investing in funds can be considerable. Also, investors may have internal constraints that prevent them from investing in one or more of the managers, or find it too costly to conduct due diligence for all 21 programs.

To get a sense of what one might expect from investing in subsets of the 21, we considered all possible portfolios ranging from 1 program (single program) to 20 programs and calculated the Sharpe ratios one would have realized over the period from January 2007–May 2008. The results of this work are shown in Exhibit 14.21.

For each portfolio size, the exhibit shows several things—the range of possible Sharpe ratios, the average Sharpe ratio, and the fraction of outcomes that produced a Sharpe ratio greater than the 21-program portfolio. The chief lessons are those we know from the rules that govern diversification and risk reduction. Most of the benefits from diversification are reaped by the time one has reached 10 managers. Even so, the likelihood of doing as well—at least by this standard—is only about 20 percent.

It is also apparent that investing in three or four short-term traders does not capture the full benefits of investing in this space. Only 3 percent of the three-program portfolios outperformed the index.

**EXHIBIT 14.21** Sharpe Ratios for All Possible STTI Constituents Sub-Portfolio (2007.1–present)

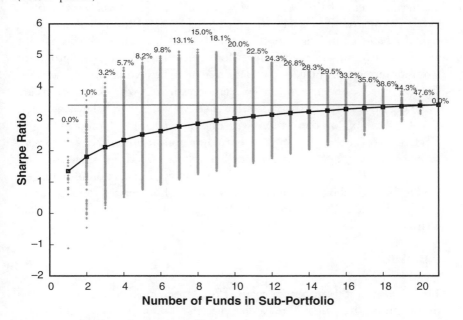

*Source:* Newedge Prime Brokerage Research.

## Cautions and Managing the Index

We should note that we rely to a large extent on self-reporting and market discipline to keep the index on track. We do not audit the managers' trades to make sure that their average holding period is 10 days or less. Rather, we rely on managers telling us what they tell their clients. Also, the $100 million criterion for assets under management for 90 percent of the index gives us confidence that these managers have passed muster with substantial investors.

Thus, our greatest concern in managing the index is with correlation. Given our prior beliefs about average holding period and return correlations, we are satisfied with the correlative properties that the index and its components have exhibited so far. For us, a red flag would be a change in implied correlation that was inconsistent with what one would expect. As we showed in Exhibit 14.11, a two-standard-deviation range around a true correlation of 0.116 would be from 0.03 to 0.20. Because we think the actual ranges of true pairwise correlations occupy a range around 0.116, our tolerances would be wider than this.

## Conclusion

The development of the *Newedge AlternativeEdge Short-Term Traders Index* has been a constructive exercise that puts to use insights from the research we originally reported in Chapters 12 and 13. Diversification when correlations are low produces superior portfolios. Moreover, when working with groups of 10 or more assets or managers, correlations tend to be predictable and we actually have more confidence in low-correlation estimates when correlations are low. In the case of short-term traders, we have every reason to believe that their returns will exhibit low correlations with one another and with those of longer-term traders because of the richer set of trading opportunities they face. So far, our expectations of low correlation have been borne out. Moreover, we are confident that we have done a good job of constructing a collection of managers who are highly and broadly representative of the short-term trading space.

The appendix that follows takes a fresh look at some of the original research.

## Appendix

The purpose of this appendix is to take a fresh look at a couple of the exhibits from the original research with the notion of commenting on

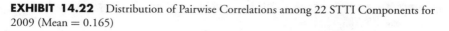

**EXHIBIT 14.22** Distribution of Pairwise Correlations among 22 STTI Components for 2009 (Mean = 0.165)

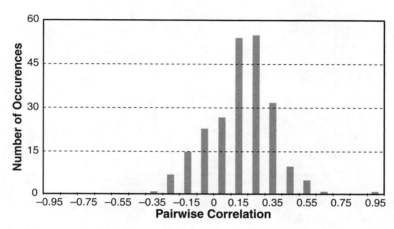

*Source:* Newedge Prime Brokerage Research.

anything that stands out or had changed from our previous analysis. We chose to update three exhibits using the daily returns of the 22 constituents in the index in 2009. Focusing on Exhibit 14.1, our first round of research showed a distribution of average pairwise correlations that was skewed right, as one would expect from a group of managers with similar styles of trading, but was fairly well distributed with a mean of 0.104. This distribution confirmed our initial thoughts on the short-term trading space, although sharing a common timeframe; most of the managers are not correlated to one another.

Taking a look at the updated exhibit (Exhibit 14.22), those same characteristics still apply. The mean of the distribution has increased slightly to 0.165 and the distribution is skewed to the right. The average pairwise correlation between managers in the short-term space is persistent and consistently low.

We used this new distribution to calculate the theoretical distribution in Exhibit 14.23. This distribution was simulated as if all the managers had a true average pairwise correlation of 0.165. Again, the new exhibit relays the same story as the original (Exhibit 14.10). The theoretical distribution is narrower than the original as it does not include the positive and negative outliers found in the actual distribution of average pairwise correlations.

**EXHIBIT 14.23**   Distributions of Pairwise Correlations among 22 STTI Components for 2009 (Mean = 0.165)

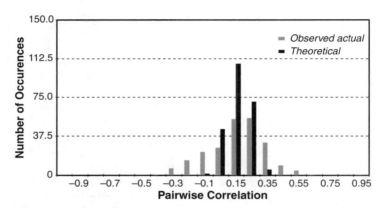

*Source:* Newedge Prime Brokerage Research.

Finally, we have updated Exhibit 14.9 to show performance through the end of 2009 (see Exhibit 14.24). We have chosen to show the NAV only from the inception of the index, January 1, 2008. In the original exhibit we showed a hypothetical backtest using manager performance from 2007. As you can see, the index had strong performance in 2008 and was down slightly in 2009. These characteristics are in complete agreement with the performance experienced by managers in the short-term space.

**EXHIBIT 14.24**   *Newedge AlternativeEdge Short-Term Trader's Index*—Updated

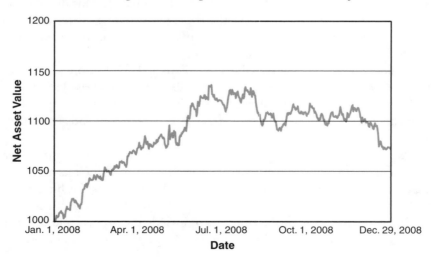

*Source:* Newedge Prime Brokerage Research.

# CHAPTER 15

# "There Are Known Unknowns"*

## The Drag of Imperfect Estimates

Donald Rumsfeld's famous quote is a perfect jumping off place for this closing chapter. What we want to explore in this chapter are those things that get in the way of improving the performance of our portfolios or that obscure our ability to know whether we have really accomplished anything useful.

Our focus in this chapter is on the challenges we face when we try to improve on the free lunch. The most significant challenges include:

1. The drag of imperfect estimates
2. A good chance of failure
3. The increased likelihood that one of our assets will seriously underperform

We consider these in turn.

Imperfect estimates of return distribution moments (mean, volatility, correlation) impede our efforts to improve portfolio performance. Under fairly plausible circumstances, we find that using estimated return moments can rob us of half or more of any improvement we might expect to get from using "optimal" portfolio weights (positive weights that maximize the Sharpe ratio using mean and covariance estimates) rather than simple volatility weights.

Because luck (randomness) so dominates skill, at least over horizons of a few years, we cannot expect too much from track records when trying

---

*Donald Rumsfeld, Feb. 12, 2002, U.S. Department of Defense newsbrief.

**EXHIBIT 15.1**    One-Standard-Deviation Bands for the Sharpe Ratio (12 Monthly Returns)

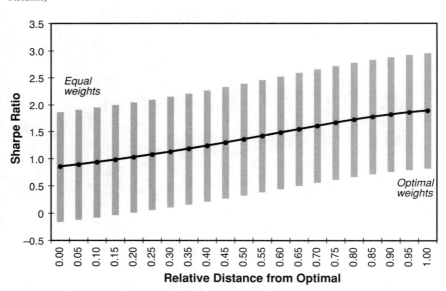

*Source:* Barclay Hedge, Newedge Prime Brokerage Research.

to evaluate the performance of an individual manager (who is running a portfolio of strategies) or a fund of funds (which is running a portfolio of managers). Large sampling variation in Sharpe ratio estimates seriously blurs the distinction between the results of naïve or simple diversification and the use of optimal weights in a portfolio with 42 managers. (See the next section for a complete description of this exercise.) Exhibit 15.1 shows one-standard-deviation bands around the expected Sharpe ratios one could achieve under the best of circumstances (that is, actually knowing the means, volatilities, and correlations of returns) but with only one year (12 monthly returns) to evaluate the results. So many of the distributions overlap that there is nearly one chance in four that equal volatility weights would result in a better Sharpe ratio than would so-called optimal weights.

Diversification has costs in the sense that we increase the likelihood that one or more of our assets will seriously underperform the market. With 5 assets in a portfolio, we can expect the worst-performing asset to produce a return that is nearly two-standard-deviations below its usual mean. With 10 assets in a portfolio, we can expect the worst-performing asset to produce a return that is nearly three standard deviations below normal.

## Improving Risk-Adjusted Returns

We know that diversification is the only free lunch in town when it comes to increasing risk-adjusted returns. In this section, we want to determine how much we can improve the Sharpe ratio of a portfolio through active or optimal weighting. For this, our benchmark is what we can achieve through naïve diversification in which we simply allocate the same amount to each asset or manager on a volatility-adjusted basis.

To illustrate this point, we began with a data set that included 42 managers for whom we had track records from 1995 through 2005 (the same data set was used in Chapter 12). We then netted interest income from each return series and normalized each manager's return volatility to 15 percent. From these series, we estimated means, correlations, and Sharpe ratios for the 11-year period. Exhibit 15.2 shows the annualized 11-year Sharpe ratios for

**EXHIBIT 15.2**    Annualized Sharpe Ratios for 42 Managers (1995–2005)

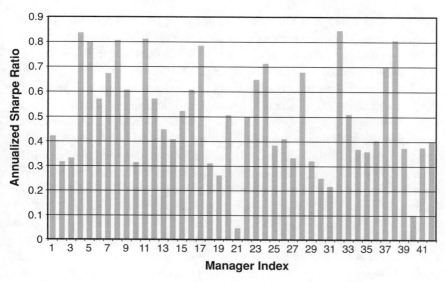

*Source:* Barclay Hedge, Newedge Prime Brokerage Research.

**EXHIBIT 15.3**   Sharpe Ratio as a Function of Distance from Optimal Weights

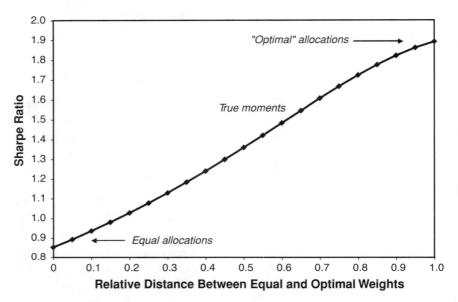

*Source:* Newedge Prime Brokerage Research.

each of the 42 managers. The names of the managers are represented by index numbers along the horizontal axis. The average Sharpe ratio was 0.49.

Now consider Exhibit 15.3, where the horizontal axis measures the distance between equal weights and optimal weights. A 0.0 represents equal weights, while 1.0 represents what would have been the optimal weights for the period had we known the true parameter values for each manager's return series. In between is the relative distance between the two. For example, if we were working with four managers, equal weights would be 0.25, 0.25, 0.25, and 0.25. Suppose, though, that the optimal weights would have been 0.15, 0.15, 0.15, and 0.55 (15% to the first three and 55% to the fourth). In this case, a value of 0.5 on the horizontal axis would represent weights that were halfway between equal weights and the optimal weights, or 0.2 (= 0.5 · .25 + .5 · .15), 0.2, 0.2, and 0.4 (= 0.5 · .25 + 0.5 · .55).

We see that equal weights for this group of managers would have produced an expected Sharpe ratio of approximately 0.85, which is a substantial improvement over the simple average Sharpe ratio of 0.49. Optimal weights, had we known the true moments of the managers' return distributions, would have produced an expected Sharpe ratio of almost 1.90. The line connecting the two measures shows the progress from one to the other as we move from equal to optimal weights. It is important to keep in mind that these are the expected values around which observed values will be distributed. As we will see in a moment, the standard deviations of these distributions can be quite large.

## We Don't Know the True Moments, Though

One of the obstacles that we face is our ignorance of the true values of the moments that govern the managers' return distributions. To the extent we use estimates or guesses for the values of these moments, the weights we derive will not equal the optimal weights. Moreover, the larger our estimating errors, the less we can expect from active weighting.

Exhibit 15.4 shows how our expected improvement is affected by the quality (standard deviation) of our estimates. To construct this exhibit, we used the estimated moments of the 42 managers' return distributions as if they were the true values to generate a large set of simulated returns. From these simulated returns, we estimated means, standard deviations, and

**EXHIBIT 15.4** Sharpe Ratio as a Function of Distance from Optimal Weights (versus Number of Observations Used to Estimate Moments of Return Distributions)

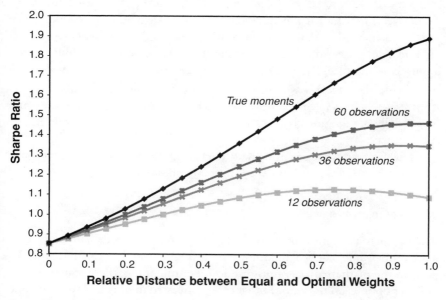

*Source:* Newedge Prime Brokerage Research.

correlations using sample sizes ranging from 12 to 60 observations. Since we were simulating what would have been monthly returns, these sample sizes represent spans ranging from one to five years. For this exercise to work, we also have to assume that the true moments of these distributions do not change over time.

We can see that having to use estimated rather than true moments puts a serious limit on how much we can expect to improve the portfolio's performance. For that matter, when working with just 12 observations, we see that the so-called optimal weights are not even the best weights. Rather, we see that a better mix is provided by weights that are themselves a weighted average of equal and optimal weights. Even with more data, though, we find that the distance between what we can expect using imperfect estimates of return moments and what we could expect if we knew the true moments is large. With 36 observations, or three years of data, the best we can expect is about halfway between what we would expect with equal weights and what we would expect if we knew the true optimal weights.

## Daily versus Monthly Data

Once we see how much ignorance can cost us, our interest in the question of whether we can learn better or faster using daily instead of monthly returns increases. If we can gather 20 or more observations per month rather than 12 per year, we can learn in three months what it would otherwise take five years to achieve. For daily data to provide this kind of boost, however, the circumstances have to be right. For one thing, we have to be confident that a one-day time slice is representative of any longer time slice except that the volatility of daily returns would be $n^{-\frac{1}{2}}$ times the volatility of monthly returns if there were $n$ days in the month. We also have to be confident that the noise in our daily observations is small and that there is no serial correlation in our daily returns.

The main drawback to using daily data is that the forces behind managers' returns can vary dramatically over longer stretches of time.

## Other Constraints on Allocations

In addition to the constraints imposed by imperfect knowledge, investors may work under some practical or long-term business constraints that have little to do with the mathematics of optimization. For one thing, there may be upper or lower bounds on the amount that can be invested in or risked with any one manager or asset. For another thing, we may invest more in a manager than the optimal weights would indicate because we want to maintain a relationship with a particular manager. And then there are the costs of reallocating our investments that make continuous rebalancing impractical.

## How Variable Are Sharpe Ratios?

The curves in Exhibits 15.3 and 15.4 represent expected values around which observed values will be distributed. How variable are Sharpe ratios? Using Andrew Lo's approximation (from *The Statistics of Sharpe Ratios*, AIMR, 2002), we have

$$SD(SR) \approx \sqrt{\frac{1 + \frac{SR^2}{2}}{T}}$$

where $SR$ is the monthly Sharpe ratio if you are using monthly returns, and $T$ is the number of months. The squiggly equals sign is standing in for "asymptotically equal to."

Because the square of a monthly Sharpe ratio is such a small number, the numerator of this expression is close to 1, so the ratio is close to 1 over the number of observations. If we are talking about 12 monthly observations, the standard deviation of a monthly Sharpe ratio would be approximately 1 over the square root of 12. The standard deviation of an annualized Sharpe ratio would be the square root of 12 times this, or about 1.0.

Exhibit 15.5 (which is the same as Exhibit 15.1) shows a one-standard-deviation band around the expected Sharpe ratios that we could achieve by combining equal weights with the true optimal weights. The scary thing about this picture is that even if we knew the true moments of the managers' return distributions, it is clear that the sampling error is so large that we would have a hard time detecting the difference between what we achieve with equal weighting and what we might have achieved through optimal weighting. The maximum possible increase in the expected Sharpe ratio is only slightly more than 1.0, which is about the size of one standard deviation of sampling error. If we use more realistic measures of the possible increase in the Sharpe ratio, all of the improvements are less than one standard deviation of sampling error.

We can, of course, decrease the standard deviation of the Sharpe ratio by increasing the sample size. As shown in Exhibit 15.6, an estimated Sharpe ratio based on 48 monthly returns would have a standard deviation of approximately 0.5. While this is better, it is still as large as the kind of

**EXHIBIT 15.5**   One-Standard-Deviation Bands for the Sharpe Ratio (12 Monthly Returns)

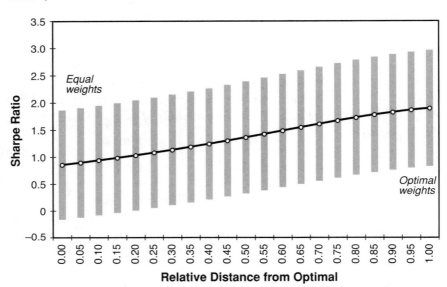

*Source:* Barclay Hedge, Newedge Prime Brokerage Research.

improvement in the portfolio's expected Sharpe ratio that we might reasonably achieve using weights based on estimated moments of the managers' return distributions.

## Correlated Track Records

To be fair, the standard deviation bands shown in Exhibits 15.5 and 15.6 paint a bleaker picture than we really face. In particular, they assume that the return streams that produce the Sharpe ratios are independent. If what we want to compare, though, is how a volatility-weighted portfolio would perform when compared with an optimally weighted portfolio, the underlying return streams of the individual assets would be the same in both cases. The only difference would be in the weighting. So, if the volatility-weighted portfolio has a good run, the optimally weighted portfolio likely would have a good run, too. So the track records of the competing portfolios would be correlated, as would the resulting Sharpe ratios.

To cope with this problem, we undertook a simulation exercise that allowed us to vary both the months used to estimate the parameters of the

**EXHIBIT 15.6**   One-Standard-Deviation Bands for the Sharpe Ratio (48 Monthly Returns)

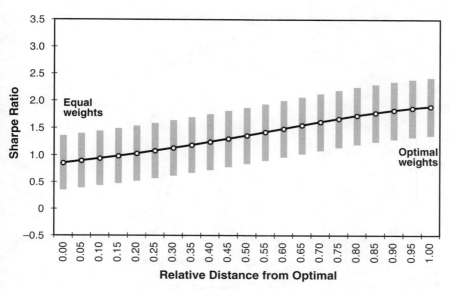

*Source:* Barclay Hedge, Newedge Prime Brokerage Research.

managers' return distributions as well as the number of months used to evaluate the results. Both the estimation and evaluation periods ranged from 12 to 60 months, although it is only the length of the evaluation period that is relevant here. For this exercise, we generated 4,000 returns paths, each of which was used to construct both a volatility-weighted portfolio and an optimally weighted portfolio.

Exhibits 15.7 and 15.8 both show three distributions. One is for the Sharpe ratio of optimally weighted portfolios. Another is for the Sharpe ratios of volatility-weighted portfolios. And the third is for the difference between the two. In both cases, we have used 60 months (five years) of return data to estimate the moments of the return distributions. In Exhibit 15.7, though, we track each of the portfolios for 12 months, while in Exhibit 15.8, we track each for 60 months. In comparing the two, we find that under the right circumstances, patience can be rewarded. With a 12-month evaluation period, the distribution of the difference in Sharpe ratios is centered to the right of zero with a mean of 0.67. Given its breadth, though, we find that 26 percent of the distribution lies to the left of zero. This means that with an evaluation period as short as one year, there is roughly one chance in four that

**EXHIBIT 15.7**  Distributions of Sharpe Ratios and Their Differences (Looking Back 60 Months and Forward 12)

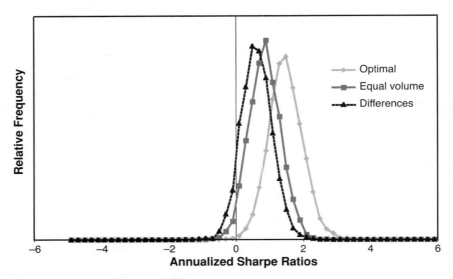

*Source:* Barclay Hedge, Newedge Prime Brokerage Research.

**EXHIBIT 15.8**  Distributions of Sharpe Ratios and Their Differences (Looking Back 60 Months and Forward 60)

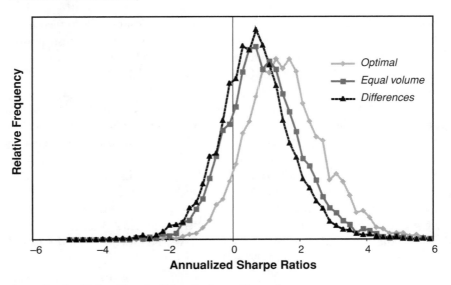

*Source:* Barclay Hedge, Newedge Prime Brokerage Research.

**EXHIBIT 15.9** What Are the Chances that Optimal Portfolios Will Outperform Equal-Volatility Portfolios? (Percentage that Optimal Is Better than Equal-Vol)

| Months Looking Back | Months Looking Forward | | | |
|---|---|---|---|---|
| | 12 | 24 | 36 | 60 |
| 12 | 61.1% | 64.1% | 66.4% | 70.0% |
| 36 | 70.1% | 76.6% | 80.9% | 85.7% |
| 60 | 74.1% | 81.0% | 85.7% | 92.2% |

the volatility-weighted portfolio would outperform the optimally weighted portfolio.

With a longer evaluation period, which is illustrated in Exhibit 15.8, our ability to discern an improvement could be substantially better. The mean of the distribution of differences in the Sharpe ratios in this case is 0.62, but only 8 percent of the distribution lies to the left of zero. And so, if we were afforded two luxuries—a long evaluation period and the confidence that the moments of the managers' return distributions would remain unchanged—we could greatly increase the odds that an optimally weighted portfolio would outperform a simple volatility-weighted portfolio.

Exhibit 15.9 shows how the odds change with changes in estimation (look-back) and evaluation (look-forward). Each cell contains the fraction of the distribution of Sharpe ratio differences that are greater than zero. In this exercise, longer estimation periods produce better estimates of the return moments and so produce higher expected outcomes for the optimal portfolios. And longer evaluation periods allow for better resolution. So as we progress from northwest to southeast in the table, things get better for the optimal portfolio.

## The Bias in Estimated Sharpe Ratios

A byproduct of this exercise was an insight into the estimation of Sharpe ratios. We found that estimated Sharpe ratios are biased upward. We also found that the estimated Sharpe ratio approaches the true Sharpe ratio as the sample size increases. This revealed itself both in the distributions of Sharpe ratios for the competing portfolios and in the differences in Sharpe ratios. This explained the decrease in the average difference in Sharpe ratios as we increased the evaluation period from 12 to 60 months.

**EXHIBIT 15.10**    Distribution of Sharpe Ratios for Randomly Selected Portfolios

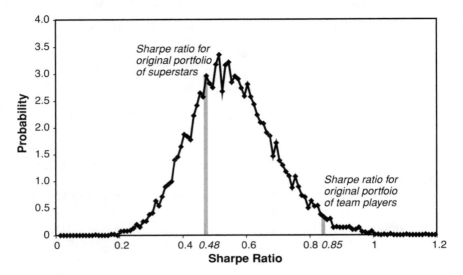

*Source:* Barclay Hedge, Newedge Prime Brokerage Research.

## Use of Historical Track Records

Our work on the distribution of Sharpe ratios led to an unexpected insight into the care we have to take in using historical data. Exhibit 15.10 (taken from Chapter 12) shows the distribution of portfolio Sharpe ratios that we would have realized from 1995 through 2005 had we formed portfolios of 10 managers at random. We observed that the Superstar portfolio was slightly below average in this distribution, while the Teamwork portfolio was well toward the upper end of the distribution.

This distribution, however, seemed too narrow in light of Lo's estimate of what the standard deviation of Sharpe ratio estimates should be. In trying to understand why, we realized that in producing the distribution, we were choosing the managers at random but were using each manager's 11-year track record over and over. We then went back and used the moments of the managers' return distributions to new return streams for each exercise and so allowed the track record of each manager to exhibit randomness as well. When we did this, the Sharpe ratio distribution that we obtained was the broader distribution shown in Exhibit 15.11. The standard deviation of this distribution proved to be 0.362, in contrast to the 0.106 that we obtained when the track records were fixed and only the manager selection was allowed to be random.

**EXHIBIT 15.11**   How Variable Are Sharpe Ratios?

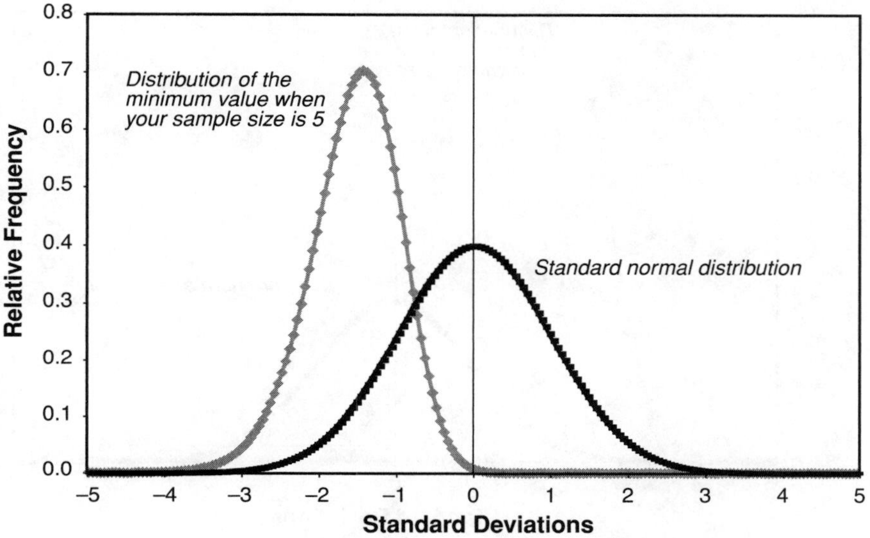

*Source:* Barclay Hedge, Newedge Prime Brokerage Research.

## Throwing Out the Losers

How do you know whether an asset or manager is doing better or worse than expected? How should your expectations for the performance of individual assets be affected by the number of assets in the portfolio or on your approach to leverage? The expected performance of the worst-performing asset gets worse as the number of assets increases. This applies both to returns and correlations. As a result, our standards for dropping an asset or firing a manager must be mapped out clearly ahead of time and suit the way we construct the portfolio.

### How Bad Is Bad?

Consider Exhibit 15.12, which shows two distributions. One is the standard normal distribution with a mean of zero and a standard deviation of 1.0. The other is the distribution of the smallest number in a sample of five draws from the standard normal. The fact that we expect this number to be negative should be no surprise. If we were drawing a single number from the standard

**EXHIBIT 15.12**   Expectations for the Worst out of 5 Draws

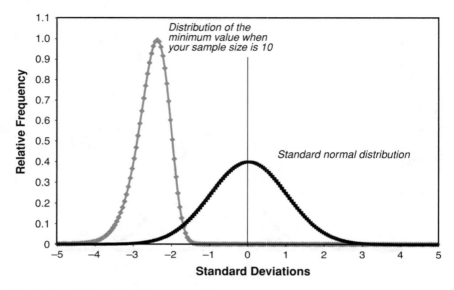

*Source:* Newedge Prime Brokerage Research.

normal, we would expect its value to be zero. If we draw two or more, though, we expect the smallest number in the sample to be negative. That is, as soon as we draw a sample of two, we actually expect one of the two values to be negative. If they were assets or money managers, we would expect one of them to underperform.

In this case, with a sample size of 5, the distribution of the minimum value in the sample is centered around a number that is close to minus 2. And, as we increase the size of our sample, we expect the value of the smallest number to get smaller still. In Exhibit 15.13, we see that with a sample size of 10, the distribution of the sample's minimum is centered around a number close to minus 3.

This aspect of sampling has profound implications for the way we evaluate individual assets or managers in a portfolio. For example, in Chapter 12, we examined the effects of dropping the worst-performing asset and replacing it with another. When we did this using returns, we found that in three instances out of eight, the manager's average return for the evaluation period was nearly two standard deviations below the manager's historical mean return. If we were evaluating the manager on a freestanding basis, this kind of value would

**EXHIBIT 15.13**   Expectations for the Worst out of 10 Draws

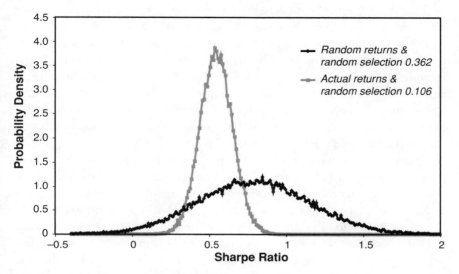

*Source:* Barclay Hedge, Newedge Prime Brokerage Research.

be enough to reject the null hypothesis of not different from normal. In a portfolio of 10 assets, however, we expect the worst-performing asset to be nearly three standard deviations below average. So, in a sense, the managers we "fired" in that exercise, although losing money, were doing better than we would have expected them to do.

Given the distributions of minimums in Exhibits 15.12 and 15.13, it looks as if a 5 percent rejection rule would require the worst asset in a 5-asset portfolio to be about three standard deviations below normal, not the usual two standard deviations. In a 10-asset portfolio, the rejection rule would call for something close to four standard deviations below normal.

## Expectations for Winners and Losers

We tried this out in practice using a larger data set that comprised 97 managers for whom we had continuous track records from December 1996 through November 2006. These managers had a minimum of $20 million under management. As with our earlier data set, we subtracted interest to produce excess returns, and we normalized the volatility of each return stream to 15 percent for the entire period.

With this data set, we estimated the means, volatilities, and correlations of the managers' returns and used them to simulate return streams from which we could sample the returns of portfolios comprising 5, 10, and 20 managers. In this way, we can produce distributions that reflect correlations as well as managers' own mean returns. The managers for these portfolios were chosen at random but then optimally weighted subject to constraints. Under these constraints, the weight given any one manager could be no more than double and no less than half what the equal weight would be. With 10 managers, for example, an equal weight would be 10 percent, so the maximum we allowed was 20 percent, and the minimum was 5 percent.

Exhibit 15.14 shows three distributions for the simulated 10-manager portfolio returns. In this particular illustration, positions in the individual managers were leveraged to produce an annualized volatility of portfolio returns of 10 percent. The middle distribution represents monthly returns for the entire portfolio. The left-hand distribution shows what to expect from the worst performer, while the right-hand distribution shows what to expect from the best performer. Taken together, these distributions tell us that the expected monthly return for the portfolio was 0.76 percent, but that in any

**EXHIBIT 15.14**  Distribution of Simulated Monthly Returns for Portfolio and Best- and Worst-Performing Assets (10 Managers, Leveraged to Produce 10 Percent Annualized Volatility of Portfolio Returns)

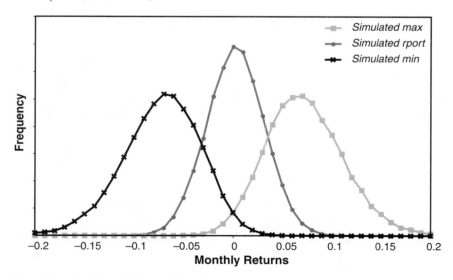

*Source:* Newedge Prime Brokerage Research.

**EXHIBIT 15.15** Actual and Simulated Monthly Returns (10 Managers, Leveraged to Produce 10 Percent Annualized Volatility of Portfolio Returns)

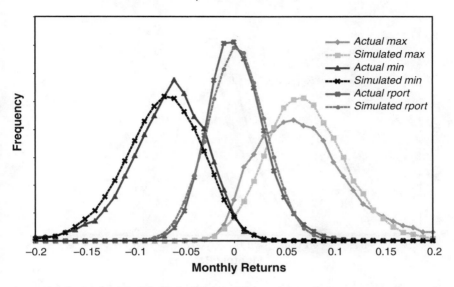

*Source:* Barclay Hedge, Newedge Prime Brokerage Research.

given month, the expected return for the worst performer in the 10-manager set would be –6.7 percent, while the expected return for the best performer would be 7.80 percent. In other words, the average spread between the best and worst return in any given month would be 14.5 percent.

Using the simulated return distributions as the standards for what we should expect, we then returned to the original track records and sampled actual returns from 10-manager portfolios formed at random from the overall set of 97 managers. These were also optimized subject to the same constraints as the simulated portfolios. Exhibit 15.15 shows that the actual distributions of monthly returns conform quite well to what we would have expected. This gives us confidence in the insights provided by the distributions derived from simulated return data.

## Moving Targets

If we now focus on what to expect of the worst-performing manager, we find that the number of managers does in fact matter. In Exhibit 15.16, we show what the distributions of the worst performer's monthly returns would have been with portfolios comprising 5, 10, and 20 managers. For this example, we

**EXHIBIT 15.16**  Distribution of Worst Performer's Monthly Return (5, 10, and 20 Managers, No Leveraging, Portfolio Vols = 9.42%, 8.24%, and 7.06%)

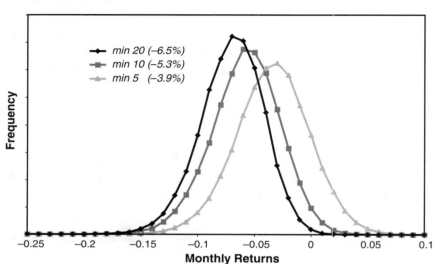

*Source:* Barclay Hedge, Newedge Prime Brokerage Research.

have not leveraged our positions in the individual managers and have allowed portfolio return volatility to fall as a natural byproduct of diversification. We find that the expected monthly return of the worst manager in any given month would have been −3.9 percent with five managers, −5.3 percent with 10 managers, and −6.5 percent with 20 managers.

## What about Leverage?

In Exhibit 15.16, we allowed portfolio return volatility to fall naturally as the number of managers increased. How would our expectations have been if we had instead leveraged our investments in each manager to maintain a portfolio return volatility of 10 percent?

Exhibit 15.17 shows what the return distributions for the worst asset would have been with the leverage needed to maintain this level of portfolio return volatility. We find, as before, that the expected return of the worst managers becomes more negative as the number of managers increases. But if we compare these results with those shown in Exhibit 15.16, we find two important differences. First, the sizes of the losses are larger than when we used

**EXHIBIT 15.17**   Distribution of Worst Performer's Monthly Return (5, 10, and 20 Managers, Leveraged to Set Portfolio Vol = 10%)

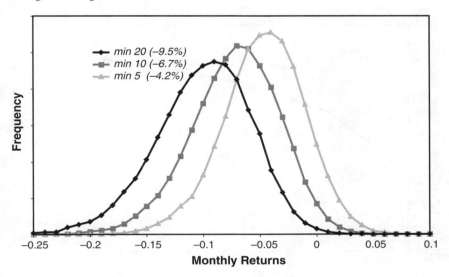

*Source:* Barclay Hedge, Newedge Prime Brokerage Research.

no leverage. Second, the spreads of these distributions are wider than when we used no leverage. As a result, the effect of leverage has been to shift the expected loss to the left and to increase the standard deviation of outcomes. Moreover, because we need more leverage with 20 assets than with 10 or 5, this effect is larger for the 20-asset portfolio than for the other two.

## The Silver Lining

If this sounds like a discouraging consequence of diversification, there are obvious upsides. For one thing, as shown in Exhibit 15.18, the expected value of the extreme outcome may increase with the number of assets, but when divided by the total number of assets, the expected contribution of the worst (or best) asset is actually reduced. A loss of 6.5 percent divided by 20 is smaller than a loss of 5.3 percent divided by 10. In addition, the likelihood of all assets losing money, or performing worse than expected, falls. And, of course, the risk-adjusted return of the portfolio is expected to go up, which is the whole point of diversification.

**EXHIBIT 15.18**   Expected Performance of Best or Worst Asset (Number of Standard Deviations Above or Below Mean)

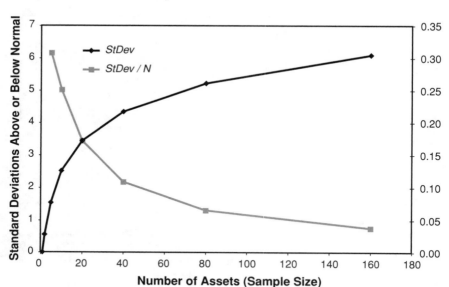

*Source:* Newedge Prime Brokerage Research.

## Due Diligence and Evaluation

What we find in this round of research would seem to have important implications for those who are doing due diligence and who have to evaluate portfolios for a living.

For one thing, because luck so dominates skill over the kinds of horizons we usually get to work with, track records are a very weak tool for evaluating the performance of a manager (who is running a portfolio of strategies) or a fund of funds (which is running a portfolio of managers). The historical track records we use to estimate the moments we need to determine portfolio weights produce imperfect estimates. As a result, there are serious limits on what we can hope to accomplish. And, once we've formed our portfolios, the ensuing track records produce sampling error that makes it very hard to know whether we've done a good job.

On this point, Stephen Ross (of Yale and MIT fame) once argued that track records tell us essentially nothing about the way a trader or investor makes money. And even if they could, do we really think that we can wait four or five years for the results we need to make reasonably good evaluations?

That does not mean we shouldn't try to do a better job. Financial theory and statistics suggest that we can improve our expected returns, so why not put the knowledge to work? In such a world, though, what we want to know is how a manager wrestles with the problem of getting better estimates of the return moments and uses his understanding of their imperfections to organize the portfolio. Due diligence in this case takes the form of inquiries into the manager's understanding of estimation procedures, sampling error, and so on. What we want to know is not only what he didn't know and when he didn't know it, but how his understanding of his ignorance guided his trading and portfolio construction decisions.

And finally, our standards for evaluating performance depend on our objectives. As we have seen, increasing the number of assets increases the likelihood that one of the assets will lose big. And we found that the distributions of best and worst performers' returns depend on the overall goal for portfolio volatility. To determine whether an asset is doing worse than we expected it to, we need a standard of performance that reflects the way we have constructed the portfolio—both in the number of assets and in the leverage used.

# Bibliography

Barclay Hedge web site, www.barclayhedge.com.

Bloomberg web site, www.bloomberg.com.

Burghardt, Galen, Jennifer Cai, Bin Chen, and LianyanLiu, "Correlations and Holding Periods," AlternativeEdge Research Note, June 9, 2008.

Burghardt, Galen, Ryan Duncan, and LianyanLiu, "What You Should Expect from Trend Following," AlternativeEdge Research Note, July 1, 2004.

———, "Two Benchmarks for Momentum Trading," AlternativeEdge Research Note, August 26, 2010.

———, "Every Drought Ends in a Rainstorm," AlternativeEdge Research Note, February 6, 2006.

———, "Understanding Drawdowns," AlternativeEdge Research Note, September 4, 2003.

———, "Superstars versus Teamwork," AlternativeEdge Research Note, May 4, 2007.

Burghardt, Galen, Jerry Hanweck, and Lauren Lei, "Measuring Market Impact and Liquidity," AlternativeEdge Research Note, May 17, 2006.

Burghardt, Galen, and Lianyan Liu, "How Important Are Daily Return Data?" AlternativeEdge Research Note, April 17, 2003.

———, "How Stock Price Volatility Affects Stock Returns and CTA Returns," AlternativeEdge Research Note, August 28, 2008.

———, "An Update on How Stock Price Volatility Affects Stock Returns and CTA Returns," AlternativeEdge Research Note, November 19, 2008.

———, "The Costs of Active Management," AlternativeEdge Research Note, November 8, 2007.

———, "There Are Known Unknowns," AlternativeEdge Research Note, September 10, 2007.

———, "A New Look at Building Teamwork Portfolios," AlternativeEdge Research Note, October 15, 2009.

Chen, Peng, Christopher O'Neil, and Kevin Zhu, "Managed Futures and Asset Allocation," Ibbotson Associates, February 2005.

de Santis, Giorgio, Bob Litterman, Adrien Vesval, and Kurt Winkelmann, "Covariance Matrix Estimation," Chap. 16 in *Modern Investment Management*, John Wiley & Sons, 2003.

Financial Industry Regulatory Authority (FINRA) web site, www.finra.org/.

Lo, Andrew W., "The Statistics of Sharpe Ratios," *Financial Analysts Journal*, Vol. 58, No. 4, July/August 2002. Available at SSRN: http://ssrn.com/abstract=377260.

Marcus, Alan J., "The Magellan Fund and Market Efficiency," *Journal of Portfolio Management*, Fall 1990.

Narang, Rishi K., *Inside the Black Box: The Simple Truth About Quantitative Trading*, John Wiley & Sons, 2009.

National Futures Association (NFA) web site, www.nfa.futures.org/basicnet/.

Rumsfeld, Donald, U.S. Department of Defense newsbrief, February 12, 2002.

Warsh, David, "Paul Samuelson Legacy," economicprincipals.com, December 20, 2009.

# About the Authors

**Galen Burghardt** is Director of Research for Newedge USA, a joint venture between Calyon and Société Général. He is the lead author of *The Treasury Bond Basis* and *The Eurodollar Futures and Options Handbook*, which are standard texts for users of financial futures. He was adjunct professor of finance in the University of Chicago's Graduate School of Business (now the Booth School). He was the head of financial research for the Chicago Mercantile Exchange and gained access to the world of futures through his work in the Capital Markets Section of the Federal Reserve Board. His PhD in Economics is from the University of Washington in Seattle.

**Brian Walls** is the Global Head of Research at Newedge Prime Brokerage, the foremost provider of brokerage services to the managed futures industry. He has worked in the financial services industry for 30 years in various capacities of trading, operations, management, and research. Brian was a pioneer in capital introduction services and is a highly sought after and trusted advisor to many Commodity Trading Advisors, Global Macro managers, funds of funds, and institutional investors. He chairs the Newedge Index Committee, which oversees both innovation and quality control in the production of the Newedge indexes of CTA performance.

# Index

*Note:* Page numbers followed by *f* refer to figures.